Vocabulary Control FOR INFORMATION RETRIEVAL

F. W. LANCASTER

Associate Professor
Graduate School of Library Science
University of Illinois

IRP INFORMATION RESOURCES PRESS
WASHINGTON, D.C. 1972

Available from--
Gothard House Publications
Gothard House
Henley, Oxon, England
U.K. and European Distributors

Available from
Information Resources Press
2100 M Street, N.W.
Washington, D.C. 20037

Library of Congress Catalog Card Number 78-186528

ISBN 0-87815-006-4

To Jude

The woof and warp of all thought and all research is symbols, and the life of thought and science is the life inherent in symbols; so that it is wrong to say that a good language is important *to good thought, merely; for it is of the essence of it.*

C. S. PEIRCE

Preface

This book deals with properties of vocabularies for indexing and searching document collections; the construction, organization, display, and maintenance of these vocabularies; and the vocabulary as a factor affecting the performance of retrieval systems. Most of the text is concerned with vocabularies for postcoordinate retrieval systems, with special emphasis on thesauri and machine-based systems. Vocabularies for pre-coordinate systems (e.g., alphabetical subject catalogs and classified catalogs) are discussed only briefly to provide historical perspective and for the light they shed on the problems of vocabulary control in general. This type of vocabulary is well covered in existing texts.

I have attempted to cover the entire range of vocabulary possibilities, from highly structured lists to free text (no control), and to point out advantages and limitations of various approaches. The book was specifically compiled as a text to accompany a course in vocabulary control presented at the Graduate School of Library Science, University of Illinois. It is therefore intended primarily for students of library and information science. In parts, however, it reflects ten years of personal experience in the design, operation, and evaluation of information retrieval systems, including work as a consultant to several agencies of the United States government. It may therefore have some value to all designers, managers, and operators of retrieval systems.

I am very grateful to the following students from the University of Illinois for participating in the first course (450 B) presented there on the subject of vocabulary control and for reviewing and criticizing the various chapters in draft form: Mary Ann Barragry, Linda Bonen, Anne Ernst, Miriam Kauffman, Arthur Ketchersid, Mary Krick, Dudley Marcum, Anna Bell McCuiston, Martha Nichols, and Margaret Smith.

I am especially grateful to Anna Bell McCuiston, my graduate assistant in the academic year 1970-71, who provided invaluable assistance in gathering material, checking references, and typing a substantial portion of the first draft. Without her, this book could not have been completed. I am also grateful to Ruth Lerner and Barbara Hoegle who undertook the final cleanup of the manuscript in the summer of 1971.

Finally I wish to thank Brian Vickery, Jack Mills, and Eugene Wall for reading my manuscript and offering many helpful suggestions.

Urbana, Illinois
August, 1971

Acknowledgments

Figure 11 is reprinted from the *British Technology Index* by kind permission of the Library Association, London, England. Figure 12 is reprinted from *Chemical Abstracts* by kind permission of the American Chemical Society. Figures 14, 38, and 42 are reprinted by kind permission of ASLIB, London, England. Figures 15 and 16 (copyright 1967), Figure 37 (copyright 1970), Figure 44 (copyright 1958), and Figure 67 (copyright 1968) are reprinted by kind permission of the American Society for Information Science (formerly American Documentation Institute), Washington, D.C. Figure 17 is reprinted from the *Exploration and Production Thesaurus* by kind permission of the University of Tulsa. Figures 18, 35, and 36 are reprinted by kind permission of GEC Power Engineering Ltd. Figure 19 is reprinted by kind permission of D. J. Foskett and the University of London Institute of Education. Figure 26 is reprinted by kind permission of the American Petroleum Institute. Figure 31 is reprinted from the *TDCK Circular Thesaurus* with kind permission of the Wetenschappelijk en Technisch Documentatie-en Informatie-Centrum voor de Krijgsmacht. Figure 32 is reprinted by kind permission of the System Development Corporation. Figures 33 and 34 are reprinted from the *EURATOM Thesaurus* by kind permission of the Commission des Communautés Européennes. Figure 43 is reprinted by kind permission of the British Institute of Management and J. F. Blagden. Figures 54–58 are reprinted by kind permission of Aspen Systems Corporation. Figure 59 is reprinted from *Automatic Information Organization and Retrieval* by Gerard Salton, copyright 1968 by McGraw-Hill Book Co., used with permission of McGraw-Hill Book Co. Figures 62 and 63 are from *Information Retrieval Systems* by F. W. Lancaster, copyright 1968, reprinted by kind permission of John Wiley & Sons, Inc.

Tables 2, 3, 4, 5, 37–49, and 56 are reprinted by kind permission of ASLIB, London, England. Table 6 (copyright 1966) is reprinted by kind permission of the American Society for Information Science (formerly American Documentation Institute), Washington, D.C. Tables 10–17 are reprinted by kind permission of the Dansk Central for Dokumentation. Table 18 is reprinted by kind permission of the Engineers Joint Council. Table 19 is reprinted by kind permission of W. Hammond. Tables 21–24 are reprinted by kind permission of the American Chemical Society and the author. Table 28 is reproduced by kind permission of the American Federation of Information Processing Societies. Table 29 is reprinted from *Automatic Information Organization and Retrieval* by Gerard Salton, copyright 1968 by McGraw-Hill Book Co., used with permission of McGraw-Hill Book Co. Tables 50 and 51 are from *Punched Cards* by Robert S. Casey, James W. Perry, Allen Kent, and Madeline M. Berry; copyright 1958, Reinhold Publishing Corporation; reprinted by permission of Van Nostrand Reinhold Company. Tables 52 and 53 are from *Tools for Machine Literature Searching*, by J. W. Perry and A. Kent (Interscience); copyright 1958; reprinted by kind permission of John Wiley & Sons, Inc. Table 58 is from "The Cost-Effectiveness Analysis of Information Retrieval and Dissemination Systems,"

ix

SOME ABBREVIATIONS AND ACRONYMS COMMONLY USED IN THIS BOOK

AEC   United States Atomic Energy Commission

AIChE   American Institute of Chemical Engineers

ANSI   American National Standards Institute

API   American Petroleum Institute

ASM   American Society for Metals

ASTIA   Armed Services Technical Information Agency (now the Defense Documentation Center)

BROWSER   Browsing On-Line with Selective Retrieval, an IBM retrieval system developed by Williams

BT   Broader term

COSATI   Committee on Scientific and Technical Information of the Federal Council for Science and Technology

COSATI Guidelines   *See* LEX Conventions

DDC   Defense Documentation Center, formerly known as ASTIA (Armed Services Technical Information Agency)

DoD   Department of Defense

EJC   Engineers Joint Council

ERIC   Educational Resources Information Center of the U.S. Office of Education

FAA   Federal Aviation Administration

IRTET   *Information Retrieval Thesaurus of Education Terms*

KWIC   Keyword-in-Context

LEX   Project LEX, a DoD development project that produced the *Thesaurus of Engineering and Scientific Terms*

LEX Conventions   Rules for thesaurus construction developed during Project LEX. Sometimes referred to as the TEST thesaurus conventions. They were subsequently adopted as guidelines for thesaurus construction by COSATI.

MEDLARS   Medical Literature Analysis and Retrieval System, a machine-based system operated by the National Library of Medicine

MeSH   *Medical Subject Headings,* the controlled vocabulary of MEDLARS

NASA   National Aeronautics and Space Administration

NT   Narrower term

Project LEX   *See* LEX

RT   Related term

SDI   Selective Dissemination of Information

SMART   An experimental, fully automatic retrieval system developed by Salton at Harvard University (now at Cornell)

TEST   *Thesaurus of Engineering and Scientific Terms,* the product of Project LEX

UF   Used for

USAEC   United States Atomic Energy Commission

WRU   Western Reserve University (now Case Western Reserve University)

Contents

xii

1 *Why Vocabulary Control?*

All the complex procedures of *information retrieval* *
are directly involved with the manipulation of classes
—classes of documents of one kind or another. When
we index a document according to its subject matter,
we assign it to one or more classes, as shown in Figure
1. To facilitate the assignment of documents to classes,
and to allow subsequent manipulation of these classes,
each class must have a name or label of some kind.
The names we give to these classes (we can regard them
as "class labels") are generically known as *index terms*
and the complete set of these index terms may conveniently be called an *index language*. In conducting
a search in an information retrieval system to satisfy
some need for information on a particular topic, we

1. Decide which document classes are most likely to
contain items relevant to the information need,
2. Examine these classes,
3. Retrieve some or all of the members.

The effectiveness of a retrieval system depends
largely upon the size and composition of the document
classes existing in the system, and upon which classes
are consulted when a search is undertaken (i.e., the
search strategy used). In general, if we create large

classes we make it easier to find all the documents on
a particular topic (i.e., achieve a high *recall*) but more
difficult to retrieve only relevant documents (i.e.,
achieve a high *precision*). Conversely, if we create
many very small classes we would expect to be able to
achieve high precision, but we may find it rather more
difficult to conduct a comprehensive search to achieve
high recall.

It is important to subsequent retrieval that, in the
indexing operation, documents be assigned to classes
according to some consistent pattern. If the classification is to be useful it must bring documents on related subjects together. This implies that we must
exercise some control over the indexing operation.
Rather than giving each indexer *carte blanche* to form
new classes indiscriminately, which would result in the
creation of many overlapping classes and lead to the
separation of related documents, most systems require
the indexer to assign documents to classes that are
predefined. This predefinition is accomplished by
giving the indexer a list of index terms that he must
use in indexing. Having decided what the document
is "about" and for what types of requests it is likely
to provide useful information, the indexer assigns it
to various document classes by labeling it with index
terms selected from the approved list. For example, a
particular document may be assigned to the classes
labeled DIET, CALCIUM, OSTEOPOROSIS, and RATS.

A controlled list of index terms is generally known as
a *controlled vocabulary* or as an *authority list*. A

* We will use this expression throughout. It is the term generally used to describe activities and systems of the type discussed
in this book even though the systems involved do not retrieve
information (an abstraction) as such. Rather, they retrieve
documents or document representations (surrogates).

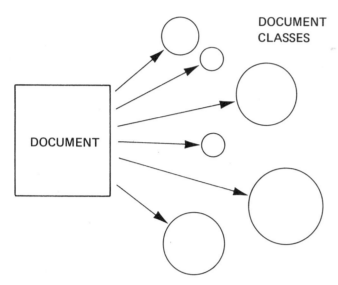

DOCUMENT CLASSES

DOCUMENT

FIGURE 1 Formation of document classes by indexing process.

controlled vocabulary is one broad type of index language. Under certain circumstances, which we will discuss later, it is possible to operate a retrieval system with essentially no vocabulary control of this type.

Vocabulary control tends to improve indexing consistency. Two indexers (or the same indexer on different occasions) are more likely to agree on the term or terms necessary to describe a particular topic if these terms are selected from a pre-established list than if they are independently concocted *de novo* at the time of the indexing operation. Moreover, when we come to conduct a search in a retrieval system, we are more likely to examine the correct classes (i.e., those containing documents related to our interests) if we can choose from a definitive list of class names.

The major role of the controlled vocabulary in an information system is demonstrated in Figure 2. It figures prominently in both the indexing and searching operations. However, the controlled vocabulary does not, or at least should not, influence the conceptual analysis of documents and the conceptual analysis of requests. The conceptual analysis stage is separate from the translation stage. We first decide what a document or a request is about and then try to translate our conceptual analysis into the terms of the index language. The two stages of conceptual analysis and translation have different effects on the performance of the retrieval system. For example, we could accurately

decide that a particular document deals with argon arc welding. This is our conceptual analysis. When we come to translate this into the index language we may need to describe the subject matter in less precise terms. The vocabulary of the system does not allow us to identify exactly the class of documents dealing with argon arc welding. Instead, we must settle for something broader, perhaps SHIELDED ARC WELDING or ARC WELDING or even WELDING.

Figure 3 shows the various steps of the retrieval operation and lists alongside each the factors most significantly affecting performance. The index language affects performance at two major points. It affects the search strategy by establishing how precisely the searcher can describe the interests of the requester, and it affects the indexing by establishing how precisely the indexer can describe the subject matter of documents. The index language obviously plays a very important part in the retrieval operation and has a major effect on overall system performance.

The index language exists primarily to bring the vocabulary of the indexer and the vocabulary of the searcher into coincidence. Normally it will provide a control over synonyms and near-synonyms to prevent different indexers from using different terms to express identical subject matter. By indicating which synonym is preferred, the vocabulary avoids separation of similar documents and tells the searcher where he need and need not look. The index language normally will also distinguish homographs such as the word "plant," which has various possible connotations, botanical and industrial among others.

The index language also has the important function of facilitating generic search. It must somehow bring related terms together so that it is possible to conduct a search on a broad subject. If we need to search on the subject of "steroids" the vocabulary should be capable of displaying all the relevant terms, linked together in some way. This spares the searcher the effort that would otherwise be involved in thinking up all possible "steroid" terms that might exist in the vocabulary, reduces the possibility of his overlooking relevant terms. and ensures that his search is in fact comprehensive. The relationships thus displayed, to assist the indexer and the searcher, will usually extend beyond formal genus-species relationships to other types, including part-whole relations and the relations between a substance or tool and its possible applications.

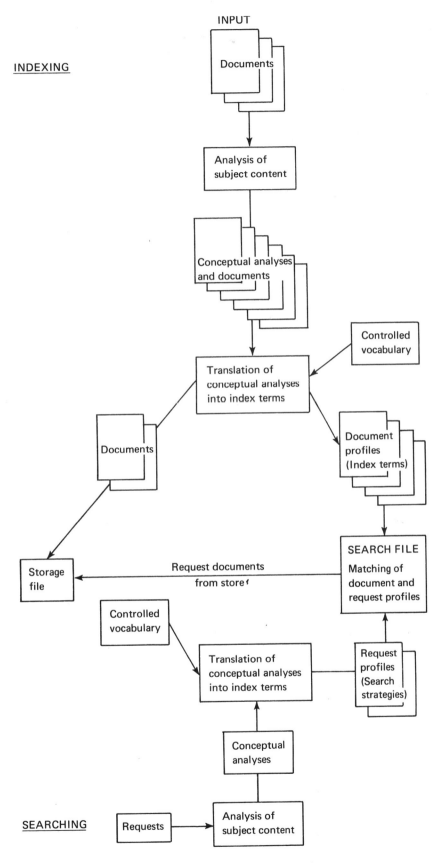

INPUT

INDEXING

Documents

Analysis of
subject content

Conceptual analyses
and documents

Controlled
vocabulary

Translation of
conceptual analyses
into index terms

Documents

Document
profiles
(Index terms)

SEARCH FILE
Matching of
document and
request profiles

Storage
file

Request documents
from store

Controlled
vocabulary

Translation of
conceptual analyses
into index terms

Request
profiles
(Search
strategies)

Conceptual
analyses

SEARCHING

Requests

Analysis of
subject content

FIGURE 2 Information retrieval: input and output processes.

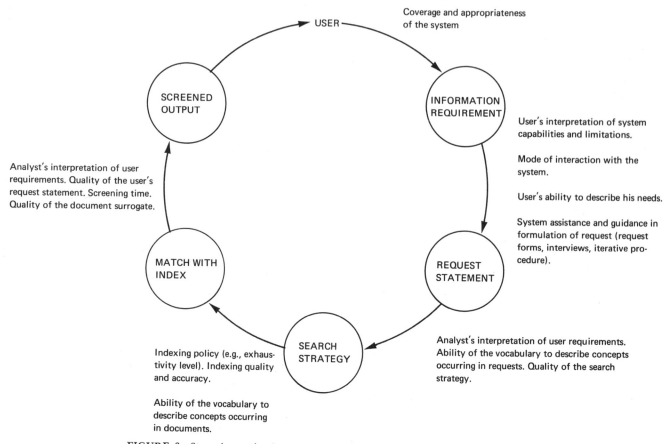

FIGURE 3 Steps in retrieval process and factors affecting success of each step.

2 Vocabulary Types: Pre-coordination and Post-coordination, Enumeration and Synthesis

The subject matter of documents tends to be complex, and the vocabulary of a modern retrieval system must be capable of expressing any degree of complexity. Consider a particular document that deals with aircraft, engines, and noise. In indexing this document we may want to assign it to all three conceptual classes because we consider it of potential relevance to requests relating to aircraft, requests relating to engines, and requests relating to noise. However, the document is highly relevant to the specific and complex topic "aircraft engine noise." We must, therefore, be able to indicate that it is a member of the specific class "documents relating to noise of aircraft engines," because the system should be capable of retrieving this document in response to a request for information on this precise topic.

Basically, there are two ways in which we can use the system vocabulary to index and retrieve documents on a complex topic such as this. One way is to create an index term which uniquely identifies this specific class. For example, if we adopt the index term AIRCRAFT ENGINE NOISE we are using a term which in itself expresses the relationships among the class "aircraft," the class "engines," and the class "noise" (Figure 4). In other words, the system vocabulary includes a label identifying a class that is the logical product (intersection) of three other classes (of documents) existing in the system. Such a vocabulary is generally known as a *pre-coordinate* vocabulary: the term AIRCRAFT ENGINE NOISE is a *pre-coordination* of the terms AIRCRAFT, ENGINES, and NOISE. In searching this type of system for documents on noise of aircraft engines, we would look at the class labeled AIRCRAFT ENGINE NOISE and expect that this class would contain items relevant to our search topic.

At the other extreme, we have systems which are largely free from pre-coordination. The vocabulary of such a system directly defines only relatively basic classes. The most obvious example is Taube's Uniterm system [3] which, at least in its original version, permitted an indexer to use only index terms consisting of single words. Thus, the topic "aircraft engine noise" is indicated by assigning to the document the separate index terms AIRCRAFT, ENGINES, and NOISE. In conducting a search in this type of system we need some way of manipulating the document classes in order to identify documents that are common to all three classes and which therefore, presumably, deal with the precise topic "aircraft engine noise." Such systems are generally known as *post-coordinate* systems. They allow us to manipulate classes, at the time of searching, in order to derive their logical sums, products, and complements.* Systems that are entirely pre-coordinate provide no such facility for manipulating classes in searching. In such systems our searches are restricted by the class relationships built into the index language

---

* The formal relations among document classes may be defined by means of Boolean algebra. The use of Boolean algebra in the construction of search strategies is discussed by Lancaster [5] and in *Principles of MEDLARS*.[7]

5

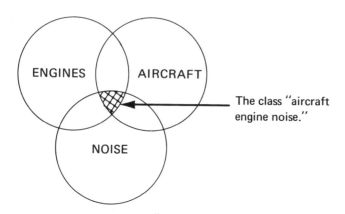

FIGURE 4 Example of pre-coordinate term expressing the intersection of three conceptual classes.

itself. It is for this reason that Bernier [2] referred to post-coordinate systems as *manipulative* and to pre-coordinate systems as *nonmanipulative*.

Post-coordinate retrieval systems have existed for less than thirty years. The earliest were developed by Batten (peek-a-boo cards using the principle of optical coincidence),[1] Mooers (edge-notched cards),[6] and Taube (Uniterm cards).[4] They are briefly described in an earlier book by Lancaster.[5] Some small retrieval systems still employ these manual or mechanical techniques for manipulating classes. However, many small systems, and most large ones, are now more fully mechanized and use digital computers, in on-line or off-line mode, to manipulate and search document classes. Others use microfilm for the same purposes.

Prior to 1940, retrieval systems were essentially pre-coordinate and nonmanipulative. Most frequently they were card catalogs or printed indexes. When arranged alphabetically such systems are known as *alphabetical subject catalogs* or *alphabetical subject indexes*.* When arranged according to the sequence of some classification scheme they are known as *classified catalogs* or *classified indexes*. Alphabetical subject catalogs have always been more popular in the United States, while classified catalogs are more prevalent in Europe. The *dictionary catalog* is merely an alphabetical subject catalog with entries for authors and titles interfiled in the same alphabetical sequence.

The distinction between pre-coordinate and post-coordinate systems is an important one. Also important is the related distinction between *enumerative* and *synthetic* vocabularies. Post-coordinate systems are, by definition, synthetic; but pre-coordinate systems may be fully enumerative or partly enumerative and partly

* Frequently the word "catalog" is restricted to a tool that describes complete works (books, reports, etc.) while "index" is reserved for a tool describing parts of works (e.g., journal articles).

synthetic. Consider two different vocabularies used to index documents. Both are lists of terms. In one instance, however, the rules of vocabulary use only allow us to employ the terms independently and do not allow us to combine these terms to express something more complex. Such a vocabulary is strictly enumerative. It lists or enumerates terms that an indexer must use in describing the subject matter of documents and provides no flexibility whereby the indexer can create new terms by combining (synthesizing) terms appearing in the enumeration. The second vocabulary, on the other hand, while it does list terms that an indexer may use in indexing, also provides rules whereby these terms may be combined in various ways to form new, more specific terms. Such a vocabulary is *synthetic*.

An enumerative system may require a document on noise of aircraft engines to be indexed under AIRCRAFT ENGINES and again, separately, under NOISE. We have no way of bringing these terms together to create a new term AIRCRAFT ENGINE NOISE. In a synthetic vocabulary, on the other hand, we can create new, more complex terms by combining existing terms. Thus, in a synthetic scheme, we would probably be able to take the "aircraft engine" term and the "noise" term and put them together in order to form a new label defining precisely the class "aircraft engine noise." Clearly, if we use a strictly enumerative vocabulary, the specificity with which we can describe subject matter is limited by the specificity of the terms provided by the compiler of the vocabulary, whereas these limitations do not exist in a synthetic vocabulary, which gives us the freedom to create new, specific terms more or less at will. Certain classification schemes (e.g., that of the Library of Congress) are almost entirely enumerative, while others (such as Ranganathan's *Colon Classification*) allow a considerable amount of synthesis. Lists of subject headings are largely enumerative but may allow some synthesis (e.g., combining of main headings with subheadings).

Conceptually, there is a clear distinction between pre-coordinate and post-coordinate systems. However, the distinction becomes less clear when we get down to the language plane. Some words in the English language, for example, are "conceptually pre-coordinate" in that they express, in themselves, a relationship between two or more concepts. For example, the word "urinalysis" means "analysis of the urine" and expresses the relationship between the topic "urine" and the topic "analysis" (Figure 5). Likewise, "proteinuria" is a word indicating the presence of protein in the urine, while "albuminuria" is a word indicating the presence of albumin in urine. There is no single word that expresses the notion of "calculi in urine," however. We must index a docu-

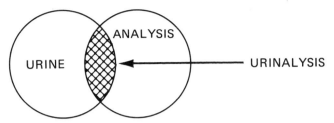

FIGURE 5 Example of "conceptually pre-coordinate" word.

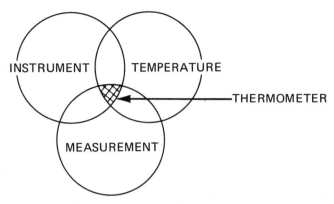

FIGURE 6 Example of semantic factoring.

ment on this topic under the term CALCULI and again under the term URINE or use some synthetic device for combining these terms; for example, using one as a subheading (as CALCULI, URINE or URINE, CALCULI) or creating an index term consisting of a phrase, CALCULI IN URINE or URINARY CALCULI. These are accidents of the English language, but they complicate the problems of vocabulary control for information retrieval. Other languages vary in the degree to which single words are used to express complex relations between concepts. German, for one, allows a high degree of conceptual pre-coordination. Lewis Carroll's "portmanteau" words are good examples of words combining concepts (e.g., "slithy"). James Joyce coined many more words of this general type. Some conflated words have found their way into the language. For example, "smog" (smoke and fog), "motel" (motorist and hotel), and "guesstimate" (guess and estimate).

Many English words that, on the surface, seem simple do not in fact represent a simple concept but may be dissected into component aspects or factors. The word "thermometer," for instance, represents an instrument for measurement of temperature (Figure 6). The analysis of words into their components and basic meanings has been called "semantic factoring." It will be discussed in more detail later.

Most modern retrieval systems are partly pre-coordinate and partly post-coordinate. Concepts that frequently occur together may be combined in a pre-coordinate term and this term may then be coordinated with others at the time of searching. For example, the vocabulary used by the National Library of Medicine (*Medical Subject Headings*) in MEDLARS includes the pre-coordination LIVER NEOPLASMS. This term must be coordinated, at the time of search, with the term RADIOTHERAPY if we are looking for literature on radiation therapy of liver tumors.

REFERENCES

1. Batten, W. E. "A Punched Card System of Indexing to Meet Special Requirements." *Report of the 22nd ASLIB Conference,* 1947, 37-39.
2. Bernier, C. L. "Correlative Indexes: 1. Alphabetical Correlative Indexes." *American Documentation* 7 (1956): 283-288.
3. Documentation Incorporated. *Installation Manual for the Uniterm System of Coordinate Indexing.* Dayton, Ohio: Document Service Center, 1953.
4. Jaster, J. J. et al. *The State of the Art of Coordinate Indexing.* Washington, D. C.: Documentation Incorporated, 1962.
5. Lancaster, F. W. *Information Retrieval Systems: Characteristics, Testing, and Evaluation.* New York: Wiley, 1968.
6. Mooers, C. N. "Zatocoding Applied to Mechanical Organization of Knowledge." *American Documentation* 2, (1951): 20-32.
7. National Library of Medicine. *Principles of MEDLARS.* Bethesda, Md., 1970.

3 The Classification Scheme in Vocabulary Control

The *Decimal Classification* of Melvil Dewey,[5] which appeared in 1876, made the first real attempt to provide a classification capable of representing the subject matter of documents. While intended primarily to allow a useful arrangement of books on library shelves, the scheme is also used to arrange classified catalogs, particularly in England. The classification is predominantly enumerative; that is, it provides a list of labels identifying various document classes, both elementary and compound. In all classification schemes of this type the actual labels assigned to documents are alphabetical or numerical codes (the notation of the classification) representing the names given to classes by the compiler of the scheme. Thus, in Dewey's scheme, the class "welding" is represented by the *class number* 671.52.

An enumerative classification, without provision for synthesis, allows us to express only class relations built into the scheme itself through pre-coordination. We are therefore limited in the degree of specificity we can achieve in indexing. We cannot be more specific than the compiler was in constructing his schedules. Through pre-coordination Dewey provided a reasonable level of specificity in certain areas even in early editions of his scheme. For example, in the 5th edition (1894) there is a number, 628.23, representing "ventilation of sewers." This number remains the same in the 16th edition (1958). A number such as 628.445, "municipal garbage disposal," is quite specific, representing the pre-coordination of three separate concepts.

While an enumerative scheme may achieve specificity in individual hierarchies, the absence of synthesis frequently prevents us from expressing precisely the complex subject relations discussed in modern technical documents. In the *Decimal Classification* we can express "welding" (671.52) and we can express "aluminum" (669.722) but we cannot exactly specify "welding of aluminum" since Dewey does not give us the capability of synthesizing the two numbers. When we classify a book on welding of aluminum we can, of course, give it both codes. For the arrangement of the book on library shelves we must choose only one of these class numbers. However, in the classified catalog an entry can appear under both, allowing us to retrieve the bibliographic reference whether we approach it via the "aluminum" route or via the "welding" route. This does *not* allow us to retrieve only those items dealing with welding of aluminum. To ensure a comprehensive search on this topic in the classified catalog, we must look at *all* the welding entries or *all* the aluminum entries or, if we are unsure that the compilers of the catalog have always made double entry, all the aluminum entries *and* all the welding entries (Figure 7). Because the system is nonmanipulative, we have no easy way of isolating the precise set of documents that belong both to the class "welding" and to the class "aluminum." There could well be many "welding" documents and many "aluminum" documents in the catalog, but the number of documents on "welding of aluminum" may be very small. A search on the pre-

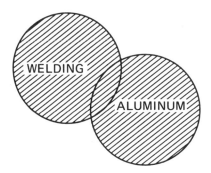

FIGURE 7 Logical sum of the class "welding" and the class "aluminum."

cise topic is inefficient because we must look at the representations of many irrelevant documents in order to retrieve representations of a small number of relevant ones.

While the *Decimal Classification* is primarily enumerative, Dewey did recognize the futility of trying to provide in advance a ready-made class number for every topic upon which literature might exist. Consequently, he made a certain amount of provision for synthesis. According to various instructions provided in the classified schedules, we can take one class number and add it to another to express the logical product of the two classes. Such synthesis is generally known as *number building*. The geographical subdivisions can be used as a synthetic device of this type, and in various parts of the classification schedules we find an instruction "Divided like 930-99," which allows us to divide a topic by geographic area. Thus, 550 (geology) may be subdivided to yield 554.2, geology of England, England being represented by 942 in the geographic schedule.* In certain other places the *Decimal Classification* includes the instruction "Divide like the main classification," and this allows us to add one subject code to another, as:

016	Bibliography
891.851	Polish poetry
016.891851	Bibliography of Polish poetry

However, the synthetic element is severely limited in the *Decimal Classification,* and Dewey cautioned against the free combination of numbers except where specific instructions were given.

The Library of Congress classification, most of which appeared in the period 1899 to 1920, is almost entirely enumerative with virtually no provision for synthesis.[7]

* In the 17th edition of the classification, geographic subdivision of this type is accomplished by an Area Table in which the British Isles is represented by 42.

Even geographic divisions are separately enumerated in many sections of the classification, although some classes (e.g., N, Fine Arts) include a table of country divisions which can be applied to certain numbers in the schedules. The scheme is highly pre-coordinate and achieves a reasonable level of specificity in many areas. In class R, Medicine, for example, RK510 represents "anesthesia in dentistry" while RL793 represents "congenital disorders of the skin." Thus, it is possible to represent the subject matter of documents specifically using the Library of Congress schedules but, again, only at the level of specificity explicitly provided by the scheme, which may be described as the "book level" rather than the level likely to be encountered in the articles of a scientific journal, for example.

An historically interesting book classification scheme, little known in the United States, is the *Subject Classification* of J. D. Brown, first published in 1906 (the last edition is the third, 1939).[3] Brown's scheme is highly synthetic. It represents an attempt to create a "one place" classification in which each main topic appears only once. The various aspects of a main topic may be expressed by a number taken from a "categorical table" which provides a list of "forms, phases, standpoints, qualifications, etc., which apply more or less to every subject or subdivision of a subject." Thus, to the main class number O350 representing "Algeria," we can add the categorical number .758, "immigration," to arrive at the code O350.758 which expresses "Algerian immigration." Likewise, we could add the categorical number for "inflammation," .524, to G703, "peripheral nervous system," to express "inflammation of peripheral nerves." Where no categorical number will serve, Brown allows the synthesis of two terms from the main schedules, as:

| F237E026 | Cuttlefish respiration |
| E154I222 | Pruning of shrubs |

The most-used classification scheme based on synthetic principles is the *Universal Decimal Classification* (UDC)[2] which first appeared, in French, in 1905. Since that date several full and abridged editions, in various languages, have been issued. While the UDC is built upon the foundation of the *Decimal Classification* and uses the same outline, it is a highly synthetic scheme. The principal device for synthesis is the colon, which can be used to combine any two terms existing in the schedules (except in cases where another device is specifically provided for this purpose and takes precedence over the colon). In UDC we can take the notation for coal mines, 622.33, and add to it the notation for ventilation, 622.41, thus creating the number 622.33: 622.41, representing "ventilation of coal mines."

Special synthetic devices, known as Auxiliary Schedules, are available to provide for:

1. *Forms of presentation:* 621.38 (03) represents encyclopedias of electronics.
2. *Place:* "youth movements in Germany" may be represented by 369.4 (430).
3. *Language:* 61 (032)=82 indicates medical dictionaries in Russian.
4. *Time:* 327 "1971," (42:43) indicates international relations between England and Germany in 1971.
5. *Race:* 378 (=924) represents higher education among Jewish people.

The UDC also employs certain special auxiliary devices (including use of the hyphen) as synthetic elements in various parts of the scheme. One example may be found in agriculture, where the crop schedules of 633 to 635 may be qualified by the agricultural problems schedules of 631 and 632, using the hyphen as connective. Thus, we can combine 633.11, "wheat," with 632.7, "insect pests," in the number 633.11-27, which represents insect pests affecting wheat. For excellent analyses of the UDC as an index language see the two contributions by Mills.[8, 10] An earlier textbook by Mills [9] gives full details on each of the classification schemes discussed in this chapter.

Synthesis in classification was carried to its logical conclusion by Ranganathan, who first published his *Colon Classification* in 1933.[11, 12] Ranganathan's scheme is based on a minimum of enumeration coupled with great freedom to synthesize notational elements at will. Ranganathan's scheme is an *analytico-synthetic* classification, and it is developed by means of a careful analysis of each subject field into its component facets, the arrangement of these facets in schedules in a helpful order, and the provision of rules whereby facets can be combined (synthesized) to express any degree of subject complexity. Consider the class L, Medicine, in the *Colon Classification.* The class number L185 represents "eye" (from the anatomic facet) and L18517 "retina," a subdivision of "eye." To this number we can add the code for "inflammation" (in the disease facet), 415, thus arriving at L18517:415, representing "inflammation of the retina" or "retinitis."

The *Colon Classification* itself has never been much used, even in India where it originated. Ranganathan's ideas, however, have been widely accepted and have had great influence on others. In particular, his principles were adopted by members of the Classification Research Group in London and have formed the basis of several excellent classification schemes devoted to special subject areas (e.g., education, engineering, sugar technology, packaging, construction industries).

Clearly, an analytico-synthetic classification, if properly constructed, can provide virtually limitless capabilities for the detailed description of the subject matter of documents. Figure 8 illustrates some sample facets, with typical subdivisions, from a hypothetical

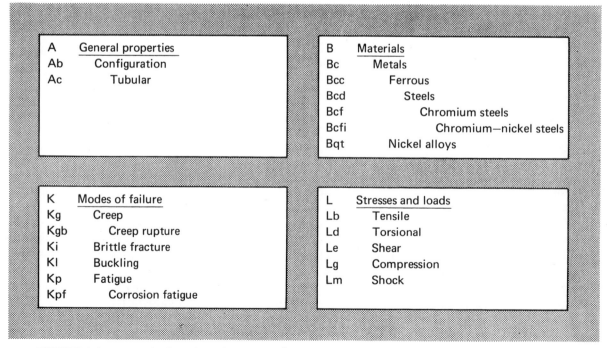

FIGURE 8 Segments of a hypothetical analytico-synthetic classification scheme in field of design engineering.

classification scheme in the field of design engineering. The various facets can be combined to express highly complex subject matter: KpBcfi represents fatigue of chromium-nickel steels, LmKpBcf represents fatigue of chromium steels under shock loading, and KgbBqtAc represents creep rupture of nickel-alloy tubes.

Through the use of synthesis, classification schemes can provide virtually unlimited specificity and are thus capable of handling extremely complex subject matter. However, all these schemes were developed for use in pre-coordinate retrieval systems, usually card catalogs or printed (book form) indexes. Such systems have one severe limitation: they are unidimensional, in that entries must be displayed in a linear fashion.

Consider a document with the hypothetical class designation BnDafiLx, representing the precise topic "radiation therapy of carcinoma of the lung," where Bn stands for "lung," Dafi "carcinoma," and Lx "radiotherapy." When a subject entry for this document is made in the classified catalog, it must file under the first element in the notation, Bn. This allows the document to be retrieved in a search relating to "lungs," because the searcher will approach the catalog at the Bn entry point, or in a search relating to "lung carcinoma" (Bn subdivided by Dafi). However, the entry does not help the searcher looking for all references to "carcinoma," because Dafi is not an entry point in this case. Conceivably the index contains many entries relating to "carcinoma," but these are dispersed throughout the index according to the organ affected. It thus becomes somewhat difficult to conduct a search on all documents relating to "carcinoma." The searcher wanting everything on "radiotherapy" is similarly inconvenienced by the filing order adopted.

Since, in a pre-coordinate index, a particular entry must file according to the initial element of the notation, a multiple-access approach to subject matter can only be achieved by duplication of entries. One way is simply to rotate entries so that each element becomes an entry point, as:

Bn Dafi Lx
Lx Bn Dafi
Dafi Lx Bn

But rotation does not necessarily provide for all useful combinations. In the foregoing example, a searcher might approach the index under Lx, seeking all references relating to "radiotherapy of malignant tumors," regardless of site. The filing order is not helpful because Lx is directly subdivided by organ affected rather than by pathologic condition.

For efficient information retrieval we need flexibility to combine topics in any way. This is allowed in a post-coordinate system, where "carcinoma," "lung," and

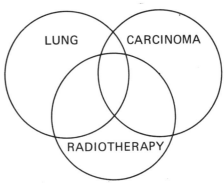

FIGURE 9 Possible combination of terms in a post-coordinate system.

"radiotherapy" would probably each be separate terms capable of being used in any possible combination (Figure 9). Thus, we can combine all these terms or any pair of terms with equal facility. To allow all possible combinations of three notational elements in a classified index, however, would mean permutation of the elements, and this would lead to six entries in the file. Obviously, permutation greatly increases file size and adds appreciably to the cost of the index.* Even strict rotation of entries will increase the bulk of the file and raise costs. The following table indicates the full cost (in bulk of file) of permutation.

Number of Terms Assigned to Document	Full Permutation
2	2
3	6
4	24
5	120
6	720
7	5,040
8	40,320

To avoid duplication of entries in a classified index while still allowing a multiple aspect approach to retrieval, Ranganathan [12] developed the principle of *chain indexing*. Using chain indexing we can restrict ourselves to a single entry in the classified file, relying on the alphabetical index to this file to provide the alternative subject approaches. A chain index is built up by systematically indexing each step in the hierarchical chain of concepts leading to the specific subject dealt with.† In the example previously used, we

---

* Sharp,[14] however, has shown in his SLIC index that complete permutation of terms can be avoided. Assuming a definite citation order is followed, a reduced number of combinations is sufficient to cover all approaches.
† The use of chain indexing presupposes that class numbers are built up by strict adherence to a well-established sequence of facets ("citation order" or "preferred order").

file the entry in the classified file under BnDafiLx, which may be dissected as follows:

B	Respiratory system
Bn	Lung
Da	Tumors
Daf	Tumors, malignant
Dafi	Carcinoma
L	Therapy
Lx	Radiotherapy

In chain procedure we provide for multiple access by indexing each step in this hierarchical chain, from right to left, and including entries for each useful access point in the alphabetical index to the classified file, as follows:

Radiotherapy: Carcinoma: Lung	Bn Dafi Lx
Therapy: Carcinoma: Lung	Bn Dafi L
Carcinoma: Lung	Bn Dafi
Malignant tumors: Lung	Bn Daf
Tumors: Lung	Bn Da
Lung	Bn
Respiratory system	B

The chain index does not refer to individual documents. It refers the user to that segment of the classified file where references to documents on a particular subject may be found. Thus, entries in the chain index may refer to a whole group of documents. We do not need to repeat the index entry "Carcinoma: Lung" each time a document on this topic is added to the system. The chain index does not grow, then, at an alarming rate, and can provide an economical way of allowing a multiple-access approach to subject retrieval.

However, subject dispersion can occur even with a well-prepared chain index, particularly if the classified file is a highly detailed index in a specialized subject area. These limitations of the chain index were well demonstrated in the first series of Cranfield studies as reported by Cleverdon.[4]

If it is based upon a well-prepared classification scheme using synthetic principles, the classified catalog can provide a highly specific subject approach. However, because the file is pre-coordinate and one-dimensional, it does not allow us the flexibility to combine facets of a topic freely, as we can in a post-coordinate index. To compensate for this, we must provide multiple-access points to complex topics, either through duplication of entries in the classified file or through the supplementary alphabetical index to the file.

Of course, there is no reason why a classification scheme must be used in a pre-coordinate way. Both Vickery[15] and Lancaster[6] have suggested that a faceted classification is highly suitable for use in a post-coor-

dinate system, and in 1958 Rosser[13] described a post-coordinate system based on a classification scheme in aeronautics. Individual notational elements would, in this case, be assigned to a document independently so that collectively they would represent its subject matter. These elements would be brought together, in whatever combination is desired, at the time of searching, using conventional post-coordinate matching mechanisms; for example, a computer or the optical coincidence principle (Figure 10).

A classification scheme can certainly be used to control the semantic problems of synonymy and homography and to offer facilities for generic search. Consider the following segment from *A Faceted Subject Classification for Engineering*[1] of the English Electric Company:

Qr	Fluid Mechanical Properties
Qrc	Viscosity
Qrd	Compressibility
Qre	Elasticity
Qrk	Capillarity, surface tension
Qrm	Thin films
Qrp	Bubbles
Qrq	Drop formation, atomisation

Notice that the term "capillarity" and the term "surface tension" are considered sufficiently close to be treated as synonyms, as also are the two terms "drop formation" and "atomisation." These nearly synonymous terms are controlled by giving each an identical class number. In the alphabetical index to the classification, both terms are referred to the same number. This effectively prevents indexers from separating "capillarity" from "surface tension" and allows retrieval

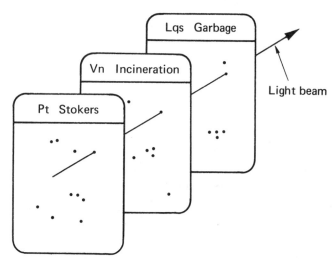

FIGURE 10 Matching notational elements by optical coincidence principle.

of documents on the topic by whichever term springs to the mind of the searcher.

In the Qr facet the makers of the classification scheme have collected together a group of terms representing fluid mechanical properties. This collection facilitates the conduct of a generic search on fluid mechanical properties. The searcher is not forced to think of all possible terms that might apply and, in the classified index, all references to documents on fluid mechanical properties are brought together into physical proximity. Cross-references between various parts of the schedules may also be used to facilitate generic search. For example, in the English Electric scheme, Kg, Seals and Glands, is linked to related terms by the reference "for Oil Seals, Hydraulic Seals, use Kdad."

Homographs are distinguished by the context in which they appear in the schedules and by their treatment in the alphabetical index, as:

Blasting: Cleaning   Vvd
Blasting: Demolition   Umze

One last important point before we leave classification schemes temporarily. The notation of a classification is merely a set of shorthand symbols for the names of classes. It has no significance beyond its function of maintaining the order of the schedules. From the viewpoints of indexing and searching it is completely immaterial whether we label documents on welding by the English-language character string WELDING or by some arbitrary code such as Vs. The important thing is what we put into a class (i.e., how we define its scope) not what we call it.

REFERENCES

1. Binns, J. and Bagley, D. *A Faceted Subject Classification for Engineering.* 3rd ed. Whetstone, England: English Electric Co., 1961.
2. British Standards Institution. *Guide to the Universal Decimal Classification (UDC).* London, 1963. B.S. 1000C: 1963.
3. Brown, J. D. *Subject Classification for the Arrangement of Libraries and the Organization of Information.* 3d ed. London: Grafton & Co., 1939.
4. Cleverdon, C. W. *Report on the Testing and Analysis of an Investigation into the Comparative Efficiency of Indexing Systems.* Cranfield, England: College of Aeronautics, ASLIB Cranfield Research Project, 1962.
5. Dewey, M. *Dewey Decimal Classification and Relative Index.* 17th ed. Lake Placid Club, New York: Forest Press, 1965.
6. Lancaster, F. W. "Engineering Information Storage: Indexing vs. Classification." *Machine Design,* 7 (January 1965): 105-107.
7. Library of Congress. *Classification.* Various parts. Washington, D.C.: Subject Cataloging Division, various dates.
8. Mills, J. "Guide to the Use of the UDC." In: *Guide to the Universal Decimal Classification (UDC).* London, 1963. B.S. 1000C: 1963.
9. Mills, J. *A Modern Outline of Library Classification.* London: Chapman & Hall, 1960.
10. Mills, J. *The Universal Decimal Classification.* New Brunswick, N.J.: Rutgers, the State University, Graduate School of Library Service, 1964.
11. Ranganathan, S. R. *Colon Classification.* 6th ed. Bombay: Asia Publications House, 1960.
12. Ranganathan, S. R. *The Colon Classification.* New Brunswick, N.J.: Rutgers, the State University, 1965.
13. Rosser, J. S. "Coordinate Indexing in an Aeronautical Library." *Library Association Record* 60 (1958): 117-119.
14. Sharp, J. R. *Some Fundamentals of Information Retrieval.* New York: London House, 1965.
15. Vickery, B. C. *Faceted Classification.* London: ASLIB, 1960.

4 Vocabulary Control by Subject Heading

As its name implies, an alphabetical subject catalog provides a subject approach by organizing classes alphabetically according to the labels given to these classes. Unfortunately, the resulting catalog is not necessarily "as simple as ABC."

The first attempt to codify rules for the construction of such a catalog was that of Charles Ammi Cutter in 1876. Prior to this, catalogers gathered material under more or less specific topical headings according to their own judgment. John Shaw Billings, director of the U.S. Surgeon General's Library, who was responsible for the compilation of the first comprehensive alphabetical catalogs of the Library, had his own simple rule for subject entry: "Those titles have been selected for subjects for which it is presumed that the majority of English-speaking physicians would look." Cutter recognized the importance of indexing according to some rules in a consistent fashion:

> The importance of deciding aright where any given subject shall be entered is in inverse proportion to the difficulty of decision. If there is no obvious principle to guide the cataloguer, it is plain there will be no reason why the public should expect to find the entry under one heading rather than another, and therefore in regard to the public it matters not which is chosen. But it is better that such decisions should be made to conform when possible to some general system, as there is then more likelihood that they will be decided alike by different cataloguers, and that a usage will grow up which the public will finally learn and profit by. . . .[3]

Cutter formulated some very useful rules for con-struction of alphabetical subject headings and it is worth considering some of these in more detail:

1. A subject is to be entered under the most specific possible heading; e.g., a book on cats under CATS rather than ZOOLOGY, MAMMALS, or DOMESTIC ANIMALS. Only when no term really exists to describe a particular topic may a more generic term be used. Cutter instances "movement of fluid in plants" which, he suggests, would need to be entered under BOTANY (PHYSIOLOGICAL).

2. A work dealing with both a subject and a country (e.g., geology of France) should receive an entry under both.

3. English expressions should be preferred to foreign wherever appropriate ones exist.

4. If two terms are exactly synonymous, one should be chosen, and a reference made from the other. Nearly synonymous terms may be similarly treated if the distinction is so minor that the separation would be unwarranted. In the selection of the preferred synonym, Cutter suggests the following criteria:

(a) Prefer the heading most familiar to the class of people who consult the library (e.g., popular names in a public library, scientific in a research collection).

(b) Prefer the heading most familiar through use in other catalogs.

(c) Prefer the heading with fewest meanings (and therefore causing least ambiguity).

14

(d) Prefer the heading that brings the subject into the vicinity of other related subjects.

5. Of terms exactly opposite, choose one and refer from the other; e.g., TEMPERANCE and INTEMPERANCE.

6. Homographs should be separated carefully or some other heading should be used in place of one of the homographs.

Cutter warned against assigning subject headings solely on the basis of title: "The title rules the title catalogue; let it confine itself to that province." He also discussed the problems involved in the use of compound headings. Five possible types of heading were recognized:

(a) Single-word: BOTANY or ETHICS
(b) Adjective-noun: CAPITAL PUNISHMENT
(c) Noun-noun: DEATH PENALTY
(d) Noun-preposition-noun: PENALTY OF DEATH
(e) Noun-conjunction-noun: NURSES AND NURSING

Cutter recognized a number of possible ways in which such compound headings could be filed. Filing under the phrase *as it reads* may be preferred for (c) and (e) and in all cases of proper names (e.g., DEMOCRATIC PARTY), with "the most significant word of the phrase" used in (b), (c), and (d); for example, ALIMENTARY CANAL, but PROBABILITY, THEORY OF. Alternatively, each phrase can be filed *as it reads* in (c), (d), (e), but (b) is governed by a special rule; namely, to reduce all adjective-noun phrases to equivalent nouns (e.g., SOCIAL SCIENCE to SOCIOLOGY) wherever possible, otherwise to invert the phrase to take the noun as heading (e.g., CHEMISTRY, AGRICULTURAL).

Cutter finally recommended that a compound subject heading be entered under the first word unless some other word "is decidedly more significant or is often used alone with the same meaning as the whole name."

Cutter advocated double entry for books dealing with more than a single topic, although there are situations where a reference will suffice instead. For example, ARCHITECTURE *see also* SPAIN, ARCHITECTURE is permissible but GOTHIC ARCHITECTURE *see also* SPAIN, ARCHITECTURE is not, because this would mean that the searcher would be forced to look at all references to Spanish architecture when he is interested solely in Gothic.

The major problems of the alphabetical subject catalog are well demonstrated by a brief review of Cutter's rules. They include synonymy, homography, and word order as well as the problem of multitopical documents.

The American Library Association (ALA) issued the first authoritative list of subject headings in 1895.[1]

Cutter served on the committee preparing the list, which was based on the practices of five major libraries, including the Peabody Institute and the Boston Athenaeum. The general principle of the ALA list was: "the heading shall be that under which it is supposed that the majority of educated Americans will look, with cross-references from other forms of heading." Other rules specified:

1. Use common names instead of technical, English instead of foreign, but not if the common or English name is ambiguous or of ill-defined extent.
2. Use singular rather than plural except where subjects are only thought of under the plural.
3. Use headings most generally found in the leading catalogs.
4. Put compound names under the first word unless some other is more significant.

The ALA list included single-word headings (FAMINES), adjective-noun headings (ELECTRIC WAVES), noun-noun headings (BANK NOTES), and phrases (VOYAGES AROUND THE WORLD). There were only a very few inversions (CELL, VOLTAIC) and no subheadings as such were used.

The first edition (1911) of the Library of Congress *List of Subject Headings*,[4] on the other hand, made extensive use of subheadings, as the following entry under BLOOD will show:

BLOOD
—Analysis and chemistry
—Buffy coat
—Circulation
—Coagulation
—Corpuscles and platelets
—Diseases
—Examination
—Jurisprudence
—Parasites
—Pressure
—Semeiology. See Blood—Examination
—Serum
—Transfusion

These early subject heading lists set the pattern for vocabulary control for alphabetical subject catalogs for many years, and standard lists of subject headings are still used for the purposes of vocabulary control in most libraries in the United States. The Library of Congress list is a widely accepted standard, now in its seventh edition (1966).

The list of subject headings is capable of serving the functions of a controlled vocabulary as these were described in Chapter 1. Expressions considered synonymous, or sufficiently synonymous for the purposes of subject cataloging, are linked by *see* references, as:

Cymric language *see* Welsh language

The reciprocal of such a reference is also indicated in the list. The entry

Welsh language
  x Cymric language

indicates that a *see* reference exists from Cymric language to Welsh language. The Library of Congress consistently used the symbol x to represent the reciprocal of a *see* reference and this convention has been adopted in other subject heading lists.

The *see* reference, besides its functions in control of synonyms, is frequently used to refer from a specific heading which is not used for indexing to the appropriate more general heading which is used, as:

Welding stresses
  See Residual stresses

In this case, the class "welding stresses" is not uniquely defined in the system but is subsumed under the broader class "residual stresses."

Homographs are distinguished by simple parenthetical scope notes:

MERCURY (METAL),
MERCURY (PLANET),

by more extensive scope notes, or by combining them into compound headings:

BASINS, RIVER

It is in its ability to provide for generic search that the list of subject headings differs most markedly from the classification scheme. In the latter, related terms are brought together by carefully applied principles of division, whereas in the subject heading list related terms may be widely separated according to their alphabetical positions. If we wish to undertake a comprehensive search on joining of metals, we may find relevant terms throughout the alphabet: COLD WELDING, ELECTRIC WELDING, GLASS-METAL SEALING, OXYACETYLENE WELDING, SOLDER AND SOLDERING, ULTRASONIC WELDING, and so on. The subject heading list indicates relationships of this type by means of *see also* references. These provide, in Cutter's words, a "syndetic structure," a sort of hidden classification scheme.

Cutter has this to say about the syndetic structure of the alphabetical index:

Its subject-entries, individual, general, limited, extensive, thrown together without any logical arrangement, in most absurd proximity—ABSCESS followed by ABSENTEEISM and that by ABSOLUTION, CLUB-FOOT next to CLUBS, and COMMUNION to COMMUNISM, while CHRISTIANITY and THEOLOGY, BIBLIOGRAPHY and LITERARY HISTORY are separated by half

the length of the catalogue—are a mass of utterly disconnected particles without any relation to one another, each useful in itself but only by itself. But by a well-devised network of cross-references the mob becomes an army, of which each part is capable of assisting many other parts.[3]

Cutter recommended making reference from general subjects to their various subordinate subjects and also to "coordinate and illustrative subjects." The catalog would thus contain a pyramid of references from the general to the specific, compiled systematically to ensure that the structure is complete. Cutter also considered that reference from the specific to the general would be necessary on certain occasions.

Following the pattern established by Cutter, the alphabetical subject catalog makes extensive use of *see also* references to tie related terms together. Consider the following sample from the Library of Congress list:

Wells
  sa Artesian wells
        Boring
        Gas, natural
        Petroleum
        Springs
        Water, Underground
        Water—supply
        Well drillers
  XX   Boring
        Hydraulic engineering
        Springs
        Water
        Water, Underground
        Water—supply

Note that the *see also* (*sa*) references are made to terms that are true species of the parent term (e.g., ARTESIAN WELLS) and also to terms that are related in other ways, including related activities, materials, and processes. These references cut across the formal hierarchical structures and provide associations that would not normally be indicated explicitly in a classified schedule. As in the case of the *see* references, reciprocals are also shown in the subject heading list. The symbol XX before the second sequence of terms above indicates that under each of these terms there appears a direction to *see also* WELLS.

In a properly constructed list of headings (and thus in catalogs based on such a list) there will be a systematic stepwise sequence of references from the general to the specific. For example, the term JOINING may refer to WELDING, WELDING to ARC WELDING, ARC WELDING to SHIELDED ARC WELDING, SHIELDED ARC WELDING to ARGON ARC WELDING and HELIUM ARC WELDING, which ends this particular chain since there are no terms in the vocabulary more specific than these last two.

References from the specific to the general are relatively rare in the alphabetical subject catalog, although they do appear in some authority lists and are strongly advocated by Coates.[2] Blanket references are also used where appropriate in many lists of headings; for example,

Draft animals
sa Draft horses
also specific animals used for draft purposes, e.g., asses and mules, oxen.

The network of *see also* references may include references to main heading/subheading combinations, as:

Bacteriology *see also* Water—Bacteriology

and from subheadings to subheadings:

Japan—Religion *see also* Buddha and Buddhism—Japan

It is obvious that the alphabetical subject catalog presents much of the same problems as the classified catalog. Through highly pre-coordinate phrase headings (e.g., "Echo Scattering Layers," "Lutherans in Georgia") and the use of topical subheadings ("Indians—Religion and Mythology," "Egg-plant—Diseases and Pests") it is possible to achieve a high level of specificity. However, the level of specificity attainable is entirely governed by the specificity provided in the list of subject headings used. A list of subject headings is an enumerative authority list just as much as an enumerative classification is. We can pre-coordinate only as far as this enumerative authority list specifies. But if we have a document on "welding of aluminum" and have no way of pre-coordinating the two facets (e.g., by using one as a subheading of the other), we are forced to resort to double entry and, as with the enumerative classification, have sacrificed specificity so that we will never be able to use the catalog to retrieve references on "welding of aluminum" and only "welding of aluminum."

Furthermore, the pre-coordinate compound heading, with which we achieve a reasonable level of specificity, presents the problem of word order first addressed by Cutter and later by many others, notably Pettee [5] and Coates.[2]

SYNTHESIS IN SUBJECT HEADINGS

In certain quarters it was eventually realized that the alphabetical subject catalog could only achieve the specificity necessary to represent highly complex subject matter by abandoning a strictly enumerative approach based on a pre-established list of subject headings and adopting, like the classified catalog, some form of synthesis. In other words, a subject heading in an alphabetical index should be a synthesis of component elements which collectively are reasonably co-extensive with the precise subject matter of the document described.

Ranganathan addressed the problem in his *Dictionary Catalogue Code*,[6] but it was really Coates [2] who developed this concept to its logical conclusion. Coates advocates an alphabetical subject catalog free from the rigidity of a list of subject headings. In fact, a subject heading should be tailor-made to fit the exact subject matter discussed in a document: the heading should be co-extensive with the subject complex to be indexed. Thus, a tailor-made subject heading may look something like:

Power Transmission Lines, Overhead, Conductors, Icing, Prevention, Heating

This type of heading is very similar to a synthesized notation. It has a number of component parts that have been put together in a particular sequence to describe a highly complex topic. Clearly, when we create a precise heading of this type, the problems of sequence are even more critical than they are in conventional subject headings. Coates uses a "significance formula" to establish a citation order for the formulation of such headings, which are the type of headings used in the *British Technology Index* (Figure 11) of which Coates is editor. This basic formula adopts the sequence: Thing, Part, Material, Action, Property, but the sequence may be modified in certain circumstances. In the heading used above, for example, the sequence is Thing, Kind, Part, Action, Agent.

Coates has also described how chain procedure can be used to derive subject headings in a systematic manner. By means of chain procedure we can determine how a complex topic would be treated in a classification scheme, and this will give us the raw material necessary to establish both a specific subject heading and a chain of appropriate hierarchical references. To revert to the simple example in the last chapter, "radiotherapy of lung carcinoma" could, by chain procedure, be reduced to the following specific heading and chain of hierarchical references:

Lung, Carcinoma, Radiotherapy
Respiratory system *See also* Lung
Carcinoma *See also* Lung, Carcinoma
Malignant tumors *See also* Carcinoma
Radiotherapy *See also* Lung, Carcinoma, Radiotherapy .

A somewhat similar approach to the creation of

EXTRUSION : Metals. See METALS : Extrusion

FABRICS
  Related Headings :
    WEAVING
**FABRICS, Cellulosic ,, Crease resistant : Cross linking :
Dimethylol-1, 3-propylene urea**
  Deferred curing [BP 1,107,796 : Sun Chemical Corp., USA] Dyer,
    Textile Printer, Bleacher & Finisher, 141 (2 May 69) p.614+
FABRICS, Cellulosic ,, Crease resistant : Finishing
  Crease-resist and wash-and-wear finishing. B.C.M. Dorset. Textile
    Manufacturer, 95 (Apr 69) p.156-63
FABRICS, Cellulosic ,, Knitted ,, Crease resistant : Finishing
  Permanent press processes for knitted fabrics. D. Haigh. Hosiery Trade
    J., 76 (May 69) p.127+. il.
FABRICS ; Cellulosic–Nylon : Dyeing, High temperature : Dyes, Reactive
  "Hot-dyeing" reactive dyes on blends [Drimarene X and Drimafon X :
    Sandoz Products Ltd, Horsforth, Leeds] [summary] P.F. Bell. Dyer,
    Textile Printer, Bleacher & Finisher, 141 (2 May 69) p.622+
**FABRICS ; Cellulosic–Polyester fibres : Dyeing, High temperature :
Dyes, Reactive**
  "Hot-dyeing" reactive dyes on blends [Drimarene X and Drimafon X :
    Sandoz Products Ltd, Horsforth, Leeds] [summary] P.F. Bell. Dyer,
    Textile Printer, Bleacher & Finisher, 141 (2 May 69) p.622+
FABRICS, Coated : Clothing. See CLOTHING : Fabrics, Coated
FABRICS : Finishing : Weft straighteners : Control system, Photoelectric
  Fabric straightening [BP 1,107,822] H. Elcken. Dyer, Textile
    Printer, Bleacher & Finisher, 141 (2 May 69) p.612+
FABRICS, Foamback : Laminating
  Versatility the key : different cloths call for different techniques. P.
    Lennox-Kerr. Hosiery Times, 42 (Apr 69) p.107-9. il.
FABRICS ; Man made fibres ,, Pile : Knitting
  Manufacture and use-development of pile fabrics in Du Pont fibres.
    J. Rest & M.R.B. Addison. Hosiery Times, 42 (Apr 69) p.88+. il.
FABRICS ; Mohair : Suitings. See SUITINGS : Fabrics ; Mohair
FABRICS : Tape. See TAPE : Fabrics
**FABRICS, Warp knit : Dyeing, High temperature : Heating : Heat
transfer oil**
  HT process heating in the modern dyehouse [Kestner-Stone-Vapor at
    Nyla-Raywarp, Long Eaton] Dyer, Textile Printer, Bleacher &
    Finisher, 141 (18 Apr 69) p.542+
FABRICS, Warp knit : Knitwear. See KNITWEAR : Fabrics, Warp knit
**FABRICS ; Wool ,, Knitted ,, Shrink resistant : Finishing : Solvents :
Perchloroethylene : Machines**
  'Bentley Rapide' solvent finishing machine for knitwear and piece-goods.
    A.G. Brooks. Hosiery Times, 42 (Apr 69) p.45+. il.
  Milling machine for knitwear [Bentley Rapide] Hosiery Trade J., 76
    (May 69) p.130+. il.
FABRICS ; Worsted : Manufactures
  What do we get from 50 packs of wool ? [W.E. Yates, Leeds] R.P.
    Hollock. Textile Manufacturer, 95 (Apr 69) p.164-5
FABRICS ; Worsted : Weaving : Costs
  Cost structure in worsted weaving [Sulzer machines] Textile
    Manufacturer, 95 (Apr 69) p.133-6
FACTORIES
  Related Headings :
    CLEAN ROOMS
    FOOD : Processing : Factories
    GLASS : Manufactures : Factories
FACTORIES : Colour
  Colour in the factory. L.R. Leworthy. Works Engng. & Factory Services,
    64 (Apr 69) p.50-3. il. refs.
FACTORIES : Conversion to shopping centres. See SHOPPING
    CENTRES : Conversion from factories
FACTORIES : Paint, Fire retardant
  Colour in the factory. L.R. Leworthy. Works Engng. & Factory Services,
    64 (Apr 69) p.50-3. il. refs.
FACTORIES : Sites
  Helping industry to move in. I.R. Holden & F.N. Brydon. Municipal J.,
    77 (30 May 69) p.1366-7. il.
FACTORY SHIPS : Stern trawlers. See TRAWLERS, Stern : Factory ships
FANS : Firing : Incinerators : Refuse. See REFUSE : Incinerators :
    Firing : Fans
FARES : Buses. See BUSES : Fares
FARM BUILDINGS
  Scottish farm buildings. R.S. Morton. Architectural Rev., 145 (Apr 69)
    p.244-5. il.
FARM BUILDINGS
  Related Headings :
    SHEEP : Shearing : Buildings
FARM MACHINERY. See AGRICULTURAL MACHINERY
    APPLES : Storage : Scald : *alpha*-Farnesene formation
alpha-FARNESENE : Formation : Scald : Storage : Apples. See

FAST NUCLEAR REACTORS. See NUCLEAR REACTORS, Fast
FAST NUCLEAR REACTORS : Irradiation : Nuclear reactor materials.
    See NUCLEAR REACTORS : Materials : Irradiation : Fast reactors
FASTENERS : Threads : Measurement : Metric system
  Metrication: data sheet 5. Light Production Engng. (May 69) p.55
FASTNESS : Colour : Carpets. See CARPETS : Colour fastness
FATIGUE, Constant strain : High tensile steel. See STEEL, High
    tensile : Fatigue, Constant strain
FATIGUE : Studded joints. See JOINTS, Studded : Fatigue
FATLIQUORS : Vacuum drying : Leather. See LEATHER : Drying,
    Vacuum : Fatliquors
FATS. See OILS
FATTY ACIDS
  Related Headings :
    GLYCERIDES
    SULPHATED OILS
FATTY ACIDS : Seed oil : Bauhinia. See BAUHINIA : Seed : Oil :
    Fatty acids
FATTY ACIDS : Seed oil : Delonix regia. See DELONIX REGIA :
    Seed : Oil : Fatty acids
FATTY ACIDS : Seed oil : Ito. See ITO : Seed : Oil : Fatty acids
FATTY ACIDS : Seed oil : Nephelium lappaceum. See NEPHELIUM
    LAPPACEUM : Seed : Oil : Fatty acids
FATTY ACIDS : Triglycerides : *n*-Alkanes substrates : Yeast. See
    YEAST : Substrates : *n*-Alkanes : Triglycerides : Fatty acids
FEED UNITS : Assembly machines. See ASSEMBLY : Machines :
    Feed units
FEEDER HEADS : Casting : Steel. See STEEL : Casting : Feeder heads
FEEDERS : Electrodes : Microplasma arc welding : Mar-ageing steel ;
    Sheets. See SHEETS ; Steel, Mar-ageing : Welding, Microplasma
    arc : Electrodes : Feeders
FEEDWATER : Boilers. See BOILERS : Feedwater
FEEDWATER : Water tube boilers. See BOILERS, Water tube : Feedwater
FERMENTATION : Protein synthesis. See PROTEIN : Synthesis :
    Fermentation
FERMENTATION : Wines. See WINES : Fermentation
FERRIMAGNETIC MATERIALS
  Related Headings :
    GARNETS ; Yttrium–Iron
FERRITIC STEEL : Cooling systems : Steam generating heavy water
    moderated nuclear reactors. See NUCLEAR REACTORS, Heavy water
    moderated ,, Steam generating : Cooling systems : Steel, Ferritic
FERROCHROMIUM. See IRON–CHROMIUM
FERRORESONANT ASYNCHRONOUS RELUCTANCE ELECTRIC
    MOTORS. See ELECTRIC MOTORS, Reluctance ,, Asynchronous ,,
    Ferroresonant
FERROUS METALS. See IRON
FERROUS METALS. See STEEL
FIBRE BOARD
  Related Headings :
    HARDBOARD
FIBRE BOARD : Building materials : Buyers' guides
  FIDOR brand list. : types, sizes and properties of fibre building boards.
    Wood, 34 (Apr 69) p.53-73
FIBRE BOARD : Building materials : International System of Units
  Metrication : some of the effects on fibre building boards. Wood, 34
    (Apr 69) p.29-30
FIBRE BOARD : Cladding : Wood ; Frames : Buildings. See BUILD-
    INGS : Frames ; Wood : Cladding : Fibre board
FIBRE BOARD : Modernisation : Housing. See HOUSING : Modernisa-
    tion : Fibre board
FIBRE BOARD ; Prefabricated house components. See HOUSES, Prefabri-
    cated : Components ; Fibre board
FIBRE GLASS : Reinforced plastics ; Panels : Houses. See HOUSES :
    Panels ; Plastics, Reinforced : Glass fibre

FIBRE GLASS–POLYESTER ; Chlorine production plant. See CHLORINE :
    Production : Plant ; Polyester–Glass fibre
FIBRE OPTICS : Image intensifiers. See IMAGE INTENSIFIERS : Fibre
    optics
FIBRE REINFORCED COMPOSITE ENGINEERING MATERIALS. See
    ENGINEERING : Materials, Composite, Fibre reinforced
FIBRES : Carbon. See CARBON : Fibres
FIBRES : Polyethylene terephthalate. See POLYETHYLENE TERE-
    PHTHALATE : Fibres
FIBRES, Textile. See TEXTILES
FIELD EFFECT TRANSISTORS. See TRANSISTORS, Field effect
FIELD ION MICROSCOPES. See MICROSCOPES, Field ion
FIGHTER AIRCRAFT, Types, MiG-15UTI
  MiG-15UTI. J. Fricker. Flight, 95 (24 Apr 69) p.669-72. il.
FILE CONVERTERS : Computers. See COMPUTERS : File converters
**FILING SYSTEMS : Trays ; Wood : Corners : Jointing : Moulding,
Spindle : Machines : Control systems**
  Automatic corner locking on a spindle moulder. F.E. Sherlock.
    Woodworking Industry, 26 (May 69) p.15-16. il.
FILLERS : Papermaking. See PAPERMAKING : Fillers

FIGURE 11 Specimen page from the *British Technology Index.*

ion (Mn^{7+}), energy levels of, transitions between, line strengths of, 69:55809a

ion (Mn^{9+}), spin-orbit coupling const. of, 69:6936f

ion (Mn^{10+}), spin-orbit coupling const. of, 69:6936f

ion (Mn^{12+}), spin-orbit coupling const. of, 69:6936f

ion (Mn^{13+}), spin-orbit coupling const. of, 69:6936f

ion (Mn^{15+}), energy levels of, transitions between, oscillator strengths for, 69:6810k

ion (Mn^{16+}), spin-orbit coupling const. of, 69:6936f

ion (Mn^{17+}), spin-orbit coupling const. of, 69:6936f

ion (Mn^{19+}), spin-orbit coupling const. of, 69:6936f

ion (Mn^{20+}), spin-orbit coupling const. of, 69:6936f

ions, contribution of, to summary d. of orbital electrons, iron-57 Moessbauer isomeric shift in relation to, 69:63221t

isotope of mass 53
  gamma rays from and nuclear energy levels of, in iron-53 decay, 69:112360y
  nuclear energy levels of, from proton bombardment of chromium-53, 69:40262t

isotope of mass 54
  half-life of, 69:7391m
  nuclear energy levels of, from alpha-ray bombardment of chromium-52, 69:56292p

isotope of mass 56
  half-life of, 69:7391m
  from uranium-238 fission by alpha-rays, 69:63764x

Knight shift of manganese-55 in aluminum and related alloys, 69:111918z

luminescence
  of calcium chloride phosphate ($Ca_{10}Cl_2(PO_4)_6$) and calcium fluoride phosphate ($Ca_{10}F_2(PO_4)_6$) contg., 69:63343j
  of glass contg., energy transfer in relation to, 69:91587k
  of lithium fluoride contg., thermal treatment effect on, 69:23415c
  of solid solns. of alk. earth halides in alk. phosphate contg., 69:48010e
  of zirconium silicates contg., 69:31804u

luminescence (cando- and cathodo-) of calcium oxide contg., radical recombination in relation to, 69:111849c

luminescence (cathodo-) of cadmium sulfide-zinc sulfide solid solns. contg., elec. field effect on, 69:62734a

luminescence (chemi-)
  in autoxidn. of oleic acid in presence of, quenching of, 69:111795g
  of hydrogen peroxideluminol mixts. contg. amines and, 69:31818b

luminescence (electro-) and resistance of tin oxide (SnO_2) doped with, 69:71739h

luminescence (electro-)
  of zinc selenide contg., 69:62740z
  of zinc sulfide contg., photocond. in relation to, 69:6172d
  of zinc sulfide doped with chloride and copper and, 69:71159q
  of zinc sulfide films contg. chloride and copper and, excitation of, mechanism of, 69:81588x

luminescence (recombination)
  of zinc silicate contg., concn. effect on, 69:48008k
  of zinc sulfate and zinc sulfide contg. at. hydrogen and, 69:6860b

luminescence (thermo-)
  of aluminum oxide and silica gel contg. zinc silicate (Zn_2SiO_4) and, 69:31820w
  of calcium halide phosphates contg., 69:23414b
  of calcium sulfate ($CaSO_4$) contg., after beta-irradiation, 69:6819v
  of calcium sulfate doped with, and applications to radiation dosimetry, 69:82732b

luminescence (tribo-) of zinc sulfide contg., during comminution with sugar, 69:39990x

magnetic hyperfine field at, in copper and copper-manganese alloys, 69:39872k

magnetic moment of
  in antimony-copper-manganese alloys, 69:22847h
  in cobalt manganese carbides, 69:101076j
  in dipotassium tetrafluoromanganate(2-), 69:14033z
  in gold-manganese compd. (AuMn), 69:91366n
  in manganese neodymium oxide ($MnNdO_3$) and manganese praseodymium oxide ($MnPrO_3$), 69:111436r
  valence in relation to localized, 69:47553x

magnetic (para-) centers in calcium sulfate contg., 69:47603p

magnetic relaxation
  in manganese(2+)-contg. solns., hyperfine coupling effect on, 69:31905c
  of protons in aq. paramagnetic solns. contg., heavy water (D_2O) isotopic effects on, 69:63456y

magnetization of Invar contg., pressure effect on, 69:81798r

magnetoresistance of gold contg., 69:91390r

magnon and phonon spectra of iron contg., neutron inelastic scattering in relation to, 69:47551v

mech.
  of aluminum-lithium-magnesium alloys contg., 69:109292x

mech.
  of aluminum-magnesium alloy castings contg., effect of coarse inclusions on, 69:109236g
  of nuclear reactor fuel element cans and plugs of magnesium alloys contg., 69:48540c

mech. properties and microstructure
  of ductile iron contg., 69:89065v
  of gray iron contg., 69:89071u
  of silicon-free iron in relation to chromium and, 69:29555v

π-mesonic atoms of manganese-55, x-ray spectrum of, 69:112236d

mol. (Mn_2), heat of dissocn. of, 69:99586e

neutron inelastic scattering by manganese-55, nuclear energy level excitation in, 69:91958g

neutron resonance integrals and self-shielding of factors manganese-55, 69:40601c

neutron resonance integrals of manganese-55, 69:73253u

neutron scattering by, symmetry term in optical potential for, 69:7295h

nodules
  gold and iridium and vanadium in, 69:108741f
  potassium and radium and thorium in, 69:88874w

nuclear magnetic resonance
  of boron-11 in calcium borate ($Ca(BO_2)_2$) contg., 69:82096x
  of copper-63 in copper contg., ground-state energy levels in relation to, 69:56106f
  of manganese-55 in α-, quadrupole effects in, 69:14692p
  of manganese-55 in iron-nickel base alloys, nuclear field interactions in relation to, 69:72675w
  of manganese-55 in manganese ferrite, steady-state, 69:101516c
  of phosphorus-31 in phosphoric acid solns. in presence of, 69:23497f

nuclear quadrupole resonance
  of manganese-55 in complexes with carbonyls and cyclopentadiene derivs., 69:23545v
  of manganese-55 in manganese cyclopentadienyltricarbonyl complexes, 69:82160p

nuclear screening in, Hartree-Fock wave functions for, 69:82143k

nuclear spin coupling with electron angular momentum of, in α-manganese sulfide (MnS), 69:56120f

optical double resonance of aluminum oxide contg., 69:56164y

oxidn. of, electrolytic, exchange current between liq. manganese and oxide melts in relation to, 69:40676f

paper pulp contg., bleaching of, 69:60138k

partition functions of, electronic, 69:89797k

partition of
  in alkali metal halides, in zone melting, 69:54427n
  between aq. soln. and tributyl phosphate in presence of salicylic acid, 69:110457m
  between aq. sulfuric acid and org. solvents, in presence of dibutyl phosphate and tributyl phosphate, 69:22515y

phys. properties of malleable iron in relation to, 69:12318x

proton inelastic scattering by manganese-55, detn. of octupole weak coupling states from, 69:91959h

quality of malleable iron in relation to sulfur and, 69:29505d

quantum mech. exchange in relation to D-parameter of cobalt chloride ($CoCl_2$) dihydrate contg., 69:111926a

recrystn.
  of iron contg., 69:98711e
  of tungsten contg., nickel effect on, 69:79658b

segregation of, in eutectic gray and white iron, 69:53752c

soly. of, in liq. plutonium, 69:70512s

sorption of
  by inorg. and org. compds., ore formation in relation to, 69:88713t
  by soil-forming minerals, 69:105373b

sound vibration spectrum in discharge of, 69:13109s

spectral lines of in stars of later type, 69:47697x

spectra (uv) of binary systems contg., evapn. and phase diagram in relation to, 69:72406j

spectra (visible and uv), of potassium chloride and rubidium bromide contg., charge transfer bands in, 69:72457b

spectrum (ir) of synthetic quartz contg., 69:6556g

spectrum of, boron and phosphorus effect on line intensity in, 69:32653f

spectrum (visible and uv)
  in argon in ballistic compressor, 69:14491x
  in elec. plasma accelerator, electron and ion temps. in relation to, 69:73144j
  in perchloric acid media contg. complexing ligands, band shifts in, 69:63241z

spectrum (visible) of, in flame, enhancement of, 69:73628v

spectrum (x-ray) of, 69:14149s
  in manganese and manganese compds. with spinel structure K_β line groups in, 69:14137m
  in manganese oxides, 69:111521q

stability of aluminum silicate (Al_2SiO_5) minerals contg., 69:90435x

structure of cesium antimonide (Cs_3Sb) films contg., 69:39477k

structure of steadite in gray iron contg., 69:89036m

sublimation of, kinetics of, 69:69771u

systems: aluminum-copper-lithium-, 69:54878k

systems: boron-, 69:70449b

systems: cadmium- and zinc—, crystal structure and quant. size factors in, 69:71200a

systems: chromium-iron- 69:69143r
  and α- and γ-phases in relation thereto, 69:90499w

systems: germanium-, 69:62090n

systems: iron-, 69:54887n, 108988s

systems: iron-phosphorus-sulfur-, 69:90491n

systems: neodymium-, 69:70371v

systems: platinum-, exchange interactions and magnetic structure in, 69:47578j

systems: tin-, 69:61125v

thermal cond. of structures from films of bismuth-indium alloys and, proximity effect in supercond. in relation to, 69:55430v

thermodynamics of aq. solns. of, dissolved oxygen effect on, 69:22619k

thermodynamics of, in copper-manganese alloy melts, 69:22690b

transfer of, between iron alloys and slags, 69:29436g

transformation of α-, Landau-Lifshitz theory of second order phase, 69:89768b

transformation of cast iron contg., and intracryst. segregation therein, 69:38125g

ultrasound velocity in iron nickel oxide ($NiFe_2O_4$) contg., in magnetic field, hysteresis of, 69:47595n

valence of, in copper manganese oxide ($CuMn_2O_4$), temp. effect on, 69:62545q

vapor pressure of, 69:22227f

wear resistance of cast iron camshafts contg., 69:P 12409c

wetting by, of diamond and graphite, 69:109290v

x-ray K fluorescence of manganese-55, hole lifetime in relation to, 69:47658k

yield strength of sodium chloride contg., 69:31000d

Manganese, reactions

alpha-ray bombardment of manganese-55, tritons from, angular distribution of, 69:91956e

aquation of, kinetics of, 69:100105f

cementation of
  with of aluminum-molybdenum-titanium alloys, fatigue strength and wear resistance in relation to, 69:61915p
  of Armco iron and steel, electrochem.-thermal treatment in, 69:45483a
  of iron and nickel powders, in prepn. of iron-manganese and nickel-manganese sintered alloys, 69:79594c
  of iron, during casting, app. for, 69:P 109128y
  of steel, induction heating in, 69:P 109132v

chromium-iron alloys contg., with fused silica, 69:60968f

corrosion of, current yield in manganese electrolysis in relation to, 69:82808f
  with furnace combustion products, 69:53882v

hydrolysis of, in disodium sulfate aq. mixts. with manganese sulfate ($MnSO_4$), 69:80995r

isotope of mass 54, electron-capture decay of, 69:112361z

isotope of mass 56
  beta-ray decay of, and γ-spectrum therein, 69:7409y
  decay of, calcn. of isospin admixt. for Fermi matrix elements for, 69:40140b
  Szilard-Chalmers reaction of, in neutron-irradiated tricarbonyl(π-cyclopentadienyl)manganese and tricarbonyl(methyl-π-cyclopentadienyl)manganese, 69:14855u

neutron bombardment of, gamma-rays from, 69:56349n

neutron bombardment of manganese-55, parametric fit of total cross sections of, 69:14953z

neutron capture by manganese-55 69:101909h
  energy dependence of cross section for, 69:7405u

neutron capture resonance integrals of manganese-55, 69:63706e

neutron cross sections of manganese-55, 69:91798e

neutron photoproduction from, 69:63662n

neutron total cross sections of 69:72936g
  nuclear structure detn. from, 69:72998d

neutron total cross sections of manganese-55, intermediate structure in, 69:72995a

nitridation of, kinetics of, 69:29665f

nitridation of molten, pressure effect on, 69:29691m

oxidn. by, of iron(2+), kinetics of, in aq. manganese(3+)-contg. solns., 69:80761m

oxidn. of, in water treatment, 69:89645j

oxidn. of manganese(2+) by ozone in aq. soln., 69:100209t

oxidn. of nickel contg., 69:38349h

oxidn.-redn. of, on magnesium oxide surfaces, E.S.R. in relation to, 69:72706g

polarography of
  alcs. in suppression of maxima in, 69:112874u
  in sulfolane, 69:112800s

FIGURE 12 Specimen page from the subject index to *Chemical Abstracts*.

solution of close-coupling equations for, 24:23789
electron excitation of, in corona, (T), 24:32579
electron reactions with Be⁺, calculation of excitation
    cross sections using classical binary-encounter
    calculation of excitation cross sections for, 24:17694
energy levels of Be III, eigenvalues and radiative
    lifetimes for 2p² ³P and 2p3p ¹P states, (T), 24:25979
energy levels of Be²⁺, oscillator strengths for, (T),
    24:42537
energy of Be²⁺, use of general spin orbitals in
    calculation of spin-projected Hartree--Fock, 24:17645
light scattering on, excitation rate coefficients for,
    24:10506(R) (ORO-3393-7)
perturbation energies of Be²⁺, calculation using Pade
    approximants and Brillouin--Wigner series, 24:37208
radii in fluorides and oxides, 24:188
spectra of, bibliography on analyses of optical,
    24:44991 (NBS-SPEC. PUBL-306-1)
wave functions for Be²⁺, 1/Z perturbation expansion for
    natural orbitals and occupation numbers, 24:35214
wave functions for Be²⁺, use of general spin orbitals in
    calculation of spin-projected Hartree--Fock, 24:17645
wave functions for excited ¹P states of Be²⁺, self-
    consistent, 24:19778
BERYLLIUM ISOTOPES
    production by alpha reactions with carbon and nitrogen at
        70 MeV, cross sections for, (E/T), 24:52456
    production with 200 MeV protons, calculation of yields
        from spallation, 24:9594 (BNL-50195)
    yields from californium-252 spontaneous fission, (E),
        24:40651
BERYLLIUM ISOTOPES Be-6
    energy levels from lithium-6 (He-3,t) reactions, (E),
        24:5389(R) (COO-1265-83)
    energy levels from resonances in helium-3--helium-3
        scattering, comparison of experimental data and
        resonating group calculations for, (E/T), 24:38084
    nuclear properties of, description using resonating-group
        method, (T), 24:28854
BERYLLIUM ISOTOPES Be-7
    abundance in Allende meteorite, (E), 24:4867
    abundance in Apollo 11 lunar samples, (E), 24:21542
    abundance in lower atmosphere, (E), 24:37291
    content in atmosphere, rainwater, and seawater during
        BOMEX, 24:39060 (BNWL-1307(Pt.1), pp 60)
    content in atmospheric dust and precipitation in Germany,
        Nov. 1969, 24:9526(R) (NYO-4061-1)
    content in atmospheric precipitation in Leningrad, 1961
        to 1965, 24:7524(T) (UCRL-Trans-10403)
    content in ground-level atmosphere at Aspendale,
        Australia, Sept. 1967 to May 1968, 24:5754
    content in near-sea surface atmosphere above Caribbean
        Sea, 24:14075 (BNWL-1051(Pt.1), pp 30-4)
    content in northeast Pacific Ocean in relation with
        depth, (E), 24:14099 (RLO-1750-54, pp 71-4)
    content of atmospheric precipitation in Croatia, 1965 to
        1968, 24:325
    content of cosmogenic, in atmosphere, (E), 24:27244
    content of cosmogenic, in ground-level atmosphere in
        Leningrad, 1963 to 1967, 24:11701(T) (AEC-tr-7128, pp
        263-87)
    content of cosmogenic, in ground-level atmosphere in USSR
        during 1965 to 1969, 24:41447
    content of eucalyptus leaves and grass at Lawrence
        Radiation Laboratory, Livermore, 24:41870
    content of excreta of Apollo astronauts, 24:12066(R)
        (BNWL-1183-1)
    content of fallout, in ground-level atmosphere in
        Leningrad, 1963 to 1966, 24:11701(T) (AEC-tr-7128, pp
        263-87)
    content of feces and urine from Apollo 12 astronauts,
        24:39501(R) (BNWL-1183-4)
    content of feces and urine of astronauts from Apollo 13
        mission, 24:48535(R) (BNWL-1183-5)
    content of feces and urine samples from astronauts during
        Apollo 11 space flight, 24:23191(R) (BNWL-1183-3)
    content of soil of east central and northeast Georgia,
        fallout, 24:17040
    content relative to cesium-137 in Indian surface
        atmosphere, 24:46358
    determination in fission product mixture containing
        inorganic salts by ion exchange and γ spectrometry,
        24:13765 (CEA-R-3877)
    determination in lunar dust and rocks from Apollo 11 by γ
        spectrometry, 24:20724
    determination in lunar materials by γ spectrometry,
        24:31252
    distribution of cosmogenic, in surface seawater,
        24:48193 (BNWL-1307(Pt.2), pp 8-10)
    electron-capture decay of, branching ratio for, (E),
        24:47637 (ANL-7610, pp 1-59)
    electron-capture decay of, half-life for, (E),
        24:28726(R) (AECL-3512)
    energy levels from lithium-6 (He-3,d) reactions, (E),
        24:45754
    energy levels from lithium-7 (p,n) reactions, isobaric
        analog, (T), 24:49707 (SINP-TH-68-4)
    fallout from troposphere, (E), 24:37364
    half-life in man and mammal, 24:25479 (CEA-CONF-1445)
    monitoring in environs of Savannah River Plant,
        24:25473(R) (DPST-70-30-1)
    production and chemical separation of carrier-free, use
        of synchrocyclotron in, 24:20793(T) (ORNL-tr-2006)

    production by 87-MeV electron reactions with carbon,
        nitrogen, and oxygen, (E), 24:40554 (AD-703259)
    production from proton spallation of argon at 310, 425,
        and 578 MeV, cross sections for, 24:35877
    production in alpha reactions with aluminum-27 at 104
        MeV, excitation functions for, (E), 24:28733 (KFK-
        1083)
    production in deuteron reactions with aluminum-27 at 52
        MeV, excitation functions for, (E), 24:28733 (KFK-
        1083)
    production in tissues of astronauts, activity-dose energy
        relations for, 24:32025(R) (N-70-15400)
    production in tissues of rats by spallation, half-life
        of, 24:44403 (CONF-691101-, pp 159-65)
    proton reactions (p,γ) with, cross-section calculations
        using single-particle model, (T), 24:40568
    radiation effects on content of, in thermal insulation
        from Apollo 12 space craft, cosmic, 24:23191(R) (BNWL-
        1183-3)
    separation from aluminum, barium, and calcium by ion
        exchange in hydrochloric acid--2-propanol mixtures,
        24:13765 (CEA-R-3877)
    separation from rainwater and soils as beryllium
        hydroxide, method for, 24:41400
    transport across placental membranes in rats, 24:4548
        (CONF-690150-7)
    use as dosimeter in determination of iodine by photon
        activation, 24:48
    use in self-diffusion studies of beryllium oxides,
        24:14959
    use of cosmogenic, in tracer studies of transport
        processes in stratosphere, 24:31493
BERYLLIUM ISOTOPES Be-8
    alpha-particle widths and molecule-like structure of,
        (T), 24:52735
    binding energy of, calculation including three-body
        forces, (T), 24:45746
    binding energy of, calculation using three-part Gaussian
        interaction, 24:3954
    binding energy of, calculation using unified shell and
        cluster models, 24:45820
    energy level at 12 MeV from beta decay of boron-8, 2⁺,
        24:13290
    energy level at 12 MeV from boron-10 (d,α) reactions,
        reduced width for, (E), 24:15793
    energy level from lithium-6 (d,p) reactions at 6.33 to
        7.14 MeV, search for lowest T = 2, (E), 24:1753
    energy level of, description of ground-state, (T),
        24:43176
    energy levels at 16.6 and 16.9 MeV from lithium-6 (Li-
        6,α) reactions, (E), 24:15811
    energy levels from beryllium-9 (p,d) reactions,
        spectroscopic factors for, (E), 24:10934
    energy levels from boron-11 (p,3α) reactions, (E),
        24:35817
    energy levels from lithium-7 (d,n) reactions, 24:47572
    energy levels from lithium-7 (p,γ) reactions, (E),
        24:6842
    energy levels from lithium-7 (p,γ) reactions, (E),
        24:6843
    energy levels in, angular correlations and Q-value
        distributions between products of Λ-⁸Li decay, (E),
        24:51919
    energy levels of, microscopic analysis of cut-off in
        ground-state rotational band, 24:49765
    energy levels of, nonresonant background interference for
        intensity-ratio dependence on emission angle for, (T),
        24:13281
    energy levels of, rescattering singularities in three-
        body formalism for, 24:20254
    energy levels of, shell model calculations of lowest T =
        2, 24:1754
    nuclear wave equations for, Hartree--Fock determination
        of single-particle cluster, (T), 24:8934
    nuclear wave functions and density distributions in,
        determination using alpha-chain type solution of
        Hartree-Fock equation, (T), 24:45744
    production in meson (π⁻) capture by carbon-12, nitrogen-
        14, and oxygen-16 at low energies in emulsions, (E),
        24:1763
BERYLLIUM ISOTOPES Be-9
    alpha decay (Be-9 → α + α + p + π⁻) of, α-α interaction
        in, (T), 24:45730 (INR-P-1179)
    alpha reactions (α,2α) at 55 MeV, angular distributions
        for, (E), 24:38098 (LYCEN-7009)
    alpha reactions (α,2α) at 55 MeV, α-α angular
        correlations for, (E), 24:3862
    alpha reactions (α,2α) at 56 MeV, analysis using
        triangular graphs, (T), 24:38100 (LYCEN-7031)
    alpha reactions (α,n) at 1.5 to 7.8 MeV, angular
        distributions for, (E), 24:52426
    alpha reactions (α,n) at 1.8 and 2 MeV, neutron
        polarization and differential cross sections for, (E),
        24:1750
    alpha reactions (α,n), as source of polarized neutrons,
        24:30675
    carbon-12 reactions with, angular distributions from,
        (E), 24:49737
    decay of Λ hypernucleus of, α-α interaction in, (E),
        24:52418

FIGURE 13 Specimen page from the subject index to *Nuclear Science Abstracts*.

highly specific, tailor-made entries may be observed in subject indexes of the *Chemical Abstracts* type, in which the entry point (term) is expanded or modified by a specific descriptive phrase. This type of subject index is well illustrated in Figures 12 and 13, from *Chemical Abstracts* and *Nuclear Science Abstracts,* respectively.

Clearly, in this type of alphabetical index, or that developed by Coates, we are able to describe the subject matter of documents of any degree of complexity. By avoiding strict adherence to a list of subject headings and putting elements together to form tailor-made headings, we are achieving results similar to those achieved in the classified catalog through synthesis.

Unfortunately, the problems occurring in the alphabetical subject catalog are very similar to those created by synthesis in the classified catalog. Although we can create index entries of any degree of specificity, we are still forced to arrange these entries in a linear sequence when we place them in a pre-coordinate card or book index. The linearity of the file precludes the use of the multi-dimensional approach possible in a post-coordinate, manipulative index. To approxi-mate the multi-dimensional approach we need to provide multiple entries or cross-references for each item indexed, using each significant facet of a subject complex as an entry point. Just as in the classified catalog, we can provide multiple access points in the alphabetical catalog, but only by multiplying entries and thus creating a bulky and costly file.

REFERENCES

1. American Library Association. *List of Subject Headings for Use in Dictionary Catalogs.* Boston, Mass.: Library Bureau, 1895.
2. Coates, E. J. *Subject Catalogues: Headings and Structure.* London: Library Association, 1960.
3. Cutter, C. A. *Rules for a Dictionary Catalogue.* 2nd ed. Washington, D.C.: U.S. Bureau of Education, 1889.
4. Library of Congress. *Subject Headings Used in the Dictionary Catalogs of the Library of Congress.* 7th ed. Washington, D.C.: Subject Cataloging Division, 1966.
5. Pettee, J. *Subject Headings.* New York: H. W. Wilson Co., 1946.
6. Ranganathan, S. R. *Dictionary Catalogue Code.* London: Grafton & Co., 1945.

5 Vocabulary Control in Post-coordinate Systems: The Thesaurus

In an earlier book,[13] I sketched the development of post-coordinate retrieval systems and the pioneering contributions made by Batten,[3] Mooers,[16] and Taube.[6] Batten developed a special classification scheme for use in his optical coincidence system, and Mooers [15] advocated the use of small vocabularies of *descriptors,* carefully defined and relatively broad in scope. In his advocacy of the Uniterm system, however, Taube indicated that careful vocabulary control was not necessary. As originally described, the Uniterm system would operate on single words extracted from the text of a document by clerical-level procedures.

The use of single-word systems, based on uncontrolled natural language, presents certain problems, however, including:

1. The synonym problem (similar documents are differently indexed).

2. The homograph problem (words that look identical have completely different meanings).

3. The generic search problem (it is difficult and tedious to conduct a broad search on such topics as "protective coatings" if we are using a large vocabulary of uncontrolled single words—how does the searcher think of all applicable terms?).

4. Problems due to ambiguous and spurious relations between words. Syntactic problems of this type lead to *false coordinations* and *incorrect term relationships.* These types of search failure will be discussed in detail in later chapters.

5. Problems due to *viewpoint.* The word "wood" may be viewed as representing a product (of the lumber industry), a raw material, or a fuel. Most single words have many possible contexts.

Because of these various problems, the Uniterm system did not last in its pure form for very long.[7, 11] The first retreat from pure Uniterms was the acceptance of certain *bound terms.* A bound term, as originally envisioned, involves a word that is always associated with one other word in the vocabulary and never with any alternative word. Rather than keep such a word as a separate Uniterm, which would be redundant since it has only one association, it is pre-coordinated with the word to which it invariably relates. Examples are the word "activated," which might always be associated with "carbon" in a particular collection and thus is bound into ACTIVATED CARBON, and the word "fragmentation," which might be bound into FRAGMENTATION AMMUNITION. Neither "carbon" nor "ammunition," in the foregoing examples, are bound terms, since both have connections with many other words in the vocabulary.

The bound term opened the door to further modifications of the pure Uniterm system. As an economy in file size, and to facilitate certain types of generic search, word endings are frequently confounded; that is, we reduce each word to its root (stem) and do not distinguish variants on a word root. Examples are

22

the words "weld," "welds," "welding," "welded," "welder," and "weldability," all reduced to the root WELD, which becomes a Uniterm for all the variants.

The bound term led naturally to the principle that became known as "judicious pre-coordination." Word combinations that occur frequently in the literature of a particular subject field are retained as precoordinate terms to avoid unnecessary manipulation at the time of searching. Good candidates would be combinations such as PRESSURE VESSELS and HEAT EXCHANGERS.

It was not long before post-coordinate systems, many of which began originally as pure Uniterm systems, began to use more and more of this "judicious pre-coordination" and the indexing principle became known as "concept coordination," [22] the implication being that "concepts" are manipulated rather than words. Concept coordination systems of this type use combinations such as AIRCRAFT ENGINES or AIRCRAFT ENGINE NOISE. It is obvious that such pre-coordinations are similar to, or identical with, conventional subject headings. Usually, however, these index terms, in a post-coordinate system, are known as *descriptors* (a debasement of the word as first used in this retrieval context by Mooers), although some organizations are still honest enough to call them *subject headings*. The National Library of Medicine, for example, which operates what is perhaps the largest post-coordinate retrieval system in existence (MEDLARS), calls its controlled vocabulary *Medical Subject Headings* (MeSH).

The move to partial pre-coordination made searching somewhat easier than it was in the Uniterm system, and it reduced the problems of ambiguous and spurious relations. It did not, however, eliminate all the problems of synonymy and homography, nor did it go all the way in facilitating generic search. Gradually it became recognized that a post-coordinate retrieval system might benefit from careful vocabulary control in much the same way as a pre-coordinate system. Thus the *thesaurus* was born.

According to Joyce and Needham,[12] investigators at the Cambridge Language Research Unit in England (notably Masterman and Parker-Rhodes) began to discuss the applicability of the thesaurus concept to information retrieval in 1956. In this context, the word first appears to have been used in print by Hans Peter Luhn of IBM in 1957.[14] To the best of my knowledge, the first thesaurus actually used for controlling the vocabulary of an information retrieval system was developed by the Du Pont organization and appears to date from about 1959.[10] The first widely available thesauri were the *Thesaurus of ASTIA Descriptors* (Department of Defense, 1960) [2] and the *Chemical Engineering Thesaurus* (American

Institute of Chemical Engineers, 1961),[1] the latter based largely on the thesaurus of Du Pont.*

The first edition of *Medical Subject Headings* appeared in 1960, but the second edition, 1963,[17] was the first designed specifically for use in the post-coordinate machine-based system, MEDLARS. The influential *Thesaurus of Engineering Terms* of the Engineers Joint Council (EJC) was published in 1964.[8] This has largely been superseded by the monumental *Thesaurus of Engineering and Scientific Terms*,[19] a project of the Department of Defense (Project LEX) together with the EJC, which was published in 1967 and contains 23,364 terms. In the decade 1960-1970 many other thesauri were developed, some widely available and others solely for internal use within an organization. Several are described or listed later in this book. Further details on the history of thesauri are given by Vickery[21] and by Henderson et al.[9]

The thesaurus, which has been widely adopted for vocabulary control in modern post-coordinate systems, is very similar in structure and organization to the conventional list of subject headings. It lists descriptors alphabetically, endeavors to control synonyms and homographs, and displays generic-specific and other relationships between terms.

Synonyms and near-synonyms are controlled by *use* references which point from an unacceptable term to the preferred descriptor that is to be used in indexing, as:

GUIDANCE WORKERS *Use* COUNSELORS

The reciprocal is usually indicated by the abbreviation UF (used for) as in the example:

COUNSELORS
   UF   GUIDANCE COUNSELORS
         GUIDANCE WORKERS

which means that COUNSELORS is the preferred descriptor and that a *use* reference appears under both variants.

The *use* reference in most thesauri is not restricted in application to synonymous expressions. Sometimes it is used to refer from a specific term that cannot be used in indexing and searching to the appropriate more generic descriptor or descriptors that must be used in its place, as in the example:

ELECTRICAL DE-ICING *Use* DE-ICING SYSTEMS

The reciprocal indicator also remains the same.

The UF reciprocal (tracing) has several purposes. First, it helps to define the scope of the preferred

---

* Because various thesauri and classification schemes are referred to on many occasions in the text, each one is usually included in the list of references only on the first occasion it appears.

term (e.g., if we see that COATING is used for "surface coatings" we learn a little more on what should be included under the descriptor COATING). Second, the reciprocal tells the user of terms that do *not* need to be looked up. In this instance the reciprocal under COATING tells the user that he does not need to look up SURFACE COATING for he will merely be referred back to COATING. Finally, the reciprocal is needed for thesaurus "housekeeping." If we delete COATING in some thesaurus revision procedure, we must also delete all references to it. We can only be sure of getting all such references if traces of them appear under the term COATING.

In the thesaurus, the homography problem may be avoided by incorporating homographs into pre-coordinate terms or by parenthetical qualifiers.

As in the subject heading list, the thesaurus employs a network of cross-references to link "related" terms together and thus provides, like the list of headings, a hidden term classification. The following illustration from the *Thesaurus of ERIC Descriptors* [18] will illustrate the phenomenon:

COUNSELORS
    UF   GUIDANCE COUNSELORS
           GUIDANCE WORKERS
    NT   ADJUSTMENT COUNSELORS
           ELEMENTARY SCHOOL COUNSELORS
           SECONDARY SCHOOL COUNSELORS
           SPECIAL COUNSELORS
    BT   GUIDANCE PERSONNEL
    RT   ADULT COUNSELING
           COUNSELING
           COUNSELOR ACCEPTANCE
           COUNSELOR CHARACTERISTICS

In addition to the UF tracing (reciprocal), there are three sets of term relationships displayed: NT, BT, and RT. The formal hierarchical relations between a genus and its species are indicated by the "narrower term" (NT) and "broader term" (BT) designators. In the foregoing example, the narrower terms are species (kinds) of the genus "counselors" which is itself a species of the BT (genus) "guidance personnel." In other words, the hierarchy indicated by these references is as follows:

GUIDANCE PERSONNEL
    COUNSELORS
        ADJUSTMENT COUNSELORS
        ELEMENTARY SCHOOL COUNSELORS
        SECONDARY SCHOOL COUNSELORS
        SPECIAL COUNSELORS

All the terms listed are valid descriptors in the vocabulary. Reciprocals (tracings) of BT's and RT's are shown in their appropriate places. Every BT will have a reciprocal NT, and vice versa. Thus, the descriptor GUIDANCE PERSONNEL will show COUNSELORS as a narrower term, while all four narrower terms listed will show COUNSELORS as a BT. There is no limit to the number of hierarchical levels that can be displayed in this way, although certain thesauri may deliberately limit the length of a hierarchy thus displayed.

The abbreviation RT stands for "related term." It is used to link together descriptors that are semantically related in ways other than the formal genus-species relationship. The descriptors marked RT in the foregoing example are neither broader nor narrower than the term COUNSELORS but they are obviously related, and a searcher for literature on counselors and counseling might well be interested in items indexed under these other terms. The thesaurus links them together by the RT reference, an indicator which says to the searcher (or indexer) "You may also be interested in these terms." The RT cuts across the formal hierarchical structure of a vocabulary. In the illustration from ERIC, people (counselors) are related to activities (counseling) and to properties (acceptance). In most thesauri, an RT is automatically reciprocated. If A shows B as a related term, B will also show A as a related term. Thus, the four RT's above also show COUNSELORS as a related term.

It is obvious from the foregoing description that the thesaurus is very similar in construction and organization to the list of subject headings. The relationships displayed in the two tools are much the same, although the devices used for displaying the relations are somewhat different. Table 1, from the thesaurus of the Bureau of Ships,[4] shows these differences.

While subject heading lists use *see* to direct from a nonacceptable to an acceptable term, the thesaurus normally indicates this by *use*. The reciprocal is indicated by x in the subject heading list and by UF (used for) in many thesauri, although some indicate the reciprocal by *includes* or *seen from*. All the BT, NT, RT relations are shown, without discrimination, by *see also* references in the list of subject headings, although references from a specific to a broader term are relatively rare. Note the variants on NT (*generic to*) and BT (*specific to, post on*) used in the DDC and AIChE thesauri. These are mere conventions and obviously have no real effect on the utility of the tools. In the 1966 revision of the ASTIA thesaurus, *Thesaurus of DDC Descriptors*,[5] the BT-NT convention was adopted.

In its display of term relationships, the thesaurus differs from the list of subject headings mainly in its conventions. In addition, it clearly distinguishes be-

TABLE 1 Comparison of Thesaurus Conventions with Traditional Library Usage

Bureau of Ships Thesaurus	Engineers Joint Council Thesaurus	Traditional Library Usage	DDC (ASTIA) Thesaurus	Chemical Engineering Thesaurus
use	use	see	use	see
includes	use for (U.F.)	see (x. ref.)	includes	seen from (S.F.)
broader terms	broader terms (B.T.)	see also (xx ref.)	specific to	post on (P.O.)
narrower terms	narrower terms (N.T.)	see also	generic to	generic to (G.T.)
related terms	related terms (R.T.)	see also	also see	related terms (R.T.)

SOURCE: Bureau of Ships.[4]

tween the broader term-narrower term relationship and the related term relationship, whereas the list of subject headings usually lumps these together and treats them all as *see also's*. Thesauri do not always restrict the BT-NT usage to the pure genus-species relationship, although it is usually desirable to do so. Sometimes an NT is not a true species of a BT. For example, the DDC thesaurus shows VOLTAGE as an NT under ELECTRICITY. Obviously, voltage is not a kind of electricity. Occasionally, certain whole-part relationships are displayed in the BT-NT form, as:

RESPIRATORY SYSTEM
    NT   BRONCHI
          LARYNX
          LUNG

The principal difference between the two tools lies in their mode of application. The subject heading stands alone in the alphabetical subject catalog, whereas the descriptor is used in conjunction with other descriptors even though in itself it may already be highly pre-coordinate (e.g., ELECTRON FLUX DENSITY, ELECTROSTATIC PRECIPITATORS, VOCATIONAL TRAINING CENTERS). Most descriptors are identical with subject headings and we can find many common terms if we compare a thesaurus with a list of subject headings in the same field. However, the thesaurus will include terms that one would never find in a list of subject headings. These terms are somewhat meaningless on their own and would never stand alone, but they are useful when used in conjunction with other descriptors to narrow the scope of a class. Examples are general property terms such as FINE or FINENESS, general characteristic terms such as EFFICIENCY, and general process terms such as TESTING or REFINING.

Schultz [20] has distinguished the functions of the information retrieval thesaurus from a thesaurus of the Roget type as follows. Roget's purpose was to give an author a *choice* of alternative words to express one concept; to display a set of words of similar meanings to allow an author to choose one that best suits his need. The information retrieval thesaurus tends to be more *prescriptive*. The thesaurus compiler chooses

one term from among several possible, and directs the user to employ this one by means of references from synonyms and other alternative forms. However, the information retrieval thesaurus clearly plays a *suggestive* role also, especially through the use of RT references.

We have by no means exhausted our discussion of the thesaurus. We will return to it, from several approaches, later.

REFERENCES

1. American Institute of Chemical Engineers. *Chemical Engineering Thesaurus*. New York, 1961.
2. Armed Services Technical Information Agency. *Thesaurus of ASTIA Descriptors*. Washington, D.C., 1960.
3. Batten, W. E. "A Punched Card System of Indexing to Meet Special Requirements." *Report of the 22nd ASLIB Conference*, 1947, 37-39.
4. Bureau of Ships. *Bureau of Ships Thesaurus of Descriptive Terms and Code Book*. 2nd ed. Washington, D.C., 1965. NAVSHIPS 0900-002-0000.
5. Defense Documentation Center. *Thesaurus of DDC Descriptors*. Alexandria, Va., 1966.
6. Documentation Incorporated. *Installation Manual for the Uniterm System of Coordinate Indexing*. Dayton, Ohio: Document Service Center, 1953.
7. Documentation Incorporated. *Studies in Coordinate Indexing*. 6 vols. Washington, D.C.: 1953-1965.
8. Engineers Joint Council. *Thesaurus of Engineering Terms*. New York, 1964.
9. Henderson, M. M. et al. *Cooperation, Convertibility, and Compatibility Among Information Systems: a Literature Review*. Washington, D.C.: National Bureau of Standards, 1966, 66-83. NBS Miscellaneous Publication No. 276.
10. Holm, B. E. and Rasmussen, L. E. "Development of a Technical Thesaurus." *American Documentation* 12 (1961): 184-190.
11. Jaster, J. J. et al. *The State of the Art of Coordinate Indexing*. Washington, D.C.: Documentation Incorporated, 1962.
12. Joyce, T. and Needham, R. M. "The Thesaurus Approach to Information Retrieval." *American Documentation* 9 (1958): 192-197.
13. Lancaster, F. W. *Information Retrieval Systems: Characteristics, Testing, and Evaluation*. New York: Wiley, 1968.
14. Luhn, H. P. "A Statistical Approach to Mechanized Encoding and Searching of Literary Information." *IBM Journal of Research and Development* 1 (1957): 309-317.

15. Mooers, C. N. "The Indexing Language of an Information Retrieval System." In *Information Retrieval Today*. Edited by W. Simonton. Minneapolis: University of Minnesota, 1963, 21-36.

16. Mooers, C. N. "Zatocoding Applied to Mechanical Organization of Knowledge." *American Documentation* 2 (1951): 20-32.

17. National Library of Medicine. *Medical Subject Headings*. 2nd ed. Bethesda, Md., 1963.

18. Office of Education. *Thesaurus of ERIC Descriptors*. 2nd ed. Washington, D.C.: Educational Resources Information Center, 1969.

19. Office of Naval Research. Project LEX. *Thesaurus of Engineering and Scientific Terms*. Washington, D.C.: 1967.

20. Schultz, C. K. *The Thesaurus—Definition and Construction*. Unpublished communication. 1967.

21. Vickery, B. C. "Thesaurus—a New Word in Documentation." *Journal of Documentation* 16 (1960): 181-189.

22. Wadington, J. P. "Unit Concept Coordinate Indexing." *American Documentation* 9 (1958): 107-113.

6 Generating the Controlled Vocabulary

In constructing a controlled vocabulary we need to:

1. Identify the precise topical areas to be covered.
2. Select appropriate terms to describe these areas.
3. Decide upon the exact form of these terms as they are to appear in the vocabulary.
4. Organize these terms in some useful way.
5. Display the terms in some useful way.

Let us first consider methods for assembling the candidate terms.

APPROACHES TO VOCABULARY CONSTRUCTION

There are at least four approaches that have been used in the past:

1. Generate the vocabulary empirically on the basis of indexing a representative set of documents.
2. Convert an existing vocabulary; e.g., convert a list of subject headings to a thesaurus.
3. Extract the vocabulary from an existing, more general thesaurus or develop a specialized thesaurus fitting within the framework of a more general thesaurus; i.e., create a microthesaurus.
4. Collect terms together from diverse sources, including glossaries and other publications and from subject specialists.

The second and third methods may be used under certain conditions, but the other two are more generally applicable and are the procedures usually followed. Basically, the two approaches may be termed the *empirical* approach and the *committee* approach. In the former the initial vocabulary is derived by means of the free indexing of a sample of documents. The candidate terms resulting from this procedure are then reviewed, grouped, and structured into a useful organization. This was the method used in the construction of the Du Pont thesaurus. It was also the method employed by Mooers in setting up his specialized Zator systems. Harold Wooster [18] has referred to this as the "stalagmitic" approach; we start at the bottom with raw candidate terms and build a structure upon these.

In the *committee* approach, we draw our candidate terms from glossaries and other published sources and, more particularly, from discussions with committees of subject specialists. The term lists thus created are then refined by an editorial staff. Only when the vocabularies are in final or semifinal form are they used to index any literature. This was essentially the method used in the construction of the *Thesaurus of Engineering Terms* of the Engineers Joint Council. Wooster described these approaches in the following way:

There are, of course, two methods of thesaurus construction which I choose to call stalactitic and stalagmitic. The stalagmitic is the way Taube and I went about constructing our index—down on the floor of the cave among the documents, slowly building towards the ceiling. The stalactitic seems to be much more fun—one convenes groups of ex-

27

perts who hang up on the roof of the cave, twittering and chirping among themselves but as far away from the actual documents as they can get.

Stalagmitic thesauruses can be constructed either by humans or computers working with actual terms in text; stalactitic thesauruses only by committees of experts. And if a thesaurus has a smooth machine produced regularity, with all terms expanded equally, it was probably produced by subject specialists jealous of the importance of their fields; if it is full of charming irregularities, with some terms almost ignored and others expanded to almost tedious depth, it was probably produced by machine, faithfully reflecting the charming irregularities of the authors.[18]

Although subject specialists may play useful roles as advisors, particularly on the structure of the vocabulary, it would be unwise to rely solely on the committee approach without empirical validation through the indexing of representative documents. The disadvantages of the committee approach are that a subject specialist:

1. May not be fully familiar with the literature and, more importantly, with the requirements of users and potential users of the system.

2. May "split hairs" and make distinctions that are not useful for retrieval purposes, complicating the tasks of indexing and searching.

3. May inflate the importance of his own specialty, causing an imbalance in the vocabulary as a whole.

A controlled vocabulary is essentially a practical tool. The prime requirement is that it be capable of describing concepts occurring in the literature and also in requests made to the system. Obviously, it needs to be based on the characteristics of documents and of requests, and it needs to be modified continuously on these same bases. An important principle, sometimes overlooked, is that of *literary warrant* (also known as *bibliographic warrant*), which was promulgated by Wyndham Hulme [10] in 1911. According to Hulme the classes into which documents are organized should not be based on any theoretical "classification of knowledge" but upon the groups that documents seem to form logically in themselves; that is, the classes upon which literature exists. In other words, the characteristics of the literature itself will determine the classes defined in the system. The system vocabulary, then, should be based on an accurate survey and measurement of the classes of literature existing in the various subject fields covered by the system. This, in Hulme's terms, is "plotting of areas pre-existing in literature."

Obviously a vocabulary derived empirically from the indexing of documents has considerable literary warrant, whereas a vocabulary constructed by the committee approach may have little true warrant. The Library of Congress classification scheme is a good example of a controlled vocabulary having considerable literary warrant because it was derived on the basis of how books appeared to "group themselves" usefully on the shelves of the library.

Goodman, discussing the *Thesaurus of ERIC Descriptors,* turns out to be a very strong advocate of literary warrant:

. . . deliberations concerning the use of any term . . . which does *not* now appear in the *Thesaurus* must be initiated by an indexer confronted by a particular document. No lexicographer can add a descriptor merely because he believes it might be useful; no member of the Panel on Educational Terminology can add a descriptor merely because he believes it might be useful; *no one* can ever add a descriptor to the *Thesaurus* unless a document is being filed under it.[7]

And again:

The minute one allows an indexer to start making up terms that he thinks might be important rather than restricting him to those which have been conceived as "musts" in dealing with actual documents, there is no logical end in sight.[7]

In a recent draft of an ANSI standard on thesaurus construction,[1] the empirical method is referred to as the *analytical* approach while the committee method is described as the *gestalt* approach. In general, the former is preferred, particularly for specialized areas of knowledge. However, the compilers of the standard indicate that the gestalt method may be more generally applicable to broad subject fields involving several disciplines and that a combination of approaches may be desirable in certain applications.

FACET ANALYSIS

Vickery [16, 17] has described procedures for constructing a faceted classification in two useful books. The raw materials for facet analysis are the terms themselves, and these are derived from a careful examination of the literature of the field, including textbooks, encyclopedias, glossaries, and abstracts. What is involved is a conceptual analysis of the subject field but it is a conceptual analysis based on the *literature* of that field, and the characteristics chosen for organizing the terms are those that actually give rise to literature (bibliographic warrant again).

Facet analysis involves sorting candidate terms into homogeneous, mutually exclusive facets on the basis of a single characteristic of division. Consider the following five chemical terms: ALCOHOL is a kind of chemical *substance,* LIQUID a *state* of the substance, VOLATILITY a *property,* COMBUSTION a *reaction,* and

ANALYSIS an *operation*. "Substance," "state," "property," "reaction," and "operation" are logical categories or characteristics of division that may be used to form facets.

In constructing a classification scheme in the field of soil science, Vickery began with a glossary of 350 terms. He assigned each of these terms to a provisional category and appended a suggested definition, as follows:

Cohesion. The property of particles sticking together to form an aggregate. *Property*.

Gravel. Particles between 2 mm. and 20 mm. in diameter. *Part of soil*.

Sticky point. Maximum moisture content at which kneaded soil ceases to stick to knife. *Measure of property*.

Working in this way he was able to isolate fourteen categories:

Category	*Example*
Soil, according to constitution	Peat soil
Soil, according to origin	Granitic soil
Soil, according to physiography	Desert soil
Physical part of soil	Gravel
Chemical constituent of soil	Nitrogen
Structure of soil	Profile
Layer of soil	Horizon
Organism in soil	Bacteria
Parent material in soil	Muck
Process in soil	Mineralization
Property of soil	Cohesion
Measure of property	Sticky point
Operation on soil	Amendment
Equipment for operation	Plough

A study of existing classifications of Soil Science suggested four new categories:

Soils, according to texture	Sandy clay
Soils, according to climate	Arctic soil
Substance used in amendment	Lime
Operations on these substances	Placement

These eighteen groups of terms became the provisional facets of the classification.

Although Vickery used these procedures in the construction of a classification scheme, they are equally applicable to the process of assembling and selecting terms for inclusion in a thesaurus. Facet analysis is potentially helpful in the construction of any type of controlled vocabulary. It helps in determining the principal categories of terms, thus establishing the major hierarchies of the vocabulary, and in displaying the most useful relations among classes (the relations that will be prime candidates for inclusion in *see also* or RT references). Facet analysis also helps us to understand the true meaning of words. Many words do not represent simple concepts. It is only when we apply facet analysis (or, alternatively, "semantic factoring") that we are able to break them down into their components and thus to understand their correct relationships with other words. For example, "colorimeter" indicates an *instrument* for *analysis* of color, while "retinitis" factors into *inflammation* of the *retina*.

The packaging classification of the European Packaging Federation [6] was constructed by examining the terms of the field, in glossaries, and in the index to an abstracting publication, and allocating them to easily recognized categories. To achieve this, many expressions occurring in the literature had to be factored into their components. For example, the simple term "tin cans" is not simple enough to appear intact in a facet. It has to be factored into its components; namely, "tin" (which belongs in the material facet) and "cans" (which belongs in the container facet). Eventually the following set of facets was identified (examples of terms from these facets are included in parentheses):

Containers (BOXES, PACKAGES, BAGS, SACHETS)
Shapes (ROUND)
Accessories (LABELS)
Materials (PLASTICS, CARDBOARD, COMPOSITES)
Operations (APPLYING, MOLDING, OPENING)
Properties (MECHANICAL, CHEMICAL)
Machines

The factoring of terms used to develop this set of useful facets would have been equally valuable in the selection and structuring of terms for a thesaurus.

THE COMMITTEE APPROACH

The committee approach to vocabulary construction is best exemplified in the methods used by the Engineers Joint Council in the compilation of the *Thesaurus of Engineering Terms*. The procedures are described in the introduction to the EJC *Thesaurus*. Work on the *Thesaurus* began in 1962 when national professional engineering societies and other organizations, including DoD and NASA, were invited to submit lists of terms. In all, eighteen organizations submitted about 119,000 terms, of which 87,550 were unique. Of the unique terms, 74,602 appeared only once and 13,948 * appeared more than once. The group of terms sub-

* These figures are quoted exactly as they appear in the EJC *Thesaurus*. Note, however, that there is a discrepancy between the total and its components.

mitted by more than one contributor became the major candidate group for further detailed processing.

The detailed term review was conducted by an Engineering Terminology Study Committee, consisting of 131 members in ten subcommittees. The subcommittees were comprised of subject specialists who donated their time to the project. A total of 130 manweeks of effort was spent in reviewing the lists of terms. During the subcommittee review, additional *unique* terms were considered, as needed, to provide a full treatment of each discipline. The subcommittees "selected terms adjudged to be of most utility within the engineering profession, resolved any serious ambiguities in term meaning, developed and recorded cross-references between terms, and provided scope notes and term definitions as needed." Eventually 10,515 unique main terms were selected, plus a large number of cross-references.

Heston Heald [9] has summarized the criteria used in selecting terms for the *Thesaurus of Engineering and Scientific Terms* (TEST) during Project LEX, as follows:

1. Is the term of a scientific and technical nature and does it have "authentic acceptability"? (Acceptability is determined by consulting dictionaries, encyclopedias, and subject specialists.)

2. What is its demonstrated usefulness in (a) communications, (b) indexing, (c) retrieval?

3. How many sources make use of the term?

4. How frequently has it been used by these organizations?

5. Is it sufficiently unique to be selected without some kind of modification in form?

6. Does it have pertinent relationships with terms already selected and thus fit into a useful hierarchical pattern?

In Appendix 1 to the *Thesaurus of Engineering and Scientific Terms* the compilers have presented these factors in a somewhat different way:

a. Frequency of prior use of a term in indexing and searching within a particular vocabulary gives a rough quantitative indication of its usefulness. The importance of frequency of use of a term depends upon the usage of other terms, the relative age of the term, and the age and scope of the collection. Terms that have been used relatively often within a given vocabulary may represent concepts that are poorly defined or too general to be useful in describing subject matter, whereas those that have been used very infrequently may represent concepts that are obscure or overly specific. Low frequency of use should not necessarily cause the rejection of a term that represents a novel concept and is a recent addition to the original vocabulary. The general rule is to establish descriptors that convey specifically the subject matter indexed. The utility

of the terms can then be evaluated by reviewing their frequency of use in indexing.

b. As construction of the thesaurus progresses and descriptors are selected, an ad hoc vocabulary framework will emerge. This structure will help form a basis for the selection of additional descriptors. Candidate descriptors should be examined to determine that they reflect a level of specificity commensurate with that of the existing structure and that they represent discrete concepts. Avoid the selection of descriptors whose meanings coincide so closely with those of established descriptors that indexers (and searchers) will have difficulty in distinguishing between or among them.

c. The acceptability of terms can be determined by consulting dictionaries, encyclopedias, other indexing vocabularies, and the opinions of subject specialists. Slang, jargon, coined terms and deprecated terminology should be excluded.

d. It is usually desirable to establish a maximum term length for the purpose of maintaining succinctness of terms or for other special purposes such as maintaining the capability for a particular page format in a printed thesaurus. A maximum of 36 characters per term is recommended.

The LEX project, which occupied the period 1965–1967 and was a joint effort of EJC and DoD, involved the following stages:

1. Acquisition and development of a data bank.
2. Formulation of rules and conventions.
3. Subject panel sessions.
4. Editing and publication.

Some 330 authority lists, dictionaries, glossaries, and similar lists of terms were assembled in the formation of the data bank. The most pertinent of these lists (145 in all) were selected, put into machine-readable form, and merged by computer to form an operating data bank of 145,000 separate terms available on both magnetic tape and microfilm.

Term lists were selected for processing on the following bases:

1. They contain scientific and technical terms.
2. They were developed from actual indexing experience and thus represented storage and retrieval requirements.
3. They are strong in thesaurus-like arrangement, preferably showing various kinds of cross-reference data, generic relationships, scope notes, and usage statistics.

Final term selection was made by the use of subject panel sessions. These were special interest groups in various subject areas, including both subject specialists and lexicographers. A typical session met for one or two weeks. More than 300 engineers participated in the sessions, which were concerned with deciding on the most important concepts to represent the field, and on the most appropriate terms to represent these con-

cepts. Final editing was conducted from machine printouts of terms selected in the panel sessions. Eventually 23,364 terms were selected; 17,810 as descriptors and 5,554 as *use* references.

It is also illuminating to consider the methods used in the construction and subsequent revision of the ASTIA thesaurus, as described by Caponio and Gillum.[3] The first edition was derived from the original ASTIA *Subject Heading List*. There were approximately 70,000 pre-coordinate terms in this list, and these were reduced to about 9,000 component terms. After synonyms were eliminated and infrequently used terms coalesced into others, a total of 7,000 terms was eventually reached. This group of terms formed the first edition of the *Thesaurus of ASTIA Descriptors,* published in 1960.

In revising the thesaurus, three guidelines were adopted on the suitability of terms:

1. Utility, as measured by records of use in searching.
2. Frequency of use in indexing.
3. Acceptability.

An example of the application of the utility criterion was the decision to drop the descriptor PHYSICAL PROPERTIES. Although this term occurs frequently in the literature, it was little used in searching—it is too general and too nebulous. Generally, a search will involve a specific property or group of properties. In applying the criterion of frequency of use in indexing, any descriptor that was found to have been used less than ten times was suspected of being of little value. Such descriptors were either coalesced into broader descriptors (e.g., APRICOTS *use* FRUIT) or they were split (e.g., PLATINUM ELECTRODES *use* PLATINUM *and* ELECTRODES). The *acceptability* criterion relates to current usage of a term within the community served; e.g., ASPIRIN may be preferred to ACETYLSALICYLIC ACID.

Candidate terms for the *Urban Thesaurus*[13] were gathered from a number of sources:

1. Library of Congress catalog cards for the last six years (the most valuable source).
2. Indexes in books on urban topics.
3. Journal articles.
4. Faculty and graduate students in the disciplines of economics, geography, history, political science, and sociology.
5. Terms that were obviously missing, after these sources were exhausted, were contributed by senior staff members of the Center for Urban Regionalism.

The first printout of the thesaurus was checked for completeness against *A Subject Heading List in Urban Planning* and against the *Urbandoc Thesaurus.*[4]

Empirical procedures were used by Barhydt and Schmidt[2] in the development of the *Information Retrieval Thesaurus of Education Terms.* The terms were derived from experience in indexing and searching several thousand research reports. The list of terms thus derived was tested through the advice and cooperation of a pilot user group. Requests representing information needs were translated into search strategies and searched in the prototype system. Responses were evaluated by both user and staff in order to modify and refine the vocabulary.

Facet analysis was applied to the lists of terms "to provide a means of keeping track of interterm relations." The authors felt strongly that ". . . the establishment of useful and valid interterm relations could be accomplished only by the conceptual analysis that is a prerequisite to faceting." The initial facets derived were very broad: activities, characteristics, people, and things. Later, the "characteristics" facet was subdivided into 14 main facets, so that a total of 17 facets resulted. Facets were divided into subfacets and subsubfacets. The purpose of this microdivision was "to provide clusters of terms in which each term could legitimately be considered a valid related term (RT) to every other term in the group."

After the faceted framework had been evolved, each candidate term was *negotiated.* The *negotiation* process posed, for each term, the following set of questions upon which a decision was made to include the term or exclude it:

1. Is the term a natural language term: i.e., has it appeared in its present form in document or question language? The natural languages aspect will not be labored, but we do feel that it (a) facilitates user/system interaction by providing an indexing language that matches that of the user and (b) is more amenable to automatic manipulation.
2. Is the term indexable: does it describe the information that is useful within the context of the system: Should it be structured, i.e., faceted, cross-referenced, etc., or is it a term that might better be considered an identifier, e.g., a trade name?
3. If it is considered indexable, does it have an unambiguous identifiable meaning?
4. If the meaning is not clear, can another, clearer term (referring to the same concept) be identified? If several indexable meanings are identified, can these be distinguished in the thesaurus by:
    (a) semantic context (when taken in combination with the meanings of other words which surround it)? For example, it may be made a bound term.
    (b) grammatical form or some use of number which establishes the plural as the thing and the singular as the process?
5. Does the term really belong in the facet, subfacet, and group in which it was originally placed?
6. What relationships can be identified between the term under consideration and other terms in the same group? In

other groups? Which of these should be displayed in the thesaurus?

7. Does inclusion of this term in the thesaurus bring to mind other candidate terms?

OTHER EMPIRICAL METHODS

Rubinoff [15] has suggested that the following procedures be used in the compilation of a small thesaurus to cover a limited subject area:

1. Obtain subject indexes from about 10 publications of the following kinds:

(a) textbooks which are widely used in colleges and universities and are widely acclaimed by experts in the field,

(b) annual indexes of journals of high repute, and

(c) outstanding handbooks in the field of specialization.

2. (Optional) Heuristically assign figures of merit or rank to each subject index based on its probable value as a microthesaurus source (file-lexicon); e.g., assign rank by closeness of match with class(es) of intended users such as engineers who may be expected to search the document file.

3. Generate a table showing the frequency of occurrence of each term in the subject indexes (weighted by merit or rank, if such have been assigned in Step 2). Terms which obviously appear infrequently need not be tabulated (see Step 4).

4. Select those terms which appear with greater than some frequency—e.g., those terms that appear in 8 out of the 10 subject indexes.

5. For each selected term, locate synonyms and near synonyms and form a new frequency list with words of synonyms.

6. Apply standards such as the EJC "Rules" to establish preferred terms, synonymic equivalences, broader-narrower relationships, homograph discriminators, and standardized format.

Rolling [14] outlines procedures used in the construction of a thesaurus in the field of metallurgy. The major steps were:

1. Assemble a term collection through analysis of several existing vocabularies in the field, including thesauri, encyclopedias, handbooks, and the indexes to abstracts journals.

2. Eliminate duplicates. This reduced the candidate list from 10,000 to 8,000 terms.

3. Divide the vocabulary into coherent subsets, covering various aspects of metallurgy. In actual fact, 37 such subsets, containing 100 to 300 terms each, were produced.

4. Display the terms corresponding to each unit in semantic charts, grouping conceptually related terms around their preferred synonyms.

5. Decide for each term whether it should appear as a preferred descriptor or as a form of reference. This step resulted in 3,800 descriptors, 1,000 A *use* B

references, 50 A *see* B_1 or B_2 references, and several thousand A *add* B references (see Chapters 7 and 10 for an explanation of these reference types).

6. Put all terms into machine-readable form for computer processing (see Chapter 11).

7. Undertake general revision and verification.

USE OF REQUESTS AND POTENTIAL SYSTEM USERS

While several of the foregoing approaches apply empirical methods to vocabulary generation, the emphasis tends to be placed on the characteristics of the documents themselves rather than the characteristics of requests made to information systems. This is a mistake. It is more important that the *warrant* of a vocabulary be established by the language of requesters than by the language of documents. To take a simple example, we might analyze a large body of reports in the field of metallurgy and derive from them a vocabulary of metallurgical terms, including many specific terms relating to welding processes. On the basis of the literature we may decide to adopt such highly specific terms as ARGON ARC WELDING and HELIUM ARC WELDING. However, although there is literary warrant for these terms, they may be used very infrequently in searching; that is, the users of our system do not need terms in the welding field at this level of specificity, so these terms may as well be eliminated.

This approach implies that we should make more use of potential system users when we generate a vocabulary. Greer [8] proposed a series of procedures for generating index terms from the vocabulary of users. Potential users contribute *search words* in the form of requests based on a representative set of problems. Greer believes that by judiciously relating carefully selected search words to an important set of problems it may be possible to produce a sensitive list of words which, in different combinations, will serve as search words for questions not previously generated. A novel and sensible approach is that used by Pickford [11, 12] in developing a controlled vocabulary in biomedical engineering for the National Institute for Medical Research, England. The draft vocabulary was developed from a representative collection of literature in the field, comprising about 1,500 reprints from some 220 journals. About a third of this data base was acquired by the interesting ploy of asking potential users to submit examples of what they considered should be included in a collection on biomedical engineering.

The reprint collection was divided into groups of articles which were circulated to potential users of the system on the basis of subject interest. The recipients

were asked to index the reprints according to a set of rules. Each reprint was circulated to two specialists so that at least two viewpoints would be represented. About 180 subject specialists cooperated in the experiment. The rules given to the indexers are presented in Table 2. The most important are those specifying that the reader's own words and phrases are to be used in indexing and that the index terms resulting are to be ranked in order of significance. The rules for ranking of index terms are shown in Table 3. The indexing worksheet used by collaborators is illustrated in Figure 14. An average of 8-9 descriptors was assigned per article.

When the worksheets were returned, the candidate descriptors were edited for grammar and spelling (see instructions in Table 4) and then punched into cards.

TABLE 2 Guide to the Allocation of Descriptors

1. First and foremost look at the paper from a bioengineering point of view.
2. Allocate as many descriptors as you wish, up to the maximum of fifteen.
3. The descriptors, in combination, should specify the contents of the article.
4. Each descriptor should represent a single concept, or idea, and may be a phrase or a single word.
5. Descriptors must be listed in descending order of importance, i.e., the first is to be the most important. The 'ranking' of your words and phrases is very important, and we suggest you make notes on the space provided, or on the back of the form, before listing them.
6. Do not use abbreviations.
7. Do not use two descriptors to describe the same idea.
8. Use the descriptor 'review' if it is a survey or review paper.
9. If you choose a word or phrase which is a member of a class of descriptors, you should consider the use of the class word as an additional descriptor, e.g., if you use 'polyvinylchloride' consider the use of 'plastics' as well.
10. Transcribe trade names and formulae into proper chemical names.
11. Avoid lone adjectives like 'long' and 'thin'. Only 'high' or 'low' may be used to qualify variables such as 'efficiency', 'power', 'speed', etc. For example, suppose a high temperature device is described—use 'temperature', or if necessary 'high temperature' not 'high' or 'hot' alone.
12. If the location of something inside or outside a body is important, use 'internal' or 'external'.
13. Use the substantive form rather than the adjectival, except where the adjective is an essential part of the descriptor. For example, 'sun' is better than 'solar' unless the 'solar system' is meant.
14. Use the participial form instead of the gerundive, e.g., use 'sintered' not 'sintering'.
15. In the case of alloys the name of the major constituent should be used in addition to the descriptor 'alloys'. Permitted exceptions are commonly used names such as 'brass', 'steels' and 'stainless steel'.
16. The function of electronic circuits, rather than their type, should be used, e.g., if a flip-flop is involved, use 'monostable' and 'circuit', or if an Eccles-Jordan circuit is used, the descriptors should be 'circuit' and 'bi-stable'.
17. Try to reveal the interesting detail which may not be indicated by the title or abstract. Please read the whole paper.
18. Whilst you are allocating descriptors please bear in mind that the words and phrases you use should be those in which you would express a request for information on the particular topic.

SOURCE: A.G.A. Pickford.[11]

TABLE 3 Guide to Putting Descriptors into Order of Importance

1. Generally, the first four or five descriptors should describe the overall subject of the article.
2. Biological engineering terms should take precedence over others.
3. The remaining descriptors should describe other interesting features of the article.
4. If the article is a particular kind of paper, e.g., a review, this should be used as a descriptor after describing the general subject of the paper, and before describing interesting features, i.e., around positions 4-7.

SOURCE: A.G.A. Pickford.[11]

TABLE 4 Additional Rules to Be Used for Editing

1. The definite and indefinite article, and prepositions preceding a descriptor, must be removed, except in cases where it has become part of the concept, e.g., 'on-line control'.
2. The plural of descriptors will be used in all cases where a class of objects or materials is meant. The use of the plural or singular form of a word or phrase must be consistent.
3. Descriptor phrases must be kept short. The absolute maximum is sixty characters, including spaces and punctuation.
4. Are any special features required, e.g., 'brief', 'Russian', 'thesis', 'conference paper', etc.?
5. Consistency must be maintained in cases like 'stimuli' and 'stimulations'.
6. Alloys:
   a. If it is pure Al isotope use 'Aluminium 27'.
   b. If it is pure natural Al with no attempt at isotopic purity, only chemically pure, use 'Aluminium'.
   c. If it is an alloy, the important thing about it being the fact that it is an Al alloy, use 'Aluminium Alloys'.
   d. If it is an alloy but its composition does not matter use 'Alloys'.
   e. If it is a class of alloys use 'Stainless Steels', 'Magnox', etc.
   f. If it is an alloy of which all constituents are important use 'Aluminium Alloys', 'Magnesium Alloys', etc.
7. Computers:
   a. If it is a digital computer use 'computers' + 'digital systems'.
   b. If it is an analogue computer use 'computers' + 'analogue systems'.
   c. If it is qualified in any other way, e.g., logical, use 'computer' + 'logical systems'.

SOURCE: A.G.A. Pickford.[11]

APPENDIX THREE

THE INDEXING WORKSHEET USED BY COLLABORATORS

	Name:	
FAIR	Date out: Date in:	Accession no:
	You are invited to make notes before putting the descriptors in order of importance. If the 'Notes' space provided below is insufficient, please use the back of this form.	

Title:

Author:

Reference:

For Project staff use only	Descriptors in order of importance:
	1
	2
	3
	4
	5
	6
	7
	8
	9
	10
	11
	12
	13
	14
	15
	Block letters please

Please return the reprint and completed list of descriptors to:

FAIR
Medical Research Council Laboratories
Holly Hill
London N W 3

Notes:

FIGURE 14 Indexing worksheet used by the National Institute for Medical Research, England, in the development of a controlled vocabulary in biomedical engineering.

Approximately 13,000 cards were thus generated and from these, 1,500 unique terms eventually emerged. Computer programs were written to select terms for the thesaurus on the basis of certain criteria, the most important being frequency of use in indexing and tendency to score high on the ranked lists.

A similar approach to thesaurus development was described by Dym.[5] The method was used in constructing a *Thesaurus for Paint Technology,* developed by the Knowledge Availability Systems Center, University of Pittsburgh, for the Federation of Societies of Paint Technology. Specimen copies of technical journals were sent to members of the Federation. A recipient was asked to review each issue cover-to-cover (including advertisements as well as articles) and to underline terms which he considered important (presumably terms representing subject matter of direct

interest to him). The marked journals were returned to Pittsburgh where all underlined terms were noted and keypunched. The printout generated from this operation was edited to remove duplicates and variant forms of the same word. The editing process reduced the original list of terms from 105,298 to about 30,000.

Each of the remaining terms was analyzed for its importance to the field of paint technology. To quote Dym:

This technique can best be described as that of a 'road map' (Figure 15) by which the areas of the field were divided into five major headings: (1) material; (2) equipment; (3) supplies; (4) process or method; and (5) property, characteristic or condition. For those terms that did not fall into one of the five areas, a miscellaneous area was established to deal with: (1) surfaces or structures to be coated; (2) terms of measurement; (3) terms not classifiable; (4) terms not known; and (5) trade names. After the initial

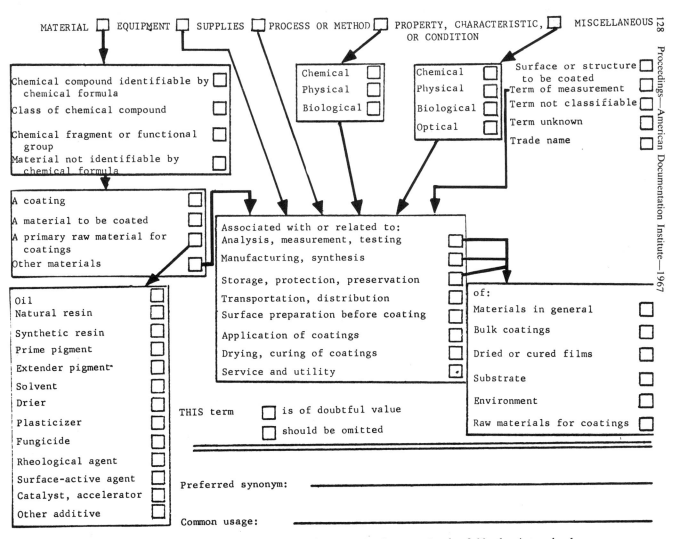

FIGURE 15 Analysis "road map" used for thesaurus development in the field of paint technology.

placement of a term into one of the above areas, subsequent decisions were made, by following the arrows, to reduce all materials or all equipment or all supplies, etc., into common locations.

Figure 16 illustrates the analysis performed for the term "vegetable oil." The term under consideration is recorded on the top line (in this case, VEGETABLE OIL). Since this term represents a material, the box beside this heading is marked. Following the arrows, it was next considered: (1) a material not identifiable by a chemical formula; (2) a primary raw material for coatings; and (3) an oil. It was now possible, from this analysis, to create sections that would list all like materials, like equipment, like supplies, etc., in one location.

From the "road maps," the terms with their analysis were recorded on punched cards and then sorted into like groupings, i.e., all oils, all natural resins, all synthetic resins, etc. Each section was then printed out and reviewed with additional terms being added where necessary and terms excluded where necessary. The number of terms remaining from this review was, approximately, 4,000.

These 4,000 terms were then examined in detail with a view to establishing *see, see also,* BT and NT relationships. The RT references were deliberately omitted from the alphabetical display of the thesaurus. Instead, a separate section of the vocabulary groups related terms together (e.g., a "synthetic resins" section, a "prime pigments" section).

The approaches of Pickford and Dym appear to be very sensible methods for generating a vocabulary, wedding in effect the important requirements of document characteristics and request characteristics (as exemplified in the viewpoints of potential users). The procedure has the following advantages:

1. It indicates terminology preferred by potential users of the system (e.g., PIGS or HOGS or SWINE).

2. It indicates the level of specificity needed by potential users.

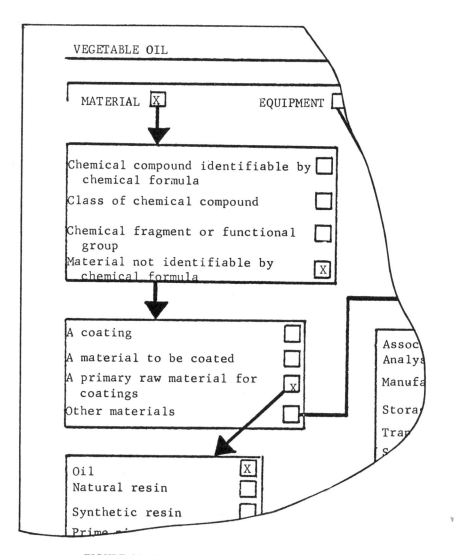

FIGURE 16. Road map analysis of term VEGETABLE OIL.

3. It indicates how exhaustively potential users would like documents indexed (reflected in the average number of terms assigned).

4. It provides both *bibliographic warrant* and *personal* (user) *warrant.*

5. It involves potential users, generates some interest, and thus has a publicity value.

REFERENCES

1. American National Standards Institute. *Guidelines for Thesaurus Structure, Construction and Use.* ANSI Z39. Draft, February 1971.

2. Barhydt, G. C. and Schmidt, C. T., comps. *Information Retrieval Thesaurus of Education Terms.* Cleveland, Ohio: Case Western Reserve University, 1968.

3. Caponio, J. F. and Gillum, T. L. "Practical Aspects Concerning the Development and Use of ASTIA's Thesaurus in Information Retrieval." *Journal of Chemical Documentation* 1 (1964): 5-8.

4. The City University of New York. *Urbandoc Thesaurus.* New York: Project URBANDOC, 1967.

5. Dym, E. D. "A New Approach to the Development of a Technical Thesaurus." *Proceedings of the American Documentation Institute* 4 (1967): 126-131.

6. European Packaging Federation. *Classification Schedule and Alphabetical Index for Packaging Documentation.* London, 1966.

7. Goodman, F. "The Role and Function of the Thesaurus in Education." In *Thesaurus of ERIC Descriptors.* 2d ed. 1-28. New York: CCM Information Corporation, 1970.

8. Greer, F. L. "User Vocabulary in Thesaurus Development." *Perceptual and Motor Skills* 21 (1965): 827-837.

9. Heald, J. H. *The Making of TEST Thesaurus of Engineering and Scientific Terms.* Washington, D.C.: Department of Defense, 1967. AD 661 001.

10. Hulme, E. W. "Principles of Book Classification." *Library Association Record* 13 (1911): 354-8, 389-94, 444-9.

11. Pickford, A.G.A. "FAIR (Fast Access Information Retrieval) Project." *ASLIB Proceedings* 19 (1967): 79-95.

12. Pickford, A.G.A. "An Objective Method for the Generation of an Information Retrieval Language." *Information Scientist* 2 (1968): 17-37.

13. Rickert, J. E., comp. *Urban Thesaurus.* Kent, Ohio: Kent State University, Center for Urban Regionalism, 1968.

14. Rolling, L. "Compilation of Thesauri for Use in Computer Systems." *Information Storage and Retrieval* 6 (1970): 341-350.

15. Rubinoff, M. "A Rapid Procedure for Launching a Microthesaurus." *IEEE Transactions on Engineering Writing and Speech* EWS-9 (1966): 8-14.

16. Vickery, B. C. *Classification and Indexing in Science.* London: Butterworth, 1958.

17. Vickery, B. C. *Faceted Classification.* London: ASLIB, 1960.

18. Wooster, H. "0.46872985 Square Inches—A Naive Look at Subject Analysis." *Digest of 1970 Annual Meeting,* 41-48. Philadelphia, Pa.: National Federation of Science Abstracting and Indexing Services, 1970.

7 Organizing and Displaying the Vocabulary

The terms selected for inclusion in the controlled vocabulary must be organized and displayed in a way useful to both the indexer and the searcher. Vickery [34, 35] again provides a useful guide on the construction of the classification scheme. The first task is to group the terms into facets and subfacets (arrays). Vickery identified eighteen facets in his classification of soil science and five subfacets under soils: soil by constitution, by origin, by physiography, by texture, and by climate. Within each facet, the individual terms ("foci" in the language of Ranganathan) may be organized hierarchically in strict genus-species display. An extract from Vickery's soil schedule is shown below:

Soils by origin (subdivide by Rock schedule)
Soils by climate
    Arctic
    Temperate
    Subtropical and tropical
        Laterite
        Red earth
        Red loam
        Terra rossa
        Regur
    Humid
    Arid
        Chernozem
        Smonitza
        etc.

Soils by texture
    Sand
    Loam
    Clay
    etc.
Soils by physiography
    Desert
    Prairie
    Forest
    Rain-forest
    Swamp
    Lake
Soils by constitution
    Allitic
    Siallitic
    Pedalfers
    Pedocals
    Peat soils
    Podzols
    Gley
    Saline and alkalies
        Solonchak
        etc.

One problem faced by the classificationist is to determine what the important categories or facets of a particular subject field should be. Over the years, attempts have been made to arrive at sets of *fundamental categories* pervasive of all fields. In 1911,

Kaiser[20] proposed the two broad categories of "concretes" and "processes." The most famous set of fundamental categories is that of Ranganathan:[28]

Personality (the "thing" itself)
Matter (constituent materials)
Energy (problem, method, process, operation, handling, technique)
Space
Time

It is possible to classify any field using categories as general (fundamental) as these. However, we usually want to be more specific in our facet structure. Vickery proposes the following expanded set of categories:

Substance (Product)
Organ
Constituent
Structure
Shape
Property
Object of Action (Patient, Raw Material)
Action
Operation
Process
Agent
Space
Time

Several of these may occur at various levels. For example, a property or process may itself have a property (e.g., rate, variation), properties can be operated on (measurement), and processes can also be operated on (initiation, control).

Campbell[5] has proposed a similar set of facets as one reasonably applicable throughout science and technology:

a. Things (tangible objects such as machines, plant, apparatus).
b. Parts of Things (components which can often form part of many different Things).
c. Substances, distinguished from Things by lacking a significant form. A gramophone record is a Thing, whereas the vinyl plastic or other substance from which it is made is not. If the substance has a form, such as flakes or powder, it is not normally significant.

Processes are conveniently divided into:

d. Operations carried out by man, and other processes which occur naturally but may be controlled by man. Distillation is an operation in this sense, evaporation is not. The other processes are so closely associated with properties and phenomena as to be best combined with them.
e. Processes, properties and phenomena. A property is often the ability or inability to undergo a process, as with corrodibility. Processes tend to be considered phenomena when first discovered.

f. Space
g. Time
h. Common subdivisions comprise: *i*, subjects which, in the special context, are important less for themselves than as associated with other subjects, such as societies, law and statistics, and *ii*, forms of documents, as bibliographies, standards and theses.

Such lists of fundamental categories must not be forced upon a subject field. They provide useful frameworks within which classes may conveniently be arranged, and they give guidance as to possible facets that should not be overlooked. However, each individual field presents a special set of problems and must be divided in the way most useful to the users of retrieval systems in that field. Table 5, based on Vickery,[35] illustrates some facets (categories) actually used in eight special classifications.

The hierarchical classification within a facet is achieved by the consistent application of a single characteristic of division. We must not end up with a schedule looking like:

Library materials
 French language
 Government publications
 Serials
 Microfilm

Such a hierarchy has not been formed by the application of a single characteristic of division. It shows a *cross-classification* in which several characteristics (language, publisher, periodicity, physical form) have been applied simultaneously. This type of inconsistent classification causes great problems when we come to classify an item on "French language serials on microfilm."

A properly constructed classification scheme will subdivide the "library materials" facet into a group of subfacets, each one created on the basis of a single principle of division, as:

Library materials
 by language
  French
  German
 by publisher
  Government
  Industry
 by periodicity
  Serial
   Weekly
   Monthly
   Annually

TABLE 5 Facets Used in Special Classifications

Occupational safety and health	Social Sciences
Industries	People, population
Special categories of worker	Psychological make-up and sex relations
Sources of hazards	Community, Society
Industrial diseases	Government, formal organization
Preventive measures	Productive, distributive, and consumptive activities
Organization and administration	Law
Occupational pathology	Communication
	Arts and crafts, culture
Insurance	Values, aims, opinions, attitudes, motivations, states,
Branch of insurance	conditions
Property insured	Ideologies
Persons insured	Environment, physical and economic
According to industry	Geographical location
According to other characteristics	Music literature
Risk insured against	Composer
Insurance operations	Executant
Insurance organization	Form of composition
	Elements of music
Office management	Character of composition
Kinds of office	Technique
Services and procedures	Container manufacture and packaging
Accommodation, equipment, supplies	Products
Personnel	Parts, components
Organization, control, finance	Materials
	Operation of manufacture
Enterprise activities	Machinery for manufacture
Aim or kind of enterprise	Machinery for processing
Size of enterprise	Packs
Personnel activities	Processing of packs
Supply, production, marketing, and public relations	Food Technology
activities	Products
Ownership, trusteeship, general, financial, office and	Parts
its activities	Materials
Management activities and general techniques	Operations

SOURCE: B. C. Vickery.[35]

```
    Nonserial
    by form
      Microform
        Microfilm
        Microfiche
          Ultramicrofiche
        Microcard
```

An entire hierarchy, from *summum genus* to most specific subclass, is known as a *chain,* and the set of subclasses formed by the application of a single characteristic of division is an *array* (in the foregoing example there is a language *array* under library materials, and several short chains, including one from microform down to ultramicrofiche).

The members of a facet should be enumerated as completely as possible, with the principle of literary warrant as the prime consideration. This is also a good time to let the subject specialists take a look at the draft schedules to identify any omissions that spring to mind. The enumeration of foci may never be complete; therefore, the classification must be capable of continuous expansion. Not only must it be expansible, it must allow new foci to be inserted into the most helpful positions in the appropriate arrays. This is not a problem until we add a notation to our schedules; the notation we use must be flexible and hospitable. We will discuss this again later.

In the printed schedules the facets must obviously appear in some order. This sequence may be important, not because the schedule order itself is critical, but because the order of the schedules is frequently the order in which terms are to be combined to form

compound subjects. *Combination order* (sometimes referred to as *preferred order* or *citation order*) is extremely important in a manual, pre-coordinate index although it is immaterial if the classification scheme is to be used in a post-coordinate system.

The combination order we seek is that which will be most logical and useful in searching the index. To determine this useful order we must know how subjects are normally approached. Do searchers think of the sequence EYE, RETINA, INFLAMMATION or INFLAMMATION, EYE, RETINA, or merely INFLAMMATION, RETINA or RETINA, INFLAMMATION? There is no one most useful grouping. Even in a particular subject area alternatives exist, and one may be preferred by audience A and another by audience B. For example, in a medical index for the general practitioner, a logical facet sequence might be ORGAN, DISEASE, DRUG; whereas, in an index for a pharmaceutical manufacturer the preferred order may be DRUG, DISEASE, ORGAN (drug therapy) and DRUG, ORGAN (pharmacology).

Again, attempts have been made to give general guidance on citation order. Ranganathan proposes a sequence of "decreasing concreteness": personality, matter, energy, space, time. Thus, in agriculture the crop (personality) is more concrete than the farming operations (energy) while, in the social sciences, people and their communities come before their activities. According to the PMEST formula, the citation order for the topic "weaving of straw mats in Peru in the eighteenth century" would be:

Mats: Straw: Weaving: Peru: eighteenth century
(P)   (M)   (E)   (S)   (T)

Vickery [35] proposes the combination order:
    P: Substance, product, organism
    O: Part, organ, structure
    C: Constituent
    Q: Property and measure
    R: Object of action, raw material
    E: Action, operation, process, behavior
    A: Agent, tool
    G: General property, process, operation
    S, T: Space and time
and gives the following as examples of its application:

1. Occurrence of caesium in fossils.
   Fossils (P): caesium (C): occurrence (E).
2. Osmotic pressure in cow intestine.
   Cow (P): intestine (O): osmotic pressure (Q).
3. Polyhedroses of insect cells.
   Insect (P): cell (O): polyhedrose (C).
4. Experimental infection of turkey with Eimeria.
   Turkey (P): infection (E): Eimeria (A).
5. Bacterial fermentation of sugar to give methane.
   Methane (P): sugar (R): fermentation (E): bacterial (A).
6. Seasonal variation of noradrenaline concentration in rat tissue.
   Rat (P): tissue (O): noradrenaline (C): concentration (Q): variation, seasonal (G).

Again, these formulas must be taken as useful guides only. As mentioned before, even within a single subject field there may be several alternative arrangements, each one particularly useful to one segment of the community. We must decide whom we are to serve and what the most useful sequence is for this population.

The order in which facets are printed in the schedules is usually the order in which they are to be cited, but in some classifications the sequence is exactly opposite; that is, the facets are cited in the reverse of schedule order. In organizing the schedules we may want to resort to *differential facets*. A differential facet is a category which does not appear in one place but is dispersed under several other facets in the classification. In the medical field a differential facet might be that of disease. Instead of listing all diseases in a single facet we may disperse them according to the organs to which they relate, as:

Respiratory system
    Parts

    Diseases
        Asthma
        Bronchitis
        Emphysema
        Pneumonia

In this example the disease facet has been split up and becomes a subfacet of various main facets in the system.

Differential facets are useful for categories that are not universal. Such terms as ASTHMA and BRONCHITIS are peculiar to the respiratory system and do not apply to other anatomical systems. In this case it may be preferable to have, in addition to the special differential facets, a general disease facet to include terms of wider applicability (e.g., TUBERCULOSIS or INFLAMMATION which may affect a number of organs.) Facets that tend to be generally applicable throughout a subject field (e.g., color, shape, language) would not normally be differential facets. Differential facets complicate the order of classification schedules, but they may be convenient in certain places, and they may, under certain conditions, reduce the length of the notation.

The sequence of terms in an *array* should also be considered in the organization of a classification

scheme. Generally we would like to bring together, in closest schedule proximity, the terms most related. Vickery suggests three possible sequences:

1. Order of increasing (or decreasing) complexity.
2. Spatial or geometrical order.
3. Chronological or evolutionary order.

He presents the following arrays as examples:

From simple to complex
Elements of language
    Phoneme (vowel, consonant)
    Syllable
    Word
    Phrase
    Clause
    Sentence
    Paragraph
    Composition

Spatial
Planets (relative to Sun)
    Mercury
    Venus
    Mars
    Asteroids
    Jupiter
    Saturn
    Uranus
    Neptune
    Trans-Neptunian

Chronological
Food technology, preliminary operations
    Transport
    Delivery, unloading
    Sorting, grading
    Trimming, peeling
    Seeding, stoning, coring
    Cleaning, washing
    Blanching
    Cutting, slicing
    Filling into containers
    Closing containers

Where no other sequence is logically preferable, one can organize the array alphabetically. Several other possible sequences are discussed by Foskett.[16]

NOTATION

In the construction of a classification scheme it is only after we have organized our terms into the most useful structure and sequence that we come to the point of assigning a notation to the set of terms. The purpose of the notation is to maintain the order of the classified schedule and, in the case of a pre-coordinate system, to maintain the order of the classified catalog, as well as to act as a convenient shorthand symbol for the terms (classes) of the scheme. A good notation should have the following properties:

1. The filing order should be immediately comprehensible. This implies the use of letters or numbers (*pure* notations) or both together (*mixed* notations).
2. It should be brief. This depends on a number of factors, one of which is the size of the notational base. An alphabetic notation (base of 26) will allow briefer symbols than a numeric notation (base of 10). A mixed notation enlarges the base and can give greater brevity. By careful apportionment of the notation it may be possible to assign proportionately more of the base to the segments of the vocabulary likely to be most heavily used. That is, the length of the class number may be made inversely proportional to the frequency of use.
3. It should be easily retained in the memory. Of course, brevity assists in this respect, but special mnemonic features may be built in. Foskett believes in pronounceable notations and adopted this principle in his *London Education Classification*. For example, *Nut* stands for theology, and sex education is represented, rather appropriately, by *Pil*.
4. The notation must be capable of infinite expansion. We must be able to add at any point. Any notation, if properly constructed, can be made infinitely expansible.

One way to achieve infinite hospitality in an expressive notation (see below) is through the *octave device*. In this case, the figure 9 is never used alone to indicate a term. It is used only to introduce a second series of figures 1–8, which are coordinate with the figures 1–8 themselves. Thus, using the octave device, we could have an array of co-equal classes numbered 1, 2, 3, 4, 5, 6, 7, 8, 91, 92, . . . 98, 991, 992.

The notation may be expressive, reflecting the order of the hierarchy; or it may be nonexpressive, as in the following illustration:

	Expressive	Nonexpressive
HEAD	Mh	Mh
EYE	Mhi	Mi
CHOROID	Mhic	Ms
RETINA	Mhir	Mt

Although, from long exposure to the *Decimal Classification*, we tend to think in terms of expressive notation, the nonexpressive notation has much to commend it. It fulfills all of its required functions and is

generally shorter, and thus more easily retained and used, than the expressive notation. It is also *much* easier to insert new terms in their appropriate places if a nonexpressive notation is used; in fact, hospitality is no problem at all. However, the nonexpressive notation is not satisfactory if we wish to move up and down hierarchies automatically—as we might in a computer system.

In a faceted classification used in a pre-coordinate fashion we need clear facet indicators or separators; that is, the notation for a complex topic must clearly reveal its component facets. One method of facet indication is to use capital letters for each main facet and lower case letters for the subdivisions. For examples, see the notations used in Chapter 3. In the notation BnDafiLx, the capital letters clearly introduce new facets.

In the classification of the European Packaging Federation,[15] the decimal point is used as the facet separating device, as in the following examples:

.14.2142.44   Plastic bags with tearstrip,
           where 14 represents "bags,"
           2142 "tearstrip," and
           44 "plastic"

13.4362.921   Machine for manufacturing corrugated boxes,
           where 13 represents "boxes,"
           4362 "corrugated," and
           921 "manufacturing machine"

Another possible way of indicating facets is by means of a retroactive notation. If we plan to use a retroactive notation, the order in which the facets are displayed in the schedules will be the reverse of the combination order. With such a notation the introduction of a new facet is indicated by reversion to an earlier letter of the alphabet. Croghan[11] used such a notation in his *Classification of the Performing Arts*. In the class number Ndh, representing "movement of actors," the reversion to the d indicates a new facet; whereas the h is not a reversion and thus is part of the d facet and not a new one being introduced. In this case the code for movement, dh, has been combined with the code for actors, N.

In addition to letters and/or figures, the notation may include some special characters; for example, the connecting colon (:) as used in UDC and the *Colon Classification*. Special characters may be used to indicate not only a connection between facets but also the *type of connection*. For example, in a metals classification we could use : to indicate a deliberate additive and ; to indicate an undesirable element (impurity). Ranganathan used indicators of this type to show "phase relations" between facets. Five phases are recognized: bias phase (e.g., mathematics *for* chemists), tool phase (e.g., design of aircraft *using* computers), aspect phase (soil from the *viewpoint* of bacteriology), comparison phase (surgery of carcinoma *compared with* radiation therapy), and influencing phase (*effect* of evaporation on soil infiltration).

For further discussion on notation see Vickery,[35] Coates,[8] and Needham.[26]

MORE ON FACET ANALYSIS

I have devoted a fair amount of space to this subject because the principles described are important and valid in the construction of thesauri as well as the making of classification schemes. The problems of facet sequence, order in array, and notational matters do not apply, of course, to the thesaurus. However, facet analysis is an extremely powerful tool in selection and definition of terms, in the grouping of terms into consistent hierarchies (thus establishing the necessary chains of BT-NT relations), and in the establishing of related term connections. In the preceding chapter, I quoted Barhydt and Schmidt, who feel that facet analysis is essential to thesaurus construction in establishing useful and valid relations between terms. As early as 1955 the Classification Research Group[7] in London published a paper urging the use of faceted classification as the basis of all systems of information retrieval, including post-coordinate systems.

The Classification Research Group is still dedicated to the belief that a formal classification scheme is essential to any efficient information retrieval operation. Current work is concentrated upon the development of a new "general" classification scheme (i.e., one for the whole of recorded knowledge) based upon the principle of "integrative levels" as described by Feibleman and others. This research, which has been supported by a grant from NATO, is fully described in two recent reports from the Library Association.[6, 17]

In an early post-coordinate system described by Wadington[36] in 1958, the descriptors of the vocabulary were grouped into facets according to Ranganathan's *Colon Classification* "to insure consistent indexing and to show necessary generic-specific relations."

Facet analysis was used extensively in construction of the *Subject Authority List* of the American Petroleum Institute (API).[1, 4, 24] Facet analysis of the petroleum literature led to the derivation of nine facets, including a "common attribute" facet, as illustrated in Table 6. The compilers of the API vocabulary claim the following advantages for facet analysis:

TABLE 6 Facet Breakdown in the American Petroleum Institute Vocabulary

[PROCESS]
(Goal-oriented activity)
  Industrial process
  (a complete multistep operation)
    e.g. Isoforming
  Chemical reaction
  (Unit process)
    e.g. Isomerization
  [Physical change]
  (a unit operation)
    Physical separation
      e.g. Distillation
    (Miscellaneous)
      e.g. Size reduction
  Analytical method
    e.g. Diffraction analysis
  Business operation
    e.g. Advertising
  [Miscellaneous]
    e.g. Maintenance
[PHENOMENON]
(a natural occurrence, happening)
  e.g. Corrosion
  e.g. Electricity
  e.g. Engine noise
MATERIAL
  [By use]
    e.g. Motor fuel
  [By composition]
    e.g. Gasoline
    e.g. Methanol
  [By phase]
    e.g. Liquid
    e.g. Emulsion
EQUIPMENT
  e.g. Petroleum refinery
  e.g. Heat exchanger
  e.g. Tube
LIVING ORGANISM
  Microorganism
  Plant
  Animal
  Man
ECONOMIC FACTOR
  e.g. Supply
  e.g. Exports
  e.g. Employment

[PLACE]

[PROPERTY]
(of materials)
  Physical property
    e.g. Melting point
    e.g. Taste
  Composition
  (of mixtures)
    e.g. Sulfur content
    e.g. Aromatic
  [Structure]
    Chemical structure
      e.g. Aromaticity
    Polymer structure
      e.g. Crosslinked polymer
    Microstructure
      e.g. Grain structure
      e.g. Hexagonal crystal
OPERATING CONDITION
(of processes and equipment)
  e.g. Temperature 100 to 200 C
  e.g. Velocity
[COMMON ATTRIBUTE]
  Shape
    e.g. Elliptical
  Arrangement
    e.g. Parallel
  Manufactured form
    e.g. Pellet
  Portion/Position
    e.g. Top
  Direction
    e.g. Crosscurrent
  Operation
    e.g. Hydraulic
  Size
    e.g. Micro
  Quantity
    e.g. Two
  Numerical relation
    e.g. Equation
  Time/Frequency
    e.g. Simultaneous
  Quality
    e.g. Standard quality
  [Origin]
    e.g. Synthetic
  [Market/Affiliation]
    e.g. European Common Market
  [Science/Technology/Industry]
    e.g. Geologic
    e.g. Petrochemical industry

SOURCE: J. G. Mulvihill and E. H. Brenner.[24]

1. It tends to ensure completeness and accuracy in establishing hierarchical relations.

2. It tends to suggest meaningful and useful *see also* (RT) relationships.

3. It tends to ensure that synonyms and near synonyms are recognized.

In the API system the facet structure is also used as a basis for linking terms together in indexing. We will discuss this in greater detail later.

Rostron,[30] an architect with no formal training in library classification, adopted a crude form of facet analysis in constructing a thesaurus relating to build-

ing and buildings. He collected the terms from various dictionaries and other published sources and then grouped related terms together on typed "concept cards." In total, 304 of these cards were developed. Card 14, for example, contained concepts that are all related to "bonding":

adhesive
adhere
glue (adhesive)
gluing
bond (join)
cement (adhesive)
gum
key (bond)
keyed
bond (gluing)
glue (process)

Cards dealing with related concepts were linked by cross-references.

McClelland and Mapleson,[23] who used classification in the construction of a thesaurus in anesthesiology, claim the following advantages for classification in vocabulary construction:

1. It draws attention to obvious omissions and incomplete hierarchies.

2. It brings together synonyms and near-synonyms and may reveal overlap and redundancy.

3. It imposes a discipline that helps to avoid loose terminology.

4. It helps to identify redundant terms.

5. The classified display helps both indexer and searcher to choose the most suitable terms and greatly facilitates the conduct of generic searches.

Another systematic approach to thesaurus construction was used by London[22] in compiling an experimental thesaurus in the field of meteorology. She discovered that scientific glossaries are potentially very valuable tools in avoiding the vagueness and lack of precision she perceived in the majority of existing controlled vocabularies. The definitions in these glossaries are usually produced as a cooperative venture by several subject specialists and are exposed to rigorous editorial review procedures; they thus represent a high level of "scientific consensus." Such definitions offer the most comprehensive, impartial, and reliable means of grouping terms by the "conceptual affinities" existing between defined terms and their cross-references and vice versa. Using two major glossaries of meteorology, supplemented by some other scientific glossaries and current textbooks, she began the construction of her experimental thesaurus. She used the network of cross-references to other meteorological

terms, embedded in the glossary definitions of each term, as the basis for grouping terms into meaningful categories and subcategories. A great deal of the initial term collection and display of relationships could be done by a typist following the leads presented in the glossaries. The initial groupings could then be subjected to detailed scholarly review and analysis. The investigator concludes that well-prepared scientific glossaries are probably the most useful sources of terms, definitions, groupings, and references for thesaurus construction, and that much of the initial term collection and organization can be done clerically or, possibly, by computer analysis. In constructing her "classed thesaurus," London was using a form of facet analysis, deriving the facets from relationships displayed in scientific glossaries.

The hierarchical relationships of the *Exploration and Production Thesaurus*[32] were also developed through the use of facet analysis and ten facets were isolated: common attribute, earth and space concepts, economic factor, equipment, material, operating condition, organism, phenomenon, process, and property. Unfortunately, although facet analysis was used in their development, the hierarchies are poorly displayed in the printed thesaurus (Figure 17) and thus difficult to follow. This brings us to the subject of display.

In a classification scheme, of course, the terms will be arranged, usually under main classes, in the systematic order of facets established by the maker of the classification. If the classification is properly presented, each facet will be clearly distinguished and the term hierarchies will use levels of indentation to show true genus-species relations. Figure 18 shows such a display, taken from *A Faceted Subject Classification for Engineering*[3] of the English Electric Co.

Note how the two main facets of the class Switches are displayed (by method of connection, by operating mechanism) and how indentation is used to show, for example, that the genus Relays has five co-equal species. Cross-references and scope notes may also appear in the schedules. In Figure 18, as an illustration, there is a general reference from Hhr, Circuit Breakers, to the F schedule for special components. Figures 19 and 20 present additional illustrations from Foskett's[18] education classification and from a special aeronautics classification devised for the ASLIB Cranfield Project.[10]

THESAURUS DISPLAY

The major display of the conventional thesaurus is an alphabetical sequence of descriptors. Figures 21 and 22 show specimen pages from the *Thesaurus of DDC Descriptors* and the *NASA Thesaurus*,[25] respectively.

```
(Common attribute)
...(Direction)
...Azimuth
...Bearing (direction)
...Circular motion
...Dip
...Steep dip
...Downward
...East
...Forward
...Inclination
...North
...Oscillating
...Radial
...Reverse
...Rotary
...South
...Spinning
...Upward
...West
..(Industry)
...Agriculture
...Chemical Industry
...Gas Industry
...Gas Transmission Industry
...Petroleum Industry
..(Location)
...Aerial
...Annulus
...Axial
....Strain Axis
...Center
...Concentric
...Connection
...Crust
....Weathering Crust
...Depth
....Basement Depth
....Charge Depth
....Penetration Depth
....Perforation Depth
....Water Depth
.....Deep Water
.....Shallow Water
```

FIGURE 17   Page from the *Exploration and Production Thesaurus,* showing poorly displayed facets.

A close examination of these pages will reveal the principal characteristics of the typical thesaurus:

1. Under each descriptor in the alphabetical display are listed the terms that are broader (BT), the terms narrower (NT), and the terms judged most related (RT).

2. Each of these three groups of terms, under a descriptor, is usually arrayed alphabetically.

3. Nonaccepted terms appear in the alphabetical sequence and are referred (*use*) to the appropriate acceptable descriptor.

4. The reciprocals (UF) of a *use* reference appear under the descriptor referred to.

5. A *use* reference may be made to more than one term (e.g., to express "bomb nose fuzes" we must use both BOMB FUZES and NOSE FUZES).

6. Scope notes are used in parentheses to define the scope of a descriptor which might not otherwise be clear.

7. Special symbols may be used in various thesauri. For example, the + sign in the DDC thesaurus indicates a term that must be expressed by the use of two or more descriptors. Under BOMB FUZES we find +BOMB NOSE FUZES, which signifies that the descriptor BOMB FUZES is only one of the descriptors *used for* BOMB NOSE FUZES (the other being NOSE FUZES).

Although most thesauri follow this general display pattern, there may be individual differences. Some thesauri limit the BT-NT relations displayed under any one descriptor to a single level in the hierarchy. For example, consider the descriptors:

```
A
   AB
      ABC
         ABCD
            ABCDE
```

Under descriptor ABC we would refer up to AB as a broader term (one hierarchical level), but not up to A (AB would refer up to A), down to ABCD, but not down to ABCDE (ABCD would refer down to this). This convention avoids excessive hierarchical listing under each descriptor.* In other thesauri a complete hierarchical listing may be presented but without discriminating the various levels of the hierarchy. See, as an example, Figure 23 from the *Thesaurus of Engineering and Scientific Terms* (TEST) where, under DIRECT POWER GENERATORS, we find listed co-equally FUEL CELLS and LIQUID METAL FUEL CELLS, the latter obviously a term subsidiary to the former but not displayed in this relation.

The display of the complete hierarchy under each descriptor conforms with the *Guidelines for the De-*

---

* Eugene Wall, in a personal communication, has indicated, however, that single-level referencing saves less than 10 percent in the number of printed thesaurus lines.

H

ANCILLARY PLANT AND COMPONENTS

ELECTRIC ANCILLARY PLANT AND COMPONENTS (cont'd.)

Hh   **Switches, Switchgear**

By method of connection:

Hhb	Interrupters
Hhc	Contactors
Hhd	Relays
Hhdd	Polarised, hinged, armature
Hhdg	Differential
Hhdl	Slugged
Hhdp	Line
Hhdy	Buchholtz
Hhe	Isolation switches
Hhf	T.R. Switches
Hhg	Selector switches
Hhgb	2-way reversing
Hhgc	Multi-way
Hhgd	Uniselectors, step switches
Hhgm	Combination switches

By operating mechanism:

Hhh	Beam switches
Hhi	Key switches
Hhj	Lever switches, knife switches
Hhl	Drum switches
Hhm	Push button switches
Hhn	Toggle action switches
Hho	Sliding switches
Hhp	Rolling switches
Hhq	Butt switches

Hhr	**Circuit Breakers** *(See F schedule for special components)*
Hhrb	Air break (OB, OBX)
Hhrd	Air blast
Hhrg	Oil break (OKF, OKM, OLK, OQF)
Hhrge	S.O.V., L.O.V., low oil breakers
Hhrh	Gas filled (SF6)
Hhrp	Current limiters
Hhrt	Fault make load break oil switches
Hhrv	Fused oil switches
Hhrw	Vacuum circuit breakers

FIGURE 18 Specimen page from the *Faceted Subject Classification for Engineering*, showing clear display of facets and hierarchies.

```
Lal    Systems of instruction (Monitorial etc.)
Lam        Lessons
Lan        Rote
Lap        Dictation
Lar        Recitation
Lav        Lecture, oral instruction
Leb        Discussion
Led        Seminar
Lef        Tutorial
Leg        Coaching
Lej        Demonstration
Lel        Experiment
Lem        Direct method
Len        Heuristic method
Lep        Group teaching
Les        Short course
Let        Part-time course
Lev        Correspondence course
Lew    Training methods
Lex        Apprenticeship, Student assistantship
Ley        In-service and on-the-job training
Lib    Teaching aids
Lid        Textbooks
Lif        Models
Lig        Toys
Lij        Laboratory equipment, apparatus
Lil        Animals
Lip        Plants, gardens
Lir        Walks
Lit        Journeys, travel
Liv        Visits
Lix        Apparatus (for Physical Education)
Lob    Audio-visual aids
Lod        Blackboard
Lof        Flannelgraph
Log        Prints, drawings
Loj        Pictures, posters
Lol        Photographs
Lom        Slides
Lop        Film, cinema
Lor        Radio and television
Los           Radio
Lot           Television
Lov              Closed-circuit
Low        Gramophone
Lox        Tape recorder
Loy        Teaching machines, automation, self-instruction
Lum    Museums   ) In schools and colleges; for
Lus    Libraries ) Educational Documentation see Bux
```

FIGURE 19 Specimen page from *The London Education Classification.*

velopment of Information Retrieval Thesauri produced by COSATI, the Committee on Scientific and Technical Information. For large hierarchies it results in the kind of display illustrated in Figure 24, from the *NASA Thesaurus,* where scores of terms of varying levels of subordination can be seen in one alphabetical sequence under the descriptor ANATOMY. This has the possible advantage that the user can find the complete set of anatomical terms in one place and does not need to flip backwards and forwards in the thesaurus to follow a complete hierarchical chain. The disadvantages are that this protocol does not effect a fully systematic display of the hierarchy (and thus needs to be supplemented by alternative displays), and that it can

result in very long term lists, as in the ANATOMY example shown in Figure 24.

A possibly more useful display is that used in the *Exploration and Production Thesaurus,*[32] in which the alphabetical display is staggered to show the various steps in the hierarchy:

MUD PUMPABILITY
  BT PUMPABILITY
    FLOW PROPERTY
      PHYSICAL PROPERTY

Here, by indentation, MUD PUMPABILITY is shown to be narrower than PUMPABILITY, which is narrower

AERODYNAMICS

	Flow elements
Ngc	Streamlines
Nge	Sources
Ngg	Sinks
Ngi	Doublets
Ngk	Vortices
Ngm	Bound Vortices
Ngn	Vortex Filaments
Ngp	Vortex Sheets
Ngs	Vortex Streets
Ngx	Jets
Nh	Waves
Nhb	Expansion waves
Nhd	Compression, shock waves
Nhf	Normal shock waves
Nhh	Oblique shock waves
Nhj	Attached shock waves
Nhk	Detached shock waves

Nhm   Mach waves   Divide by S, Mechanical vibration –
                                  e.g. Attenuation: Shock waves Nhd Sfr

	Attributes
Ni	Velocity (Aerodynamics)
Nic	Mass flowrate
Nie	Velocity Gradient
Nj	Similarity parameters
Njb	Mach number
Njd	Critical Mach number
Njf	Mach number of divergence
Njh	Prandtl number
Njj	Nusselt number
Njm	Reynolds number
Njp	Froude number
Nkb	Profile
Nkd	Thickness ratio
Nkf	Circulation
Nkh	Vorticity
Nm	Hydrodynamic characteristics
Nmd	Spray

FIGURE 20 Specimen page from the *Facet Classification Schedules and Index* (of Aeronautics).

BOM - BOM

```
    BT  ORDNANCE
        >BOMB AUXILIARY EQUIPMENT


BOMB CARRIERS
    19 02
    BT  ORDNANCE
        >BOMB AUXILIARY EQUIPMENT


BOMB CASES
    19 02
    BT  ORDNANCE
        >BOMB COMPONENTS


BOMB CLUSTERS
    19 02
    (CLUSTERS OF CONVENTIONAL BOMBS USED
    TO INCREASE THE NUMBER OF BOMBS IN
    A LAUNCHING CONFIGURATION.)
    UF  +CLUSTER ADAPTERS
    BT  ORDNANCE
        >BOMBS


BOMB COMPONENTS
    19 02
    (PARTS OF BOMBS WHEN CONSIDERED AS
    SEPARATE ENTITIES.  FOR BOMB HANDLING
    AND STORING DEVICES, SEE $BOMB AUXILIARY$
    $EQUIPMENT$.)
    BT  ORDNANCE
        >BOMBS
    NT  BOMB CASES
        BOMB FINS
        BOMB FUZES


BOMB DAMAGE ASSESSMENT
    USE
    DAMAGE ASSESSMENT


BOMB DIRECTORS
    19 05
    (DEVICES USED TO ADJUST COMPONENTS OF
    BOMB LAUNCHING EQUIPMENT TO PROVIDE
    CORRECTIONS IN THE EARLY PART OF BOMB
    TRAJECTORIES.)
    BT  ORDNANCE
        >FIRE CONTROL SYSTEM COMPONENTS


BOMB DISPOSAL TOOLS
    USE
    BOMBS
    AND
    ORDNANCE DISPOSAL TOOLS


BOMB EJECTOR CARTRIDGES
    USE
    BOMB EJECTORS
    AND
    CARTRIDGES(PAD)


BOMB EJECTORS
    19 05
    UF  +BOMB EJECTOR CARTRIDGES
    BT  ORDNANCE
        >BOMB AUXILIARY EQUIPMENT
        >FIRE CONTROL SYSTEM COMPONENTS
        EJECTORS(ORDNANCE)

BOMB FINS
    19 02
    BT  AERODYNAMIC CONFIGURATIONS
        >AERODYNAMIC CONTROL SURFACES
        ORDNANCE
        >BOMB COMPONENTS
        CONTROL SURFACES
        >FINS
```

```
BOMB FRAGMENTATION DAMAGE
    USE
    AMMUNITION DAMAGE
    AND
    BOMBS
    AND
    FRAGMENTATION AMMUNITION


BOMB FRAGMENTS
    USE
    AMMUNITION FRAGMENTS
    AND
    BOMBS


BOMB FUZES
    19 01
    UF  +ARMING WIRES
        +ATHWARTSHIP FUZES
        +BOMB ARMING UNITS
        +BOMB ATHWARTSHIP HYDROSTATIC FUZES
        +BOMB NOSE FUZES
        +BOMB TAIL FUZES
        +BOMB TAIL HYDROSTATIC FUZES
    BT  ORDNANCE
        >BOMB COMPONENTS
        >FUZES(ORDNANCE)


BOMB HANDLING VEHICLES
    13 06
    (GROUND TRANSPORTATION DEVICES FOR
    BOMBS AND AIRCRAFT ROCKETS.)
    UF  BOMB LIFTS
    BT  ORDNANCE
        >BOMB AUXILIARY EQUIPMENT
        VEHICLES
    NT  BOMB TRUCKS


BOMB HOISTS
    19 02
    BT  ORDNANCE
        >BOMB AUXILIARY EQUIPMENT


BOMB LIFTS
    USE
    BOMB HANDLING VEHICLES


BOMB NOSE FUZES
    USE
    BOMB FUZES
    AND
    NOSE FUZES


BOMB RACKS
    19 02
    UF  +BOMB SHACKLE RELEASES
        BOMB SHACKLES
    BT  ORDNANCE
        >BOMB AUXILIARY EQUIPMENT


BOMB SHACKLE RELEASES
    USE
    BOMB RACKS
    AND
    RELEASE MECHANISMS


BOMB SHACKLES
    USE
    BOMB RACKS


BOMB SHELTERS
    USE
    SHELTERS
```

FIGURE 21 Specimen page from the *Thesaurus of DDC Descriptors.*

```
      ELECTRON TRANSFER
      GASEOUS SELF-DIFFUSION
      IONIC DIFFUSION
      PLASMA DIFFUSION
      THERMAL DIFFUSION
ELECTRON DISTRIBUTION
   2401 2403 2404 2405
   BT  #DENSITY (NUMBER/VOLUME)
       #DISTRIBUTION (PROPERTY)
       PARTICLE DENSITY (CONCENTRATION)
   NT  ELECTRON DENSITY PROFILES
   RT  CHARGE DISTRIBUTION
       CURRENT DISTRIBUTION
       #DENSITY (NUMBER/VOLUME)
       ELECTRON DENSITY (CONCENTRATION)
       THOMAS-FERMI MODEL
       VERTICAL DISTRIBUTION
ELECTRON EMISSION
   0604 0902 0905 1001 2304 2402
   BT  #DECAY
       EMISSION
       PARTICLE EMISSION
   NT  FIELD EMISSION
       PHOTOELECTRIC EMISSION
       SECONDARY EMISSION
   RT  CATHODES
       ELECTRIC DISCHARGES
       ELECTRON SOURCES
       ELECTRON TRANSITIONS
       #ELECTRON TUBES
       EMITTERS
       PAIR PRODUCTION
       PHOTOELECTRIC MATERIALS
       PHOTOELECTRONS
       PHOTOIONIZATION
       PHOTOVOLTAIC EFFECT
       RADIO FREQUENCY DISCHARGE
       SELF SUSTAINED EMISSION
       STIMULATED EMISSION
       THERMAL EMISSION
       THERMIONIC EMISSION
       WORK FUNCTIONS
ELECTRON ENERGY
   0604 2304 2311 2402 2403
   UF  ELECTRON TEMPERATURE
       ELECTRONIC LEVELS
   BT  #PARTICLE ENERGY
   NT  ELECTRON STATES
   RT  ACTIVATION ENERGY
       ELECTRON DENSITY (CONCENTRATION)
       ELECTRON MASS
       ELECTRON PRECIPITATION
       ELECTRON PRESSURE
       ELECTROSTATIC PROBES
       ENERGY
       FORBIDDEN BANDS
       IONOSPHERIC TEMPERATURE
       KINETIC ENERGY
       PLASMAS (PHYSICS)
       PROTON ENERGY
       SPACE TEMPERATURE
       SURFACE ENERGY
       #TEMPERATURE
ELECTRON FLUX
   USE  ELECTRONS
        FLUX (RATE)
ELECTRON FLUX DENSITY
   2401 2403
   (ELECTRON EMISSION OR DETECTION RATE
   PER UNIT AREA)
   UF  ELECTRON INTENSITY
   BT  FLUX DENSITY
       PARTICLE FLUX DENSITY
       RADIANT FLUX DENSITY
       #RATES (PER TIME)
   RT  ELECTRON COUNTERS
       ELECTRON PRESSURE
       ELECTRON RADIATION
       IRRADIANCE
       RADIANCY
       SOLAR FLUX DENSITY
ELECTRON GAS
   0604 1704 2403
   BT  #GASES
   RT  COSMIC GASES
       ELECTROHYDRODYNAMICS
       ELECTRON PLASMA
       FREE ELECTRONS
       IONIZED GASES

       PLASMONS
       RAREFIED GASES
       SCREEN EFFECT
       SUPERCONDUCTORS
ELECTRON GUNS
   0710 0905 1504 2403 3404
   RT  CATHODE RAY TUBES
       CROSSED FIELD GUNS
       ELECTRON BEAMS
       ELECTRON TRAJECTORIES
       GUNS
       MAGNETIC LENSES
       #PARTICLE ACCELERATORS
       PLASMA GUNS
       TUBE ANODES
       TUBE CATHODES
       TUBE GRIDS
ELECTRON IMPACT
   2403 3201
   BT  IMPACT
   RT  ELECTRON BEAMS
       ELECTRON TRAJECTORIES
       ION IMPACT
       POINT IMPACT
       PROTON IMPACT
ELECTRON INTENSITY
   USE  ELECTRON FLUX DENSITY
ELECTRON INTERACTIONS
   USE  ELECTRON SCATTERING
ELECTRON IONIZATION
   USE  #IONIZATION
ELECTRON IRRADIATION
   1002 1504 2402 2403 3404
   BT  #IRRADIATION
   RT  AURORAL IRRADIATION
       ELECTRON ATTACHMENT
       ELECTRON BEAMS
       ELECTRON PRESSURE
       ELECTRON RADIATION
       ION IRRADIATION
       SECONDARY EMISSION
ELECTRON MASS
   2402 2403
   BT  #MASS
       PARTICLE MASS
   RT  ELECTRON ENERGY
       ELECTRONS
ELECTRON MICROSCOPES
   0501 1406 2310 2403 3404
   UF  ELECTRON MICROSCOPY
   BT  MICROSCOPES
   RT  ELECTRON DIFFRACTION
       ELECTRON OPTICS
       ELECTRON PHOTOGRAPHY
       FIELD EMISSION
       ION MICROSCOPES
       MAGNETIC LENSES
       MICROANALYSIS
       OPTICAL MICROSCOPES
       PHOTOMICROGRAPHY
       REPLICAS
ELECTRON MICROSCOPY
   USE  ELECTRON MICROSCOPES
ELECTRON MOBILITY
   0604 2302 2403 2603
   BT  CARRIER MOBILITY
       #ELECTRICAL PROPERTIES
       MOBILITY
       #TRANSPORT PROPERTIES
   RT  AMBIPOLAR DIFFUSION
       CHARGE CARRIERS
       ELECTROHYDRODYNAMICS
       ELECTROMIGRATION
       ELECTRON PRECIPITATION
       HOLE MOBILITY
       MAJORITY CARRIERS
       MINORITY CARRIERS
       SOLID STATE PHYSICS
ELECTRON MULTIPLIERS
   USE  PHOTOMULTIPLIER TUBES
ELECTRON OPTICS
   2307 2310 2402 2403
   RT  BEAM SWITCHING
       BRILLOUIN FLOW
       CATHODE RAY TUBES
       ELECTRO-OPTICS
       ELECTRON BEAMS
       ELECTRON DIFFRACTION
       ELECTRON MICROSCOPES
```

FIGURE 22 Specimen page from the *NASA Thesaurus*.

Direction finding antennas 0905
BT Antennas
     Navigational antennas
NT Wullenweber antennas
RT Sense antennas
Direction finding signals 1703
RT Direction finding
Direction finding stations 1703
RT Direction finding
Directivity
USE Orientation
Direct labor 0501
RT Direct costs
     Management control reports
Directories 0502
BT Documents
RT Indexes (documentation)
Direct power generation
USE Direct electric power generation
Direct power generators 1002
UF Nonrotating generators
BT Electric generators
NT Bacon fuel cells
     Biochemical fuel cells
     Cesium thermionic converters
     —Closed cycle MHD generators
     —Electrostatic generators
     Fossil fuel thermionic converters
     —Fuel cells
     Liquid metal fuel cells
     Liquid metal MHD generators
     —Magnetohydrodynamic generators
     Nuclear thermionic converters
     Open cycle MHD generators
     Plasma closed cycle MHD
      generators
     Portable thermionic converters
     Portable thermoelectric generators
     Pulsed power MHD generators
     Radiation resistant solar cells
     Radioisotope thermoelectric
      devices
     Regenerative fuel cells
     —Solar cells
     —Thermionic converters
     —Thermoelectric generators
     Thermophotovoltaic converters
     Van de Graaff generators
RT Auxiliary power plants
     Spacecraft electric power units
Direct quenching
USE Quenching (cooling)
Direct rolling
USE Hot rolling
Dirichlet problem 1201
BT Analysis (mathematics)
     Boundary value problems
     Differential equations
     Partial differential equations
     Real variables
Dirichlet series 1201
BT Analysis (mathematics)
     Calculus
     Real variables
     Series (mathematics)
Dirigibles
USE Airships
Dirt 1407
RT —Dust
     —Soils
Disaccharides 0601
BT Carbohydrates
     Oligosaccharides
     Polysaccharides
     Sugars
NT Cellobiose
     Lactose
     Maltose
     Sucrose
Disarmament
USE Arms control
Disassembly 1505
*The process of taking equipment apart
so that its components can be reused*
RT Dismantling
Disasters 1312
RT —Accidents
     Anxiety
     Stress (psychology)
Disazo compounds 0703
Compounds with two azo groups
UF Bisazo compounds
BT Azo compounds
Discharge 1407
Use of a more specific term is

*recommended; consult the terms
listed below*
     Detonation
     Dispersing
     Disposal
     Drainage
     Effluents
     Ejection
     Electric arcs
     Electric discharges
     Elimination
     Emission
     Emptying
     Exhausting
     Explosions
     Releasing
     Relieving
     Unloading
     Venting
Discharge lamps 1301
BT Electric lamps
     Lamps
NT Arc lamps
     Flash lamps
     Fluorescent lamps
     Glow lamps
     Mercury lamps
     Neon tubes
     Sodium lamps
     Ultraviolet lamps
     Xenon lamps
RT Carbon arcs
     Electroluminescent lamps
     Glow discharges
     Incandescent lamps
Discharge tubes
USE Gas discharge tubes
Discharging (personnel)
USE Disciplining
Disciplining 0509
UF Discharging (personnel)
RT Industrial relations
     Labor relations
     Morale
     Penalties
Discoloration 1407
RT Color
     Coloring
     —Damage
     —Degradation
     Fading
     Spotting
     Staining
     Tarnishing
Discone antennas 0905
BT Antennas
     Biconical antennas
     Broadband antennas
Disconnect fittings 1305
BT Fittings
NT Self sealing disconnect fittings
RT Hose fittings
     —Pipe fittings
     Plugs
     Quick release fasteners
     Release mechanisms
     Sleeves
     Tube fittings
     —Valves
Discontinuity (mathematics) 1201
BT Analysis (mathematics)
     Measure and integration
     Real variables
RT Continuity (mathematics)
Discontinuous grain growth
USE Grain growth
Discounted cash flow 0503
UF Discounted cash flow method
BT Cash flow
RT Breakeven point
     Economic analysis
     Interest rate of return
     Payout time
     Present worth
     Return on investment
     Return on sales
     Turnover ratio
Discounted cash flow method
USE Discounted cash flow
Discovery allowables
USE Production allowables
Discovery wells
USE Exploratory wells
and Producing wells
Discrete distribution functions
1201
BT Functions (mathematics)

     Probability distribution functions
     Statistical analysis
     Statistical distributions
RT Binomial density functions
     Continuous distribution functions
     Histograms
     Normal density functions
     —Skewed density functions
Discriminate analysis 1201
BT Statistical analysis
RT Clumps
     Clustering
     Factor analysis
Discrimination 1407
NT Background discrimination
     Target discrimination
RT —Acuity
     —Resolution
     Selectivity
Discrimination learning 0510
BT Learning
RT Maze learning
     Overlearning
     Reversal learning
     Trial and error learning
Discriminators 0901
BT Circuits
NT Frequency discriminators
     Phase discriminators
     Pulse discriminators
RT Comparator circuits
Discs (storage)
USE Magnetic disks
Disease carriers
USE Disease vectors
Diseases 0605
UF Disorders
*Use of a more specific term is
recommended; consult the terms
listed below*
     Abscesses
     Animal diseases
     Biliary system diseases
     Blood diseases
     Breast diseases
     Calculi
     Cardiovascular diseases
     Chromosome abnormalities
     Collagen diseases
     Congenital abnormalities
     Diagnosis
     Disease vectors
     Ear diseases
     Endocrine diseases
     Epidemiology
     Etiology
     Eye diseases
     Gastrointestinal diseases
     Growth abnormalities
     Hereditary diseases
     Iatrogenic diseases
     Immunologic diseases
     Infectious diseases
     Inflammatory diseases
     Inoculation
     Insect control
     Integumentary diseases
     Lymphatic diseases
     Mental disorders
     Metabolic diseases
     Musculoskeletal disorders
     Neoplasms
     Nervous system disorders
     Nutritional deficiency diseases
     Occupational diseases
     Oral diseases
     Pancreatic diseases
     Plant diseases
     Pregnancy complications
     Psychosomatic disorders
     Public health
     Respiratory diseases
     Reticuloendothelial disorders
     Signs and symptoms
     Therapy
     Toxic diseases
     Traumatic disorders
     Tropical diseases
     Urogenital diseases
     Vaccines
     Vitamin deficiency diseases
Disease vectors 0606
UF Disease carriers
     Vectors (etiology)
NT Insect vectors
RT Epidemiology
     Etiology

     Parasitology
Disengagement (military forces)
0504 1507
*Geographic separation of opposing
nonindigenous forces without
directly affecting indigenous forces*
RT —Arms control
     Demilitarization
Disengaging 1407
RT Detaching
     Dismantling
     —Separation
Dishing
USE Bulging
Dishwashers 0608
BT Electric appliances
Dishwashing compounds 1111
BT Cleaning agents
RT Detergents
     —Soaps
Disilane 0702
BT Hydrides
     Silicon hydrides
     Silicon inorganic compounds
Disinfectants 1107
UF Antiseptics
RT —Antiinfectives and antibacterials
     Bactericides
     Biocides
     —Drugs
     Fungicides
     —Pesticides
Disinfection 0606 0609
RT Fumigation
     Microorganism control (water)
     —Pest control
     Sterilization
Disintegration 1113
UF Powdering
RT Atomizing
     Chalking
     —Comminution
     —Damage
     Decay
     Decomposition
     —Deterioration
     Flaking
     Granulation
     Grinding (comminution)
Disintegrators
USE Grinding mills
Disk brakes 1306
BT Brakes (motion arresters)
RT Brake disks
     Drum brakes
     Hydraulic brakes
     —Pneumatic brakes
     Power brakes
Disk filters 1311
BT Fluid filters
     Separators
RT —Pressure filters
     Rotary filters
     Vacuum filters
Disks (agricultural)
USE Agricultural machinery
Disks (shapes) 1409
RT —Aerodynamic configurations
     Bodies of revolution
Disks (storage)
USE Magnetic disks
Dislocations (materials) 1113
RT —Creep properties
     —Crystal defects
     —Crystal dislocations
     —Fatigue (materials)
     —Geological faults
     —Mechanical properties
Dismantling 1505
*The process of taking equipment apart
for disposal*
RT Disassembly
     Disengaging
Disorders
USE Diseases
Dispatching
USE Distributing
Dispenser bombs 1902
BT Bombs (ordnance)
NT Leaflet bombs
RT Biological bombs
     Bomblets
     Chaff
     Chemical bombs
     —Countermeasures
     —Firebombs

FIGURE 23 Specimen page from the *Thesaurus of Engineering and Scientific Terms* (**TEST**), showing hierarchical listing presented without discrimination of levels.

ANALYTICAL CHEMISTRY
(CON'T)

RT   CHEMICAL ANALYSIS
       CHEMISTRY
       INORGANIC CHEMISTRY
       QUALITATIVE ANALYSIS
       QUANTITATIVE ANALYSIS
       VOLUMETRIC ANALYSIS
ANALYZERS
    0701 0801 0902 0905
    (EXCLUDES DEVICES FOR PERFORMING
    MATHEMATICAL ANALYSIS)
BT #MEASURING INSTRUMENTS
NT ENGINE ANALYZERS
      SIGNAL ANALYZERS
RT #CONTROLLERS
      DETECTORS
      MONITORS
      SELECTORS
      TEST EQUIPMENT
ANALYZING
    0601 0802 1505 3406 3407
    (USE OF A MORE SPECIFIC TERM IS
    RECOMMENDED--CONSULT THE TERMS
    LISTED BELOW)
UF ANALYSIS
      INSTRUMENTAL ANALYSIS
RT #ALGEBRA
      #ANALYSIS (MATHEMATICS)
      APPLICATIONS OF MATHEMATICS
      CHEMICAL ANALYSIS
      CREEP ANALYSIS
      DIAGNOSIS
      DIFFERENTIAL GEOMETRY
      DIFFERENTIAL THERMAL ANALYSIS
      EVALUATION
      EXAMINATION
      FIGURE OF MERIT
      #FORECASTING
      NETWORK ANALYSIS
      PHOTOINTERPRETATION
      POSTFLIGHT ANALYSIS
      PREFLIGHT ANALYSIS
      SIGNAL ANALYSIS
      SPECTRUM ANALYSIS
      #STATISTICAL ANALYSIS
      #STRESS ANALYSIS
      #STRUCTURAL ANALYSIS
      SYSTEMS ANALYSIS
      TERRAIN ANALYSIS
      TESTS
      TRAJECTORY ANALYSIS
      WEIGHT ANALYSIS
      X RAY ANALYSIS
ANAPHYLAXIS
    0404 0405 0408
  RT SENSITIZING
ANASTIGMATISM
    0404 0405 0408
  RT OPTOMETRY
      VISION
ANATASE
    0603 1804
  UF OCTAHEDRITE
  BT #CHALCOGENIDES
      METAL OXIDES
      OXIDES
      #TITANIUM COMPOUNDS
      TITANIUM OXIDES
  RT #MINERALS
      PIGMENTS
      RUTILE
#ANATOMY
    0402 0404
  NT ADRENAL GLAND
      AORTA
      ARM (ANATOMY)
      ARTERIES
      BARORECEPTORS
      BLADDER
      BLOOD VESSELS
      BONES
      BRAIN
      BRAIN STEM
      BRONCHI
      BRONCHIAL TUBE
      CAPILLARIES (ANATOMY)
      CARDIAC AURICLES
      CARDIAC VENTRICLES
      CARDIOVASCULAR SYSTEM
      CARTILAGE

CEREBELLUM
CEREBRAL CORTEX
CEREBRUM
CHEMORECEPTORS
CHEST
CHIN
CHOROID MEMBRANES
CIRCULATORY SYSTEM
COCHLEA
COLLAGENS
CONGENERS
CONJUNCTIVA
CONNECTIVE TISSUE
CONSTRICTORS
CORNEA
CORPUSCLES
CORTI ORGAN
CRANIUM
DIAPHRAGM (ANATOMY)
DIASTOLE
EAR
EARDRUMS
ELBOW (ANATOMY)
ENDOCRINE GLANDS
EPICARDIUM
ERYTHROCYTES
ESOPHAGUS
EUSTACHIAN TUBES
EYE (ANATOMY)
FEMUR
FINGERS
FLEXORS
FOREARM
FOVEA
GENITOURINARY SYSTEM
GLANDS (ANATOMY)
GLOMERULUS
GONADS
GRAVIRECEPTORS
HAND (ANATOMY)
HEAD (ANATOMY)
HEART
HEMATOPOIESIS
HEMATOPOIETIC SYSTEM
HIPPOCAMPUS
HUMAN BODY
INTRACRANIAL CAVITY
JOINTS (ANATOMY)
KIDNEYS
KNEE (ANATOMY)
LABYRINTH
LEG (ANATOMY)
LEUKOCYTES
LIMBS (ANATOMY)
LIVER
LUNGS
LYMPHOCYTES
MAMMARY GLANDS
MARROW
MASTOIDS
MECHANORECEPTORS
MIDDLE EAR
MUSCULOSKELETAL SYSTEM
MYOCARDIUM
NECK (ANATOMY)
NOSE (ANATOMY)
OCCIPITAL LOBES
OCULOMOTOR NERVES
ORGANS
OTOLITH ORGANS
OVARIES
PANCREAS
PARATHYROID GLAND
PELVIS
PHARYNX
PHOTORECEPTORS
PINEAL GLAND
PITUITARY GLAND
PROPRIOCEPTORS
PROSTATE GLAND
PUPILS
RESPIRATORY SYSTEM
RETINA
SALIVARY GLANDS
SCAPULA
SCIATIC REGION
SEBACEOUS GLANDS
SEMICIRCULAR CANALS
SENSE ORGANS

FIGURE 24 Specimen page from the *NASA Thesaurus,* showing complete hierarchy (under ANATOMY) without discrimination of levels.

than FLOW PROPERTY, which is narrower than PHYSICAL PROPERTY.

Although the alphabetical descriptor display is generally regarded as the major display in a thesaurus, many thesauri supplement the alphabetical display with alternative arrangements of the descriptors.

It is common to have a display of descriptors arranged alphabetically under broad subject categories. Frequently this display follows the subject categories presented in the *Subject Category List* of the Committee on Scientific and Technical Information (COSATI), which organizes knowledge into 22 broad fields (e.g., 01 AERONAUTICS, 02 AGRICULTURE . . . , 22 SPACE TECHNOLOGY) with group subdivisions. In the *Thesaurus of ERIC Descriptors,* the descriptors are organized into 52 subject groups, as shown in Table 7. Figure 25 shows a sample page from the ERIC descriptor group display.

Another possibility is the hierarchical display, which is really an alphabetico-classed display used as a supplement in thesauri which do not use the alphabetical display to show hierarchical indentation. The following is an example from the *Thesaurus of DDC Descriptors:*

ACTINIDE SERIES COMPOUNDS
   ACTINIUM COMPOUNDS
   PROTACTINIUM COMPOUNDS
   THORIUM COMPOUNDS
   TRANSURANIUM COMPOUNDS
      AMERICIUM COMPOUNDS
      BERKELIUM COMPOUNDS
      CALIFORNIUM COMPOUNDS

A similar hierarchical display is used in the *NASA Thesaurus.* Figure 26 illustrates a hierarchical display derived by facet analysis, as used in the *Subject Authority List* of the American Petroleum Institute.[1]

A fourth display which has become common is the permuted descriptor display. Such a display takes every significant word in a multiword descriptor and uses it as an entry word. Figure 27 is an example from the *NASA Thesaurus.* Note that the display under FLUX includes descriptors beginning with FLUX and descriptors with the word FLUX in other positions. Thus, all contexts of the word are brought together, even though they might be widely separated hierarchically. Figure 28, from the *Thesaurus of ERIC Descriptors,* shows the equivalent permuted display in a somewhat different format.

Goodman [19] illustrates the utility of the permuted display, as follows:

The words "culture," "cultural," and "culturally" illustrate the advantages of having a "Rotated Descriptor Display."

TABLE 7 ERIC Descriptor Groups

010	ABILITIES
020	ADMINISTRATION
030	ARTS
040	ATTITUDES
050	AUDIOVISUAL MATERIALS AND METHODS
060	BEHAVIOR
070	BIOLOGY
080	COMMUNICATION
090	COUNSELING
100	CULTURE
110	CURRICULUM
120	DEMOGRAPHY
130	DEVELOPMENT
140	EDUCATION
150	EMPLOYMENT
160	ENVIRONMENT
170	EQUIPMENT
180	EVALUATION
190	EVALUATION TECHNIQUES
200	EXPERIENCE
210	FACILITIES
220	FINANCE
230	GOVERNMENT
240	HANDICAPPED
250	HEALTH AND SAFETY
260	HUMANITIES
270	INSTRUCTION
280	INSTRUCTIONAL PROGRAM DIVISIONS
290	LANGUAGE AND SPEECH
300	LANGUAGES
310	LEARNING AND COGNITION
320	LIBRARY MATERIALS
330	LIBRARY SCIENCE
340	MATHEMATICS
350	OCCUPATIONS
360	OPPORTUNITIES
370	ORGANIZATIONS (GROUPS)
380	PERSONNEL AND GROUPS
390	PHYSICAL EDUCATION AND RECREATION
400	PHYSICAL SCIENCES
410	PROGRAMS
420	PSYCHOLOGY
430	RACE RELATIONS
440	READING
450	RESEARCH
460	RESOURCES
470	SCHOOLS
480	SOCIAL SCIENCES
490	SOCIOLOGY
500	STANDARDS
510	TECHNIQUES
520	TESTS

If one were to begin by looking up the term Culturally Disadvantaged in the *Thesaurus,* he would be presented with three narrower terms, all of which are variations on the "disadvantaged" portion of the term, e.g., Disadvantaged Youth. The RT entries lead to the closely related term Cultural Disadvantagement and to the word Culture, along with concepts like Acculturation. All together, there are seven related terms. There is no particular reason to ex-

DESCRIPTOR GROUP DISPLAY

EDUCATIONAL RADIO	PROGRAMED TEXTS	COVERT RESPONSE
EDUCATIONAL TELEVISION	PUBLIC TELEVISION	CRIME
ELECTROMECHANICAL AIDS	RADIO	DELINQUENCY
EXHIBITS	RAISED LINE DRAWINGS	DELINQUENT BEHAVIOR
FACSIMILE TRANSMISSION	REALIA	DISCIPLINE
FILM PRODUCTION	SINGLE CONCEPT FILMS	DISCIPLINE PROBLEMS
FILMS	SLIDES	DRUG ABUSE
FILMSTRIPS	SOUND EFFECTS	DRUG ADDICTION
FILM STUDY	SOUND FILMS	EATING HABITS
FIXED SERVICE TELEVISION	SOUND TRACKS	ECHOLALIA
FLES MATERIALS	STUDENT DEVELOPED MATERIALS	GROUP BEHAVIOR
FOREIGN LANGUAGE FILMS	STUDENT WRITING MODELS	HYPERACTIVITY
GRAPHS	SUPPLEMENTARY TEXTBOOKS	IMMATURITY
HANDWRITING MATERIALS	TALKING BOOKS	INFANT BEHAVIOR
HEALTH ACTIVITIES HANDBOOKS	TAPE RECORDINGS	INFORMAL LEADERSHIP
HEALTH BOOKS	TEACHER DEVELOPED MATERIALS	INTEGRITY
HIGH INTEREST LOW VOCABULARY BOOKS	TEACHING MACHINES	LEADER PARTICIPATION
HISTORY TEXTBOOKS	TELEGRAPHIC MATERIALS	LEADERSHIP
HORIZONTAL TEXTS	TELEVISION	MISBEHAVIOR
ILLUSTRATIONS	TELEVISION COMMERCIALS	NEGRO LEADERSHIP
INSTRUCTIONAL AIDS	TELEVISION VIEWING	OVERT RESPONSE
INSTRUCTIONAL FILMS	TEXTBOOKS	PARENT REACTION
INSTRUCTIONAL MATERIALS	THREE DIMENSIONAL AIDS	PARENT ROLE
INSTRUCTIONAL MEDIA	TOYS	PATTERNED RESPONSES
INSTRUCTIONAL TELEVISION	TRANSPARENCIES	PLAGIARISM
INSTRUCTOR CENTERED TELEVISION	VERTICAL TEXTS	REACTIVE BEHAVIOR
KINESCOPE RECORDINGS	VIDEO TAPE RECORDINGS	RESPONSE MODE
LABORATORY MANUALS		SCHOOL VANDALISM
LANGUAGE AIDS		SOCIAL IMMATURITY
LANGUAGE RECORDS (PHONOGRAPH)	BEHAVIOR 060	SOCIALLY DEVIANT BEHAVIOR
LARGE TYPE MATERIALS		SPONTANEOUS BEHAVIOR
MANIPULATIVE MATERIALS		STIMULUS BEHAVIOR
MAPS	AFFECTIVE BEHAVIOR	STUDENT BEHAVIOR
MASS MEDIA	ANTI SOCIAL BEHAVIOR	STUDENT LEADERSHIP
MASTER TAPES (AUDIO)	ATTENDANCE PATTERNS	STUDENT REACTION
MATHEMATICS MATERIALS	ATTENTION	STUDY HABITS
MECHANICAL TEACHING AIDS	ATTENTION SPAN	TEACHER BEHAVIOR
MICROFICHE	BEHAVIOR	TEACHER RESPONSE
MICROFILM	BEHAVIOR CHANGE	TRUANCY
MULTICHANNEL PROGRAMING	BEHAVIOR PATTERNS	VIOLENCE
MULTICULTURAL TEXTBOOKS	BEHAVIOR PROBLEMS	WITHDRAWAL
OPEN CIRCUIT TELEVISION	BEHAVIOR THEORIES	
ORIENTATION MATERIALS	BEHAVIORAL OBJECTIVES	
OVERHEAD TELEVISION	CHEATING	BIOLOGY 070
PHONOGRAPH RECORDS	CONDITIONED RESPONSE	
PHONOTAPE RECORDINGS	CONDITIONED STIMULUS	
PHOTOGRAPHS	CONDUCT	AGE
PICTORIAL STIMULI	CONFORMITY	AGE DIFFERENCES
PROGRAMED MATERIALS	CONSTRUCTED RESPONSE	AGRICULTURAL PRODUCTION

FIGURE 25 Descriptor group display from the *Thesaurus of ERIC Descriptors.*

pect that a dense network of terms involving the idea of "cultural" exists in the *Thesaurus.* Yet looking up the term in the "Rotated Descriptor Display" reveals forty-five terms involving either "culture," "cultural," or "culturally." About a dozen of these terms refer to specific cultures, but even some of these specific references, such as Puerto Rican Culture, might be of high interest to the searcher. The "Display" reveals such terms as Cultural Background, Cultural Factors, Culturally Advantaged, and Culture Free Tests. Indeed, many of the terms are likely to be of high interest to the searcher.

A permuted descriptor display is also included in the *Information Retrieval Thesaurus of Education Terms.*[2] This thesaurus was constructed by means of facet analysis. It therefore includes a faceted display of terms, illustrated in Figure 29. The existence of a faceted display reduces the RT load on the alphabetical sequence (Figure 30), where it is possible to

make blanket references to facets in which related terms may be found. Thus, the descriptor INTERPERSONAL CONFERENCE refers to the facet 2018. When we go to the 2018 facet (Figure 29) we can find a set of terms related to the term we began with.

GRAPHIC DISPLAY

So far we have discussed the methods of display used in the major thesauri published in the United States. There is a completely different way of presenting a thesaurus, involving the use of graphic displays. The first thesaurus to present terms graphically in this way was the so-called "circular thesaurus" of TDCK,*

* Technisch Documentatie-en Informatie-Centrum voor de Krijgsmacht.

28M

```
EQUIPMENT(CONTINUED)
  MANIFOLD(CONTINUED)
    INTAKE MANIFOLD
  PIPE
    SEAMLESS PIPE
    THIN WALL PIPE
    TRANSFER LINE
    WELDED PIPE
    STANDPIPE
    HOSE
    TUBE
      CAPILLARY TUBE
      FINNED TUBE
      HILSCH VORTEX TUBE
      VENTURI TUBE
    ORIFICE
    INLET
    OUTLET
    NOZZLE
      JET NOZZLE
    DISPENSER
    FITTING
    SLEEVE
    COLLAR
    FLANGE
  MOTOR VEHICLE
    AUTOMOBILE
      COMPACT CAR
      ELECTRIC AUTOMOBILE
    BUS
    EXCAVATING MACHINERY
      BACKHOE
      DRAGLINE
    MOTORCYCLE
    MOTOR SCOOTER
    TRACTOR
      BULLDOZER
    TRUCK
      FORK LIFT TRUCK
      TANK TRUCK
    TRAILER
    LOCOMOTIVE
    RAILROAD CAR
      GONDOLA
      TANK CAR
    GROUND EFFECT MECHANISM
    MONORAIL
  SHIP
    BARGE
      FLEXIBLE BARGE
    DREDGE
    TANKER
      BRIDGE AFT TANKER
      REFRIGERATED TANKER
    TUG
  AIRCRAFT
  SPACECRAFT
    ROCKET
  MAN MADE SATELLITE
  GUIDED MISSILE
```

29M

```
EQUIPMENT(CONTINUED)
  NAVIGATION EQUIPMENT
    RADAR
    WIND TUNNEL
    RAILROAD TRACK
    TRANSPORTATION TERMINAL
      AIRPORT
      BUS TERMINAL
      DOCK
      PIPELINE TERMINAL
      RAILROAD TERMINAL
      TRUCK TERMINAL
  PIPELINE
    BRANCH PIPELINE
    GATHERING LINE
    PIPELINE BYPASS
    PIPELINE CROSSING
    TRUNK PIPELINE
    PUMPING STATION
  STORAGE FACILITY
    TANK
      CONE ROOF TANK
      FLOATING ROOF TANK
      FUEL TANK
      INFLATED DOME ROOF TANK
      INGROUND TANK
      REFRIGERATED TANK
      STORAGE SPHERE
      SURGE TANK
    GAS HOLDER
    RESERVOIR
    TANK FARM
    UNDERGROUND STORAGE FACILITY
  CONTAINER
    BAFFLE
    AMPOULE
    BOTTLE
    CAN
    CARBOY
    CARTON
    DRUM
    PRESSURIZED STORAGE CYLINDER
  INSTRUMENT
    ANEMOMETER
    BALANCE
    BAROMETER
    BOLOMETER
    BRIDGE CIRCUIT
    CALIPER
    CALORIMETER
    CLOUD CHAMBER
    COUNTER
    DILATOMETER
    DYNAMOMETER
    EBULLIOMETER
    FLOWMETER
      ORIFICE METER
      PITOT TUBE
      POSITIVE DISPLACEMENT METER
      ROTAMETER
```

30M

```
EQUIPMENT(CONTINUED)
  INSTRUMENT(CONTINUED)
    FLOWMETER(CONTINUED)
      TURBINE METER
      VENTURI METER
    GAGE
    HALF CELL
    HYDROMETER
    HYGROMETER
    INTERFEROMETER
    MAGNETOMETER
    MANOMETER
    OSCILLOSCOPE
    OSMOMETER
    PENETROMETER
    PERMEAMETER
    POLARIMETER
    POLAROGRAPH
    PROBE
    PYROMETER
    RADIATION DETECTOR
    SPECTROSCOPE
    STROBOSCOPE
    THERMOCOUPLE
    THERMOMETER
    THERMOSTAT
    CRYOSTAT
    TIMER
    TITRIMETER
    VISCOMETER
      ELASTOVISCOMETER
  PROCESS CONTROL EQUIPMENT
    GOVERNOR
  SAFETY EQUIPMENT
    ALARM
    BLOWDOWN SYSTEM
    FIRE EXTINGUISHER
    GAS MASK
    RESPIRATOR
    SPRINKLER SYSTEM
  COMMUNICATION EQUIPMENT
    OPTICAL COMMUNICATION EQUIPMENT
    RADIO
      AM RADIO
      FM RADIO
      MICROWAVE RADIO
    TELEGRAPH
    TELEMETER
    TELEPHONE
    TELETYPE
    TELEVISION EQUIPMENT
  MATERIALS TESTER
    ALMEN EP LUBRICANT TESTER
    BOWDEN-LEBEN TESTER
    FALEX TESTER
    FLASH POINT TESTER
    FOUR BALL TESTER
    GREASE WORKER
    KUGEL FISCHER GREASE TESTER
    RYDER TESTER
```

FIGURE 26 Hierarchical display from the *Subject Authority List* of the American Petroleum Institute, showing faceted structure.

PROTACTINIUM FLUORIDES
SODIUM FLUORIDES
STRONTIUM FLUORIDES
SULFUR FLUORIDES
TECHNETIUM FLUORIDES
THORIUM FLUORIDES
TUNGSTEN FLUORIDES
URANIUM FLUORIDES
ZINC FLUORIDES
FLUORINE
FLUORINE COMPOUNDS
FLUORINE ORGANIC COMPOUNDS
FLUORO
FLUORO COMPOUNDS
FLUOROMETHANE
TRIS (DIFLUORAMINO) FLUOROMETHANE
FLUOZIRCONATES
SODIUM FLUOZIRCONATES
FLUTTER
FLUTTER ANALYSIS
PANEL FLUTTER
SUBSONIC FLUTTER
SUPERSONIC FLUTTER
TRANSONIC FLUTTER
FLUX
ELECTRON FLUX DENSITY
FLUX (RATE)
FLUX DENSITY
HEAT FLUX
HIGH FLUX ISOTOPE REACTORS
MAGNETIC FLUX
NEUTRON FLUX DENSITY
PARTICLE FLUX DENSITY
PLASMA FLUX MEASUREMENTS
PROTON FLUX DENSITY
RADIANT FLUX DENSITY
SOLAR FLUX
SOLAR FLUX DENSITY
FLY
VENUS FLY TRAP ROCKET VEHICLE
FLYBY
FLYBY MISSIONS
FLYING
FEAR OF FLYING
FLYING PERSONNEL
FLYING PLATFORMS
SUNDERLAND 5 FLYING BOAT
FM
FM/PM (MODULATION)
FOAM
POLYURETHANE FOAM
FOCUSING
SELF FOCUSING
FOIL
FOIL BEARINGS
FOILS
FOILS (MATERIALS)
METAL FOILS
FOKKER
FOKKER AIRCRAFT
FOKKER-PLANCK EQUATION
FOLDING
FOLDING FIN AIRCRAFT ROCKET VEHICLE
FOLDING STRUCTURES
FOLIC
FOLIC ACID
FOLLOWING
TERRAIN FOLLOWING AIRCRAFT
FOOD
FLOUR (FOOD)
FOOD INTAKE
GRAINS (FOOD)
FOODS
FROZEN FOODS
FOOTWEAR
BOOTS (FOOTWEAR)
FOR
BRAKES (FOR ARRESTING MOTION)
LUNAR EXPLORATION SYSTEM FOR APOLLO
NUCLEAR ENGINE FOR ROCKET VEHICLES
FORBIDDEN
FORBIDDEN BANDS
FORBIDDEN TRANSITIONS
FORBUSH
FORBUSH DECREASES
FORCE
CABLE FORCE RECORDERS
CENTRIFUGAL FORCE
CENTRIPETAL FORCE

FORCE DISTRIBUTION
FORCE-FREE MAGNETIC FIELDS
LINES OF FORCE
LORENTZ FORCE
ZERO FORCE CURVES
FORCED
FORCED CONVECTION
FORCED VIBRATION
FORCES
AERODYNAMIC FORCES
ARMED FORCES
ARMED FORCES (FOREIGN)
ARMED FORCES (UNITED STATES)
ELECTROMOTIVE FORCES
HYPERSONIC FORCES
INTERATOMIC FORCES
INTERMOLECULAR FORCES
LOAD DISTRIBUTION (FORCES)
LOADS (FORCES)
NONCONSERVATIVE FORCES
PONDEROMOTIVE FORCES
VAN DER WAAL FORCES
FORD
WEST FORD PROJECT
FOREBODIES
NOSES (FOREBODIES)
FORECASTING
LONG RANGE WEATHER FORECASTING
NUMERICAL WEATHER FORECASTING
STATISTICAL WEATHER FORECASTING
WEATHER FORECASTING
FOREIGN
ARMED FORCES (FOREIGN)
FOREIGN BODIES
FOREIGN POLICY
FOREIGN TRADE
FORK
TUNING FORK GYROSCOPES
FORM
FORM FACTORS
JORDAN FORM
FORMALDEHYDE
PHENOL FORMALDEHYDE
FORMATION
ENERGY OF FORMATION
HEAT OF FORMATION
ICE FORMATION
FORMHYDROXAMIC
FORMHYDROXAMIC ACID
FORMIC
FORMIC ACID
FORMING
BRAKES (FORMING OR BENDING)
ELECTROHYDRAULIC FORMING
EXPLOSIVE FORMING
FORMING TECHNIQUES
MAGNETIC FORMING
PRESSING (FORMING)
ROLL FORMING
STRETCH FORMING
FORMS
CANONICAL FORMS
DOMES (STRUCTURAL FORMS)
FORMS (PAPER)
SHELLS (STRUCTURAL FORMS)
FORMULA
BETHE-HEITLER FORMULA
BLATON FORMULA
CAUCHY INTEGRAL FORMULA
LANGEVIN FORMULA
FORMULAS
FORMULAS (MATHEMATICS)
FORTISAN
FORTISAN (TRADEMARK)
FORWARD
FORWARD SCATTERING
SWEPT FORWARD WINGS
FOSTER
FOSTER THEORY
FOULIS
FOULIS THEOREM
FOUNDATIONS
PILE FOUNDATIONS
FOUR
FOUR BODY PROBLEM
TWENTY-FOUR HOUR ORBITS
FOURIER
FOURIER ANALYSIS
FOURIER LAW

FIGURE 27 Specimen page from the permuted descriptor display of the *NASA Thesaurus.*

```
ROTATED  DESCRIPTOR  DISPLAY              ROTATED  DESCRIPTOR  DISPLAY
         VOCATIONAL APTITUDE                   CITY WIDE PROGRAMS
         VOCATIONAL COUNSELING                      WILDLIFE MANAGEMENT
         VOCATIONAL DEVELOPMENT                     WINDOWLESS ROOMS
         VOCATIONAL DIRECTORS                       WITHDRAWAL
         VOCATIONAL EDUCATION                       WITHDRAWAL TENDENCIES (PSYCHOLOGY)
   ADULT VOCATIONAL EDUCATION                       WOLOF
         VOCATIONAL EDUCATION TEACHERS              WOMEN PROFESSORS
         VOCATIONAL FOLLOWUP                        WOMEN TEACHERS
         VOCATIONAL HIGH SCHOOLS            WORKING WOMEN
         VOCATIONAL INTERESTS                       WOMENS EDUCATION
         VOCATIONAL REHABILITATION                  WOODWORKING
         VOCATIONAL RETRAINING                      WORD FREQUENCY
         VOCATIONAL SCHOOLS                         WORD LISTS
    AREA VOCATIONAL SCHOOLS                         WORD RECOGNITION
         VOCATIONAL TRAINING CENTERS               WORD STUDY SKILLS
         VOGUL                             FUNCTION WORDS
         VOICE DISORDERS                            WORK ATTITUDES
     EYE VOICE SPAN                                 WORK ENVIRONMENT
         VOLUNTARY AGENCIES                         WORK EXPERIENCE
         VOLUNTARY INTEGRATION                      WORK EXPERIENCE PROGRAMS
         VOLUNTEER TRAINING                         WORK LIFE EXPECTANCY
         VOLUNTEERS                    SHEET METAL WORK
 STUDENT VOLUNTEERS                                 WORK SIMPLIFICATION
         VOTER REGISTRATION                  SOCIAL WORK
         VOTING                  STUDENT PERSONNEL WORK
         VOTING RIGHTS                              WORK STUDY PROGRAMS
         VOWELS                            VERTICAL WORK SURFACES
 MINIMUM WAGE LAWS                                  WORKBOOKS
 MINIMUM WAGE LEGISLATION                   MIGRANT WORKER PROJECTS
 MINIMUM WAGE                               NURSERY WORKERS (HORTICULTURE)
         WAGE STATEMENTS                 CHILD CARE WORKERS
         WAGES                             CLERICAL WORKERS
   CLASS WALLS                                ENTRY WORKERS
   CIVIL WAR (UNITED STATES)           FOOD SERVICE WORKERS
         WAREHOUSES                          FOREIGN WORKERS
         WATCHMAKERS                      INTERSTATE WORKERS
         WATER RESOURCES                     MIGRANT WORKERS
         WEEDS                                 SALES WORKERS
         WEEKEND PROGRAMS             SCHOOL SOCIAL WORKERS
         WEIGHT                          SEMISKILLED WORKERS
         WELDERS                            SERVICE WORKERS
         WELDING                        SHEET METAL WORKERS
         WELFARE                            SKILLED WORKERS
         WELFARE AGENCIES                    SOCIAL WORKERS
   CHILD WELFARE                          UNSKILLED WORKERS
         WELFARE PROBLEMS                           WORKING HOURS
         WELFARE RECIPIENTS                   METAL WORKING OCCUPATIONS
         WELFARE SERVICES                          WORKING PARENTS
 MIGRANT WELFARE SERVICES                          WORKING WOMEN
  SOCIAL WELFARE                                   WORKMANS COMPENSATION
 STUDENT WELFARE                                   WORKSHEETS
 TEACHER WELFARE                                   WORKSHOPS
         WESTERN CIVILIZATION                 DRAMA WORKSHOPS
     NON WESTERN CIVILIZATION                PARENT WORKSHOPS
         WHITE COLLAR OCCUPATIONS          PRESCHOOL WORKSHOPS
         WHOLE NUMBERS                      SHELTERED WORKSHOPS
         WHOLESALING                          SUMMER WORKSHOPS
    CITY WIDE COMMISSIONS                    TEACHER WORKSHOPS
```

FIGURE 28 Specimen page from the permuted descriptor display of the *Thesaurus of ERIC Descriptors*.

the Netherlands Armed Forces Technical Documentation and Information Center,[21, 27] dating from 1963 (Figure 31). The *Circular Thesaurus* presents term displays in the form of concentric circles, each circle representing a level of the hierarchy, with the summum genus at the center of the graph. Over 10,000 terms are thus displayed in this thesaurus.

Lauren Doyle [12, 13] also advocated a pictorial display, using arrowgraphs (Figure 32) to depict strengths of association between terms. In this case the associations are derived from statistical data on frequency of co-occurrence of words in a corpus. In Figure 32, the words in largest type are those of greatest prevalence in the corpus. Doyle called his display a "semantic road map." It was really intended for use in an on-line retrieval system using a cathode ray tube, but it is also suitable for use in a printed format.

Graphic display of this type is also used in a trilingual thesaurus (English, French, German) developed by the French Road Research Laboratory with the cooperation of the Bureau d'Etudes Van Dijk.[33] Intended for use by the road research laboratories of OECD member countries, it uses arrowgraphs to show relations between terms and a superimposable grid to display equivalents in other languages.

The best-known graphic display is that of the

```
        FACET        2
        SUB-FACET    2013


ANTICIPATION METHOD
CLUING
CUEING
PROMPTING

CLASSICAL CONDITIONING
CONDITIONING
EXTINCTION
INSTRUMENTAL CONDITIONING
OPERANT CONDITIONING
RESPONSE GENERALIZATION
STIMULUS GENERALIZATION

APPLICATION
TRANSFER

CONFIRMATION
NEGATIVE REINFORCEMENT
NEGATIVE REWARD
PUNISHMENT
REINFORCEMENT
REWARD



        FACET        2
        SUB-FACET    2014


DISTRIBUTED PRACTICE
DRILL
EXERCISE
MASSED PRACTICE
MASSING
PRACTICE
REPETITION
WARM UP

ASSIGNMENT
CLASS PREPARATION
CLASSWORK
HOMEWORK
PREPARATION
TASK



        FACET        2
        SUB-FACET    2015


LEARNING
LEARNING TO LEARN
OVERLEARNING
SET LEARNING
TRIAL AND ERROR LEARNING

ASSOCIATIVE LEARNING
INCIDENTAL LEARNING
MOTOR LEARNING
PERCEPTUAL MOTOR LEARNING
SLEEP LEARNING
SOCIAL LEARNING

ATTITUDE FORMATION
HABIT FORMATION
HABITUATION

LANGUAGE DEVELOPMENT
LANGUAGE USAGE
ORAL LANGUAGE DEVELOPMENT
SECOND LANGUAGE LEARNING
USAGE(LANGUAGE)
VERBAL LEARNING
VOCABULARY BUILDING
WRITTEN LANGUAGE DEVELOPMENT

CORRESPONDENCE STUDY
DIRECTED STUDY
DISCOVERY LEARNING
GUIDED LEARNING
GUIDED STUDY
INDEPENDENT STUDY
NON DIRECTED STUDY
```

```
        FACET        2
        SUB-FACET    2015


SELF DIRECTED STUDY
STUDY HABITS
STUDYING

MEMORIZATION
PAIRED ASSOCIATE LEARNING
ROTE LEARNING
SERIAL LEARNING

MEMORY SPAN
RECALL
RECOGNITION
REMEMBERING
RETENTION

LEARNING INHIBITION
PROACTIVE INHIBITION
RECIPROCAL INHIBITION
RETROACTIVE INHIBITION



        FACET        2
        SUB-FACET    2016


COGNITION
COGNITIVE PROCESSES

CONCEPTUALIZATION
CREATIVE THINKING
CRITICAL THINKING
DECISION MAKING
LOGICAL ORGANIZATION
ORGANIZING
PROBLEM SOLVING
REASONING
SEARCHING BEHAVIOR
THINKING
VISUALIZATION

DEDUCTION
GUESSING
INDUCTION
INFERENCE
INTUITION

ABSTRACTION
CONCEPT FORMATION
CONCEPTION
GENERALIZATION

APPREHENSION
AUDITORY COMPREHENSION
COMPREHENSION
LANGUAGE COMPREHENSION
MECHANICAL COMPREHENSION
READING COMPREHENSION
UNDERSTANDING
VISUAL COMPREHENSION

AUDITORY DISCRIMINATION
DISCRIMINATION
VISUAL DISCRIMINATION
WORD DISCRIMINATION

APPERCEPTION
AUDITORY PERCEPTION
ECCENTRIC PROJECTION
INTERSENSORY PERCEPTION
LOCALIZATION
PERCEPTION
SOCIAL PERCEPTION
SPACE PERCEPTION
SUBCEPTION
TACTUAL PERCEPTION
VISUAL PERCEPTION

SENSORY ADAPTATION
```

```
        FACET        2
        SUB-FACET    2017


ANSWER
BEHAVIOR
CONSTRUCTED RESPONSE
COVERT RESPONSE
MOTOR RESPONSE
ORAL RESPONSE
OVERT RESPONSE
REACTION
RESPONSE
RESPONSE MODE
SENSORY DISCRIMINATION
VERBAL RESPONSE



        FACET        2
        SUB-FACET    2018


COMMUNICATING
INFORMATION SERVICE
LIBRARY SERVICE
PUBLISHING

ADVERTISING
PROPAGANDA
PUBLIC RELATIONS

ARTICULATION
COMMENTARY
FINGERSPELLING
NARRATION
SHOW AND TELL
SPEAKING
SPEECH
VERBALIZATION

INTERVIEW
INTERVIEWING
JOB INTERVIEW
QUESTION ASKING

CONFERENCE(INTERPERSONAL)
CONFERENCE(PROFESSIONAL MEETING)
INTERPERSONAL CONFERENCE
PROFESSIONAL MEETING
SYMPOSIUM



        FACET        2
        SUB-FACET    2019


CREATIVE WRITING
EXPOSITORY WRITING
REWRITING
WRITING

AUDING
LEISURE LISTENING
LISTENING
LISTENING HABITS

LEISURE READING
LIP READING
MAP READING
MUSIC READING
ORAL READING
READING
READING HABITS
SIGHTSINGING
SILENT READING
SKIMMING
SPEECH READING

VIEWING HABITS
```

FIGURE 29 Specimen page from *Information Retrieval Thesaurus of Education Terms*, showing faceted display of terms.

```
                HOSPITAL●
                INSTITUTIONALIZED●
                MENTAL ILLNESS

INSTITUTIONALIZED
        RT   8001
                INSTITUTIONAL CARE●

INSTRUCTION
        USE  TEACHING

INSTRUCTION RATE
        USE  PACING

INSTRUCTION TIME
        SN   TOTAL TIME SPENT FOR A GIVEN BLOCK OF
                INSTRUCTION
        RT   4001

INSTRUCTIONAL TELEVISION
        USE  TELEVISED INSTRUCTION

INSTRUCTIONAL TEST
        SN   A TEST INTENTIONALLY USED AS AN
                INSTRUCTIONAL DEVICE
        RT   2002
                PROGRAMMED INSTRUCTION●

INSTRUCTOR
        USE  TEACHER

INSTRUCTOR TRAINING
        USE  TEACHER EDUCATION

INSTRUMENT PANELS
        RT   15016

INSTRUMENTAL CONDITIONING
        USE  OPERANT CONDITIONING

INSTRUMENTAL MUSIC
        RT   17011
                MUSICAL INSTRUMENTS●

INSTRUMENTS
        USE  EQUIPMENT

INSUFFICIENCY
        USE  ADEQUACY

INSURANCE
        SN   *
        RT   13001

INTEGRATION[RACIAL]
        USE  RACIAL INTEGRATION

INTELLIGENCE
        SN   *
        UF   GENERAL ABILITY
                MENTAL ABILITY
        RT   6001
                INTELLIGENCE TEST●
                MENTAL DEVELOPMENT●

INTELLIGENCE QUOTIENT
        UF   IQ
        RT   6001

INTELLIGENCE TEST
        UF   MENTAL TEST
        BT   PSYCHOLOGICAL TEST
        NT   ABILITY TEST
                APTITUDE TEST
        RT   2002
                INTELLIGENCE●
                MENTAL DEVELOPMENT●

INTELLIGIBILITY
        UF   COHERENCE
                UNDERSTANDABILITY
        RT   11001
                LOGICAL ORGANIZATION●
                PERCEPTIBILITY●
```

```
INTENSITY
        RT   3001

INTERACTION
        SN   *
        UF   INTERPLAY
        RT   2023
                INFLUENCE

INTERCOMMUNICATION SYSTEM
        SN   *
        RT   15014

INTEREST
        SN   PSYCHOLOGICAL SENSE
        RT   7003
                INTEREST TEST●
                MOTIVATION●

INTEREST TEST
        BT   PSYCHOLOGICAL TEST
        RT   2002
                INTEREST●

INTERFERENCE
        SN   LIGHT AND SOUND WAVES
        RT   9004

INTERGROUP RELATIONS
        SN   *
        RT   12003
                GROUP DYNAMICS●

INTERMEDIATE GRADES
        UF   MIDDLE GRADES
        BT   ELEMENTARY SCHOOL
        NT   GRADE FIVE
                GRADE FOUR
                GRADE SIX
        RT   14001

INTERPERSONAL CONFERENCE
        SN   FACE TO FACE COMMUNICATION, AS BETWEEN
                TEACHER AND STUDENT
        UF   CONFERENCE[INTERPERSONAL]
        RT   2018
                COUNSELING●
                INTERPERSONAL RELATIONS●

INTERPERSONAL RELATIONS
        SN   *
        RT   12003
                FRIENDLINESS●
                INTERPERSONAL CONFERENCE●
                SOCIAL APTITUDE●
                SOCIAL DIFFERENCES●
                SOCIAL INTERACTION●
                SOCIAL PROBLEMS●

INTERPLAY
        USE  INTERACTION

INTERPRETATION
        SN   *
        RT   2001

INTERRUPTION
        SN   *
        RT   4001
                DISRUPTIVE BEHAVIOR

INTERSENSORY PERCEPTION
        SN   PERCEPTION INVOLVING SEVERAL SENSE
                MODES
        RT   2016
                MULTISENSORY PRESENTATION●
                SENSE MODE

INTERSTUDENT RELATIONS
        RT   12003
                SOCIOMETRIC TEST●
```

FIGURE 30 Specimen page from the alphabetical display of the *Information Retrieval Thesaurus of Education Terms.*

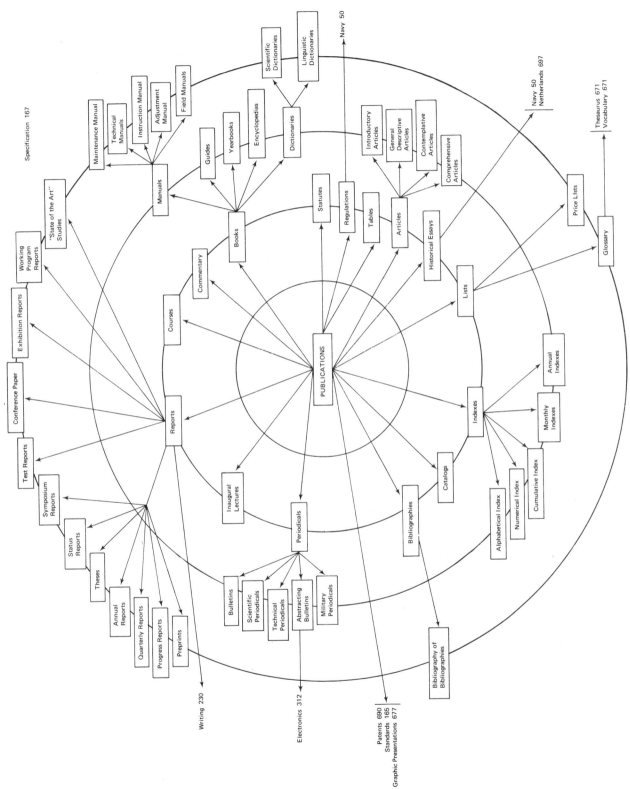

FIGURE 31 Specimen page from *TDCK Circular Thesaurus System.*

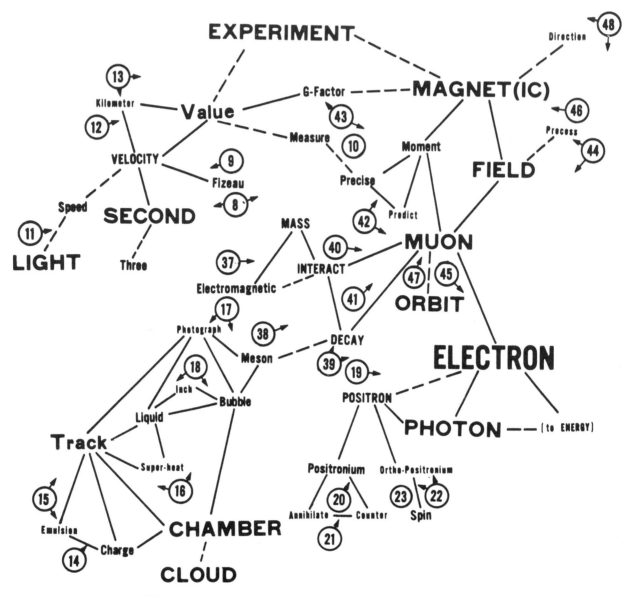

FIGURE 32 Specimen "semantic road map" as presented by Doyle.

EURATOM Thesaurus,[14] the justification for which is well presented by Rolling.[29] This thesaurus includes both an alphabetical display and a graphic display. Because the graphic display is used, the alphabetical display does not need either cross-references or hierarchy.

The graphic display used in the first edition consisted of arrowgraphs (Figure 33). Within each keyword group, the hierarchical and associative relationships are represented by arrows. These replace the cross-referencing encountered in a conventional thesaurus. Some arrows also point to related keywords in other graphs. For example, in Figure 33, NEUTRONS is related to NEUTRON FLUX, which appears in chart 82. The direction of the arrows is usually from the higher to the lower generic level; related keywords of the

same generic level are linked with two-way arrows. In the second edition of the thesaurus a somewhat modified display was adopted (Figure 34). Here semantically related terms are grouped to form clusters (domains) around the keywords, which appear in upper case. Nonkeyword *accepted* terms (synonyms and terms at lower generic level — the *use* references in a conventional thesaurus) are in lower case and *forbidden* words appear in italics. The difference between these two is that the *accepted* terms may be used in indexing and searching while the *forbidden* terms may not. The *see also* or RT references of the classical thesaurus are replaced by links between terms in the arrowgraphs, the thickness of the line indicating the strength of the link; that is, the strength of the "semantic relationship." Related graphs are referred to along the pe-

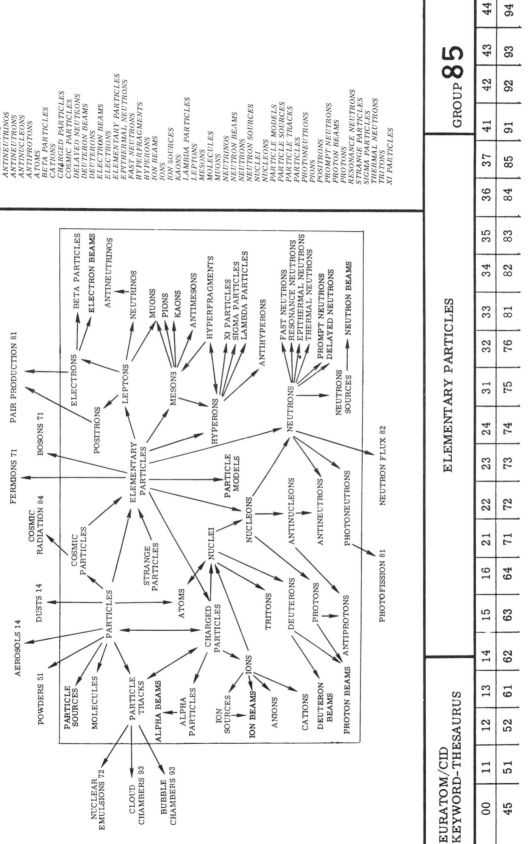

FIGURE 33 Specimen page from *EURATOM Thesaurus*, first edition. Note use of arrowgraphs.

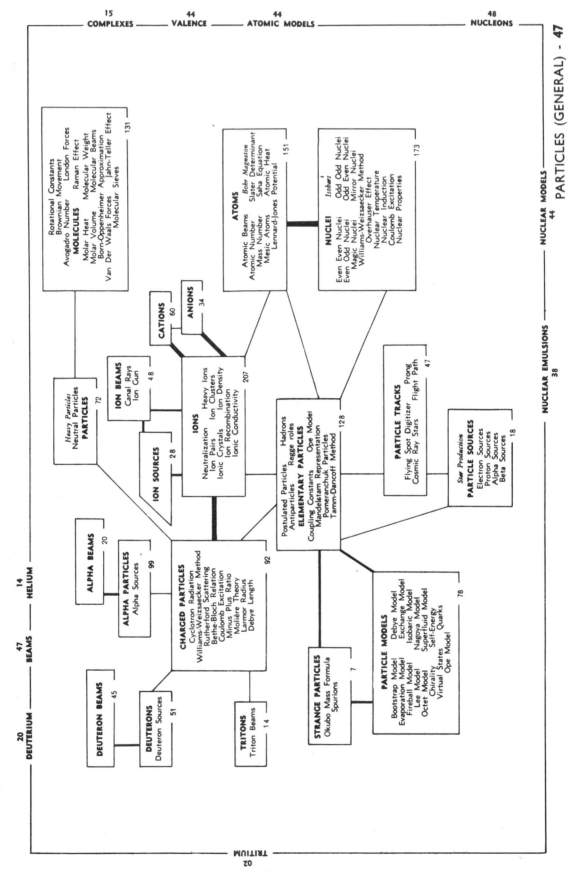

FIGURE 34   Specimen page from *EURATOM Thesaurus*, second edition. Note modification of graphic display used in first edition.

riphery of each diagram. Thus in Figure 34 DEUTERON BEAMS is connected to DEUTERIUM, which appears in graph 20, relating to radioisotopes. According to Colbach,[9] these displays "do away with the need for extensive cross-referencing and scope notes defining the conceptual coverage of the keywords, since the scope of every keyword is defined by the surrounding nonkeyword terminology and limited by the existence of its keyword neighbors."

Graphic display is effective in all forms of communication. It has appeal in the thesaurus context because, like the faceted classification scheme, it brings related terms into physical proximity and allows an indexer or searcher to view a complete conspectus of these associations at a glance. The alphabetical display does not do this; to get the full picture we must dodge backwards and forwards as the related term references direct us. However, extremely large hierarchies involving multiple relationships and levels are difficult to display intelligibly in graphic form.

A brief report on thesaurus display, including a discussion of the pros and cons of various methods, was issued by Surace [31] in 1970. However, the report ignores graphic display entirely.

REFERENCES

1. American Petroleum Institute. *Subject Authority List.* 3rd ed. New York, 1966.
2. Barhydt, G. C. and Schmidt, C. T., comps. *Information Retrieval Thesaurus of Education Terms.* Cleveland: Case Western Reserve University, 1968.
3. Binns, J. and Bagley, D., comps. *A Faceted Subject Classification for Engineering.* 3rd ed. Whetstone, England: English Electric Co., 1961.
4. Brenner, E. H. and Mulvihill, J. G. "American Petroleum Institute Information Retrieval Project *Subject Authority List.*" *Bulletin de l'Association Internationale des Documentalistes et Techniciens de l'Information* 5 (1966): 81-84.
5. Campbell, D. J. "Making Your Own Indexing System in Science and Technology." *ASLIB Proceedings* 15 (1963): 282-302.
6. Classification Research Group. *Classification and Information Control.* London: Library Association, 1969. L. A. Research Publication No. 1.
7. Classification Research Group. "The Need for a Faceted Classification as the Basis of all Methods of Information Retrieval." *Library Association Record* 57 (1955): 262-268.
8. Coates, E. J. "Notation in Classification." *Classification Research Group Bulletin* 2 (1957): D1-D19.
9. Colbach, R. "Thesaurus Structure and Generic Posting." In *Handling of Nuclear Information: Proceedings of a Symposium.* Vienna, 16-20 February 1970. Vienna: International Atomic Energy Agency, 1970, 585-595.
10. College of Aeronautics. *Facet Classification Schedules and Index* (of Aeronautics). Cranfield, England: ASLIB Cranfield Research Project, 1960.
11. Croghan, A., comp. *Classification of the Performing Arts.* London: Anthony Croghan, 1968.
12. Doyle, L. B. *Indexing and Abstracting by Association.* Part 1. Santa Monica: System Development Corporation, 1962.
13. Doyle, L. B. "Semantic Road Maps for Literature Searchers." *Journal of the Association for Computing Machinery* 8 (1961): 553-578.
14. European Atomic Energy Community. *EURATOM Thesaurus: Indexing Terms Used Within EURATOM's Nuclear Documentation System.* 2nd ed. 2 vols. Brussels: 1966-67. EUR 500.e.
15. European Packaging Federation. *Classification Schedule and Alphabetical Index for Packaging Documentation.* London: 1966.
16. Foskett, A. C. *The Subject Approach to Information.* Hamden, Conn.: Archon Books, 1969.
17. Foskett, D. J. *Classification for a General Index Language.* London: Library Association, 1970. L. A. Research Publication No. 2.
18. Foskett, D. J., comp. *The London Education Classification.* London: University of London, Institute of Education, 1963.
19. Goodman, F. "The Role and Function of the Thesaurus in Education," In *Thesaurus of ERIC Descriptors.* 2d ed. New York: CCM Information Corporation, 1970, 1-28.
20. Kaiser, J. *Systematic Indexing.* London: Vacher and Sons, 1911.
21. Koekkoek, M. and Schuller, J. A. "The TDCK—Compact System." *Journal of Documentation* 18 (1962): 176-182.
22. London, G. *A Classed Thesaurus as an Aid to Indexing, Classifying and Searching.* New Brunswick, N.J.: Rutgers, the State University, Graduate School of Library Service, 1966.
23. McClelland, R. M. A. and Mapleson, W. W. "Construction and Usage of Classified Schedules and Generic Features in Coordinate Indexing." *ASLIB Proceedings* 18 (1966): 290-299.
24. Mulvihill, J. G. and Brenner, E. H. "Faceted Organization of a Thesaurus Vocabulary." *Proceedings of the American Documentation Institute* 3 (1966): 175-183.
25. National Aeronautics and Space Administration. *NASA Thesaurus.* Washington, D.C., 1967.
26. Needham, C. D. *Organizing Knowledge in Libraries.* London: Andre Deutsch, 1964.
27. Netherlands Armed Forces Technical Documentation and Information Center. *TDCK Circular Thesaurus System.* The Hague, 1963.
28. Ranganathan, S. R. *The Colon Classification.* New Brunswick, N.J.: Rutgers, the State University, 1965.
29. Rolling, L. *The Role of Graphic Display of Concept Relationships in Indexing and Retrieval Vocabularies.* Brussels: European Atomic Energy Community, 1965. EUR 2291.e.
30. Rostron, R. M. "The Construction of a Thesaurus," *ASLIB Proceedings* 20 (1968): 181-187.
31. Surace, C. J. *The Displays of a Thesaurus.* Santa Monica, Calif.: Rand Corporation, 1970. P-4331.
32. University of Tulsa. *Exploration and Production Thesaurus.* 3rd ed. Tulsa, 1968.
33. Van Dijk, M. "Un Thésaurus Multilingue au Service de la Coopération Internationale," *Bulletin de l'Association Internationale des Documentalistes et Techniciens de l'Information* 5 (1966): 85-87.
34. Vickery, B. C. *Classification and Indexing in Science.* London: Butterworth, 1958.
35. Vickery, B. C. *Faceted Classification.* London: ASLIB, 1960.
36. Wadington, J. P. "Unit Concept Coordinate Indexing." *American Documentation* 9 (1958): 107-113.

8 The Thesaurofacet

A controlled vocabulary must provide both alphabetical and classified arrangements of the terms it contains. The traditional thesaurus displays its classification covertly in its BT-NT reference structure and perhaps by supplementary term groupings. The faceted classification provides an alphabetical approach in its alphabetical subject index. Another way of providing both approaches is the *Thesaurofacet*,[1] which is sufficiently novel and interesting to deserve a brief chapter of its own. It was produced by Aitchison et al.[2] in 1969. Containing 16,000 approved terms and 7,000 "entry terms" (references), this controlled vocabulary completely integrates the thesaurus and the faceted classification. The vocabulary contains both a complete classification and a complete thesaurus, one complementing the other, and is thus able to achieve the full advantages of both.

The faceted classification (Figure 35) is conventional. The thesaurus (Figure 36) also looks fairly conventional. *Use* references are employed to control synonyms and to provide entries for specific terms that are not used for indexing or searching. The UF reciprocals also appear. Against each descriptor in the thesaurus is placed its class number. Thus, TELEVISION CAMERA TUBES is given the class number MCE. When we go to this number in the classification schedules, the faceted display reveals the complete hierarchy of broader terms (CATHODE RAY TUBES, ELECTRON BEAM DEFLECTION TUBES, ELECTRON TUBES) and narrower terms

(TELEVISION COLOUR CAMERA TUBES). It also shows the terms that are most closely related; that is, the co-equal terms in the same array (for example, STORAGE TUBES, IMAGE CONVERTER TUBES) and the terms subsidiary to these. The advantage over the conventional thesaurus is that the display shows all these relations for any term at a glance and shows the correct relations among these terms.

The thesaurus section of the *Thesaurofacet* also contains some RT's and some BT's, but does not duplicate any feature of the classified section. The related terms are terms from other facets. TELEVISION CAMERA TUBES is shown to be related to PHOTOTUBES, PHOTOMULTIPLIERS, and TELEVISION CAMERAS. None of these terms belongs in the same array as TELEVISION CAMERA TUBES and thus might well be overlooked if the faceted display alone were used.

The related terms shown in the thesaurus are not terms related hierarchically. The thesaurus displays other relationships (e.g., between a whole and a part or between an object and its properties). The more important of these relationships are indicated in Table 8.

Likewise, the thesaurus does not display the same BT relationship as shown in the faceted structure. However, a particular concept may quite properly belong in several hierarchies. The faceted display shows only the principal hierarchy. Others are revealed in the thesaurus. In the case of TELEVISION

MBE	**Electron wave tubes**
MBF	Travelling wave tubes
MBH	Backward wave tubes
MBJ	Carcinotrons
MBM	Magnetrons
MBP	Velocity modulated tubes
MBQ	Klystrons
MBT	**Electron beam deflection tubes**
MBV	Indicator tubes (tuning)
MBW	Trochotrons
MC	Cathode ray tubes
MC2	Image converter tubes
MC4	Image intensifiers
MC6	Storage tubes
MCE	Television camera tubes
MCI	Television colour camera tubes
MCL	Television picture tubes
MCO	Television colour picture tubes
MCQ	**X ray tubes**
MCS	**Phototubes**
MCT	Photomultipliers
MCW	**Electron multipliers**
	˙ Photomultipliers MCT

By number of electrodes:

MD	Diodes (tubes)
	˙ Plasma diodes (tubes) MAR
MD3	Triodes (tubes)
	˙ Thyratrons MAI
MD5	Multielectrode tubes
	˙ Trochotrons MBW
MD6	Phasitrons
MD7	Reactance tubes
MDA	Tetrodes
MDB	Dynatrons
MDC	Resnatrons
MDG	Pentodes
MDH	Pentagrid converters
MDL	Multiple unit tubes

By application:

	˙ Storage tubes MC6
	˙ Television camera tubes MCE
	˙ Television picture tubes MCL
MER	Counting tubes
	˙ Indicator tubes (numerical) MB7
	˙ Trochotrons MBW
MET	Dekatrons

For other applications combine notation for Electron tubes with application. For manual systems the preferred order is application followed by tube, but permuted entries may be made, for example:—
˙ Electron tube amplifiers LE/MA
˙ Electron tube demodulators LW/MA
˙ Electron tube mixers LX/MA
˙ Electron tube modulators LV/MA
˙ Electron tube oscillators LL, MA
˙ Electron tube rectifiers JPL

By components:

MF	Electron tube components
	˙ Electrodes KP
	˙ Electron guns EHT
	˙ Electron lenses EHL
	˙ Fluorescent screens DWQ
MF3	Grids (tube components)
MF5	Filaments (tube components)
MF6	Heaters (tube components)

By techniques:

MFM	Electron tube production techniques

Combine with appropriate notation from Production engineering and other schedules.
˙ Brazing TQ
˙ Glass metal seals QNS
˙ Soldering TQO
˙ Vacuum engineering PV
˙ Welding TN

MG	*Semiconductors*
	˙ Crystals FB
	˙ Semiconductor physics EKH
MG2	**SEMICONDUCTOR MATERIALS**
MGB	Binary semiconductor materials
MGC	Ternary semiconductor materials
MGF	Intrinsic semiconductor materials
MGG	Extrinsic semiconductor materials
MGJ	Impurity elements
MGK	Acceptors
MGL	Donors
MGN	N type semiconductor materials
MGP	P type semiconductor materials
MGR	Bulk semiconductor materials
MGS	Multivalley semiconductor materials
MGV	Mixed valence semiconductor materials
MGW	Semiinsulators

For individual semiconductor materials combine with the notation from the materials schedules, for example:—

MG2/GLR	Silicon semiconductor materials
MG2/GLS	Germanium semiconductor materials
MG2/HFG/HLP	Gallium arsenide semiconductor materials

MH	**SEMICONDUCTOR DEVICES**
	˙ Semiconductor amplifiers LE/MH
	˙ Semiconductor demodulators LW/MH
	˙ Semiconductor lasers MOF
	˙ Semiconductor masers MNL
	˙ Semiconductor modulators LV/MH

FIGURE 35 Specimen page from faceted classification portion of the *Thesaurofacet*.

Teletypewriters   463   **Television Time Bases**

    Telegraph receivers
    Telegraph transmitters
BT(A) Automatic typewriters
    Typewriters

Television   **NH**
RT   Television and radio manufacturing
      industries
    Television broadcasting
    Television films
    Television recording
    Television telephone calling
      apparatus
    Vehiclar communications

Television Aerials   **NSN**
RT   Television masts
    Television receivers
    Television stations
    Television transmission systems
    Television transmitters
    Towers
BT(A) Television apparatus

Television and Radio Manufacturing
Industries   **ZKFW**
UF   Radio industry
RT   Radio
    Television

Television Apparatus   **NJ**
RT   Television switching
NT(A) Colour television apparatus
    Fluorescent screens
    Radiofrequency transformers
    Telecine equipment
    Television aerials
    Television receivers
    Television recording cameras
    Television telephone calling
      apparatus
    Television transmitters
    Vision mixers

Television Broadcasting   **ZLSJD**
RT   Colour television
    Subscription television
    Television
    Television stations
    Television studios
    Television wire transmission
      systems

Television Cameras   **NJ3**
RT   Television camera tubes
    Television transmitters
NT(A) Colour television cameras
    Television recording cameras
BT(A) Television studio apparatus

Television Camera Tubes   **MCE**
UF   Camera tubes (television)
    Emitrons
    Iconoscopes
    Image iconoscopes
    Image orthicons
    Orthicons
    Pick up tubes (television)
    Vidicons
RT   Phototubes
    Photomultipliers
    Television cameras
BT(A) Television apparatus

Television Centres use
Television Studios

Television Channels   **NHC**
UF   Channels (television)
RT   Television links

Television Circuits   **NJA**
RT   Clamping circuits
    Television interference
    Television receivers
    Television scanning
    Television synchronisation
    Television transmitters
    Video circuits
NT(A) Colour television circuits
    Combining amplifiers

    Equalising pulses
    Horizontal deflection oscillators
    Limiters
    Phase detectors
    Scanning circuits
    Synchronising pulse generators
    Synchronising separators
    Television time bases
    Vertical deflection oscillators
    Videofrequency amplifiers
    Vision mixers

Television Colour Camera Tubes   **MCI**
UF   Colour camera tubes (television)
    Colour cell
    Pick up tubes (colour television)
    Plumbicons
RT   Colour television cameras
BT(A) Colour television apparatus

Television Colour Picture Tubes   **MCO**
UF   Apple tubes
    Banana tubes
    Colour picture tubes (television)
    Chromatrons
    Display tubes (television colour)
    Flat picture tubes
    Gabar tubes
    Kaiser Aiten thin tubes
    Kinescope
    Reflected beam kinescope
    Shadowmask tubes
    Television display tubes (colour)
RT   Colour television receivers

Television Communication Systems use
Television Transmission Systems

Television Display Tubes (colour) use
Television Colour Picture Tubes

Television Distribution Systems use
Television Transmission Systems

Television Fields   **ENS**
RT   Interlaced scanning
    Television scanning

Television Films   **A5U**
UF   Cine films (television)
    Films (television)
RT   Optical television recording
    Photographic film
    Telecine equipment
    Television
    Television studio apparatus
BT(A) Films

Television Guidance   **WIG**

Television Interference   **NI4**
RT   Snow (spurious signals)
    Television circuits
    Television transmission systems
NT(A) Colour television interference
    Crossview
BT(A) Interference (radio wave)

Television Interference Suppression
    NI4/MXS
Synth
S RT   Television interference
    NT(A) Colour television interference
        suppression
S BT(A) Interference suppression

Television Links   **NJN**
UF   Links (television)
    Point to point television links
    Television relay systems
    Vision links
RT   Communication satellites
    Microwave communication systems
    Radio links
    Radio towers
    Television channels
    Television networks

Television Masts   **NJK**
UF   Television towers

    Towers (television)
RT   Radio towers
    Television aerials
    Television transmission systems
    Television transmitters
    Television transmitting aerials
    Towers
BT(A) Masts

Television Modulation   **NH2**
RT   Chrominance modulators
    Colour television transmission
      systems
    Colour television transmitters
    Television transmitters
BT(A) Modulation

Television Networks   **NHA**
RT   Television links
BT(A) Communication networks

Television Picture Tubes   **MCL**
UF   Display tubes (television)
    Kinescope
    Picture tubes (television)
RT   Fluorescent screens
    Phosphors
    Raster
    Television receivers
BT(A) Television apparatus

Television Receiver Control   **NIQ**
RT   Television receivers
    Television synchronisation
    Tuning
NT(A) Colour television receiver control

Television Receivers   **NVU**
RT   Fluorescent screens
    Television aerials
    Television circuits
    Television picture tubes
    Television receiver control
    Television receiving aerials
    Television reception
    Television synchronisation
BT(A) Television apparatus

Television Receiving Aerials   **NSQ**
UF   Receiving aerials (television)
RT   Television receivers
NT(A) Communal television aerials

Television Reception   **NI**
RT   Signal detection
    Signal processing
    Television receivers
NT(A) Colour television reception
BT(A) Reception

Television Reception Quality   **NI2**
NT(A) Colour television reception
      quality
BT(A) Reception quality

Television Recording   **WRH**
UF   Video recording (television)
RT   Recording receivers
    Television
    Video tape recorders

Television Recording Cameras   **WRW**
UF   Recording cameras (television)
    Telecine cameras
RT   Optical television recording
BT(A) Television apparatus
    Television cameras
    Television studio apparatus

Television Rediffusion use
Television Wire Transmission Systems

Television Relay Systems use
Television Links

Television Scanning   **NIB**
RT   Raster
    Television circuits
    Television fields
NT(A) Colour television scanning
    Interlaced scanning
BT(A) Scanning

Television Screens use
Fluorescent Screens

Television Signal Frequency use
Videofrequency

Television Signals   **NHE**
UF   Signals (television)
NT(A) Colour signals

Television Standards Convertors   **NJ7**
UF   Convertors (television standard)
    Image transfer standards convertors
    Standard convertors television
RT   Bandwidth compression
    Low pass filters
    Magnetic recording

Television Standard Signals   **NHJ**
UF   Colour television standard signals
RT   Colour signals
    Standardisation
BT(A) Standards

Television Stations   **NJD**
UF   Stations (television)
RT   Television aerials
    Television broadcasting
    Television transmission systems
    Television transmitters
    Television transmitting aerials

Television Studio Apparatus   **NJH**
UF   Control rooms (television)
    Sound control (television)
    Vision control (television)
RT   Optical television recording
    Television films
NT(A) Luminaires
    Microphones
    Sound mixers
    Telecine equipment
    Television cameras
    Television recording cameras
    Vision mixers

Television Studios   **NJF**
UF   Studios (television)
    Television centres
RT   Radio studios
    Television broadcasting

Television Switching   **NH6**
UF   Switching (television)
    Video switching
RT   Switches
    Television apparatus

Television Synchronisation   **NIE**
UF   Synchronising signals
RT   Hold control
    Horizontal deflection oscillators
    Oscillators
    Sweep generators
    Synchronising separators
    Television circuits
    Television receiver control
    Television receivers
    Television time bases
    Television transmitters
    Vertical deflection oscillators
NT(A) Colour television synchronisation
BT(A) Synchronisation (electric)

Television Systems   **NJM**
NT(A) Television telephone calling
      apparatus
    Television wire transmission
      systems
    Walkie talkies

Television Telephone Calling Apparatus
    N7O
RT   Television wire transmission
      systems
BT(A) Television apparatus
    Television systems

Television Time Bases   **LKJ**
UF   Frame generators
    Line generators

FIGURE 36 Specimen page from the thesaurus portion of the *Thesaurofacet*.

TABLE 8 Types of Relationships Displayed in the Thesaurus Portion of the *Thesaurofacet*

THING	
Thing/part	Boilers
	RT Steam pipes
Thing/property	Lasers
	RT Coherence
Thing/process	Ships
	RT Shipbuilding
Thing/thing as attribute	Arcs
	RT Arc furnaces
Thing/application	Adaptive Filters
	RT Signal processing
PROPERTY	
Property/process	Charge (electric)
	RT Charge measurement
Property/property as attribute	Skew
	RT Skew girders
PROCESS	
Process/thing (agent)	Landing (flight)
	RT Landing gear
Process/property	Detonation
	RT Detonation waves

SOURCE: J. Aitchison et al.[2]

CAMERA TUBES the additional hierarchy, indicated by the abbreviation BT (A), is the hierarchy of "television apparatus."

The thesaurus similarly lists additional narrower terms, indicated by NT (A). As an illustration, consider the term JETS. This appears in the faceted schedules as follows:

CWJ	Jets
CWK	Jet streams
CWL	Plumes
CWM	Wall jets
CWO	Couette flow
CWP	Jet mixing
CWQ	Propulsive jets

This is the primary "jets" hierarchy; the jets listed here are all fluid dynamic jets. But there are other types of jets, as we well know, and these additional hierarchical linkages are shown as NT (A)'s under Jets in the thesaurus:

Jets
  NT (A) Jets (hovercraft)
      Plasma jets

Used in this way, jointly, the classification scheme and the thesaurus reveal the "multiple hierarchical linkage" of terms.

In the *Thesaurofacet*, the thesaurus replaces the alphabetical subject index that would normally accompany the schedules in a conventional faceted classification. Likewise, the faceted classification replaces the usual hierarchical structure built into a thesaurus by means of BT-NT references. In a sense the *Thesaurofacet* achieves the best of all worlds. It benefits from careful facet analysis and thus consistently displays the most important relationships between terms and provides consistent control of synonyms. The faceted schedules facilitate generic search, while the thesaurus portion facilitates immediate access to a specific term and also provides inter-term relationships that cut across the faceted structure. The tool can be used equally well as a terminological authority in a pre-coordinate system (using notational synthesis) or a post-coordinate system.

It should be pointed out that the *Thesaurofacet* is very similar to the *Information Retrieval Thesaurus of Education Terms* in providing both thesaurus and facet displays. However, the facet structure in the former is derived with greater care, and the term relationships are also more carefully displayed. In addition, the *Thesaurofacet* goes further in making the two elements entirely complementary.

During 1971 a *Construction Industry Thesaurus* was in the process of being compiled in England by the Polytechnic of North London and the Brixton School of Building. Publication, by the Department of the Environment, is planned for late 1971. This tool also combines the thesaurus and faceted classification approaches. It seems likely that, in England at least, the thesaurofacet will become the norm for controlled vocabularies used for both indexing and searching purposes.

REFERENCES

1. Aitchison, J. "The *Thesaurofacet*: a Multipurpose Retrieval Language Tool." *Journal of Documentation* 26 (1970): 187-203.
2. Aitchison, J. et al., comps. *Thesaurofacet: a Thesaurus and Faceted Classification for Engineering and Related Subjects.* Whetstone, England: English Electric Co., 1969.

9 Some Thesaurus Rules and Conventions

The compiler of a thesaurus has certain decisions to make regarding such matters as descriptor form and punctuation. A considerable amount of experience in thesaurus construction has already been accumulated and recorded, notably by Wall [12] in 1962, by Project LEX [3] in 1966, COSATI [2] in 1967, and the Educational Resources Information Center (ERIC) of the Office of Education [9] in 1966 and again in 1969. It will be useful to review some of the rules and conventions presented in these and other sources.

WORD FORM

By LEX convention, noun forms are used wherever possible; e.g., ROUGHNESS rather than ROUGH. Adjectives or equivalent expressions may be used where no noun is available to specify the required concept exactly; e.g., the words AIRBORNE, MOBILE, PORTABLE. Verbs are never used as descriptors; ANALYSIS is preferred to ANALYZE, and the gerund POURING to the active verb POUR. The ERIC thesaurus uses some adjectives to take the place of nouns; e.g., DISADVANTAGED and BLIND, which really stand for "disadvantaged people" and "blind people." The draft ANSI standard on thesaurus construction [1] recommends that noun phrases be written to exclude prepositions wherever possible (e.g., CARBOHYDRATE METABOLISM rather than METABOLISM OF CARBOHYDRATES).

NUMBER

Project LEX has adopted the following convention:

1. The plural form is preferred for "count" nouns (i.e., nouns that respond to the question "how many?") such as TUBES, FILTERS, CITIES.
2. The singular form is preferred for "mass" nouns (i.e., responding to the question "how much"?) such as RADIATION and WOOD.
3. The singular is preferred for specific processes, properties, or conditions.

The complete set of LEX guidelines on number is given in Table 9.

Many thesauri follow these conventions, but others have their own rules. The *Exploration and Production Thesaurus* uses the singular form except in those cases in which the meaning of the word is changed by a final "s." For example, CUTTING, a process, is distinguished from CUTTINGS (ROCK).

FORM OF ENTRY

In TEST direct entry is preferred to inverted entry: RADAR ANTENNAS rather than ANTENNAS, RADAR. Most thesauri follow this convention. An exception is *Medical Subject Headings* which uses the principle of

TABLE 9 LEX Guidelines on Number

Type of Term	Use Singular Form	Use Plural Form

Material terms, such as:
  chemical compounds
  mixtures
  materials
	When term is specific, as:
	  urea
	  cellophane
	  beeswax
		When term is generic, as:
		  amines
		  solvents
		  plastics

Terms representing properties,
  conditions, characteristics
	When term is specific, as:
	  viscosity
	  temperature
	  purity
	  opacity
		When term is generic, as:
		  physical properties
		  process conditions

Terms representing equipment,
  devices, physical objects, and
  elementary particles
	Do not use singular	Use plural, as:
		  pulverizers
		  regulators
		  mesons
		  teeth
		  stars

Class of use terms	Do not use singular	Use plural, as:
		  adhesives
		  catalysts

Process terms	Use singular, as:
	  constructing
	  installing
	  modulating
		Do not use plural

Proper names (A proper name is
  defined as the name for a
  single unique item)
	Use singular, as:
	  Hookes Law
	  Pluto
		Do not use plural

Disciplines, fields, subject areas	Use singular according to common
	  usage, as:
	  chemistry
	  hydraulics
	  engineering
		Do not use plural (Words such
		  as "hydraulics" are actually
		  singular)

Events or occurrences	Do not use singular	Use plural, as:
		  ambushes
		  explosions
		  discharges

SOURCE: Department of Defense.[3]

inversion to bring closely related terms into physical proximity:

TUBERCULOSIS, AVIAN

TUBERCULOSIS, BOVINE

TUBERCULOSIS, CARDIOVASCULAR

TUBERCULOSIS, CUTANEOUS

TUBERCULOSIS, ENDOCRINE

This is a useful practice. The typical searcher is much more likely to think of "tuberculosis, variety avian" than he is to approach the index under AVIAN TUBERCULOSIS. Moreover, this type of inversion reveals to the searcher, at a glance, the entire tuberculosis picture and, more importantly, groups all entries relating to tuberculosis of any kind together in the printed *Index Medicus*. In a sense, such inversion is equivalent to the

use of subheadings in conventional alphabetical subject catalogs:

TUBERCULOSIS. AVIAN

TUBERCULOSIS. BOVINE

TUBERCULOSIS. CARDIOVASCULAR

It should be pointed out, however, that MeSH does not display BT-NT relations. If it did, there would be little need for inversion since the terms for types of tuberculosis would be displayed under the generic term TUBERCULOSIS.

Inversion is also used in the *Exploration and Production Thesaurus* where considered appropriate: DRILLING (WELL) rather than WELL DRILLING, REFLECTION (SEISMIC) rather than SEISMIC REFLECTION.

The alphabetical subject catalog incorporates a con-

siderable amount of inversion to bring related classes together as a searching aid. This is less important in a post-coordinate system; although, as in the case of MEDLARS, such systems may generate printed indexes. Moreover, if the thesaurus is used by people who are not information specialists, inversion may still be a useful device to aid the searcher. While consistency is always desirable, and while the straight natural-language approach is certainly appealing, it sometimes does lead to some unusual descriptors. For example, the ERIC thesaurus contains such headings as SIXTEEN MILLIMETER PROJECTORS and OFF FARM AGRICULTURAL OCCUPATIONS. It is difficult to believe that the person not fully familiar with the thesaurus would enter it initially under SIXTEEN or OFF.

DEFINITIONS AND SCOPE NOTES

Homographs and other words whose meanings could be misinterpreted are handled in TEST in the following ways:

1. By the use of modifying terms; e.g., in the descriptor AIR CLEANERS the meaning of the word "cleaners" is quite evident.

2. By using parenthetical qualifiers which become part of the descriptor:

MERCURY (METAL)
MERCURY (PLANET)

3. By varying word endings: "ing" for processes and "ion" for materials and properties, where necessary to distinguish them; e.g., CONCENTRATION and CONCENTRATING, PRECIPITATION and PRECIPITATING.

4. When a parenthetical qualifier will not suffice, a fuller scope note may be added to a descriptor to show how it is to be used. Such a scope note is not part of the descriptor but an explanation of it, as in this entry from the *FAA Thesaurus of Technical Descriptors:* [4]

DAMPING
(The suppression of motion in a vibrating or oscillating system, usually by conversion to heat.)

Wall distinguished between *instructional scope notes* (which tell how a descriptor is to be applied in indexing) and *definitive scope notes* (dictionary-type definitions used with unfamiliar or exotic terms). An example of the former is the instruction under the descriptor DISEASE to "Use also the part of the body affected and the causative organism, if known." Mulvihill [8] has strongly emphasized the value of instructional scope notes in place of definitive ones.

The scope note appended to a descriptor should define the meaning of that descriptor within the context of the indexing system in which it is used rather than attempting a general purpose dictionary definition. It is most useful in preventing ambiguity, in the case of a descriptor whose meaning may not otherwise be clear. For example, in the *Thesaurus of ERIC Descriptors,* the term ACCELERATION is defined as "The process of progressing through the school grades at a rate faster than that of the average child."

Perhaps the most elaborate set of thesaurus scope notes is that included in the *Information Retrieval Thesaurus of Education Terms* (IRTET). This publication includes a clear discussion of the scope note policy. The compilers avoid parenthetical scope notes wherever possible although they recognize the potential value of a scope note that is an integral part of a descriptor and thus defines its scope at a glance. This would be important when the descriptor appears, for example, in a printed index, at the top of a peek-a-boo card, or in the "tracings" that appear as part of the printout in some machine-based systems, including MEDLARS.

In IRTET, as in TEST, homographs are frequently avoided by the use of an appropriate modifier: MENTAL DEPRESSION is not ambiguous but DEPRESSION alone might be. I prefer the construction DEPRESSION (MENTAL) on the grounds that a user, unfamiliar with the thesaurus conventions, is much more likely to look under DEPRESSION. In fact I cannot conceive of him thinking in terms of MENTAL DEPRESSION. Of course, a *use* reference is made from DEPRESSION (MENTAL) but this still puts the user through an additional step. However, in preferring the uninverted straight natural-language construction, the compilers of IRTET are following the conventions of most thesauri in use in the United States.

The following types of scope notes are recognized in this education thesaurus:

1. Positive limitation in the scope of a term:

RETRAINING
Training for a change in occupation.
(Such a note limits the scope of the term and distinguishes it from other related terms such as REHABILITATION.)

2. Negative limitation:

LICENSING
Excluding school accreditation and teacher certification.
(Such a scope note not only excludes but may direct a user to concepts he may have had in mind when approaching the thesaurus under LICENSING. I

prefer a scope note that refers unequivocally to other descriptor forms, as

"Excludes aspects covered by the descriptors SCHOOL ACCREDITATION and TEACHER CERTIFICATION.")

3. True definition:

SPACE ERROR
Tendency to be biased by the spatial position of stimuli in relation to the observer.

4. Combination of definition and positive limitation:

PLAYBACK
Of a visual or sound recording enabling a person to evaluate or react to his own recorded performance.

The *Thesaurus of Engineering Terms* includes some broad terms which are to be used only as a last resort. Such terms (e.g., CONVERTERS) carry the general scope note, "Use more specific term if possible."

SYNONYMS

We have discussed this aspect previously. There are very few true synonyms, other than spelling variations (sulphur and sulfur) and abbreviations (MHD and magnetohydrodynamics). For indexing and searching purposes, terms that are considered sufficiently equivalent to make a distinction unnecessary are treated as synonyms; one is chosen and a *use* reference made from the other.

The compilers of the *Information Retrieval Thesaurus of Education Terms* are careful to point out that terms used synonymously in this tool are synonyms only in this special context (e.g., AIM *use* GOAL) and not "universal" synonyms. In choosing between synonyms the "least ambiguous" version is preferred. They recognize a number of types of "synonymy":

1. *Grammatical form.* INTERVIEW *use* INTERVIEWING (alternative spellings would also be included: MOULD-ING *use* MOLDING).
2. *Trade-name.* IBM CARDS *use* PUNCHED CARDS.
3. *Word order.* INTEGRATION (RACIAL) *use* RACIAL INTEGRATION.

These are in addition to the "true synonyms" and the application of the *use* references, which direct from a specific term that is not a descriptor to the appropriate more generic descriptor. As pointed out by Mandersloot et al.,[7] multiword synonyms are most difficult to handle. For example, "shear stress at a wall" is synonymous with "skin friction."

QUASI-SYNONYMS

In TEST and most other thesauri, quasi-synonyms are treated like synonyms. TEST regards the following as quasi-synonyms:

1. Terms that represent different viewpoints on the same property continuum, such as SMOOTHNESS and ROUGHNESS, RESISTANCE and CONDUCTIVITY. The justification here is that a user interested in one aspect will usually be interested, by implication, in the other. Thus, if a user is seeking information on conductivity he should be equally interested in documents discussing electrical resistance.
2. Terms representing concepts that have considerable semantic overlap, as LIGHTING and ILLUMINATION, DURATION and TIME.

Mandersloot et al.[7] have discussed the treatment of antonyms in some detail. They distinguish those best treated as quasi-synonyms from those best retained as separate terms, as follows:

1. *Reciprocals and complements*

e.g., HARDNESS, SOFTNESS
DRYNESS, WETNESS
ACCURACY, ERROR

Should be treated as quasi-synonyms.

2. *Unequivalent and diametrical opposites*

e.g., ORGANIC, INORGANIC
REST, MOTION

Should be treated as separate terms. The distinction between these terms and those in the former group is that these are mutually exclusive whereas the others are not (they represent degrees on a continuous scale).

3. *Reversals*

e.g., POTENTIAL, COUNTERPOTENTIAL

Should be treated as separate terms.

PUNCTUATION

By LEX conventions, punctuation marks in descriptors are avoided wherever possible or are used very sparingly. Parentheses are used for brief scope indicators, but commas, periods, apostrophes, and most hyphens are avoided since they are difficult to handle consistently and they complicate machine processing of the thesaurus data. Thus, HIGH TEMPERATURE is preferred to HIGH-TEMPERATURE and BIOMEDICAL to BIO-MEDICAL. The use of the comma is obviously unavoidable if we adopt inverted headings as used in *Medical Subject*

Headings (MeSH). MeSH also uses apostrophes in descriptors relating to syndromes derived from proper names (e.g., VON WILLEBRAND'S DISEASE).

ABBREVIATIONS

Abbreviations are generally avoided wherever possible in most thesauri. The compilers of TEST avoid them because:

1. They may not be universally recognized,
2. Their meaning may be dependent on context, or
3. Their recognition may depend on capitalization and punctuation, which are constraints on computer processing.

Where abbreviations are well accepted, however, they are allowed in TEST; for example, ACTH for adrenocorticotropic hormone and VTOL AIRCRAFT for vertical takeoff and landing aircraft. Well-established acronyms (e.g., LASER, RADAR) are accepted in most thesauri. An exception to the general thesaurus pattern is MeSH, which does not use abbreviations even where these are commonly accepted in the literature (e.g., it prefers CORTICOTROPIN to ACTH and LYSERGIC ACID DIETHYLAMIDE to LSD).

In contrast, the *NASA Thesaurus* makes extensive use of abbreviations well-accepted in the aerospace sciences, as ORBITING SOLAR OBSERVATORY use OSO.

PRE-COORDINATION

One of the most difficult problems facing the thesaurus compiler is to decide how much pre-coordination to include. Some thesauri, such as the *Isotopes Information Center Keyword Thesaurus*,[6] rely rather heavily on Uniterms while others are heavily pre-coordinate.

The LEX guidelines tackle this important problem as follows:

Specific multiword descriptors often facilitate retrieval of specific information, but may add to the cost of indexing by increasing substantially the number of descriptors in the index. On the other hand, proper use of individual descriptors in indexing for later combination upon retrieval will serve to control the size of the vocabulary and to promote consistency in the use of terminology. Decisions on the formation of specific descriptors require consideration of the following factors. If reasonable doubt remains, a specific multiword descriptor should be established because, if it eventually proves to be of little utility, it can easily be reduced to a combination of individual descriptors. The converse is not easily accomplished.

a. A specific multiword descriptor should be established when suitable more general descriptors are not available in the vocabulary. To provide adequate representation of the specific concept, a combination of general descriptors must include at least one descriptor that is a member of the same hierarchical class as the specific concept. Observation of this principle will promote more consistent and complete retrieval, whereas the use of a combination in which neither descriptor bears a generic relationship to the specific concept may lessen retrieval efficiency.

b. A specific, multiword descriptor should be established when the specific concept is encountered so frequently that the ability to index and search directly would be both expeditious and economical or when one or both of the more general descriptors is so often used in indexing as to make searches awkward or inaccurate.

c. Two or more individual descriptors should be used instead of establishing a specific multiword descriptor when the specific concept is a member of the same generic class as each of the more general descriptors; for example, ARC OXYGEN CUTTING is a member of the classes ARC CUTTING and OXYGEN CUTTING, so may be represented by those descriptors. When individual descriptors are employed in preference to a specific descriptor, the appropriate cross-reference should be added to the Thesaurus.

The following philosophy is that adopted in the *Thesaurus of ERIC Descriptors:*

In most coordinate indexing schemes, the basic objective is to break down the language or terminology into its simplest components while still retaining definition. In many information systems, this is reflected in a thesaurus comprised mostly of single-word terms. In this Thesaurus, however, there is an abundance of compound (multiword) terms. This can be explained in terms of the educational process itself. Basically, this process involves students, teachers, and an educational environment; and the events occurring during this process can often be equally applicable to either the students, the teachers, or the environment. In a coordinate indexing system, it is almost impossible to distinguish the source of an action and the recipient of an action without defining each of them in the terminology of the system. Thus, if there is a document dealing with "the effect of the teacher on the attitudes of students," according to an ideal coordinate indexing scheme it should be possible to index such a document by coordinating the concepts of "attitudes," "teachers," and "students." However, in searching the system, how is one to know whether he is retrieving documents that deal with "student attitudes" or "teacher attitudes"? These two concepts can be distinguished by indexing the documents by the concepts "student attitudes" and "teachers." This involves the addition of the term "student" to the term "attitudes" in order to avoid confusion. In an environment as complex and highly specific as the educational process, this type of compounding (binding) of terms is unavoidable.

This is a particularly vexing problem in a subject field described in large part by compound terminology. Multiword concepts offer a greater possibility of disagreement and inconsistency than do single-word concepts simply because of the combinations possible in multiword concepts. An example of this situation arose in the use of "student" and "pupil" in multiword terms. In this Thesaurus, the concept "student" was adopted to represent the person receiving education. The concept "pupil" by itself or in compound terms was identified as synonymous with the concept "student." Therefore, when the term "pupil dis-

tribution" occurred in indexing, it became synonymous with "student distribution," for the purpose of maintaining consistency with the basic decision to select "student" as the preferred descriptor form.

Beyond the considerations of the logic of such a system there is the question of how people think and express themselves in the language of the subject field. In developing this Thesaurus, every attention was given to using natural language that would be meaningful and recognizable to thesaurus users. Much of the language of education consists of compound terminology, which has been preserved here for clarity and utility.

Goodman,[5] however, warns against the extensive proliferation of multiword terms:

The extensive proliferation of terms which can occur if multiword terms are made the basic indexing units does seem to mean that documents can be described in more "precise" terms than if only more general, single word, descriptors were used. The cost of this kind of "precision" can be seen in two ways, however. Documents which could have been described by one descriptor may now be described by either or both of two descriptors, or perhaps by even more. For example, it might be dangerous to have the following four descriptors: Group Tests, Group Intelligence Tests, Group Testing, and Group Intelligence Testing. A searcher might search on one or two of these terms and assume that he had found all the relevant documents. With such a proliferation of multiword terms, the cost can be viewed in terms of relevant documents not found. On the other hand, the cost may be seen in terms of the energy required to perform the more elaborate search made necessary by a level of "precision" necessary so as not to miss relevant documents.

In creating the *Thesaurofacet* a distinction was made between a "concept" (which may be represented by a single descriptor) and a "theme" (which will involve more than one concept and should not be represented by single descriptors). A theme, according to the compilers, is "a group of concepts in relationship which together comprise the subject matter or part of the subject matter of a document." A rough distinction is that a concept will indicate a *type* of thing, process, or property, while a theme will represent interrelationships between things, parts, processes, and properties. Some examples are as follows:

Concepts
One term	Oceans
Two terms	Central heating (process/type)
Three terms	Impulse water turbines (thing/type)
Four terms	Air cell combustion chambers (thing/type)
Six terms	Two rotor rotary piston diesel engines (thing/type)

Themes
Impulse water turbines/blades (thing/part)
Diesel engines/big ends/clearance measurement (thing/part/process)

Sometimes data processing considerations place an artificial limit on the length of a descriptor. NASA, for example, restricts descriptor length to 42 characters, including spaces. A maximum of 36 characters is recommended in the LEX conventions.

In 1970 UNESCO issued a set of guidelines for the construction of monolingual thesauri [10] and a draft of similar guidelines for multilingual thesauri.[11] The UNESCO rules and conventions are very similar to the LEX/COSATI rules except that the alphabetical display of terms is not considered by UNESCO to be the major thesaurus display. Classified (systematic) or graphic display appears to be preferred. UNESCO also encouraged the development of two clearinghouses dealing with thesauri; one at the School of Library Science, Case Western Reserve University, for English languages, and the other at the Centralny Instytut Informacji Naukowo-Technicznej i Ekonomicznej, Warsaw, for languages other than English.

In 1969 a new subcommittee of Sectional Committee Z39 of the American National Standards Institute was established to develop a draft standard for thesaurus construction. A draft of a standard was issued in 1971. This draft, which closely follows the LEX/COSATI guidelines, should eventually become a U.S. national standard on the subject.

In concluding this chapter it is worth noting that, while some of the conventions discussed (e.g., the degree of pre-coordination) will have a significant impact on the performance of a retrieval system, other conventions (e.g., direct versus inverted entry) will have virtually no effect on system performance. Clearly, for indexing and searching purposes, it makes not the slightest difference whether a descriptor takes the form TUBERCULOSIS, PULMONARY or PULMONARY TUBERCULOSIS as long as we use one consistently, refer from the other, and have a clear statement of the scope of the heading. Many of the thesaurus conventions relate to convenience factors. We try to choose the heading that the majority of users will be likely to think of, and we refer from variants of this. How important some of these convenience factors are will depend on who is to use the thesaurus. If it is to be used primarily by information specialists, it is less important to base descriptor format on preferred usage in the field. The information specialist can learn that the subject of tuberculosis, for example, is spread throughout the thesaurus under such descriptors as AVIAN TUBERCULOSIS, BOVINE TUBERCULOSIS and PULMONARY TUBERCULOSIS. If the tool is to be used by working scientists, however, more consideration must be given to the form of descriptor that would best suit this audience. Under these conditions it might be preferable to group all the "tuberculosis"

descriptors under inverted forms to bring them all together.

In computer-based systems using batch processing, where a human intermediary is always interposed between user and system, form of descriptor is not particularly important. In on-line systems and printed indexes, where practitioners in a field are likely to conduct their own searches, it is much more important that descriptors correspond with the language and viewpoint of the practitioner himself.

REFERENCES

1. American National Standards Institute. *Guidelines for Thesaurus Structure, Construction and Use.* ANSI Z39. Draft, September 1971.
2. Committee on Scientific and Technical Information (COSATI). *Guidelines for the Development of Information Retrieval Thesauri.* Washington, D.C., 1967.
3. Department of Defense. *Manual for Building a Technical Thesaurus.* Washington, D.C., 1966. AD 633 279. (Revised and published as Appendix 1 of the *Thesaurus of Engineering and Scientific Terms,* 1967).
4. Federal Aviation Administration. *FAA Thesaurus of Technical Descriptors.* 3rd ed. Washington, D.C., 1969. AD 686 837.
5. Goodman, F. "The Role and Function of the Thesaurus in Education." In *Thesaurus of ERIC Descriptors.* 2d ed. New York: CCM Information Corporation, 1970, 1-28.
6. Isotopes Information Center. *Isotopes Information Center Keyword Thesaurus.* Oak Ridge, Tenn.: Oak Ridge National Laboratory, July 1969. ORNL-IIc-24.
7. Mandersloot, W. G. B. et al. "Thesaurus Control—the Selection, Grouping, and Cross-Referencing of Terms for Inclusion in a Coordinate Index Word List." *Journal of the American Society for Information Science* 21 (1970): 49-57.
8. Mulvihill, J. G. *Supplementing Thesaural Relationships with Usage Notes.* New York: American Petroleum Institute, 1968.
9. Office of Education. *Rules for Thesaurus Preparation.* Washington, D.C.: Educational Resources Information Center, 1969.
10. UNESCO. *Guidelines for the Establishment and Development of Monolingual Scientific and Technical Thesauri for Information Retrieval.* Paris, 1970.
11. UNESCO. *Guidelines for the Establishment and Development of Multilingual Scientific and Technical Thesauri for Information Retrieval.* Second Draft. Paris, 1970.
12. Wall, E. *Information Retrieval Thesauri.* New York: Engineers Joint Council, 1962.

10 *The Reference Structure of the Thesaurus*

In earlier chapters we have mentioned the thesaurus reference structure, involving *use*, NT, BT, and RT indicators. It will be worthwhile devoting a little more time to a consideration of this reference structure, which is very similar to the syndetic structure of the alphabetical subject catalog, as described by Cutter.

THE USE *REFERENCE*

As mentioned earlier, the *use* reference directs from a term that cannot be used in indexing and searching to a term that can be used. The *use* reference directs from synonyms, abbreviations, near-synonyms, quasi-synonyms, alternative spellings, and alternative word sequences. In all of these cases the two terms involved (referred from and referred to) are essentially equivalent.

The *use* reference is also employed to direct from specific terms not used in indexing or searching to appropriate more generic terms, as PLANT WAXES *use* WAXES. In this application, the two terms are not in any sense equivalent. However, it has been decided that the term PLANT WAXES is unnecessarily specific and that the more generic term WAXES will suffice for retrieval purposes.

Although *use* is the usual thesaurus convention for these situations, some vocabularies prefer *see* to serve the same function. *See* is used in *The New York Times Thesaurus of Descriptors;* [7] e.g.:

BEDS *see* FURNITURE

Medical Subject Headings (MeSH) also uses *see* to handle synonyms and near-synonyms (HYPOXEMIA *see* ANOXEMIA), but it uses the form *see under* in the case of the specific term referred to a generic term (HYPOXIA *see under* ANOXIA). MeSH is one of the few authority lists that distinguishes the synonymous expression from the specific expression in this respect.

In many thesauri the *use* reference is also employed to effect one-to-many mapping. To index "ferromagnetic films" in TEST we must use both the descriptor FERROMAGNETIC MATERIALS and the descriptor FILMS. This policy is prescribed in the vocabulary by the form:

FERROMAGNETIC FILMS
   use   FERROMAGNETIC MATERIALS
   and   FILMS

In the Bureau of Ships thesaurus this format is merely:

DIRECTION FINDING ANTENNAS
   use
     ANTENNAS
     DIRECTION FINDING

While in the *Exploration and Production Thesaurus* the format is:

PIPELINE VIBRATION
   use   PIPELINE
   plus   VIBRATION

In the reciprocals some convention is usually adopted to signify that the descriptor referred to is only one of two (or more) descriptors used to represent the term referred from. In TEST the convention is to use a dagger (†) as in the example,

AIR
UF   † air bubbles
      † air drilling

which signifies that AIR is only one of the descriptors referred to from the terms AIR BUBBLES and AIR DRILLING.

In the *EURATOM Thesaurus* (Second Edition, 1966) a unique distinction is made between the *use* reference and the *see* reference. Also, two types of *use* reference exist. In the example,

JASON *use* RESEARCH REACTORS

we *may* index under the specific reactor name if we wish. If we do, however, we *must* also use the generic descriptor referred to. On the other hand, in the example,

—ION CHAMBERS *use* IONIZATION CHAMBERS

the dash indicates a forbidden term. We may *not* use this; we *must* use the descriptor referred to.

The *see* reference, at EURATOM, indicates optional assignment (whereas the *use* indicates compulsory assignment). It is used particularly with words that have many possible contexts, e.g.,

LAMPS *see* INFRARED RADIATION
       or   LIGHT
       or   ULTRAVIOLET RADIATION

This means that we should probably index a document on ultraviolet lamps under both LAMPS and ULTRAVIOLET RADIATION.

The makers of the *Urban Thesaurus* do not believe in the use of preferred synonyms. Any synonym may be used; all are linked together by an OR indicator, as

RECTANGULAR PLAN
   OR   GRIDIRON PLAN
   OR   GRID PATTERN
   OR   GRID PLAN
   RT   PLANNING
         STREET SYSTEMS

They justify this decision on the grounds that "it would be presumptuous to suggest preferred terms where a number of disciplines and professions are using the same thesaurus, each having its own set of preferred terms for nearly identical concepts." Unfortunately the thesaurus is confusing in that each synonymous term is not given the same set of relationships with other terms in the vocabulary. RECTANGULAR PLAN shows STREET SYSTEMS as an RT while one synonym, GRIDIRON PLAN, shows STREET SYSTEMS as a BT and a second synonym, GRID PLAN, has URBAN FORM as an RT. No relationship is shown between URBAN FORM and either RECTANGULAR PLAN or GRIDIRON PLAN. Such inconsistencies are confusing and difficult to explain.

BT-NT RELATIONS

The BT-NT relations are reciprocals of one another. If *ab* is a term narrower than *a*, then *a* is a term broader than *ab*. The BT-NT relationship should generally be restricted to the formal genus-species relation, but in some thesauri the relation is extended beyond this to certain part-whole relations (e.g., CHICAGO regarded as a term narrower than ILLINOIS).

Although the BT-NT relation appears to be simple and straightforward, it is not completely so. The major difficulty is that any term may quite legitimately belong to several hierarchies and we must decide how many of these we wish to display explicitly. Bernier and Heumann [2] have discussed this problem of multiple hierarchical linkage, using as an illustration "aniline" which may be regarded as an amine, a benzene derivative, a six-carbon compound, a seven-hydrogen compound, a one-nitrogen compound, a dye intermediate, an oily substance, a toxic substance, a combustible, or a base, among other possible relationships.

Some authorities, including the *Thesaurofacet*, display more than one hierarchical affiliation for a term. The term AVALANCHE DIODES is an NT to both DIODES and SEMICONDUCTOR DEVICES in TEST, for example. In most cases, however, a term is placed in a single hierarchy. The problem is to decide which of several possible hierarchies to use. In a thesaurus covering a very wide area, it is best to restrict the formal hierarchies to those formed on the basis of inherent, invariable characteristics. This is the policy generally followed in TEST. For example, "platinum" could be categorized as a metal or as a catalyst, among other things. However, platinum is always a metal and thus belongs invariably in the "metals" hierarchy. It is *not* always a catalyst; catalysis is merely a possible application or function of platinum. In a general thesaurus, platinum should probably not be listed in the "catalyst" hierarchy but should be in the "metals" hierarchy.

This distinction is also made in the *Information Retrieval Thesaurus of Education Terms* where, as an illustration, the descriptor FOREIGN LANGUAGES is *not*

shown as a BT for such descriptors as FRENCH or GERMAN on the grounds that French or German are not always foreign languages (not in France or Germany anyway).

This principle of "inherent property" or "invariable hierarchy" will not always be applicable. Choice of appropriate hierarchical structure should depend upon the viewpoint and convenience of the particular user population to be served. In a specialized thesaurus devoted exclusively to welding technology, ARGON might quite properly be placed in the hierarchy SHIELDING GASES on the grounds that the term has only one significant context in the field. Likewise, in another thesaurus, WOOD and BARK might well appear only as narrower terms under FUELS.

Although it is founded on facet analysis, the *Information Retrieval Thesaurus of Education Terms* deliberately adopts certain "hierarchies of convenience" that do not reflect true genus-species relations. In fact, some of these hierarchies include terms having varying relationships with the parent term. Consider the following list, all narrower terms under MENTAL HANDICAP:

AGRAPHIA
ALEXIA
ATHETOSIS
BRAIN INJURY
CEREBRAL PALSY
DYSGRAPHIA
DYSLEXIA
MENTAL RETARDATION
MONGOLISM
SPASTICITY

Clearly, not all of these terms represent kinds of mental handicap. In fact, the relationship between BRAIN INJURY and MENTAL HANDICAP is that of cause and effect. This type of hierarchy is justified on the grounds that, in the education context, a user interested in "mental handicap" would be likely to be interested in documents indexed by any of the NT's listed. Such "hierarchies of convenience" are legitimate if used carefully and deliberately but should not be overdone.

As a rule of thumb we might ask the question "If we do a generic search on A are we likely to be happy with items indexed under any of the terms subordinate to A in the hierarchy?" If the answer is "no" for any particular term it is best omitted from this hierarchy.

Another thesaurus that departs fairly radically from strict genus-species hierarchies is the *Bureau of Ships Thesaurus of Descriptive Terms and Code Book,* which includes such hierarchies as

LAUNCHING
  NT CATAPULTS
      GUIDED MISSILE LAUNCHERS
      ROCKET LAUNCHERS
      TORPEDO LAUNCHERS
      UNDERWATER LAUNCHING

Only the last term is a true species of the genus "launching"; the others represent means of accomplishing the launching operation.

Mandersloot et al.[5] recognize the following distinctions in relation to the NT-BT relationship:

1. *"is always."* A *mouse* is always a *rodent* but only occasionally a *pet*. *Rodent* is therefore a broader term than *mouse,* but *pet* is simply an additional term, which indicates a specific function: *mouse* in the role of a *pet*.

2. *"consists of."* This applies when the concept described by a narrower term consists of parts which are described by a broader term. "Consists of" is then synonymous to *"being a specific form or state of." Dust, grit, powder,* and *slurry* all consist of *particles* (broader term) and as discussions on dust, etc., almost invariably deal with the particles, posting on this broader term is compulsory.

3. *"is part of."* In the case of the part-whole relation the "whole" is *not* automatically a broader term than the "part." A *province* is part of a *state,* but it *is not* a state. Legislation on air pollution control in (by) a specific province does *not* apply to the rest of the state, but it does apply somewhere *in* that state. One can envisage the retrieval questions "air pollution control legislation (anywhere) in the U.S.A." and "air pollution control legislation of the U.S.A. (as a whole)." There is obviously a need to distinguish between (a) the whole-and-the-component parts and (b) the whole-as-a-unit. One posting method which solves the problem is to have one term (code) for each, with compulsory posting on (a) whenever there is posting on (b). Alternatively, a separate indexing term "the whole-as-a-unit" can be introduced. The latter approach may give rise to "noise," but it creates only one additional term, which may be used for all such cases.

The question of *automatic generic posting* or *autoposting* is relevant to a discussion on the BT-NT relationship. Autoposting is common in many systems and is advocated in the Bureau of Ships thesaurus and also in the *Information Retrieval Thesaurus of Education Terms.* Autoposting involves the automatic posting-up of a document reference (number) from a narrower term to a broader term. Consider, in the Bureau of Ships system, the descriptor CANTILEVER BEAMS. This is an NT under BEAMS (STRUCTURAL). Whenever the term CANTILEVER BEAMS is assigned to a document by an indexer, the BT BEAMS (STRUCTURAL) is also assigned automatically. In some systems, including that of EURATOM, such generic posting goes up to the ultimate level in the hierarchy: abcd is posted up to abc, to ab, and eventually to a.

The technique of autoposting is built in to facilitate the conduct of generic searches. If a searcher is in-

terested in documents on structural beams, he might be interested not only in documents indexed under the descriptor BEAMS (STRUCTURAL) but also in documents indexed under terms for specific structural beams (BOX BEAMS, CANTILEVER BEAMS, WEB BEAMS). *The principle is valid and useful as long as the term hierarchies are well constructed and do not contain odd anomalies.* A possible disadvantage is that autoposting does not allow the retrieval system to distinguish between general documents and specific documents. It is conceivable that some searcher might be interested in any documents indexed under the general descriptor LAUNCHING but would *not* be interested in items bearing the specific descriptors noted above as NT's under LAUNCHING. If autoposting is used, we lose the distinction between (a) descriptor assigned by indexer and (b) descriptor posted as a result of more specific descriptor assigned by indexer.* In most cases this may not be important, but in some cases it may be.

This type of autoposting is obsolete in computer-based systems. Autoposting was developed for use in nonmechanized systems such as peek-a-boo. In such a system it is extremely tedious to conduct a generic search without the device. In the case of "mental handicap," in the foregoing example, a generic search would involve the examination of no less than twelve cards, and probably the coordination of each of these with one or more other cards. Autoposting to MENTAL HANDICAP avoids this tedious manipulation as a means of effecting a generic search. In a mechanized system, however, we can build the BT-NT relations into a machine thesaurus which will allow the search programs to bring in the NT's automatically when appropriate. Thus, we can search the descriptor MENTAL HANDICAP alone or we can specify "MENTAL HANDICAP (generic search)" which would bring in the additional descriptors shown as subordinate to MENTAL HANDICAP in the thesaurus. This kind of system has greater flexibility.

THE RT REFERENCE

The RT relationship is rather more vague than the BT-NT relationship. Wall calls this type of relationship an "unspecifiable relationship," although "unspecified" might be more appropriate. The RT reference

is used to link a term to other terms semantically related to it but not in a synonymous or hierarchical relationship. In a sense, every thesaurus term is related to every other thesaurus term at varying strengths of semantic association. (We can test this by a thesaurus game in which we take term A and term Q and find the minimum path between the two, the length of the path being defined by the number of linking descriptors needed to relate A to Q). The problem is to decide which terms are sufficiently closely related to warrant RT connections. The makers of TEST recognize four types of RT references; they link descriptors that:

1. Are closely related in meaning or concept, including those in different hierarchical structures.
2. Are near synonyms.
3. Have viewpoint interrelationships based on usage; for example, an RT for DEVIANT BEHAVIOR would be DELINQUENCY.
4. Represent concepts bearing a part-whole relationship with each other.

A more complete list of nonhierarchical relationships, taken from the *Thesaurofacet,* was given in Table 8 of Chapter 8.

In the *Information Retrieval Thesaurus of Education Terms* (IRTET) considerable effort has been expended in defining the possible relations that would justify the RT connection between terms. In this thesaurus three broad types of RT relationship are recognized: (1) whole-part, (2) near-synonym, (3) "other terms closely related conceptually." The first of these we have already discussed and it is relatively straightforward. The near-synonym relationship is rather more difficult to pin down. Two terms that are nearly synonymous are frequently treated as synonyms, and a *use* reference is employed to direct from one to another. But the two terms may represent shades of meaning that may be important for retrieval in a particular subject field. If this is so we may want to maintain their separate identities and link them by the RT reference. Examples, from IRTET, are CLARITY and PERCEPTIBILITY, EXPERIENCE and LENGTH OF SERVICE. Near-antonyms may be treated in a similar fashion.

The "other conceptual relationship" is even more vague. In the education thesaurus the following are among those specifically recognized:

(a) Between device or medium for carrying out a process and the processes

      PROGRAMMED INSTRUCTION
      RT TEACHING MACHINE

(b) Between a quality and that which the quality characterizes

---

* Although, in a computer-based system, the descriptors assigned by autoposting can obviously be tagged in some way.

GIFTED CHILDREN
    RT HIGH INTELLIGENCE
VISION
    RT VISUAL HANDICAP
INTERPERSONAL RELATIONS
    RT FRIENDLINESS

(c) Between a specific measure or measuring device and that which is normally measured

    VISION
        RT THRESHOLD

(d) Between process and product

    PAINTING
        RT PAINTINGS

(There will be further mention of this particular example under [p].)

(e) Between a product and a device for producing the product

    PHOTOGRAPHS
        RT STILL CAMERA

(f) Between a thing, process, or state and a place frequently connected with its presence, occurrence, or manipulation

    MID CHILDHOOD
        RT ELEMENTARY SCHOOL
    FOREIGN LANGUAGES
        RT LANGUAGE LABORATORY

(This latter example is also close to example [a].)

(g) Between a process and a possible quality of the unnamed object of the process

    ORDERABILITY
        RT ORGANIZING

(h) Between (SN *) terms and alternative more specific terms

    POSITION
        SN *
        RT ANGLE
            OCCUPATION
            RANK
            SEQUENCE
            STANCE

(i) Between a scope-noted term and other possible meanings of that term in natural language which have been excluded by the scope note

    MOBILITY
        SN   CAPACITY FOR PHYSICAL
                MOVEMENT OR CONTRACTION
        RT   GEOGRAPHICAL MOBILITY
                SOCIAL MOBILITY

(j) Between a multimeaning term which has been limited

* The asterisked SN (scope-noted) term is a very broad one that should never be used if a more specific term can be found in the vocabulary.

in meaning by being made a BT or NT in a particular hierarchy and the other possible meanings of that term

    RECOGNITION
        BT REMEMBERING
        RT AWARDS
            PRAISE

(k) Between two persons considered from a special point of view who interact in the resultant special status

    FOREIGN STUDENT
        RT FOREIGN STUDENT ADVISOR

(l) Between two processes which may occur in a sequence

    PHYSICAL EXAMINATION
        RT DIAGNOSIS

(m) Between a situation or condition and what may occur in that situation or condition

    LEISURE TIME
        RT LEISURE READING

(n) Between possible cause and effect

    JUVENILE DELINQUENCY
        RT HOSTILITY

(o) Between apparent opposites which, however, can also be construed as interacting factors

    FRUSTRATION
        RT ACHIEVEMENT

With regard to these latter two examples (n and o) it is not clear that a cause-and-effect relationship is a desirable type of RT. It is possible that such a relationship would simply add a multitude of RT's that are not useful. On the other hand, they could conceivably function as helpful indicators of types of combinations of terms indexed in the file or at least generally dealt with in the field.

(p) Between person and process habitually associated with that person

    COUNSELOR
        RT COUNSELING

Although these RT relationships have possibly been worked out more carefully in IRTET than in any other thesaurus, except for the *Thesaurofacet,* the complementary faceted listing reduces the need for RT's in the alphabetical section of this thesaurus. Many lengthy lists of RT's are avoided by making a blanket reference to a particular subfacet in the faceted display (Figure 29).

In some thesauri RT's are automatically reciprocated; that is, if A is shown to be related to B, then B is also shown to be related to A. This is the case in the *Thesaurus of ERIC Descriptors.* In other thesauri, including IRTET, some RT's are reciprocal and some are not.

The retrieval system of the American Petroleum Institute is unusual in that it autoposts certain RT's as well as BT's. For example, the BT for ROAD ASPHALT is PAVING MATERIAL, while the RT is ASPHALT. Both are autoposted when ROAD ASPHALT is assigned. This policy

reflects the recognition of multiple hierarchical linkage. In the foregoing example, ROAD ASPHALT is legitimately a species of both PAVING MATERIAL and ASPHALT. Another example is the pair ISOFORMING and ISOMERIZATION, which are linked by an RT reference. When either one is assigned the other is automatically posted. Thus a chemical process is related to the principal chemical reactions or physical changes involved. In the API system the RT reference is restricted to this "autoposting" relationship. Most related terms are merely linked by a *see also* reference. It is worth mentioning that the equivalent of the RT in *Medical Subject Headings* is the reference *see also related*.

The introduction to the *Thesaurus of ERIC Descriptors* recognizes two major functions of the RT reference:

A term listed as RT clarifies scope, that is, provides further definition of a main descriptor entry. It does this mainly by better describing the context in which the main descriptor entry should be interpreted. The second function of an RT entry is to alert the user to terms other than the main descriptor in which he may be interested, either as an indexer or a searcher. RT entries provide the collateral word relationships in a thesaurus that would not ordinarily be apparent if the user were to think only in terms of the hierarchical scheme.

If the RT reference structure in a thesaurus is developed systematically and conscientiously, the resulting tool is likely to become bulky (perhaps unwieldly and difficult to use) and expensive in terms of printing costs. Possible economies in the RT structure, which would not significantly reduce the effectiveness of the tool, would be welcome. One possible economy, not practiced in all vocabularies, is to eliminate RT references between terms that appear in very close alphabetical proximity. For example, there appears to be little need to show CORROSION, CORROSIVE GASES, and CORROSIVE LIQUIDS as RT's if the three terms appear adjacent to one another in the thesaurus.*

This matter has been investigated by Papier and Lin.[9] They point out that related term references are designed to refer the user to terms he might not think of without the thesaurus guidance, and they hypothesize that a searcher is most likely to think of related terms having the same initial letter as the search term he begins with. Thus, if a user begins with CORROSION he is more likely to think of CORROSIVE GASES than he is to think of, say, DEGRADATION or OXIDATION. If thesauri refer users primarily to other terms they would think of themselves, or terms in close alphabetical proximity, they are not serving their true function.

The investigators studied the tendency of four thesauri (ERIC, ASTIA, *Medical Subject Headings*, and the *Medical and Health Related Sciences Thesaurus* [6]) to use related term references from descriptors to other descriptors of the same initial letter. The analysis was based on ten letters of the alphabet: A, E, I, J, K, L, M, S, W, Z. First the *expected* frequency of RT references to descriptors of the same initial letter was calculated, based upon the total number of descriptors in each thesaurus that begin with each of the letters studied. For example, if in one thesaurus there are two descriptors beginning with K, while as many as 400 begin with A, the expected frequency of related term references between K and A is much greater than the expected frequency between K and K, all other things being equal. The difference between expected frequency of related term references and actual frequency, when applied to references between descriptors of the same initial letter, is a measure of the tendency of a thesaurus to include a disproportionate number of RT's between descriptors of the same initial letter.

In the thesauri studied, related term references from descriptors to others having the same initial letter were more than four times the expected frequency. The authors postulate that this phenomenon is likely to be particularly prevalent in thesauri constructed by the committee approach because subject experts, like thesaurus users, are more likely to think of associated terms beginning with the same initial letter as the starting term.

An earlier but related investigation, reported by Papier and Cortelyou,[8] attempted to arrive at systematic guidelines to determine what types of relationships are prime candidates for inclusion in a thesaurus as interterm connections. The thesaurus in question was one being developed for the U.S. Naval Propellant Plant, in which five major categories of terms were present: fields, objects, processes, properties, and substances. The study was conducted by presenting short lists of representative terms to library users and asking them to supply the first technical term suggested by each term on this association list. The types of association made were then categorized by term type, as in the following examples:

Starting Terms	Types of Terms Associated				
	Field	Object	Process	Property	Substance
ELASTICITY (property)	0	2	2	7	2
NITRATION (process)	1	0	5	0	7
NOZZLE (object)	0	7	3	1	0

---

* In a large printed index, however, there may be several pages separating CORROSION from CORROSIVE GASES and a reference may be desirable in this case.

ELASTICITY, a property term, was associated with other property terms by seven users; but NITRATION, a process term, was strongly associated with substance terms and not at all with property terms. The purpose of this type of study, conducted in only a very small way by Papier and Cortelyou, is to determine what types of association the user is most likely to make for himself, thus allowing the thesaurus to concentrate on other types of associations.

Mandersloot et al.[5] have produced a frequency distribution of cross-references from the EJC thesaurus, based on a random sample, and have compared this distribution with that in their own word list (Chemical Engineering Group, Council for Scientific and Industrial Research, South Africa). These distributions, illustrated in Figure 37, are very similar except that the CEG-CSIR list contains rather more terms with no cross-references. This is explained by the fact that the CEG-CSIR list tends to include proportionally more single-word terms than the EJC list. Single-word terms tend to be less heavily cross-referenced than multi-word terms.

Kochen and Tagliacozzo[4] have studied the question of how one can determine the optimal cross-reference structure for a given index and for a given community of users. For samples drawn from the Library of Congress (L of C) *Subject Headings* (7th edition), *Medical Subject Headings* (1967), and the *Thesaurus of ASTIA Descriptors* (2nd edition), they estimated:

1. *Connectedness Ratio* (the ratio of cross-referenced terms to total number of terms).
2. *Accessibility Measure* (the average number of index terms referring to one index term).

These two measures are suggested to define the "level of cross-referencing" of an index. The results from the sample were as follows (a later accessibility figure for TEST was also added):

	Connectedness	Accessibility
MeSH	.573	.381
L of C	.799	1.032
ASTIA	.956	1.492
TEST	—	2.923

These findings tend to indicate that there is a strong tendency toward increasing the cross-referencing (*see, see also*) in the more recently developed vocabularies. Figure 38 shows, for the three vocabularies studied, the frequency distribution of the number of index

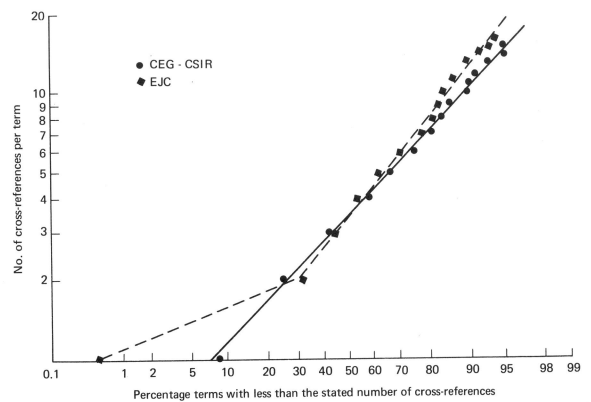

FIGURE 37 Comparison of frequency distribution of cross-references from the EJC *Thesaurus* with distribution from the CEG-CSIR word list.

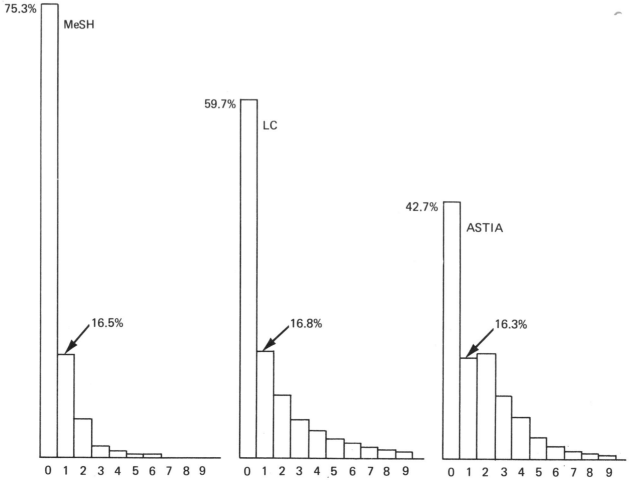

FIGURE 38   Frequency distribution of number of index terms referring to particular index term (ACCESSIBILITY), for three vocabularies.

terms referring to a particular index term (ACCESSI-BILITY). All three are quite similar in the percentage of index terms that are the target of a single cross-reference, but MeSH includes many more terms that are not targets of any references and many fewer terms that are the targets of multiple references.

Kochen and Tagliacozzo also discuss the problems of choosing the "preferred term" between two synonyms or nearly synonymous expressions. They suggest that the most reasonable factor governing preference is the relative frequency of use in the literature of the field. Taking a group of 80 single-word *see* references from *Psychological Abstracts,* they examined the frequency of occurrence of referring term and target term in the titles of papers indexed under the target term. They found that in 71 of the 80 cases (88.8 percent) the preferred term occurred in titles more frequently than the referring term. Assuming that the titles of papers are representative of the language habits of readers, this indicates that in *Psychological Abstracts* the reader is usually led from less-

used to more-used terms. In other words, papers are generally indexed under the headings that the majority of users will think of first.

Rolling [10] has mentioned the desirability of weighting RT relationships to reflect degree of "semantic similarity" between terms. If two terms can be given a numerical similarity value, a computer can be programmed to elaborate upon an original search strategy in order to select and incorporate additional related terms having a similarity to the starting terms above some given cut-off value. The result of such a search would be presented as a ranked output in order of degree of match between the document and the strategy. For example, given a request for A in relation to B in relation to C, a document indexed A * B * C would be given a weight of 100 percent by the search procedures; one indexed A_2 * B * C, where A_2 is related to A with a strength of 0.8, would be given a weight of 80 percent; and a document indexed A_2 * B_2 * C, where B_2 is related to B with a strength of 0.9, would receive a weight of 72 percent (i.e., the

document weight is calculated on the basis of the *product* of the similarity factors involved.) Rolling suggests that similarity factors between terms would need to be established by human intellectual decisions. However, it is possible that similarity factors could be derived automatically, based on the tendency of two terms to co-occur (i.e., to have been used together in indexing).

DISPLAY OF ASSOCIATIONS

Most thesauri present the various types of references and their reciprocals in separate lists, according to conventions established in LEX, as follows:

DIENE RESINS
  UF Nitrile rubber
     Polydiene resins
  BT Addition resins
  NT ABS resins
     Butyl resins
     Chloroprene resins
     Polybutadiene
     Polychloroprene
     Polyisoprene
     Styrene butadiene resins
  RT Thermoplastic resins
     Thermosetting resins

The New York Times Thesaurus of Descriptors, however, presents all relationships in a single sequence, indicating type of relationship parenthetically:

BEAUTY CONTESTS
  Refer from
    Contests and Prizes (BT)
    Miss America (NT)
    Miss International (NT)
    Miss Universe (NT)
    Miss USA (NT)
    Miss World (NT)
    Mrs. America (NT)

There appears to be no particular advantage in this form of display.

We are indebted to Angell[1] for a complete survey of the form in which term relations are presented in ten controlled vocabularies. The types of relation studied by Angell are shown in Table 10, where A represents the term referred from and B, C . . . N the descriptors referred to. Type I covers the case where A must not be used and one or more other terms are substituted for it. The relation indicators for this situation, as presented in the ten vocabularies studied by Angell, are shown in Tables 11, 12, 13, and 14.

TABLE 10 Classification of Term Relations

Statement number	Formula statement
	I. A forbidden, B . . . instead
1	a. B
2	b. B and C
3	c. B and C and . . . N
4	d. B or C or . . . N
	II. A permitted, B . . . also required
5	a. B
6	b. B and C
7	c. B and C and . . . N
	III. A permitted, consider B . . . also
8	a. B
9	b. B or C or . . . N
	IV. A permitted, consider B . . . instead
10	a. B
11	b. B or C or . . . N

SOURCE: R. S. Angell.[1]

Type II is the situation in which, if term A is assigned, one or more additional terms must also be assigned. Table 15 illustrates this situation. Note that only the API and EURATOM thesauri include this type of compulsory autoposting. Type III is the situation in which, if A is assigned, one or more additional terms may be assigned and are suggested by the thesaurus. Type IV is the common situation in which the user who consults A is directed to other terms (BT, NT, RT) that may be more appropriate. The various applications of the *see* and *use* references are presented in Table 16. The reference structure of the *EURATOM Thesaurus* is rather unconventional, as mentioned previously. It is illustrated in Table 17.

The *Urbandoc Thesaurus* includes some interesting structural elements not contained, to my knowledge, in other tools. These include "C terms," "M terms," "S terms," and "P terms." A C term is one which, in the view of the thesaurus compilers, might usefully be coordinated with the term under which it is listed. Thus CONSERVATION shows NATURAL RESOURCES as a C term. This indicates to the indexer that he should use both terms in describing a report on conservation of natural resources. Likewise, the relationship is brought to the attention of the searcher. The C relationship is like a conventional RT reference, but stronger. It may be regarded as a strong hint to indexers to use both terms under a particular set of conditions. The same effect could obviously be achieved by an entry term CONSERVATION OF NATURAL RESOURCES *use* CONSERVATION *and* NATURAL RESOURCES. An M is assigned to a "subdescriptor" (really a type

TABLE 11 References from Single Term to "Equivalent" Single Term

| | For A forbidden, B instead | | Relation of B to A | | | | |
	Expressed as A . . . B	Recorded under B as	Synonym	Antonym	Alternative form	More general term	More specific term
AIChE	see	sf (seen from)	*	*		*	
API	use	used for	*	*	*	*	
BuRec [1]	use	—	*		*		
BuShips	use	includes	*		*	*	
DDC	use	UF (used for)	*			*	
EJC	use	UF (used for)	*	* [2]	*	*	* [2]
EURATOM [3]	use	—	*			*	
	see	—	*				*
LC	see	X	*		*	* [4]	
NASA	s (see)	—			*		
NLM	see	X	*		*		*
	see under [5]	XU				*	

SOURCE: R. S. Angell.[1]   [1] "BuRec" is an abbreviation for the thesaurus of the U.S. Bureau of Reclamation.[3]
[2] Uncommon in EJC 1964.   [3] For examples, see Table 17.
[4] The *see* reference to a more general term was abandoned in Library of Congress subject heading practice many years ago. Some examples remaining in the list are being eliminated.
[5] NLM also employs "see under" for statement 4. See Table 14.

TABLE 12 References from Single Term to Two Terms Regarded as "Equivalent"

| | For A forbidden, B and C instead | | | |
	Expressed as A . . .	Recorded under B as	Recorded under C as	Relation of B and C to A
AIChE				
API	use B plus C	UF A plus C	UF A plus B	More general terms, whose intersection is synonymous with A
BuRec				
BuShips	use B C	—	—	same as API
DDC	use B and C	UF + A [1]	UF + A [1]	same as API
EJC	use B C	UF A [2]	UF A [2]	same as API
EURATOM	use B + C	—	—	same as API
LC				
NASA				
NLM				

SOURCE: R. S. Angell.[1]   [1] DDC tracings are to be read, respectively, as "B and another term are used for A" "C and another term are used for A"   [2] In TEST, tracings show that two or more terms are used for A.

TABLE 13 References from Single Term to N Terms Regarded as "Equivalent"

	For A forbidden, B and C and . . . N instead			
	Expressed as A . . .	Recorded under B as	Recorded under C . . . N as	Relation of B, C . . . N to A
EJC	use B c . . . N	UF A [1]	UF A [1]	more general terms
EUR-ATOM	use B + c . . . + N	—	—	more general terms

SOURCE: R. S. Angell.[1]
[1] In TEST, tracings show that two or more terms are used for A.

of modifier of a descriptor) that is recommended for use with the descriptor under which it is listed. COMPENSATORY EDUCATION shows as M terms both the subdescriptor AFTER-SCHOOL and the subdescriptor PRE-SCHOOL. The reciprocal entry is an S term. Thus, both of these subdescriptors show COMPENSATORY EDUCATION as an S term. The P relationship is one of prohibition. Under INDUSTRY we find LOCATION as a P term. That is, we should not use these two together in indexing and searching because a separate descriptor (INDUSTRIAL LOCATION) exists to express the concept represented by their joint use.

These special relationships are unique to the *Urbandoc Thesaurus*. They are forms of indexing instructions that have been cleverly combined in the thesaurus structure itself to reduce the need for a separate manual of indexing protocols.

TABLE 14 References from Single Term to Several "Alternative" Terms

	For A forbidden, B or C or . . . N instead			Relation of B, C, . . . N to A		
	Expressed as A . . .	Recorded under B as	Recorded under C . . . N as	Components, divisions, examples	Alternative form	Various
AIChE						
API	see B c . . . N	—	—	*	*	*
BuRec						
BuShips						
DDC						
EJC						
EURATOM [1]	see B or c . . . or N	—	—	*	*	
LC	see B c . . . N	x	x	*		
NASA	S B c . . . N	—	—	*		
NLM	see under B, C, . . . N	XU	XU	*		

SOURCE: R. S. Angell.[1]
[1] For examples, see Table 17.

TABLE 15 Reference from Single Term to Other Term that Must Be Used With It

		For A permitted, B . . . also required		Relation of B . . . N to A	
		Expressed as A . . .	Recorded under B . . . as	More general term	Various
B only	API	Broader terms (autoposted) B	Narrower terms A	*	
		Related terms (autoposted) B	See also A *	*	*
	EURATOM	Use B	—	*	
B and C	API (1)	Broader terms (autoposted) B C . . . N	Narrower terms A	*	
B and C and . . . N		Related terms (autoposted) B C . . . N	See also A *	*	*
	EURATOM (2)	Use B +C . . . +N	—	*	

SOURCE: R. S. Angell.[1]   (1) In some of the 2-term cases B and C together define A, but most relations are looser.
(2) In the 2-term case, B and C together define A. In the 3 or more terms case, B, C . . . N are members of class A or attributes of A.

TABLE 16 *See* and *Use* References: Terminology, Meaning, Occurrence

Vocabulary	A see B	A use B	A use B and C	A use B and C and . . . N	A see B or C or . . . N
	[1] A is a forbidden term— assign B instead		[2] A is a forbidden term— assign both B and C instead	[3] A is a forbidden term— assign B and C and . . . N instead	[4] A is a forbidden term— assign B or C or . . . N instead
AIChE	*				
API		*	*		*
BuRec		*			
BuShips		*	*		
DDC		*	*		
EJC		*	*	*	
LC	*				*
NASA	*				*
NLM	*				* (1)
EURATOM	*	*	*	*	*
		[5] If A is an accepted term, assign B also.	[6] If A is an accepted term, assign both B and C also.	[7] If A is an accepted term, assign B and C and . . . N also.	

SOURCE: R. S. Angell.[1]   (1) NLM's "see under" is also used for this reference.

TABLE 17   Reference Structure of the *EURATOM* Thesaurus

Type of Term	Examples			Symbolic
1. Keywords (no references)	ACETIC ACID			K
2. Accepted Index Terms (only USE references)	ACETYL RADICALS	USE	ACETIC ACID	A———►K
	ACETYLATION	USE	ACETIC ACID	A———►K₁
		+	CHEMICAL REACTIONS	►K₂
	ACETOLYSIS	USE	ACETYL RADICALS	A———►A₂
		+	DECOMPOSITION	►K
3. Forbidden Terms (Synonyms and Abbreviations) (only USE references)	—COLUMBIUM	USE	NIOBIUM	—F———►K
	—ADU	USE	AMMONIUM COMPOUNDS	—F———►K₁
		+	URANATES	►K₂
	—ADRENOCORTICOTROPIC HORMONE	USE	ACTH	—F———►A
4. Forbidden Terms (Homographs) (only SEE references)	—CONDUCTIVITY	SEE	ELECTRIC CONDUCTIVITY	—H/?/ K₁
		OR	THERMAL CONDUCTIVITY	K₂
	—BADGES	SEE	FILM BADGES	—H/?/ A
	—MPA	SEE	MERCAPTOPROPYLAMINE	—H/?/ A₁
		OR	MP-ACTIVITY	A₂

SOURCE: R. S. Angell.[1]

REFERENCES

1. Angell, R. S. *The Language of Term Relation Designations in Subject Access Vocabularies.* Copenhagen: Danish Centre for Documentation, 1968. FID/CR Report No. 8.
2. Bernier, C. L. and Heumann, K. F. "Correlative Indexes. III. Semantic Relations Among Semantemes—the Technical Thesaurus." *American Documentation* 8 (1957): 211-220.
3. Bureau of Reclamation. *Thesaurus of Descriptors: a List of Keywords and Cross-References for Indexing and Retrieving the Literature of Water Resources Development.* Denver, 1963.
4. Kochen, M. and Tagliacozzo, R. "A Study of Cross-Referencing." *Journal of Documentation* 24 (1968): 173-191.
5. Mandersloot, W. G. B. et al. "Thesaurus Control—the Selection, Grouping, and Cross-Referencing of Terms for Inclusion in a Coordinate Index Word List." *Journal of the American Society for Information Science* 21 (1970): 49-57.
6. National Institutes of Health. *Medical and Health Related Sciences Thesaurus.* Bethesda, Md.: Division of Research Grants, 1970. PHS Pub. No. 1031 (1970 ed.).
7. New York Times Co. *The New York Times Thesaurus of Descriptors.* New York, 1968.
8. Papier, L. S. and Cortelyou, E. H. "Use of a Technical Word Association Test in the Preparation of a Thesaurus." *Journal of Documentation* 18 (1962): 183-187.
9. Papier, L. S. and Lin, T. L. "First Letter Frequency of Related Term References in Four Technical Thesauri." *Proceedings of the American Documentation Institute* 3 (1966): 409-417.
10. Rolling, L. "Compilation of Thesauri for Use in Computer Systems." *Information Storage and Retrieval* 6 (1970): 341-350.

11 *Computer Manipulation of Thesaurus Data*

The computer can play several important roles in the handling of thesaurus data:

1. It can manipulate and edit the input data, generate reciprocals, sort and print the thesaurus.
2. It facilitates thesaurus updating and maintenance.
3. In a computer-based system, the thesaurus will be available in machine-readable form to allow certain mappings and term substitutions to be conducted automatically, and to provide statistics useful in indexing, searching, and vocabulary control functions.

Computer programs for editing thesaurus data and for organizing and printing the final thesaurus were developed by Hammond while working with the ARIES Corporation, and these programs have been used in the generation of several thesauri including the *NASA Thesaurus* and the *Water Resources Thesaurus*.[1] The programs were described by Hersey and Hammond[4] in 1967 but have been modified and improved since that time.* The programs are designed to produce thesauri conforming to the COSATI guidelines. Another set of thesaurus programs, now commercially available, was developed by Owens-Illinois, Inc.† Other useful papers on thesaurus applications of the computer have been published by: Martinez et al.[6] dealing with the *Exploration and Production Thesaurus;* by Wolff-Terroine et al.[12] dealing with a cancer thesaurus, and by Rolling[8] (the *EURATOM Thesaurus*). Way[10] has described computer programs for generating a list of subject headings. These programs all have basic similarities.

THE COMPUTER IN THESAURUS CONSTRUCTION

For thesaurus input, it is customary to prepare a master descriptor form for each descriptor to be included in the vocabulary. Such a form would record the exact descriptor, its scope note if any, any synonymous or other terms to be referred to it (UF's), its BT's, NT's, and RT's. Figure 39 shows a typical form of this type, and Figure 40 shows an alternative, more elaborate, form as used for input to the ERIC thesaurus.

The data from such a form are put into machine-

---

* The latest and most sophisticated version of Hammond's program is known as AVOCON and is available from Infodata Systems, Inc., Arlington, Va. AVOCON is described in the following publications:
  1. Infodata Systems, Inc. *AVOCON Users Guide.* Arlington, Va., June 1971.
  2. Hammond W. *The Economics of Computerized Processing in Thesaurus Construction and Maintenance.* Arlington, Va.: Infodata Systems, Inc., 1970.

† For further information on these programs, written in COBOL, contact LEX-INC., 7037 Wolftree Lane, Rockville, Md. 20852.

1A Descriptor Ident. Code	1B Descriptor - In Upper Case	1C Descriptor Origin
2A Descriptor in Final Print Format (SN)		
2B Subject Categories (SC)	2C Scope Notes (SN)	
3 Use or "Post On" Descriptor (US)		
4 Use for - Reciprocal Use (UF) Cross-Reference		
5 Broader Descriptors (BT)	7 Related Descriptors (RT)	
6 Narrower Descriptors (NT)		
	8 Nonreciprocally Related (RR) Descriptors	
9 Date of Final Review	10 Date Added to Thesaurus Corpus	

FIGURE 39 Master descriptor form used for thesaurus input.

ERIC DESCRIPTOR JUSTIFICATION AND DATA INPUT FORM

ERIC FACILITY USE ONLY

M D S	ADD
	DELETE
	CHANGE
	PURGE
L	REMOVE

☐ Entering New Term   ☐ Modifying an Existing Term

ELITE (12 pitch) typewriters stop at first mark.
PICA (10 pitch) typewriters stop at end of block.

Action Codes for Modifications **Only**.

A – ADD   C – CHANGE   D – DELETE

1. Main Term (34 Character Limit)   2. Group Code   Act

TERM _   GROUP _ ☐

3. Scope Note (380 Character Limit)   ELITE (12 pitch) typewriters use first four lines only.

SCOPE _

                                                                Act.

4. Broader Terms   Act.   5. Used For (i.e. Synonyms)   Act

BT _   UF _

6. Narrower Terms

NT _   7. Related Terms

                                                 RT _

DO NOT KEY DATA BELOW THIS LINE

8. Justification Information (Use reverse side if necessary)

A. Indexer & CH	C. Accession No(s).
B. Supervisory Approval & Date	D. Applicable PET Rules

E. Authorities used

F. Definition of Term

EFF - 11 (4/71)

FIGURE 40 Form used for input to *Thesaurus of ERIC Descriptors*.

readable form via punched cards. Actually, if the compilation programs are properly constructed, only the following input data are needed: the descriptor, its scope note, its BT's, and its RT's. Everything else can be generated automatically from this input. Consider the following examples:

Descriptor: ABCD
BT: ABC
UF: PQ
RT: LM
             LN
             LO

From this input the computer program will:

1. Format the correct entry under ABCD.
2. Develop the reciprocal to the BT; that is, under the entry ABC (which is generated from its own input form) it will add ABCD as an NT. If desired, the program can generate the NT references throughout the full hierarchy, showing ABCD as a narrower term under ABC, AB, and A.
3. Develop the reciprocal of the UF; that is, generate a reference to read "PQ *use* ABCD."
4. Develop the RT reciprocals; that is, show ABCD as an RT under the descriptors LM, LN, and LO. If we do not want a particular RT reciprocated, we must distinguish it on the input form (section 8 in Figure 39).
5. Identify and eliminate duplicate entries.

In addition to generating the complementary entries automatically (a tedious and error-prone operation if conducted manually), the computer programs will handle many other editing functions, including checking for blind references and checking for consistency in descriptor format (e.g., the descriptor ABCD must appear in exactly this format throughout the thesaurus, wherever it appears as an NT, BT, or RT under another descriptor, and wherever it appears as the target of a *use* reference; it may also appear in a scope note for another descriptor). A vast amount of manual checking is thus eliminated. Finally, the programs will sort all descriptors and references into the correct alphabetical sequence and will produce a machine printout of the thesaurus suitable for offset reproduction. Alternatively, the computer output can be automatically formatted for input to a photocomposition device. Lists of subject headings tend to include more punctuation marks (hyphens, apostrophes, commas, parentheses) than thesauri and thus present greater problems for machine manipulation. Some of these problems have been described in detail by Harris.[3]

After the thesaurus has been printed we are left with a machine-readable thesaurus, usually on mag-

netic tape. This thesaurus tape will be used in updating and maintenance activities. New descriptors can be added, according to the procedures used in generating the initial list, and they will be checked for consistency within the existing thesaurus framework. These new descriptors will be identified as such, and the thesaurus tape can then be used to generate printed supplements containing new descriptors. New descriptors will usually be added at the bottom of term hierarchies. They will have BT's but probably no NT's.

When a descriptor is deleted or altered in some way (e.g., spelling is changed, or the references to or from are altered), a change card is generated for this descriptor only. The necessary changes in other parts of the thesaurus will then be generated automatically. If ABCD is deleted, or changed to ABCX, entries will need to be changed under PQ, LM, LN, LO, ABC (and possibly AB and A), and any terms that show ABCD as a broader term. Such a procedure is difficult to conduct manually (with the danger of leaving inconsistencies or blind references) but very easy for the computer to handle completely and consistently.

ROLE OF THE MACHINE-READABLE THESAURUS

The computer can play a valuable role in generating a printed thesaurus. The machine-readable thesaurus also has important functions to undertake in mechanized post-coordinate retrieval systems.

The machine-readable thesaurus is a fully authoritative record of the system vocabulary, and it is completely up-to-date. Let us call it the "master vocabulary tape" or MVT. In addition to providing thesaurus printouts of various types, the MVT has the following functions in a computer-based retrieval system:

1. It checks for consistency and acceptability of terms used by indexers and terms used by searchers. Should an indexer or searcher use a term that is not recognized by the MVT, the input record or search strategy will be rejected with an appropriate notification to indexer or searcher. In addition to checking for appearance and spelling of descriptors, the MVT will check on acceptability of combinations. For example, it will check on the validity of descriptor/subheading combinations.
2. In some systems the MVT may undertake certain automatic mapping activities. For example, the indexer or searcher may be allowed to use any of several synonyms recognized in the thesaurus, the MVT automatically substituting the preferred term. Only when a term used by indexer or searcher is completely unrecognized by the MVT will the input record be

rejected. Mapping can be from synonymous expressions (e.g., ASPIRIN *use* ACETYLSALICYLIC ACID) or from combinations (e.g., LUNG PHYSIOLOGY *use* LUNG/PHYSIOLOGY, where PHYSIOLOGY has become a subheading under LUNG).

3. A special form of mapping is associated with term history. Vocabularies used in indexing and searching do not remain static. Changes are made over time, usually to make the vocabulary increasingly specific or to reflect current preferences in terminology. It is difficult and tedious to maintain the history of a large vocabulary by manual processes. The computer can do this very easily. Suppose, for example, that the term CIRCADIAN RHYTHM was first introduced into the vocabulary on 5/9/65. Prior to that date the more generic term PERIODICITY was used for this specific concept. The printed thesaurus now shows CIRCADIAN RHYTHM as an accepted term so the indexer has no problem in handling documents on this topic. But what about the searcher? He must use the term PERIODICITY for material prior to 5/9/65 if he wishes a comprehensive search. Of course, the MVT can be used to generate printouts showing terminological changes, but this would mean that the searcher must always consult such printouts and must use all variants (with date restrictions) in conducting a search. It is preferable to have the searcher use only the latest descriptor, allowing the search programs to substitute earlier versions automatically. Thus, in this example, if the searcher used CIRCADIAN RHYTHM the search programs would automatically substitute PERIODICITY in searching records input before 5/9/65.

4. The MVT maintains certain useful statistics which would be almost impossible to maintain manually. First and foremost, it maintains a record of the number of "postings" or "tallies" under each term; i.e., the number of times a descriptor has been used in indexing. Such data can be presented in printouts (it appears, for example, in the *EURATOM Thesaurus,* and in special machine listings generated by MEDLARS) or it can be displayed at a terminal in an on-line system. Information on the frequency with which a term has been used in indexing is valuable in the searching operation because it allows the searcher to estimate how many citations will be retrieved in response to a particular search strategy or, at the very least, it will tell him the maximum number of citations that could possibly be retrieved.

Statistics on frequency of assignment in indexing are also important in vocabulary control activities. A descriptor that has been used very infrequently in the past twelve months may be a good candidate for deletion from the vocabulary.

Statistics on frequency of use of terms in searching are also extremely valuable in vocabulary control activities (perhaps even more valuable than the statistics on indexing use), but these statistics are kept much less frequently in automated systems although they are no more difficult to collect.

5. A record of the complete hierarchical structure of the vocabulary should appear on the MVT. This facilitates the conduct of generic searches. Only the parent term need be specified in searching, the descendants of it being substituted automatically from the MVT. This procedure is used in MEDLARS, for example, where the hierarchical structure of the vocabulary is fully recorded on the MVT and also in printed *Medical Subject Headings Tree Structures,*[7] as shown in Figure 41.

Suppose we wanted to conduct a search on some aspect of tuberculosis but were interested in all types of tuberculosis. Without the MVT we would need to incorporate all tuberculosis terms in our search strategy in an *or* relationship by listing, as TUBERCULOSIS *or* TUBERCULOSIS, AVIAN *or* TUBERCULOSIS, BOVINE *or* . . . With about thirty terms to choose from in this case, such listing is a tedious and unnecessary procedure. To accomplish such a generic search in MEDLARS, where it is referred to, rather violently, as an *explosion,* we need list only the appropriate generic term or, more exactly, its category number. In this instance, if we say "C1.90 (explosion)," the MVT will automatically expand to include all subdivisions of C1.90 and incorporate these automatically, in an *or* relationship, into the search strategy.

6. Using statistics on frequency of term assignment in indexing, the MVT may be used in the automatic optimization of a search strategy. Consider the Boolean strategy (A *or* B) *and* (L *or* M *or* N) *and* Y. To satisfy this search formula a citation must have been indexed under either term A *or* B *and* (L *or* M *or* N), *and also* under term Y. Suppose that Y is a very broad term and has been used 10,000 times, A and B have collectively been used 750 times, and L, M, N have collectively been used only 84 times. In searching the system it would be grossly inefficient to first look for Y records and then examine these 10,000 records to see if, first, A *or* B and then L *or* M *or* N are present. This is the worst possible strategy to use from the viewpoint of machine processing. The efficient procedure is to identify the *least-heavily posted* component of the strategy that must be present for retrieval. In this example it is the term group L, M, N, which collectively have been applied to only 84 citations. In searching the file efficiently, we look for the group of citations indexed under L *or* M *or* N, finding a maximum of 84 (there may be some overlap in the assignments); then we examine these 84 to see if either A *or*

C1 - INFECTIOUS DISEASES

INFECTIOUS DISEASES (NON MESH) (CONTINUED)
SPIROCHAETALES INFECTIONS (NON MESH) (CONTINUED)
TREPONEMAL INFECTIONS (CONTINUED)

PINTA	C1.70.48.1	C12.94.40.		
SYPHILIS	C1.70.48.1	C1.30.55.1	C1.80	
YAWS	C1.70.48.1	C12.94.56		
SYPHILIS	C1.80.	C1.30.55.1	C1.70.48.1	
NEUROSYPHILIS	C1.80.11.	C10.45.37.		
PARESIS	C1.80.11.1	C10.45.37.1		
TABES DORSALIS	C1.80.11.1	C10.45.37.1	C10.99.56.	
SYPHILIS, CARDIOVASCULAR	C1.80.22.	C8.71.		
SYPHILIS, CONGENITAL	C1.80.33.	C16.70.55.		
HUTCHINSON'S TEETH	C1.80.33.1	C16.35.56.1		
SYPHILIS, CUTANEOUS	C1.80.44.	C12.94.48.		
SYPHILIS, LATENT	C1.80.55.			
TUBERCULOSIS	C1.90.	C1.10.32.1		
TUBERCULOMA	C1.90.3.			
TUBERCULOSIS, AVIAN	C1.90.6.	C15.9.54.		
TUBERCULOSIS, BOVINE	C1.90.9.	C15.16.48.		
TUBERCULOSIS, CARDIOVASCULAR	C1.90.12.	C8.84.		
TUBERCULOSIS, CUTANEOUS	C1.90.15.	C12.94.51.		
LUPUS	C1.90.15.1	C12.94.51.1		
TUBERCULOSIS, ENDOCRINE	C1.90.18.	C7.90.		
TUBERCULOSIS, GASTROINTESTINAL	C1.90.21.	C4.36.48.		
TUBERCULOSIS, HEPATIC	C1.90.24.	C4.58.58.		
TUBERCULOSIS IN CHILDHOOD	C1.90.27.			
TUBERCULOSIS, LARYNGEAL	C1.90.30.	C5.33.11.1	C5.77.58.	
TUBERCULOSIS, LYMPH NODE	C1.90.33.	C9.75.56.		
TUBERCULOSIS, MENINGEAL	C1.90.36.	C10.45.21.1		
TUBERCULOSIS, MILIARY	C1.90.39.			
TUBERCULOSIS, OCULAR	C1.90.42.	C11.39.58.		
TUBERCULOSIS, OSTEOARTICULAR	C1.90.45.	C3.50.55.		
TUBERCULOSIS, SPINAL	C1.90.45.1	C3.50.55.1	C3.100.54.	
TUBERCULOSIS, PERITONEAL	C1.90.48.	C4.88.56.		
TUBERCULOSIS, PLEURAL	C1.90.51.	C5.44.59.	C5.77.60.	
EMPYEMA, TUBERCULOUS	C1.90.51.1	C5.44.9.1	C5.44.59.1	C5.77 60.1
TUBERCULOSIS, PULMONARY	C1.90.54.	C5.22.57.	C5.77.62.	
SILICOTUBERCULOSIS	C1.90.54.1	C5.22.33.1	C5.22.57.1	C5.77.62 1
TUBERCULOSIS, SPLENIC	C1.90.57.	C9.91.56.		
TUBERCULOSIS, UROGENITAL	C1.90.60.	C6.96.		
TUBERCULOSIS, FEMALE GENITAL	C1.90.60.1	C6.18.42.	C6.96.16.	
TUBERCULOSIS, MALE GENITAL	C1.90.60.1	C6.12.54.	C6.96.32.	
TUBERCULOSIS, RENAL	C1.90.60.1	C6.96.48.	C6.108.18.1	
VIRUS DISEASES	C1.100.			
ADENOVIRUS INFECTIONS	C1.100.3.			
ARBOVIRUS INFECTIONS	C1.100.5.			
'COLORADO TICK FEVER	C1.100.5.1			
DENGUE	C1.100.5.1			

* INDICATES PROVISIONAL HEADING

FIGURE 41 Specimen page from the hierarchical "tree structures" used in MEDLARS.

B are present; we then examine this subset to determine if Y is present. From posting statistics on the MVT, an efficient machine search program will automatically optimize the strategy; i.e., it will identify the least-heavily posted component, the next least-heavily posted, and so forth, ordering the strategy in ascending order of posting and searching the file in this sequence to economize on computer time.

7. The MVT may be used to generate automatically *see* and *see also* references in printed indexes. For example, if an entry is to appear in the printed index under DECORATION, the reference INTERIOR DECORATION *see* DECORATION is generated automatically and will appear in the printed index. Likewise, if DEMODULA-

TORS and MODULATORS are both used as headings in an issue of a printed index, because they are linked by RT indicators in the machine thesaurus, the printed *see also* references are generated automatically. The machine thesaurus of the *Engineering Index* [5, 11] is used in this way.

Several thesauri are now available on magnetic tape and may be purchased in this format. The *Thesaurus of Engineering Terms* was made available some years ago, and TEST is also available in machine-readable form. The EJC layout and format, as presented by Speight,[9] are illustrated in Table 18. The LEX tape layout, as presented by Hammond,[2] is shown in Table 19.

TABLE 18   EJC Layout and Format

Thesaurus Magnetic Tape Logical Record Layout		Thesaurus Print and Punch Format ($8\frac{1}{2} \times 11$ in. continuous forms are assumed, but any width greater than $8\frac{1}{2}$ in. may be used).	
Position	Description	Position	Description
1-5	«Main Term» Alphabetic Sequence Code.	1-3	EJC Identifier.
6	Record Type Code.*	4	Record Type Code.*
7-9	Subterm Type Identification (No identification if «Main Term» or «Scope Note»).	11-15	«Main Term» Alphabetic Sequence Code.
10-14	Subterm Alphabetic Sequence Code.	19-21	Subterm Type Identification as follows:
15-20	Print Sequence Code (assigned in order of each sequential line of information).		Blank —Main Term.
			Blank —Scope notes.
21-56	Main term of subterm (except scope notes).		USE —«Use» reference.
60	USE tag (if applicable),—identifies main term record to which «USE» subterm records are posted.		UF —«Used For» reference.
			NT —Narrower Term.
21-60	Scope note (if applicable).		BT —Broader Term.
* 1—Main term.			RT —Related Term.
2—Scope note.		24-28	Subterm Alphabetic Sequence Code (when applicable).
3—Subterm.		32-37	Print Sequence Code.
		41-80	Alphabetic Description.

SAMPLE OF EJC THESAURUS TAPE PRINT FORMAT

10001			100000	ABANDONMENT
10001	UF	36249	100008	ESCAPE ABANDONMENT
10001	RT	27057	100016	COSTS
10001	RT	29633	100024	DEPLETION
10001	RT	29681	100032	DEPRECIATION
10001	RT	51905	100040	LIFE
10001	RT	54193	100048	MAINTENANCE
10001	RT	60097	100056	OBSOLESCENCE
10001	RT	74497	100064	SALVAGE
10001	RT	75137	100072	SCRAP
10009			100080	ABATEMENT
10009	RT	14961	100088	ATTENUATION
10009	RT	28513	100096	DAMPING
10009	RT	29041	100104	DECONTAMINATION
10009	RT	30745	100112	DILUTION
10009	RT	31225	100120	DISPERSING

SOURCE: F. Y. Speight.[9]

TABLE 19 Description of LEX Magnetic Tape Layout

FIELD CONTENT

109 CHARACTER RECORD—13 FIELDS—IBM MODE * 1)

Field	Position(s)	Content
A	1-7	Reserved [1] * 2)
B	8	Term relationship code; see code key below.
C	9-14	Reserved
D	15	Line sequence code for scope note; type of pseudo scope note; see code key below.
E	16-19	Reserved
F	20-21	Reserved
G	22-23	Reserved
H	24	Reserved for term tag * 3)
I	25-60	36-character term entry, scope note line, or subject category codes; this field is also referred to as the *sub-term field;* see key below.
J	61-66	Reserved; used for carrying numeric surrogate of sub-term in Field I (25-60) or for extending capacity of sub-term field from 36 to 42 characters.
K	67-102	36-character term entry; this field also referred to as *main-term field.*
L	103-108	Reserved; used for carrying numeric surrogate of main term in Field K (67-102) or for extending capacity of main-term field from 36 to 42 characters.
M	109	Reserved; used for record indicator when required for computer configurations other than IBM 360.

LEX RECORD IDENTIFICATION CODE KEY

Main-term record (MT) is identified by a 1 in position 8.
Scope Note (SN) is identified by a 2 in position 8 and a numeric line sequence code (1 through 9) in position 15.
COSATI Subject Category Code is identified by a 2 in position 8 and a c in position 15. Each subject category is represented by a set of 4 numeric digits, beginning in position 25, with a blank between each 4-digit set. Thus, seven category codes may be carried in a single record. If more than seven codes are required, an additional record is formed.
A "USE" cross-reference is identified by a 3 in position 8.
A "Used for" (UF) cross-reference (reciprocal of USE) is identified by a 4 in position 8.
A "Broader term" (BT) cross-reference is identified by a 5 in position 8.
A "Narrower term" (NT) cross-reference is identified by a 6 in position 8.
A "Related term" (RT) cross-reference is identified by a 7 in position 8.
* 1 800 bpi, 9 Track, 300 records per block
* 2 7-digit numeric line sequence code
* 3 System/360, 8-bit code shown below indicates:
  Ø1ØØ1Ø11 = narrower terms listed in thesaurus
  Ø1ØØ111Ø = refer to main term entry

SOURCE: W. Hammond.[2]
[1] Unless otherwise specified, the content of reserved fields varies with the application.

REFERENCES

1. Department of the Interior. *Water Resources Thesaurus.* Washington, D.C.: Office of Water Resources Research, 1966.
2. Hammond, W. "Satellite Thesaurus Construction." In *The Thesaurus in Action: Background Information for a Thesaurus Workshop at the 32nd Annual Convention of the American Society for Information Science.* San Francisco, Calif., October 1969: 14-20. AD 694 590.
3. Harris, J. L. *Subject Analysis: Computer Implications of Rigorous Definition.* Metuchen, N.J.: Scarecrow Press, 1970.
4. Hersey, D. F. and Hammond, W. "Computer Usage in the Development of a *Water Resources Thesaurus.*" *American Documentation* 18 (1967): 209-215.
5. Hohnecker, W. and Newmark, M. "Automated Maintenance of a Highly Structured Thesaurus of Engineering Index." *Proceedings of the American Documentation Institute* 4 (1967): 132-136.
6. Martinez, S. J. et al. "Computer Processing of Thesaurus Data." *Proceedings of the American Society for Information Science* 6 (1969): 269-275.
7. National Library of Medicine. *Medical Subject Headings Tree Structures.* Bethesda, Md.: National Library of Medicine, 1969.
8. Rolling, L. "Compilation of Thesauri for Use in Computer Systems." *Information Storage and Retrieval* 6 (1970): 341-350.
9. Speight, F. Y. "What is *The Thesaurus of Engineering Terms* Developed by the Engineers' Joint Council (EJC)?" *Bulletin de l'Association Internationale des Documentalistes et Techniciens de l'Information* 5 (1966): 29-36.
10. Way, W. "Subject Heading Authority List, Computer Prepared." *American Documentation* 19 (1968): 188-199.
11. Whaley, F. R. and Flanagan, C. M. "The Engineering Index Thesaurus." *Bulletin de l'Association Internationale des Documentalistes et Techniciens de l'Information* 5 (1966): 45-52.
12. Wolff-Terroine, M. et al. "Use of a Computer for Compiling and Holding a Medical Thesaurus." *Methods of Information in Medicine* 8 (1969): 34-40.

12 Vocabulary Growth and Updating

A controlled vocabulary for indexing and searching cannot be static; it must grow. Of course, a vocabulary developed through an actual indexing operation will grow very fast at first, but it will reach a plateau after X papers have been indexed. Figure 42 illustrates a typical growth curve, taken from McClelland and Mapleson,[7] although this is a vocabulary in a very limited subject area (anesthesiology). These authors believe that, in practice, most specialized fields will get by with from 5,000 to 8,000 terms and that the whole of science and technology would require about 20,000 terms. This has since been confirmed by actual experience. The MEDLARS vocabulary (*Medical Subject Headings*), covering the whole of biomedicine, is of the order of 8,000 descriptors, whereas the *Thesaurus of Engineering and Scientific Terms* contains 23,000 terms. How large the vocabulary will be depends not only on the subject field but on the specificity of the terms and the type of terms used. A pre-coordinate vocabulary will be larger than a simple Uniterm vocabulary, and a vocabulary of basic semantic factors could be quite small indeed.

Figure 43 presents a growth curve, reported by Blagden,[2] for a thesaurus in the management sciences. This vocabulary had leveled off at about 800 terms after 2,000 documents had been indexed.

The rate of vocabulary growth will also depend upon what the terms are describing. The growth curve shown in Figure 44, taken from Wadington,[10] is unusual in that no real plateau had been reached after 10,000 documents had been indexed. However, the true subject descriptors began to level off relatively early. Most of the continued growth was in "materials" terms. These are mainly terms for chemicals and include terms for specific chemical combinations. Clearly this type of vocabulary could be very large and could continue to grow for a long time, as long as documents on new chemical compounds are encountered in indexing.

In the development of an indexing vocabulary, it is presumably important to have some fairly objective way of evaluating its degree of completeness before putting it into use or offering it for review by other individuals or organizations. D.C. Snow,[9] of the United Kingdom Patent Office, described such an evaluation procedure in 1965, and this has since become known, affectionately, as the "Snow Test." Snow's procedure aims at establishing, in a very short time (about two working days): "(1) the nature and extent of pertinent aspects of the subject matter which have been overlooked; (2) whether the depth of indexing provided is commensurate with the state of the art; (3) whether the term list is reasonably balanced; i.e., mostly contains terms which have a high probability of being useful and is not overloaded with terms having only a low probability of usefulness."

The test is founded upon two very reasonable assumptions: (1) that the only terms essential to a retrieval system are those occurring in search requests, and (2) that in patent searching these terms will neces-

98

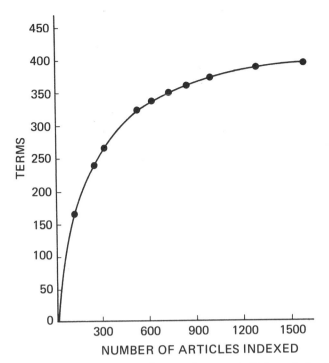

FIGURE 42 Typical growth curve for a controlled vocabulary.

of being matched, at what level they can be matched) by terms in the list. Snow explains the procedure as follows:

Briefly, a random sample of about 40–45 new applications is taken and the cumulative total of terms required for matching the features of the broadest claims in the sample application and available in the tentative term list is plotted against sample size (curve A). In addition the cumulative total of features in the claims which cannot be matched by terms in the list is also plotted against sample size (curve B). To obtain a numerical measure of the efficacy of the term list, for each sample size or for every other sample size (i.e., 2, 4, 6, etc.), the ratio of the cumulative total of the number of features that cannot be matched to the sum of the cumulative total of these features and the cumulative total of available terms that have been used to match characteristics in the broadest claims is calculated. This ratio, (which necessarily lies between 0 and 1) can again be plotted against sample size (curve E). The value of the ratio at the end of the sample and the slope of the last half of this curve (which is almost linear over the last half) appear to be useful parameters.

In addition, the features which cannot be matched by available terms are split into two groups: (1) those relating to aspects or sub-aspects which are missing from the system; (2) those representing detail for which a close generic term is available in the system. It is useful to plot the cumulative totals of these two groups against sample size (curve C and curve D).

If the tentative term list is reasonably satisfactory the following characteristics will be observed.

1) The ratio referred to above will be about 0.75 or more at the end of the sample.

sarily bear a very close relationship to the claims made in new patent applications. The procedure involves a comparison of the broadest claims in current applications with the tentative term list to determine which features of these claims can be matched (and if capable

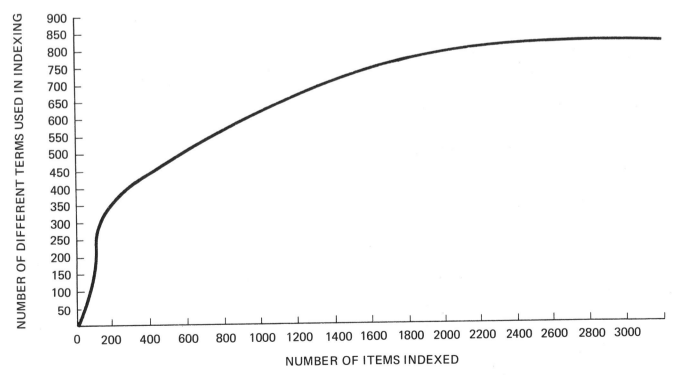

FIGURE 43 Growth curve for a thesaurus in the management sciences.

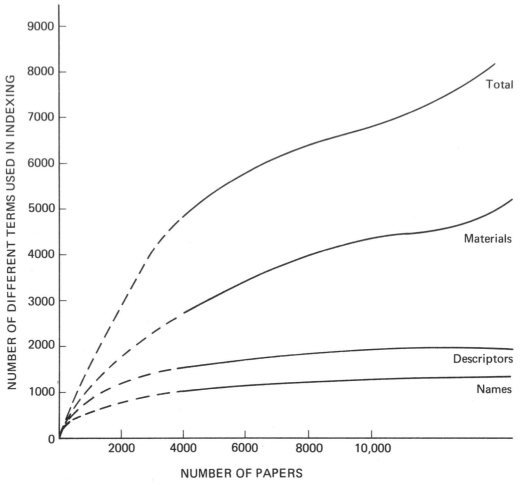

FIGURE 44 Growth curve showing rate of addition of terms of various types.

2) The slope of the last part of curve E will be about minus 0.001.

3) The curve for the cumulative total of available terms used for matching purposes (curve A) will still be rising fairly steeply at the end of the sample and the total at the end of the sample will be about one third or more of the total number of terms in the list.

4) The curve for the cumulative total of features which cannot be matched and which relate to missing aspects or sub-aspects, (curve C), will show signs of leveling off.

5) The curve for the cumulative total of features which cannot be matched but which represent detail for which close generic terms are available in the tentative term list, (curve D), will have a relatively small slope.

In applying this test to a number of draft term lists, it was found that a ratio of 0.75 is necessary if the list is to be regarded as satisfactory for further development. If the ratio is as low as 0.5, the tentative term list will probably need considerable revision. A value much below 0.5 would indicate that the list is quite inadequate and only in an early stage of development. The ratio does not involve any distinction between the two kinds of deficiencies represented by curves C and

D, but represents an overall measure of the degree to which the draft vocabulary is able to represent topics occurring in typical search requests. In fact, it simply represents the proportion of all terms required that are actually present in the list.

As the measured ratio increases, the modulus of the slope of the second half of the curve E (almost linear) decreases. For a ratio of 0.75, the modulus of the slope is small (0.001) and probably decreasing, thus indicating that the total theoretical number of terms required in the system will increase only very slowly with time and that the final vocabulary resulting from the various stages of development (the ratio for the final list should be very much greater than 0.75) should be stable and have a long life expectancy.

Snow's procedure has apparently been used successfully in the monitoring of small vocabularies intended for indexing patents in a particular restricted subject area (e.g., graft polymers). A typical vocabulary of this type is illustrated in Figure 66, Chapter 21. The procedure could probably be modified to test any draft vocabulary covering a relatively small subject area.

In the nonpatent environment, abstracts of recent papers (e.g., those being presented at current meetings) could probably be substituted for the patent claims.

DISTRIBUTION OF TERM USAGE

A matter related to vocabulary growth is the distribution of index term usage. This aspect has been reviewed by Arthur D. Little, Inc.,[1] by Houston and Wall,[6] and by Wall.[11, 12] The A.D. Little investigators claim that the distribution of term usage within an indexing vocabulary corresponds closely to the distribution of word usage in natural-language texts as investigated by Zipf.[13] Zipf's studies showed that a comparatively small percentage of words in the English language account for a very large percentage of the total word usage. The Zipfian distribution of term usage in a technical information system is illustrated in Figure 45. This figure was first presented in the A.D.

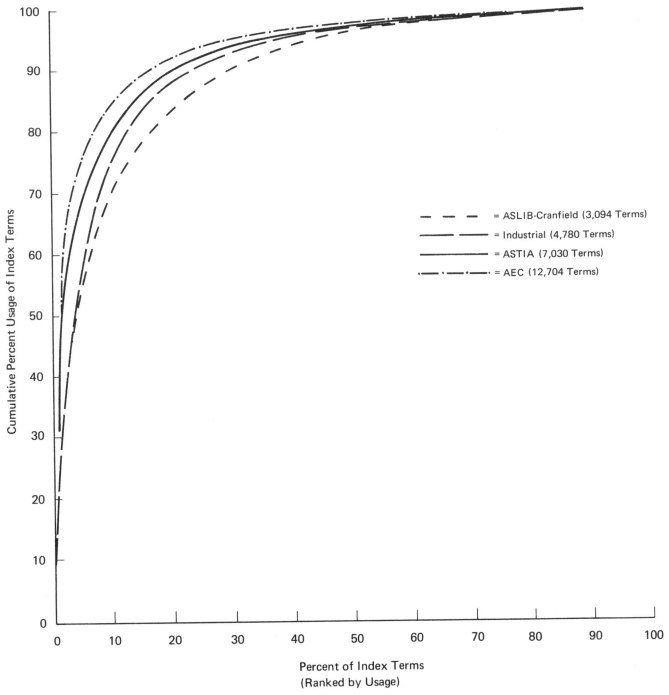

FIGURE 45 Distribution of term usage.

Little report and was later added to by Cleverdon et al.[3] The distributions illustrated are based on an industrial information system, an information system of the U.S. Atomic Energy Commission, the information system of ASTIA (now the Defense Documentation Center), and the experimental corpus established in the Cranfield study itself. In this last corpus, the 10 percent of most-used terms accounted for 68 percent of all the postings, and the 30 percent of most-used terms accounted for no less than 92 percent of the postings, after which the curve flattens out. In Figure 45, *cumulative percentage* of term usage is plotted against *cumulative percentage* of terms contributing to this usage.

Wall,[11] on the other hand, claims that the distribution of term usage in all indexes is log-normal rather than Zipfian. The form of the relationship between vocabulary size (T) and total number of index entries (P) is:

$$T = a \ \log_{10} \ (P+b) - c$$

where a, b, and c are constants approximated by the values 3,000, 7,100, and 11,000, respectively. He presents numerical procedures whereby accurate predictive values of vocabulary size, average term usage, and typical term usage can be determined by computer as functions of index size. Predictive estimates of maximum term usage can also be obtained.

There are many other statistics that can be maintained on a controlled vocabulary and which may be useful in various types of study. Heald[5] reports many interesting statistics on the *Thesaurus of Engineering and Scientific Terms* (TEST). Figure 46 shows the distribution of sources contributing to TEST, and Table 20 presents further statistics on the composition of the vocabulary and length of descriptors. Note that 64.5 percent of the descriptors contain more than one word and that there are 13,012 unique words in the

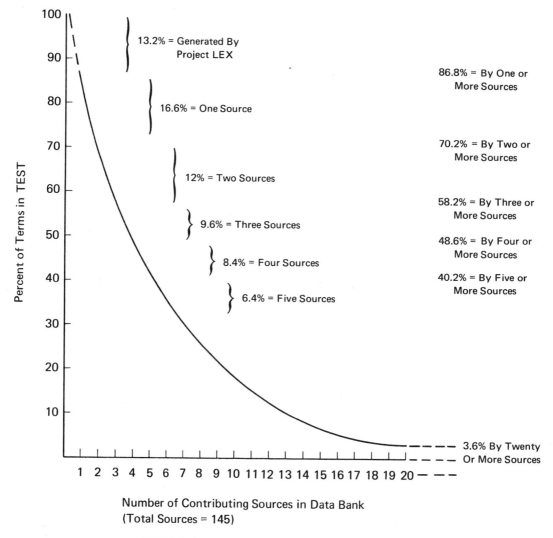

FIGURE 46 Source distribution of terms in TEST.

TABLE 20 Statistics on Composition and Characteristics of Vocabulary in TEST

Thesaurus of Terms	
Descriptors	17,810
USE References	5,554
Total terms	23,364
Scope Notes	1,178
USED FOR'S	6,102 *
Broader Terms	23,907
Narrower Terms	23,907
Related Terms	76,257
Line entries	162,657
Avg. number of entries under each descriptor	7.48
Descriptors having one or more BT's	11,424
Descriptors having one or more NT's	3,512
Descriptors having one or more RT's	14,792
Percent of One-word terms	35.5
Percent of Two-word terms	52.2
Percent of Three-word terms	10.8
Percent of Four-word terms	1.5
Permuted Index	
Line entries	47,758
No. of unique words	13,012
Subject Category Index	
Line entries	20,223
Descriptors	17,810
Avg. categories per descriptor	1.14
Hierarchical Index	
Line entries	13,310
Descriptor heads of families	607
Avg. number of entries per descriptor	21.9

SOURCE: J. H. Heald.[5]
* The difference between this figure and that for USE references is caused by several USE references having more than one USED FOR.

vocabulary. In other words, if this were a Uniterm system, 13,012 Uniterms would suffice.

UPDATING THE VOCABULARY

Once a vocabulary has grown to a leveling-off point we can expect continued gradual growth, to increase specificity and to accommodate new topics, but there should not be any sudden bursts of growth (unless the information center happens to move into completely new subject areas). The continued growth of the vocabulary should come from within the system itself. It should be based on literary warrant: new terms will be derived from the indexing and searching operations. They will be terms needed to express items of subject matter, occurring in documents and in requests, that

cannot be expressed in the terms of the vocabulary as it stands. This will be the principal criterion governing the addition of new terms to the vocabulary. Other general criteria have already been mentioned in our discussion of initial vocabulary generation, in Chapter 6.

Normally, in an information center or network of information centers, a vocabulary control group (sometimes called a "lexicographic staff") is created to review the vocabulary on a continuous basis and, in particular, to consider recommendations for new terms made by indexers and searchers. Eller and Panek[4] have described procedures used in continued thesaurus development in the Educational Resources Information Center Network. In the ERIC network, each participating clearinghouse has responsibilities for input to the vocabulary control functions.

If an indexer at an ERIC clearinghouse encounters a topic that cannot adequately be represented in the vocabulary, he may generate a new "candidate" descriptor. Justification for the new descriptor is based on the subject analyst's own expertise, thesaurus rules and conventions, dictionaries, handbooks, and other reference materials. The candidate descriptor is entered on a Descriptor Justification Form (Figure 40), together with proper reference (UF, BT, NT, RT) relationships with the descriptors currently in the thesaurus, and a scope note if this is deemed necessary. Descriptor Justification Forms (DJF's) are reviewed by lexicographers working under contract with the ERIC headquarters staff in Washington. The review is made in terms of compliance to thesaurus rules, errors of omission, and need for adjusting the scope-note or reference connections. If the descriptor is accepted, the DJF is forwarded for machine input and thesaurus update procedures. Machine printouts of new descriptors are generated and circulated among all ERIC clearinghouses to allow further group review and to update working vocabulary tools.

In some systems it is customary to introduce a new descriptor for a trial period, observe its use patterns (manner and frequency of use), and retain or discard it after, say, twelve months. This is done in MEDLARS, for example, where the new descriptors are known as "provisional headings."

Besides adding new terms to the vocabulary, thesaurus updating will also include some term deletion, although the amount of deletion is unlikely to equal the amount of addition. A term may be deleted and replaced by a synonymous or nearly synonymous expression. This is likely to reflect a change in the accepted terminology of the field. Alternatively, a term may be deleted and referred, by a *use* reference, to another term of broader scope. For example, the term

CUMULUS CLOUDS is relegated from a descriptor to a reference (*use* CLOUDS).

The decision to delete a specific term, and map instead to a broader one, is usually based on the fact that the specific term has not been used very much in indexing (hence the value of term postings to vocabulary control activities). Therefore it is felt that the term could be removed from the vocabulary without much loss. Statistics of indexing use are certainly valuable indicators in vocabulary updating operations, and these statistics are generally maintained in most systems. Strangely enough, statistics on term usage in searching are almost never recorded. In a sense these statistics are more important than the statistics of use in indexing. However often a term is used in indexing, it is unjustified if, for instance, over a two-year period it has never been used in searching. This would indicate fairly clearly that the term is unnecessarily specific.* Indexers use it because it is available and documents exist on the specific topic. However, requests are never made this specifically in this particular subject area so that a term at this level of specificity is redundant.

This re-emphasizes the very important fact that an efficient vocabulary must be tailored to the types of requests made to the retrieval system. It also highlights an important, twofold need that is frequently overlooked in the operation of such a system:

1. System users must make initial requests in their own natural-language terms and *not* in the terms of the system vocabulary.
2. These natural-language requests must be recorded and analyzed for input to vocabulary updating procedures.

It is highly undesirable to require a user to make his initial request in the terms of a controlled vocabulary because:

1. His request will be unnaturally constrained by the terminology of the system; i.e., he will ask not for what he wants but for what he thinks the system can give him, which may be several removes from his actual information need.
2. If requesters always use the terminology of the system, we will tend not to become aware of inadequacies in the system caused by lack of specificity in the vocabulary. For example, many requesters would like to be able to search on terms indicating specific oxides or groups of oxides (e.g., alkaline earth oxides) but they do not make their requests this specific. In-

stead they say OXIDES, because this is the only descriptor existing in this area. Consequently, we are not made aware of the fact that, to meet user needs adequately, we need to subdivide the descriptor OXIDES further.

It is important, therefore, that all requests made to a retrieval system should be initially recorded in the requester's own words (on a search request form or at an on-line terminal), and that the translation into system terminology should take place *after* the natural-language statement is recorded.

Addition of new terms to a vocabulary, at least on a provisional basis, will occur continuously. But term deletion involves the analysis of statistics on term usage, and this can only be done through complete vocabulary review procedures on a periodic basis. Sometimes such complete review is done annually, leading to the production of a revised edition of the tool. *Medical Subject Headings,* for example, is reissued in revised form every year.

CONSOLIDATION OF VOCABULARIES

Occasionally we may be faced with an unusual vocabulary updating situation, such as the consolidation of two or more separately existing thesauri. This situation was faced by Du Pont, which began consolidating the activities of nine separate information centers in 1964. These centers collectively indexed some 50,000 reports and processed about 3,000 queries annually. Schirmer[8] has reviewed the vocabulary updating procedures used by Du Pont to build a consolidated thesaurus for nonchemical terms. Selection of terms for the consolidated thesaurus was based on an analysis of the degree of overlap between terms from the various centers, the type and frequency of terms used in searching, the relationship between terms used in indexing and terms used in searching, and the density of postings for both indexing and search terms (Table 21).

TABLE 21 Density of Postings for Indexing and Search Terms

Postings	Index Terms (Incl. Chemicals)	Search Terms (Excl. Chemicals)
1	47%	2%
More than 1	53%	98%
More than 5	22%	92%
More than 10	13%	87%
More than 20	8%	75%
More than 50	4%	51%

SOURCE: R. F. Schirmer.[8]

* Alternatively, it might indicate that the scope of the collection no longer matches the interests of the clientele!

A total of 25,700 separate nonchemical terms was obtained from the nine separate systems. Of these, 7,500 were found to be exact duplicates representing 2,790 different nonchemical concepts. The extent of duplication is represented by the following table:

Number of duplications	Number of terms
2	1,650
3	660
4	280
5	120
6	60
7	20
	2,790

Further manual analysis revealed that an additional 11 percent of the nonchemical terms could be combined with the 2,790 because they were simple variants (spelling differences, singular versus plural, word ending differences). The total number of *different* nonchemical terms was eventually reduced to 15,310. These terms were divided into nine broad categories, as shown in Table 22.

A study of searching patterns in the three largest systems showed that only 2,010 (18 percent) of the available 11,300 nonchemical terms had been used in 2,100 computer searches over a one-year period. All of the search terms were classified by category, and data on frequency of usage were recorded (Table 23). The results showed that the 2,010 nonchemical con-

TABLE 22 Categories of Different Nonchemical Terms

1. Proper Names: Plants, Geographical Locations.
   Examples: American Can Co., Beaumont Works, Texas, Germany
2. Trade or Code Names.
   Examples: "Carbowax," "Lucite," "Orlon."
3. Materials: Mixtures, States of Materials.
   Examples: Chemicals, Ceramics, Costs.
4. Energy: Forms of Energy.
   Examples: Heat, Electricity, Ultraviolet Radiation.
5. Devices: Equipment, Tools, Components.
   Examples: Dryers, Drills, Mandrels.
6. Shapes: Forms.
   Examples: Bars, Interfaces, Chips.
7. Processes: Operations, Technologies.
   Examples: Spinning, Polymerization, Mathematics.
8. Qualities: Properties, Conditions.
   Examples: Elasticity, Temperature, Velocity.
9. Adjectives: Modifiers.
   Examples: Blue, Cold, Dimensional.

SOURCE: R. F. Schirmer.[8]

cepts previously identified were used more than 5,300 times; 52 percent occurred once only, 72 percent once or twice, and 90 percent occurred five times or less.

The number of occurrences of each category of terms in the 2,100 searches was then calculated, as shown in Table 24. In this table proper names occur once only, trade names once in every 45 searches, and process terms in every single search.

A further analysis of the search terms from the three systems revealed that an average of 89 percent of all

TABLE 23 Classification of Search Terms by Category and Frequency of Usage

Frequency	Proper Names	Trade Names	Shapes	Energy	Adjectives	Devices	Qualities	Materials	Processes	Total	%
1	1	32	18	13	41	216	182	192	341	1,036	52
2	0	1	8	6	24	77	67	74	148	405	20
3	0	0	7	6	8	36	48	42	56	203	10
4	0	0	1	3	4	10	21	21	33	93	5
5	0	0	1	2	2	7	13	18	27	70	3
6-10	0	2	1	0	5	13	29	32	46	128	6
11-49	0	0	0	2	1	7	13	26	26	75	4
Total	1	35	36	32	85	366	373	405	677	2,010	
%	0	2	2	2	4	18	19	20	33		100
Frequency of Terms Searched	1	47	71	92	193	745	1,014	1,347	1,816	5,326	
%	0	1	1	2	4	14	19	25	34		100

SOURCE: R. F. Schirmer.[8]

TABLE 24 Ratio of Terms Searched Per Question
by Category

Category	Ratio
Proper Names	1:2100
Trade Names	1:45
Shapes	1:30
Energy	1:23
Adjectives	1:11
Devices	1:3
Qualities	1:2
Materials	1:1.5
Processes	1:1

SOURCE: R. F. Schirmer.[8]

nonchemical terms used in searching (89 percent of the concepts used in System 1, 96 percent of those used in System 2, and 80 percent of those used in System 3) could be converted to the 2,790 concepts on the overlap list. These results were considered to indicate that a relatively small, well-defined thesaurus would adequately meet the requirements of a consolidated Du Pont retrieval system. This is a functional example of a study of thesaurus requirements based on records of past use of terms in both the indexing and searching activities.

Although continuous vocabulary review is essential if a retrieval system is to remain responsive to user needs, terminological changes over time do complicate the searching process. However, by using the computer to maintain term histories and to substitute terms in strategies automatically where necessary, searching problems of this type are minimized.

REFERENCES

1. Arthur D. Little Inc. *Centralization and Documentation.* Cambridge, Mass., 1963.
2. Blagden, J. F. *Management Information Retrieval: a New Indexing Language.* London: British Institute of Management, 1969. (2nd edition, 1971).
3. Cleverdon, C. et al. *Factors Determining the Performance of Indexing Systems. Vol. 1, Design.* Cranfield, England: College of Aeronautics, ASLIB Cranfield Research Project, 1966.
4. Eller, J. L. and Panek, R. L. "Thesaurus Development for a Decentralized Information Network." *American Documentation* 19 (1968): 213-220.
5. Heald, J. H. *The Making of TEST Thesaurus of Engineering and Scientific Terms.* Washington, D.C.: Department of Defense, 1967. AD 661 001.
6. Houston, N. and Wall, E. "The Distribution of Term Usage in Manipulative Indexes." *American Documentation* 15 (1964): 105-114.
7. McClelland, R. M. A. and Mapleson, W. W. "Construction and Usage of Classified Schedules and Generic Features in Coordinate Indexing." *ASLIB Proceedings* 18 (1966): 290-299.
8. Schirmer, R. F. "Thesaurus Analysis and Updating." *Journal of Chemical Documentation* 7 (1967): 94-98.
9. Snow, D. C. "Development and Monitoring of Indexing Systems: Evaluation of Term Lists by Comparison with a Sample of Claims in New Patent Applications." Paper presented at the Annual Meeting of ICIREPAT (International Cooperation in Information Retrieval among Examining Patent Offices), London, September 1965.
10. Wadington, J. P. "Unit Concept Coordinate Indexing." *American Documentation* 9 (1958): 107-113.
11. Wall, E. "Further Implications of the Distribution of Index Term Usage." *Proceedings of the American Documentation Institute* 1 (1964): 457-466.
12. Wall, E. "Indexing Control in the Technical Information Center." In *Technical Information Center Administration,* edited by A. W. Elias. Washington, D.C.: Spartan Books, 1964, 72-103.
13. Zipf, G. K. *Human Behavior and the Principle of Least Effort.* Cambridge, Mass.: Addison-Wesley, 1949.

13 *The Influence of System Vocabulary on the Performance of a Retrieval System*

Before we can study the effect of the vocabulary on the performance of a retrieval system we need to consider:

1. Criteria by which we may evaluate performance.
2. Procedures by which we may conduct such an evaluation.

I have discussed these matters in considerable detail in a previous book [2] and will not repeat them here, except in the briefest possible form.

USER REQUIREMENTS

In evaluating the *effectiveness* of a retrieval system we attempt to determine how well it meets the needs of its users. In general, *any* operation can be evaluated in terms of its performance with respect to (1) quality, (2) time, and (3) cost, and there are always tradeoffs among these criteria. In the retrieval environment we can recognize the following set of performance criteria as important:

1. *Quality.*
    a. The *coverage* of the data base.
    b. The ability of the system to retrieve relevant documents from this data base in response to a subject request. This is usually known as *recall* and may be expressed quantitatively by means of a *recall ratio*.
    c. The ability to hold back nonrelevant documents at the same time, which is usually known as *precision* and may be expressed quantitatively by means of a *precision ratio*.

    d. Form and format of output for easiest and most convenient use.
2. *Effort.* The amount of effort involved in use of the system. Eventually this is reduced to *cost* of using the system.
3. *Response time.*

All users of a retrieval system have one fundamental requirement in common: they expect the system to be able to retrieve one or more documents that contribute to the satisfaction of some information need (*relevant documents*). All users are presumed to have an information need — otherwise they would not have approached the system in the first place. Actually, this "fundamental requirement" is a slight oversimplification. In some, comparatively rare, situations the user wants the system to retrieve nothing. This is the situation where the user believes and hopes nothing exists (e.g., certain patent searching situations). Under these circumstances (nothing existing), the system behaves perfectly if it retrieves nothing.

In most situations, however, the user wants and expects the system to retrieve some relevant documents. It is possible to express quantitatively the degree of system success in retrieving relevant literature from its data base. The appropriate ratio is the *recall ratio*, which may be defined as:

$$\frac{\text{the number of relevant documents retrieved by the system}}{\text{the total number of relevant documents contained in the system}} \times 100$$

Suppose that for a particular subject request made to some retrieval system we are able to establish that there are only ten relevant documents in the entire data base. We conduct a subject search using normal system procedures, and retrieve seven of these ten documents. The recall ratio of this search is 7/10 × 100, or 70 percent.

The recall ratio is one very important measure of the success of a search; but it is not the only important measure. In fact, on its own it is somewhat meaningless: we can always get 100 percent recall for any search in any system if we are prepared to search broadly enough and to retrieve a sufficiently large portion of the collection. An information retrieval system is essentially a filter and, as in the case of other types of filters, it should be capable of letting through what we want while withholding what we don't want. The recall ratio expresses the ability of the system to let through what we want, but we also need a companion measure which will express the ability of the system to withhold what we don't want.

One such measure is the precision ratio, which may be defined as:

$$\frac{\text{the number of relevant documents retrieved by the system}}{\text{the total number of documents retrieved by the system}} \times 100$$

Returning to the hypothetical search previously mentioned, we may find that the system retrieved a total of 50 documents (or references), 7 of them relevant and 43 not. The precision ratio for this search is thus 7/50, or 14 percent, and the search has operated at 70 percent recall and at 14 percent precision. These two measures, used jointly, indicate the filtering capacity of the system. They give a good picture of system effectiveness whereas either one, on its own, is inadequate.

The precision ratio measures the efficiency with which the system is able to achieve a particular recall ratio. Clearly, achievement of 70 percent recall at a precision of 7/14 (50 percent) indicates greater efficiency than the attainment of the same recall at 7/50 (14 percent) precision or 7/100 (7 percent) precision; greater filtering capacity has been brought into play. In a sense, the precision ratio may be regarded as a measure of the effort required from the user of the system to achieve a particular recall ratio. This effort is expended after the search results have been delivered by the system, in order to separate the relevant items retrieved from the irrelevant items. Obviously, it takes longer to separate 7 relevant from 93 irrelevant (7 percent precision) than it does to separate 7 relevant from 43 irrelevant (14 percent precision), and the latter case requires more effort than the separation

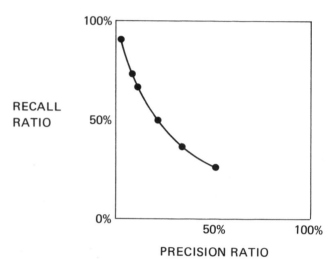

FIGURE 47 Typical performance curve when recall is plotted against precision.

of 7 relevant from an equal number of irrelevant (50 percent precision). Viewed in this light, the precision ratio is clearly a valid and useful measure of search efficiency.

Recall and precision tend to vary inversely in searching; that is, whatever we do to improve recall (by broadening a search) will also tend to reduce precision; and whatever we do to improve precision (by searching more stringently) will tend to reduce recall. In fact, if we conduct one search, or a whole group of searches, at varying strategy levels from very broad to very stringent, we can derive a series of performance points that will allow us to draw a performance curve resembling that of Figure 47.

Although the vocabulary of a retrieval system has no effect on the coverage of that system, it may affect the amount of user effort needed to exploit the system and it may indirectly affect response time. It certainly has a very direct influence on system recall and precision capabilities.

EVALUATION PROCEDURES

When we conduct a search in a retrieval system in response to a particular subject request, the results of this search may be presented in the form of a 2×2 table, as shown in Figure 48. In evaluating a retrieval system, we must put values, or at least estimates, into this table for a representative set of requests (searches). Three of these values are directly observable: the total collection size $(a+b+c+d)$, the total number of items retrieved $(a+b)$, and the total not retrieved $(c+d)$. The other values we need to establish, or at least

USER RELEVANCE JUDGMENT

		RELEVANT	NOT RELEVANT	TOTAL
SYSTEM RELEVANCE PREDICTION	RETRIEVED	a Hits	b Noise	a + b
	NOT RETRIEVED	c Misses	d Correctly Rejected	c + d
	TOTAL	a + c	b + d	a + b + c + d (total collection)

FIGURE 48 2×2 contingency table for search results.

estimate, in our evaluation program. The values a and b can be established relatively easily. A search has been conducted for a requester and has retrieved a number of documents or document surrogates $(a+b)$. We present these to the requester and have him tell us which items he considers relevant (a) and which he considers irrelevant (b). Usually we will want him to judge relevance on some type of scale ("major relevance," "minor relevance," "no relevance" will probably suffice). Although the topic of "relevance" has generated much literature and heated discussion, and although a great many factors influence a requester's relevance decisions, when we are evaluating an operating system in its entirety we must accept that a "relevant" document is one that contributes to the satisfaction of the information need of the requester and an "irrelevant" document is one that does not. Therefore, relevance assessments are value judgments placed on documents by individuals with information needs.

Once the requester has made these relevance assessments for us, we have a precision ratio $(a/a+b)$ for the search under review. In practical application, these relevance assessments should be recorded by the requester on assessment forms. We should also ask the requester to indicate reasons for his various judgments; i.e., why is one document of major relevance, a second of no relevance, a third of minor relevance. These recorded reasons will be extremely useful in our analysis of the search performance.

We still have two values to place in the 2×2 table, namely, c and d. These are the difficult ones to determine, but we need them in order to establish a recall ratio. To be truthful, there is only one way to arrive at these values absolutely (and thereby derive a "true" recall figure), and that is by having the requester examine all the nonretrieved items $(c+d)$ and tell us which of them are relevant (c) and which are not

(d). If this can be done, we can establish an absolute value for c and thus can derive an absolute recall ratio $(a/a+c)$. In the evaluation of experimental or small prototype systems it is sometimes possible to do just this. However, in most operating systems which function at all effectively, $c+d$ will be a very large portion of the entire collection, and it will be quite impossible to expect the requester to examine all of these items or even a large part of them. Moreover, $c+d$ will usually be so large (in relation to c) that we cannot even use conventional random sampling procedures; that is, an extremely large sample would need to be drawn from $c+d$ to achieve any expectation of finding even one relevant document therein.

If we are evaluating a retrieval system of any size, we may just as well abandon the idea of trying to establish true recall and be satisfied with the best possible *recall estimate* we can come up with. Probably the most reasonable method of doing this is that employed by Lancaster[1] and justified statistically by Shumway.[3] The situation is illustrated in Figure 49.

For any particular subject request posed to the collection, I, there will be a set of documents, A, that the requester would judge relevant if he saw them. If we knew this set, A, and we knew what portion of this set was retrieved by a search in the collection, we would be able to establish absolute recall. But, as previously indicated, we usually cannot establish the composition of A in a system of any significant size. However, we *can* find a portion of A, the subset A_1, and we can base our recall estimate on the proportion of A_1 retrieved by a search in the system. The subset A_1 is a group of documents *contained in the data base of the system* and judged to be relevant by the requester but found by methods extraneous to the system to be evaluated. For example, A_1 can be composed of rele-

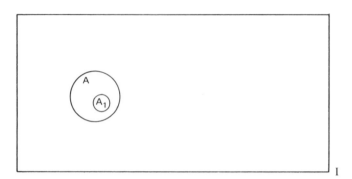

FIGURE 49   Method of estimating recall by extrapolation from "hit rate" for known population, A_1, to "hit rate" for unknown population, A.

vant documents known to the requester at the time he first approaches the system and makes his request. Alternatively, it can be composed of documents found by the evaluator through outside sources (e.g., other information centers or published indexes), submitted to the requester for his assessment, and judged relevant by him. The subset can also be comprised of items partly from the first source and partly from the second. For example, a scientist comes to an information system and makes a subject request, at which time he already knows two relevant items. The evaluator does a parallel search in another source or sources and finds twelve "possibly relevant" items. Of these twelve, eight are judged relevant by the requester. We now have a group of ten documents that we know to be relevant to the request (the two the requester knew originally and the eight found subsequently). Assuming that all ten appear in the data base of the system, we have established a *recall base* of ten relevant items; i.e., the subset A_1. We now check the results of the search actually conducted by the system and find that seven of the ten items were retrieved and three were not. Our recall estimate is, then, $7/10 \times 100$, or 70 percent. If A_1 is a representative sample of A, it is then reasonable to assume that the hit rate (recall ratio) for the entire set A will approximate the hit rate for the subset A_1.

The recall ratio and the precision ratio are very valuable measures of effectiveness, and we can use them as indicators of how the system performs under various conditions or modes of operation. However, the figures do not in themselves explain why the system behaves as it does. To determine the "why," we need to apply a high level of intellectual analysis. Since evaluation is essentially a diagnostic (and eventually therapeutic) procedure, we are particularly concerned with the identification of sources of system failure. The system failures of most interest are the failures to retrieve relevant documents (*recall failures*) and the failures

to screen out irrelevant documents (*precision failures*). Failure analysis is in fact the most important aspect of evaluation because eventually it will suggest ways to improve the system. It involves the examination of documents, indexing records, request statements, search strategies, completed relevance assessment forms, and whatever further information can be obtained from users participating in the study. On the basis of all of these records we determine the precise reasons why various failures occur in the system.

The principal sources of failure will fall within the four major subsystems of a complete retrieval system: the indexing subsystem, the vocabulary subsystem, the searching subsystem, and the user-system interface. These various sources of failure are shown in Figure 3. Although each one is extremely important, this book is about vocabulary control (or lack of it), and we will therefore concentrate on the vocabulary as a source of system failure and the influence of the vocabulary on the performance of a retrieval system.

VOCABULARY FAILURES

Retrieval failures contributed by the system vocabulary are due primarily to: lack of specificity in the vocabulary, or ambiguous and spurious relationships between terms. Lack of specificity is by far the more important. Consider a technical information system including documents on metallurgical engineering. Some of the documents in the collection deal with arc welding using argon as a shielding gas (i.e., with argon arc welding). The vocabulary of the system is not sufficiently specific to allow us, in indexing these documents, to identify this class of documents uniquely. Instead, we must index them under the more general term SHIELDED ARC WELDING. In other words, the class "argon arc welding" is subsumed under the broader class "shielded arc welding" and thus loses its separate identity.

As a result, when we are asked to conduct a search on the precise topic "argon arc welding" we will not be able to retrieve this class of documents as a unique entity; we can only retrieve the broader class of "shielded arc welding" (Figure 50). Clearly, it is unlikely that a search on argon arc welding will achieve a very high precision since not everything in the class "shielded arc welding" is relevant to argon arc welding (other shielding gases may be used). Here the inability of the vocabulary to express the precise concept of the request has led inevitably to precision failures. If the vocabulary is even less specific, and we must use ARC WELDING for all varieties of arc welding, precision will obviously be further reduced.

What effect will this lack of specificity have on the

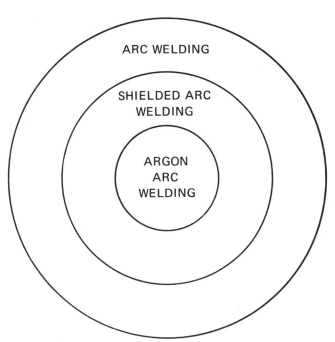

FIGURE 50   Levels of specificity in document classes.

recall ratio of a search on argon arc welding? It need have no deleterious effect, providing indexers and searchers know unequivocally that documents on argon arc welding must always be indexed, and thus found, under the term SHIELDED ARC WELDING. It is extremely important that the vocabulary make this fact explicit to indexers and searchers by means of a *see* or *use* reference, as:

Argon Arc Welding *use*
SHIELDED ARC WELDING

Without such an explicit instruction, different indexers (or even the same indexer on separate occasions) may index documents on argon arc welding in various ways. For example, some documents may be indexed under the even broader heading ARC WELDING (where the indexer did not know that argon arc welding is a form of shielded arc welding), and some may be put under other terms, such as GAS WELDING. Lack of an appropriate reference or signpost will lead to inconsistency in the indexing of this precise topic and the subject matter will become dispersed.

When we begin a search on a subject, and the vocabulary does not tell us explicitly where to look, we may not think of the right term or terms to use. If the indexing has been inconsistent, the searcher may think of some of the headings under which documents have been indexed, but not all, and recall failures will occur.

Lack of specificity will always cause precision failures but need not cause recall failures as long as the

appropriate references are included in the vocabulary. If no specific term exists, and no references are made from it, both recall and precision failures are likely to occur in a search on the specific topic.

The specificity of the vocabulary is the principal factor affecting the precision capabilities of a retrieval system. We can be only as specific in indexing and searching as the language of the system allows us to be.

There is, however, some tendency for a highly specific vocabulary to reduce recall at the same time that it improves precision. The problem is that consistent indexing becomes increasingly difficult the greater the number of terms in the vocabulary and, hence, the finer the shades of meaning that the vocabulary can express. The finer the shades of meaning possible, the more subject expertise may be required of indexers and searchers. For example, all indexers can agree that a particular document deals with welding, but there may be less agreement that it is about arc welding, and even less that it is on shielded arc welding. The nonspecific vocabulary improves indexing consistency and, as far as recall goes, simplifies the searching task. With a broad vocabulary we can be reasonably sure that everything on argon arc welding has been indexed under WELDING. With a highly specific vocabulary we may find that some documents are indexed under ARGON ARC WELDING, some under SHIELDED ARC WELDING (either because the indexer did not recognize the fact that argon was used as a shielding gas or because the document in question discusses several types of shielded arc welding and was indexed at the generic term rather than under the specifics), some under ARC WELDING (where the indexer did not recognize the fact that a shielding gas, namely argon, was involved, or where the indexer did not recognize a synonym for shielded arc welding, e.g., "submerged arc"), and even some under GAS WELDING (on the grounds that argon is a gas). If the searcher sticks rigidly to the term ARGON ARC WELDING he may, in the specific vocabulary system, be missing some relevant documents, both

1. documents on the specific topic that have been incorrectly indexed, and
2. more general documents on shielded arc welding, including some discussion on argon arc welding.

In summary, a highly specific vocabulary will allow high precision but may cause lower recall, while a nonspecific vocabulary is likely to allow high recall but will certainly cause low precision.

The situation is illustrated rather simplistically in Figure 51. A specific vocabulary allows us to place a document into many small classes, enabling us to search on small classes and thus to achieve high pre-

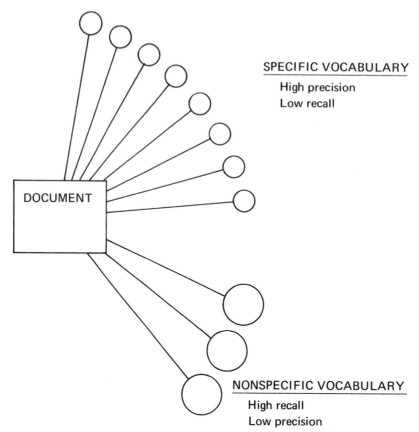

SPECIFIC VOCABULARY

High precision
Low recall

NONSPECIFIC VOCABULARY

High recall
Low precision

FIGURE 51   Relation of specific and nonspecific vocabularies to recall and precision.

cision, but complicating the search when we want to expand to achieve high recall. The nonspecific vocabulary facilitates the generic search and minimizes indexing inaccuracies, thus improving recall, but it lacks the facility for high precision. On the whole, it is better to err on the side of the specific vocabulary. To attain high recall, where this is essential, we can broaden the scope of our search strategies (e.g., by retrieving everything on any type of shielded arc welding or any type of arc welding), thus compensating for indexing inaccuracies and for the fact that more general reports may include discussions on specific aspects. However, we cannot compensate for lack of specificity in order to improve precision. If "argon arc welding" is subsumed under "shielded arc welding" it loses its separate identity, and no search strategy will enable us to retrieve this specific class uniquely.

The second major source of system failure, attributable to the vocabulary, is caused by ambiguous or spurious relationships among terms. There are two distinct types: false coordinations and incorrect term relationships. Both types of failure occur because words, by themselves, lack syntax. Index terms assigned to a document frequently lack syntax, especially if these terms are single words (Uniterms).

The two types of failure are illustrated in the following simple examples.

FALSE COORDINATION

Document Indexing	*Request*
ALUMINUM	Cleaning of aluminum
CLEANING	
COPPER	*Search Strategy*
ULTRASONIC	
WELDING	ALUMINUM *and* CLEANING

INCORRECT TERM RELATIONSHIP

Document Indexing	*Request*
COMPUTERS	Design of computers
DESIGN	
AIRCRAFT	*Search Strategy*
	COMPUTERS *and* DESIGN

In the first example, the document is retrieved in response to a search on cleaning of aluminum, but it turns out to be completely irrelevant to this topic.

In fact, it discusses the fabrication of various electronic components, including the welding of aluminum and the cleaning of copper parts by means of ultrasonics. There is no direct relationship between the index term CLEANING and the index term ALUMINUM. This is a *false coordination:* the two terms causing retrieval are essentially unrelated in the document. Similar false coordinations could occur in response to searches on various other legitimate topics, including "welding of copper" and "ultrasonic welding." Clearly, in a system without syntax, the more index terms assigned the greater the likelihood that false coordination will occur. This type of failure is especially prevalent in Uniterm and natural-language systems. It is less prevalent in systems in which the vocabulary is more pre-coordinate (and hence more specific) and more carefully controlled. False coordination can be avoided by "linking" related terms together and separating these linked terms from others unrelated to them, as discussed in Chapter 15.

The second example is rather different. Here the document is retrieved in response to a request relating to the design of computers. It is not relevant. It deals not with the design of computers but with the design of aircraft using the computer as a tool in the design function. This is an *incorrect term relationship:* the two terms causing retrieval are indeed directly related, but they are not related in the way that the requester (or searcher) wants them related. Again, incorrect term relationships are most prevalent in Uniterm systems. They occur less frequently where more pre-coordinate vocabularies are used. For example, the foregoing precision failure would not have occurred had the more specific index term COMPUTER DESIGN (or AIRCRAFT DESIGN) existed in the vocabulary.

Incorrect term relationships *cannot* be avoided by a simple linking device. In the example given, for instance, both the word COMPUTER and the word DESIGN would appear in the same link since they are directly related. Incorrect term relationships can be avoided by the use of devices that indicate relationships between terms. Such devices include so-called "role indicators" and subheadings. However, this type of device essentially increases the specificity of the vocabulary and makes it possible to express fine shades of meaning. Consequently, indexing consistency is reduced and, while precision is likely to improve, it becomes increasingly difficult to achieve a high recall.

In addition to these direct effects on system performance, the vocabulary will have less direct effects on the indexing and searching functions. The structure of the vocabulary is likely to have a profound effect on the searching operation. The more highly structured, the more relationships displayed, the more

useful the vocabulary will be in the construction of search strategies. If the vocabulary does not bring all related terms together in some way (by hierarchical organization, cross-reference structure, or both), there is a strong possibility that the searcher will not think of all terms relevant to a particular topic, and that search failures will result. For example, in a particular thesaurus, FAILURE is shown to be related to FATIGUE and to have as narrower terms FRACTURE and RUPTURE. However, a search on failure of structural panels might not be completely successful on this group of terms alone. Reports on failure of structural parts will frequently use the terminology "instability" or "stability" rather than "failure." The term STABILITY (which includes "instability") also appears in the vocabulary and has in fact been used in indexing to express the notion of structural stability. The searcher is guided by the thesaurus and uses only FAILURE, FATIGUE, and RUPTURE. Recall failures occur because the searcher was not guided to the term STABILITY.

The vocabulary also exerts a strong influence on the indexing process. Again, the structure of the vocabulary should aid the indexer in the choice of most appropriate terms. The reference or hierarchical structure of the vocabulary is important in this respect. It should lead the indexer who thinks first of ARC WELDING down to subordinate terms such as SHIELDED ARC WELDING and ARGON ARC WELDING, allowing him to choose these more specific descriptors where they are appropriate. Similarly, reverting to an earlier example, an explicitly stated relationship between STABILITY and FATIGUE should aid the indexer in term selection in this area. Term definitions and scope notes are also important in aiding the selection of terms.

The use of *see* or *use* references is particularly valuable in ensuring indexing consistency and accuracy of searching. Such references should be made both from synonymous expressions and from specific terms that are not used as descriptors in the system. If there is no reference from ARGON ARC WELDING to SHIELDED ARC WELDING, there is no guarantee that an indexer will know how to express the specific concept or that a searcher will know where to look for it.

Finally, the vocabulary may have associated with it various auxiliary devices which may refine the indexing and searching functions. An example is the device of *weighting,* which allows indexers to indicate those aspects of a document that are most important or treated in greatest detail. These auxiliary devices will be discussed further in Chapter 15.

In summary, the specificity of the vocabulary is its most important characteristic where retrieval is concerned. Vocabulary specificity directly controls the

level of precision it is possible to attain in searching because it controls the size of the classes into which documents are placed. *The size of the classes defined by a vocabulary is much more important than the arrangement of these classes.* Consider the two displays

presented in Figure 52. Under A is a set of class labels arranged in a hierarchical display, as they would appear in a classification scheme or a classified catalog. Under B is the same set of labels arranged in a strictly alphabetical order, as they would appear in a thesaurus or alphabetical subject catalog. Clearly, both schemes are identical in the specificity with which they can index the literature on vision disorders. Providing system B supplies references showing BT-NT-RT relationships to help indexers and searchers choose the most appropriate terms, both systems will offer identical retrieval capabilities; that is, both can obtain the same recall and precision figures for a particular set of requests. The fact that the two systems arrange the classes, or their labels, in different sequences is comparatively unimportant.

```
A                        B

VISION DISORDERS         AMBLYOPIA
                         ANISEIKONIA
   AMBLYOPIA             ASTIGMATISM
   BLINDNESS             BLINDNESS
   COLOR BLINDNESS       COLOR BLINDNESS
   DIPLOPIA              DIPLOPIA
   HEMERALOPIA           HEMERALOPIA
   HEMIANOPSIA           HEMIANOPSIA
   NYCTALOPIA            HYPEROPIA
   REFRACTIVE ERRORS     MYOPIA
      ANISEIKONIA        NYCTALOPIA
      ASTIGMATISM        PRESBYOPIA
      HYPEROPIA          REFRACTIVE ERRORS
      MYOPIA             SCOTOMA
      PRESBYOPIA         SNOWBLINDNESS
   SCOTOMA               STRABISMUS
   SNOWBLINDNESS
   STRABISMUS
```

FIGURE 52 The same set of class labels arranged in a classified sequence (left) and alphabetically (right).

REFERENCES

1. Lancaster, F. W. *Evaluation of the MEDLARS Demand Search Service.* Bethesda, Md.: National Library of Medicine, 1968.
2. Lancaster, F. W. *Information Retrieval Systems: Characteristics, Testing, and Evaluation.* New York: Wiley, 1968.
3. Shumway, R. H. "Some Estimation Problems Associated with Evaluating Information Retrieval Systems." In *Evaluation of Document Retrieval Systems: Literature Perspective, Measurement, Technical Papers.* Bethesda, Md.: Westat Research, Inc., 1968, 78-96.

14 *Characteristics and Components of an Index Language: The Vocabulary*

So far in this book, we have used various words rather loosely, including the expressions "vocabulary," "term," and "index language." Now we need to tighten up our definitions of some of these expressions. It is well known that a language of any kind will have as its components:

1. A vocabulary (i.e., a set of terms).
2. A syntax (i.e., grammatical structure).
3. Rules for use of the language and for controlling changes in it.

An index language also includes these three components. We have already spoken at various times of rules for using an index language (e.g., how notational elements are to be synthesized in a faceted classification) and methods for effecting changes.

TYPES OF TERMS

We have also spoken of the "vocabulary" and indicated that this vocabulary is composed of terms that we have loosely referred to as "index terms." These terms are essentially "labels" assigned to document classes. However, it is important to distinguish three types of terms or labels in an index language. For these various types I now prefer the terminology:

1. Descriptors
2. Specifiers
3. Entry terms

This represents a change in terminology over that used previously. In my earlier writings I used "code terms," "index terms," and "entry terms," but this terminology proved confusing. The distinction among these three categories is not generally made. However, it is an important distinction, worth clarifying.

The terms an indexer assigns to a document to describe its subject matter may conveniently be referred to as *descriptors*. Descriptors may be of various kinds: generic, specific, single-word, or multiword. These descriptors are also used, in various combinations, to conduct searches in the system. The descriptors are the working terms of the vocabulary: they are used by indexers and searchers, and they are the terms to which document numbers, or document surrogates, are posted.

By using a single descriptor, we can uniquely identify (*specify*) a particular document class. The descriptor ARC WELDING, for instance, uniquely identifies the class of documents dealing with arc welding and distinguishes this class from all other classes in the system. In other words, it is possible to retrieve the class of documents dealing with arc welding precisely and not as part of some larger class. All descriptors are also *specifiers* (i.e., labels that uniquely specify a particular document class).

However, in a post-coordinate retrieval system, we will usually have many more specifiers than descriptors. The reason is that, if we use the vocabulary

115

intelligently, we should be able to identify document classes uniquely by means of various combinations of descriptors. For example, we could say that the class of documents dealing with argon arc welding is uniquely identified (specified) by the joint use of the descriptor ARGON and the descriptor SHIELDED ARC WELDING. If we record this decision in our vocabulary as

Argon arc welding *use* ARGON and SHIELDED ARC WELDING,

we are providing the capability for the unique identification of the class and, therefore, the ability to retrieve it uniquely. "Argon arc welding," then, is also a specifier because, even though there is no descriptor ARGON ARC WELDING, we have provided a unique label composed, in this case, of two separate descriptors.

Suppose that, instead, we decide not to define uniquely the class of documents dealing with argon arc welding but to subsume it under the broader class "shielded arc welding." This decision should be recorded in the vocabulary in the form: Argon arc welding *use* SHIELDED ARC WELDING. Clearly, in this case, "argon arc welding" is not a descriptor since it is not one of the working terms of the vocabulary. Nor is it a specifier, because the class of documents is not uniquely identified in the system. It is merely an *entry term* (i.e., a term appearing in the vocabulary and providing some type of entry into the system).

All specifiers will be entry terms and some of these will also be descriptors. All descriptors are also entry terms (referring, if you like, to themselves). But not all entry terms are specifiers or descriptors. In a well-constructed, post-coordinate retrieval system, there will be many more entry terms than specifiers and many more specifiers than descriptors.

Why is it important to maintain these distinctions? It is important because we should understand the composition of a complete index language, the functions that these various terms play, and their effects on the retrieval process.

The size of the descriptor vocabulary (i.e., the working terms assigned by indexers and used by searchers) bears no direct relationship to the specificity that it is possible to achieve in a system, but the size of the specifier vocabulary does. That is, the specificity of the vocabulary, and thus the precision capabilities of the system, is dependent upon the number of classes that the vocabulary can uniquely identify (i.e., the number of specifiers) rather than the number of descriptors available to the indexers and searchers.

Consider a pre-coordinate retrieval system based on 5,000 subject headings. In this system the size of the descriptor vocabulary and the size of the specifier

vocabulary are identical. We cannot combine terms to make more specific labels so that the size of the specifier vocabulary is exactly 5,000. Put another way, the vocabulary can uniquely identify 5,000 classes and 5,000 classes only. The size of the entry vocabulary will likely be much greater because it will include additional specific terms that are referred to the 5,000 subject headings by means of *see* references.

We may be able to reduce these 5,000 subject headings to a smaller number of less pre-coordinate descriptors suitable for use in a post-coordinate retrieval system. For example, we split the heading AIRCRAFT ENGINE NOISE into two separate descriptors, AIRCRAFT ENGINES and NOISE, including a reference in our vocabulary in the form:

Aircraft engine noise *use* AIRCRAFT ENGINES *and* NOISE

If we want to go further we might split the headings into simple Uniterms, as:

Aircraft engine noise *use* AIRCRAFT *and* ENGINES *and* NOISE

By doing this we are not reducing the number of specifiers in our vocabulary. The concept of "aircraft engine noise" is uniquely identified in all three systems: in one by a single subject heading, in the second by two descriptors, and in the third by three single-word descriptors. (Of course, although we have this theoretical capability for unique identification, false coordinations may well occur in the post-coordinate systems whereas they would not in the pre-coordinate). Since AIRCRAFT ENGINES, NOISE, AIRCRAFT, and ENGINES are all expressions that are likely to occur in many of the original 5,000 subject headings, by reducing the amount of pre-coordination in this way we are actually reducing the number of descriptors in the vocabulary without reducing the number of specifiers. The 5,000 classes that we are able to identify uniquely by 5,000 descriptors in the first vocabulary, we may be able to identify uniquely by, say, 2,000 descriptors in the second vocabulary, and by perhaps 1,000 descriptors (single-word) in the third. This was the pattern observed when the subject heading list (pre-coordinate) of the Armed Services Technical Information Agency was dissected to form descriptors for post-coordinate retrieval application (the first *Thesaurus of ASTIA Descriptors*). In this case 70,000 subject headings were reduced to about 7,000 eventual descriptors.

In analyzing and comparing various vocabularies we should be careful to distinguish the descriptor vocabulary from the specifier vocabulary. If system A uses 15,000 *terms* and system B, 5,000 *terms*, it would not necessarily be correct to assume that A can achieve greater specificity, and thus precision, than B. Before

we can make such an assumption we need to know what types of terms we are dealing with. If A contains 15,000 *specifiers* and B, 5,000 *specifiers,* it would be correct to say that A can uniquely identify 15,000 classes whereas B can uniquely identify only 5,000. Therefore, A has greater specificity and will allow greater search precision, on the average, than B (assuming that both systems are in the same subject field).

It is possible to operate an information retrieval system with quite a small vocabulary of descriptors. The record is probably that set by Whelan [4] at the Royal Radar Establishment in England. Whelan claimed to operate a retrieval system using a vocabulary of about 75 broad concept groups; for example:

    2 ADD (gain, superimpose, sum, application, join, towards)
    28 GENERATE (excitation, construct, make, produce, prepare, design)
    41 MICRO (miniature, small, narrow)
    73 STAR (solar flares, prominences, ellipse, meteors, sun)

These conceptual groups are so fundamental, Whelan claims, it is possible to identify a large number of classes using various unique combinations of the basic groups.

THE ENTRY VOCABULARY

We have already pointed out that all descriptors and all specifiers may be regarded as entry terms but that not all entry terms are necessarily specifiers or descriptors. The entry vocabulary has an extremely important part to play in the complete index language. Consider again the example displayed in Figure 50. If we do not uniquely identify the class "argon arc welding" (e.g., by the descriptor ARGON ARC WELDING or by the joint use of the descriptors ARGON and SHIELDED ARC WELDING), we cannot obtain high precision in a search on this specific topic. Recall, however, need not be affected (as pointed out in Chapter 13) *providing the specific term is included in the entry vocabulary* with appropriate instructions as to how the class is to be treated:

Argon arc welding *use* SHIELDED ARC WELDING

What will happen if the specific term is not put into the entry vocabulary? First, inconsistencies in indexing are likely to occur. Whenever a document on "argon arc welding" is encountered, the indexer must decide how it is to be treated. In a large system involving many indexers we cannot be certain that all indexers will put it in the same place, much less in the

best place (i.e., under the most immediately generic descriptor or descriptors). Thus, related material becomes dispersed for want of an appropriate entry term.

Lack of an adequate entry vocabulary is likely to have a significant effect on the performance of searches conducted in a retrieval system. When we undertake a search on argon arc welding, where are we going to look? The entry vocabulary does not include the specific term, so again we must determine where the topic is likely to have been indexed. Perhaps we will hit upon SHIELDED ARC WELDING, but perhaps we will be misled (or ignorant) and search under ARC WELDING, GAS WELDING, or some other term too general or not directly related. Even if we use SHIELDED ARC WELDING we may not get a high recall because lack of an entry term has caused various indexers to treat the subject differently.

In my evaluation of MEDLARS,[3] I discovered many instances in which lack of an adequate entry vocabulary led to indexing inconsistencies and eventually to recall failures in searching. One classic example was a search on "premature rupture of the fetal membranes," a not-too-exotic medical phenomenon which, nevertheless, did not appear in the MEDLARS entry vocabulary. Consequently, documents on this subject were indexed under various term combinations, including:

FETAL MEMBRANES *and* RUPTURE
FETAL MEMBRANES *and* RUPTURE, SPONTANEOUS
FETAL MEMBRANES *and* LABOR COMPLICATIONS
FETAL MEMBRANES *and* PREGNANCY COMPLICATIONS
FETAL MEMBRANES *and* LABOR, PREMATURE

The searcher hit upon some of these combinations, but not all, and recall in the search was reduced accordingly, a failure readily avoidable with a simple entry term.

Results of the MEDLARS study also served to indicate that lack of suitable entry terms may occasionally lead to indexing errors of omission. For example, an indexer is faced with a medical case study, one aspect of which is the premature rupture of the fetal membranes. He is, I feel, more likely to omit this aspect of the document if he is not sure how to index it, whereas he is more likely to include it if the entry vocabulary tells him unequivocally how to treat it.

The entry vocabulary serves another useful function. It at least indicates that documents on a particular topic exist in the system, even if we cannot retrieve the class uniquely. The reference

Argon arc welding *use* ARC WELDING

shows that there are documents relevant to the specific

topic in the data base and tells us where to look for them. It also informs us that our search is likely to have a rather low precision. Nevertheless, the entry should at least encourage us in our search. Without it we have no guarantee that there are any documents on the specific topic in the system being interrogated. We may therefore abandon our search unnecessarily.

Finally, the entry vocabulary, if conscientiously and fully developed over a period of time, should reduce the intellectual burden on the indexing staff. This may allow us to use indexers with less training and experience or it may speed up the indexing process, allowing us to index more documents with the same level of manpower. In the early months of operation of a retrieval system, virtually all of the indexing will involve fairly high-level intellectual decisions. The indexer must decide which particular combinations of descriptors best represent a particular item of subject matter. For example, in an aerodynamics collection the indexer may encounter documents on Poiseuille flow and on Prandtl-Meyer flow. No specific descriptors for these concepts occur in the controlled vocabulary of the system so he must represent each with one or more existing descriptors. This requires a certain amount of research on his part; at least he needs to consult a glossary or textbook to find out what is involved in these flow phenomena. Eventually he decides that Poiseuille flow should be indexed under LAMINAR FLOW and PIPE FLOW and that Prandtl-Meyer flow should be indexed under SUPERSONIC FLOW and EXPANSION FLOW. He records his decisions in the system entry vocabulary in the form:

> Poiseuille flow *use* LAMINAR FLOW *and* PIPE FLOW
> Prandtl-Meyer flow *use* SUPERSONIC FLOW *and* EXPANSION FLOW

The next time that a document on one of these phenomena appears for indexing, the decision about how to treat it will have already been made. The intellectual burden on the indexer is reduced — he need only follow the precedent already established.

As the entry vocabulary is developed, the intellectual effort of indexing is reduced. Once a well-established entry vocabulary exists it is possible to reduce the personnel level at which indexing is conducted. As an alternative, if the same personnel level is maintained, we can expect the availability of the entry vocabulary to reduce the amount of time needed for the indexing operation. The entry vocabulary, therefore, has important implications for the cost-effectiveness of a retrieval system. Carried to its logical end, the *translation* phase of indexing (as opposed to the conceptual analysis stage — deciding what a document is about) becomes a mechanical operation. If we recog-

nize that a document is about Prandtl-Meyer flow, the entry vocabulary tells us exactly how this concept is to be translated into system descriptors. If the entry vocabulary is recorded in machine-readable form, the translation into system descriptors can be effected automatically by a computer. We will return to this later.

Rather surprisingly, Angell [1] has produced a paper in which he criticizes certain systems for including what he calls "specific to general *see* references." By a "specific to general *see* reference" he means an entry term pure and simple, as in the example, Argon arc welding *use* SHIELDED ARC WELDING. He feels that it is misleading to direct a user to a class that is not uniquely defined in the system. This is an extremely misguided notion, for the several reasons explained, born of lack of direct experience with, and appreciation of, large machine-based retrieval systems and the problems associated with such systems.

For some further clarification of the three types of terms, examine the specimen page from the *FAA Thesaurus of Technical Descriptors* presented in Figure 53. Notice the descriptors on this page; they include HELIUM GROUP GASES, HELMETS, HEMATOLOGY, and HEMISPHERICAL SHELLS. These are also specifiers. The label HIGH-ALTITUDE FLIGHT is another specifier because the class "high-altitude flight" is uniquely identified by the descriptors FLIGHT and HIGH-ALTITUDE. There are many terms on this page that are simply entry terms. For example, HEMOCHROMATOSIS, which is referred to the much broader descriptor METABOLISM DISORDERS, and HEPATIC DUCTS, which is referred to the broader BILIARY SYSTEM.

In a manual system, such as peek-a-boo, the size of the descriptor vocabulary may become rather critical because the number of aspect cards increases with the size of this vocabulary. This adds to costs and increases the size of the file, making searching more cumbersome. Blagden [2] has described a number of possible methods of reducing vocabulary in such a system:

1. By grouping of synonyms and near-synonyms.
2. By grouping of homonyms, even when the meaning of these is completely different.*
3. By breaking terms into linguistic parts (splitting or fragmentation); e.g., DEFORMING *use* DE *and* FORMING.
4. By splitting into "meaningful constituents"; e.g., HOT into HIGH + TEMPERATURE. This is really semantic factoring.
5. By splitting of chemical compounds; e.g., TETRA + ETHYL + LEAD.

---

* This is justifiable because the terms are placed in context when coordinated with others. For example, STRIKE and RAILROADS obviously refers to a labor strike, whereas STRIKE and BEDOUIN most probably refers to a strike force.

Specific to:
  HELIUM GROUP GASES
  NON-METALS

HELIUM GROUP GASES
  (Chemical Compounds)
  Includes:
    Inert gases
    Rare gases
  Specific to:
    NON-METALS
  Generic to:
    ARGON
    HELIUM
    NEON

HELMETS
  (General Services & Supplies)
  Includes:
    Visors
  Specific to:
    ARMOR

HEMATOLOGY
  (Hematology)
  Includes:
    Blood chemistry

Heme
  use HEMOGLOBIN

Hemin
  use HEMOGLOBIN

HEMISPHERICAL SHELLS
  (Geometric Forms)
  Specific to:
    BODIES OF REVOLUTION
    GEOMETRIC FORMS
    STRUCTURAL SHELLS
  Also see:
    CONICAL BODIES
    CURVED PROFILES
    PARABOLIC BODIES
    SPHERES

Hemochromatosis
  use METABOLISM DISORDERS

Hemocyanin
  use CHROMOPROTEINS

HEMOGLOBIN
  (Proteins)
  Includes:
    Heme
    Hemin
    Hemosiderin
    Myoglobin
  Specific to:
    BLOOD PROTEINS
    CHROMOPROTEINS
    ORGANIC PIGMENTS
    PROTEINS
    PROTEINS (CONJUGATED)
  Also see:
    BLOOD CELLS

Hemolymph
  use BLOOD

Hemophilia
  use BLOOD DISORDERS

Hemopoiesis
  use HEMOPOIETIC SYSTEM

HEMOPOIETIC SYSTEM
  (Anatomy)
  Includes:
    Blood forming organs
    Hemopoiesis
  Generic to:
    BONE MARROW
    SPLEEN
  Also see:
    BLOOD
    RETICULOENDOTHELIAL SYSTEM

Hemorrhagic shock
  use SHOCK (PATHOLOGY)

Hemosiderin
  use HEMOGLOBIN

Hepatic ducts
  use BILIARY SYSTEM

Herbst's corpuscles
  use END ORGANS

Heredity
  use GENETICS

Hermite functions
  use SPECIAL FUNCTIONS (MATHEMATICAL)

Hermite transforms
  use INTEGRAL TRANSFORMS

Hermitian forms
  use MATRIX ALGEBRA

HEXOSES
  (Carbohydrates)
  Specific to:
    CARBOHYDRATES
    MONOSACCHARIDES
  Generic to:
    GLUCOSE

Hierarchal models
  use STATISTICAL ANALYSIS

HIGH FREQUENCY
  (Frequency)
  (3 to 30 mc.)
  Specific to:
    FREQUENCY
    RADIOFREQUENCY

High octane gasoline
  use AVIATION FUELS

HIGH-ALTITUDE
  (Modifiers)
  (Over 15,000 feet.)

High-altitude flight
  use FLIGHT
  and HIGH-ALTITUDE

FIGURE 53 Page from the *FAA Thesaurus of Technical Descriptors,* illustrating the use of descriptors, specifiers, and entry terms.

Some of these are decidedly dangerous, however. For example, a searcher for articles on "lead" is not likely to be interested in tetraethyl lead.

We may summarize the salient points in this discussion on the component vocabularies of a complete index language as follows:

1. The size of the *descriptor* vocabulary bears no direct relationship to the specificity of the vocabulary.

2. The number of *specifiers* (classes uniquely defined) directly controls specificity and thus the precision capabilities of the system.

3. If we do not define a class uniquely, we cannot obtain high precision in a search relating to this specific class.

4. Even if we choose not to define a particular class uniquely, the name of this class should appear in the *entry vocabulary* with a reference to the more generic descriptor (descriptors) that is (are) to be used for it. Without this, indexing inconsistencies and hence recall failures are likely to occur.

5. All the terms in the vocabulary may be regarded as entry terms. Some of these terms are also specifiers and some are also descriptors. The entry vocabulary in a post-coordinate system is larger than the specifier vocabulary, and this is larger than the descriptor vocabulary.

Before leaving the subject of vocabulary we should mention the "identifier." The identifier is usually a name of something—an aircraft, a ship, or possibly a personal name or trade name. If identifiers of this type are important as retrieval handles we may allow our indexers to assign them to documents. However, because of the volume of potential identifiers, we may attempt no control over them. Certainly we do not list them all in our controlled vocabulary. In some systems a separate identifier file, with associated document numbers, is maintained. This avoids increasing the bulk of the major search file with a great many unique terms which are searched very infrequently. Where necessary, a search that involves matching of postings between terms in both files is conducted. In a medical collection, trade names of drugs might be good candidates for inclusion in an identifier file. Sometimes identifiers are regarded as provisional descriptors. They may be added to the thesaurus at a later date if volume of use warrants it.*

A possible way of handling identifiers in a peek-a-boo system is to represent each identifier by a unique trigraph. The identifier file consists of 26 cards, one for each letter of the alphabet. Each identifier is given a unique trigraph. For example, "Peter Jones" may be represented by AQL. A search on this identifier will involve the comparison of postings on the A card, the Q card, and the L card.

---

* Identifiers are sometimes referred to as "open-ended terms."

REFERENCES

1. Angell, R. S. *The Specific-to-General See Reference in Thesaurus Construction.* FID/CR Report No. 8. Copenhagen: Danish Centre for Documentation, 1968.

2. Blagden, J. F. "How Much Noise in a Role-Free and Link-Free Coordinate Indexing System?" *Journal of Documentation* 22 (1966): 203-209.

3. Lancaster, F. W. *Evaluation of the MEDLARS Demand Search Service.* Bethesda, Md.: National Library of Medicine, 1968.

4. Whelan, S. "Library Retrieval." *Royal Radar Establishment Journal.* (October, 1958): 59-68.

15 Characteristics and Components of an Index Language: Auxiliary Devices

In addition to the actual terms, a complete index language may include certain devices which can be used with the terms themselves to achieve various results. These devices may conveniently be referred to as "index-language devices." Essentially, they may be divided into two groups:

1. Devices that group terms together into classes of one type or another. Such devices will reduce the size of the specifier vocabulary and will allow improvements in recall. We will call them *recall devices*.

2. Devices that, when used in association with terms, increase the shades of meaning it is possible to express. These devices increase the number of specifiers in the vocabulary and allow improvements in precision. We will call them *precision devices*.

The most important of these index-language devices are the following:

Recall Devices	*Precision Devices*
Control of synonyms	Coordination (including pre-coordination)
Control of quasi-synonyms	
Control of word forms	Linking of terms
Hierarchical grouping	Relational indicators
Grouping by statistical association	Term weighting

We may conveniently regard these various devices as forming the syntax of the index language, although not all the devices are syntactical in the strict sense of the term. As a point of departure, let us consider a very primitive system. It involves the indexing of documents by means of single words (Uniterms) only and allows us to search on single words only, with no ability to combine terms. Such a system has a vocabulary only; it does not have any index-language devices; and it offers extremely limited retrieval capabilities. We have little possibility, except simple word substitution, for varying a search strategy in order to improve recall or to improve precision.

SYNONYM CONTROL

If we want to refine the system, perhaps the first thing we should do is to control synonyms. In actual fact, there are very few true synonyms in the English language, apart from abbreviations and acronyms. If we control a true synonym by choosing one version and referring from the other (e.g., VTOL *use* VERTICAL TAKE-OFF PLANES), we tend to improve recall, since we avoid separation of identical documents and provide the possibility of retrieval by whichever synonym springs to the mind of the searcher.

When we speak of synonym control in information retrieval, however, we usually mean *near-synonyms* (i.e., terms that, while not completely synonymous, are sufficiently close that we feel the distinction is not worth making within the confines of a particular retrieval system). We control a near-synonym in the

121

same way that we control a true synonym, by choosing one version and referring from the other. Again, this device tends to improve recall. As an illustration, we may decide that the terms EVAPORATION and VAPORIZATION are conceptually so close that, in our particular retrieval environment, the distinction is not worth making. We decide, therefore, to use EVAPORATION and to refer from VAPORIZATION. By so doing we:

1. Reduce the number of specifiers in the vocabulary. Previously there were two separate terms, with a fine distinction between them. Now there is only one.

2. Form a larger class which we can call "evaporation and vaporization."

The net result is a probable improvement in recall. If the terms were not controlled in this way a searcher might use one but not the other. Since the two terms are closely related conceptually this might well mean a loss of some relevant documents. On the other hand, we must realize that by combining these near-synonyms we have lost the ability to make a certain fine distinction. In certain searches, then, precision is likely to be reduced by this conflation. For example, in the *FAA Thesaurus of Technical Descriptors* the distinction between evaporation and vaporization is maintained, the term VAPORIZATION being reserved for discussions of intentional production of vapor (e.g., industrial processes). Certain searchers may want to maintain this distinction. Control of near-synonyms, therefore, will tend to improve recall but will also tend to reduce precision. A very complete discussion of the synonym problem is provided by Sparck Jones.[25]

Exactly the same thing is true of the control of quasi-synonyms. Quasi-synonyms include words that represent opposite extremes on a descriptive continuum (e.g., "stability" and "instability," "roughness" and "smoothness"), and words that are, to all intents and purposes, equivalent in a particular context but not in other contexts (e.g., in aerodynamics, the expressions "supersonic flight," "supersonic flow," and "supersonic speed" are essentially equivalent, indicating a phenomenon taking place above a speed of Mach 1, although "flow," "flight," and "speed" are not synonymous terms in nonaerodynamic contexts).

WORD ENDINGS

In Uniterm systems and in computer systems based on search of natural-language text (see Chapter 16), it is customary to reduce words to root form, using the root only as a descriptor in the vocabulary. We can call this process "control of word endings." Salton[21] refers to the process as "stem-suffix cutoff." The justifi-

cation for this procedure is that words derived from the same etymological root are semantically related; in fact, the various endings (suffixes) represent various facets of the root concept. As an example, the words "weld," "welds," "welding," "welded," "weldable," "weldability," and "welder" may all be reduced to the root "weld," which becomes a descriptor in the vocabulary. When we conduct a search on the root descriptor WELD, we are dropping the distinctions among the various parts of speech and essentially looking for all possible aspects of the basic notion. We would expect this, on the whole, to improve recall since a searcher seeking information on the *process* of welding as applied to titanium, for instance, might well be interested in a document discussing the *property* of weldability of titanium, or in one which discussed welded titanium *products*. As with synonym control, however, we are losing a fine gradation of meaning when we confound word endings in this way. In some searches we may lose a valid distinction that it is important to make. Someone seeking reports on vacuum melting of steels, for instance, would probably not want to retrieve all reports discussing properties and applications of steels that happen to have been vacuum melted. Dropping of word endings, like control of synonyms, will tend to improve recall, but at the same time to reduce precision.

HIERARCHICAL STRUCTURE

The most obvious recall device is that of hierarchical grouping of terms. As already pointed out, it is possible to impose a hierarchical structure on a vocabulary by means of a formal classificatory organization (overt classification) or through an appropriate network of cross-references (covert classification). If the hierarchical relationships are carefully derived and displayed, the same end results can be obtained from either method. Consider the following partial hierarchy.*

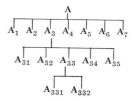

This hierarchical structure guides us in the conduct of searches in the system. We may begin with a highly specific term, A_{331}, and find that this alone does not

---

* In actual practice most hierarchies in information retrieval systems are not pure tree structures, but term networks.

give us an adequate recall. Following the hierarchy we may go up to the parent term, A_{33}, and conduct a generic search on this larger class (i.e., A_{33} and all its subdivisions), which we can expect to yield a higher recall but a reduced precision. If we still must have a greater recall in the search we may decide to go up one further level in the hierarchy and to conduct a generic search on A_3 and all its subdivisions. In this case we are using the hierarchy of the vocabulary to facilitate searching of increasingly larger document classes. To improve recall we might, to use one of our earlier examples, move up from ARGON ARC WELDING to SHIELDED ARC WELDING to ARC WELDING.

We regard hierarchical structure as primarily a recall device because it groups classes together and forms them into larger classes. In practical application we can use the hierarchical structure to guide us in the progressive narrowing of a search; that is, we may first think of the term A_3, but be led down from this to A_{33}, and eventually to A_{331}, which we recognize as representing the precise topic of our interest. If we are really interested in A_{331}, the refinement of our search from all of A_3 to A_{33} and then to A_{331} will progressively improve our precision but reduce our recall.

STATISTICAL ASSOCIATION

In a computer-based system we can group terms together, and thus form broader classes, in ways that it would be virtually impossible to implement in a nonmechanized system. In particular, we can use the statistical characteristics of terms as a basis for class-forming operations. For example, we can say that technical term B is related in some way to technical term Q if, in a particular corpus of documents, whenever the term B occurs in a document, Q also frequently occurs. This type of statistical association between terms can be used to derive classes that may be useful for retrieval purposes. The process is sometimes referred to as "clumping" or "clustering" of terms. We will discuss it in greater detail in later chapters.

COORDINATION

We now need to consider the precision devices of an index language. The most potent precision device is the obvious one of term coordination. By the logical intersection of classes, we reduce their size, achieve greater specificity, and improve precision. If we begin with term A, and then coordinate this term with term

P, we are reducing the size of the class under consideration ("A in relation to P" rather than "A alone"). Classes may be coordinated at the time of indexing (pre-coordinate vocabulary) or at the time of searching (post-coordinate). Class coordination is a very powerful precision device, but it tends to have the effect of reducing recall. Consider a search on the topic of "renal amyloidosis as a complication of tuberculosis." This has three facets: kidney, amyloidosis, and tuberculosis. To achieve high precision in a post-coordinate system we need to include all three facets in an *and* relationship in our search strategy, as:

AMYLOIDOSIS *and* TUBERCULOSIS *and* any term in the vocabulary that indicates kidney involvement.

In other words, we are coordinating three conceptual classes. Although precision in this search is likely to be high, recall could well be low because we are not compensating for the possibility of less than perfect indexing. In some of the relevant documents, for example, the indexer may have omitted a term indicating kidney involvement. We miss these with our stringent (*exhaustive*) search strategy, but we could retrieve them if we searched at a lower coordination level (reduced *exhaustivity*); i.e., AMYLOIDOSIS *and* TUBERCULOSIS. Of course, while recall improves, precision will be reduced, because not everything indexed under these two search terms will relate to kidney involvement. All index languages must provide some facility for the coordination of classes, either at the time of indexing (e.g., through notational synthesis) or at the time of searching. In many modern systems we find a partly pre-coordinate vocabulary which can be further coordinated in searching operations.

LINKS

In an earlier chapter we mentioned the possibility of false coordinations occurring in post-coordinate retrieval systems. False coordinations can be avoided by the use of a linking device, which ties together related terms and separates terms that are not related. Consider again the example of the document indexed as follows:

ALUMINUM

CLEANING

COPPER

ULTRASONICS

WELDING

Among other things, it might possibly deal with the welding of aluminum and the cleaning of copper by means of ultrasonics. Unless steps are taken to avoid it,

false coordination between terms will occur in response to all of the following simple search strategies:

ALUMINUM *and* COPPER (searcher looking for an aluminum-copper alloy or the coating of one metal on a substrate of the other)
ALUMINUM *and* ULTRASONICS
ALUMINUM *and* CLEANING
COPPER *and* WELDING

This type of false coordination can be avoided by the simple device of a *link*. In the example

ALUMINUM	A
CLEANING	B
COPPER	B
ULTRASONICS	B
WELDING	A

we have used a letter code to group together the terms that are related and to separate them from terms that are not related. For a document to be retrieved in such a system, it must not only contain the terms searched upon but must contain them in the same link. Each of the four false coordinations previously discussed would be avoided in a system using links.

Cleverdon et al.[5] have used the term "interlocking" to describe the general concept of linking terms together in this way. They recognize two possible levels of interlocking: the theme level and the word level. Most technical documents do not deal with a single topic but with several topics, although these topics may be very closely related. If we analyze a document conceptually we can determine that it deals with several distinct themes. Take the following hypothetical example, in which a document has been divided into four distinct themes:

1. Sweptback wing—supersonic flow—low angle of attack—drag
2. Delta wing—transonic flow—high angle of attack—drag
3. Low aspect ratio wing—transonic flow—high angle of attack—drag
4. Tail—supersonic flow—flutter

Without some linking device in the vocabulary there are several possibilities for false coordinations between words in various themes (e.g., "tail" and "transonic flow"). These can be corrected by linking together all the words in a particular theme. This level of linking is referred to as *partitioning* (whereby a document is partitioned into various distinct themes). But there is still a possibility of false coordinations (in Uniterm systems at least) within themes. For example, the adjective "low" must be shown to govern "aspect ratio," and the adjective "high" to govern "angle of attack,"

otherwise two false coordinations are possible. An intratheme linking device can also be used for greater indexing and searching accuracy, if this is considered desirable. Cleverdon calls this level of linking "interfixing."

At the American Petroleum Institute, the facets that were derived in the formation of a thesaurus are also used as the basis of term linking.[19] Terms are linked together only when certain relationships obtain:

1. Common attribute terms must be linked to other facets that they modify.
2. Terms from the Structure facet must be linked to the material they describe.
3. Terms from the *By Use* and *By Composition* subdivisions of the Material facet must be linked when used to describe the same substance; e.g., PARAFFIN WAX is linked to COATING when indexing a PARAFFIN WAX COATING.

ROLE INDICATORS

Linking devices, whatever they are called, merely link terms together and indicate that a relationship exists between them; they do not indicate the *type* of relationship. Links do not, therefore, solve the problem of *incorrect term relationships*. In the example of the three terms DESIGN, COMPUTERS, and AIRCRAFT, where we wish to distinguish "design of computers" from "design by means of computers," a simple linking device will not suffice, because all three terms are related and all three should appear in the same link. To solve this type of syntactic problem we need a device capable of indicating the precise relationship between terms.

Before examining such devices we should recognize the fact that there are two fundamental kinds of relationships between terms that are important for retrieval purposes. Consider the two groups of relationships displayed in the following table.

ALUMINUM

Related to	*Related to*
METALS	PANS
LIGHT METALS	WELDING
MAGNESIUM	COATING
ALUMINUM-	EXPORT
COPPER ALLOY	POISONING

The relationships on the left are permanent relationships that the concept "aluminum" bears. It is permanently related, as a species, to metals and to light metals, as a genus to aluminum-copper alloy, and as a sibling to magnesium. These are true genus-species relations and they are independent of particular docu-

ment collections. The group of concepts on the right bears only a transient relationship to aluminum. A pan *may* be made of aluminum; aluminum *may* be welded, coated, or exported; or it *may* cause poisoning. These are not permanent relationships. This type of relationship varies with the characteristics of the document collection: aluminum may be related to poisoning in a medical retrieval system but not so related in a collection on foreign trade. Gardin [9] calls the first set of relations *paradigms* and the second set *syntagmas*. In an information retrieval system the paradigmatic relationship is taken care of by the hierarchical structure of the index language. This type of relationship is usually relatively unambiguous. The syntagmatic relationship, however, is not displayed in the hierarchical structure, and it is frequently ambiguous in a post-coordinate retrieval system (aluminum can be used as a coating or it can itself be coated; computers can be designed or they can be used in design). When we speak of "incorrect term relationships" as a cause of retrieval failures we are referring to ambiguities in the syntagmatic relationships between terms.

Let us return to the simple example involving the terms COMPUTERS, DESIGN, and AIRCRAFT. One way to resolve this ambiguity in a post-coordinate system is by the use of *roles* or *role indicators*. A role indicator is a symbol added to a descriptor in order to indicate the relationship the descriptor bears to the other descriptors used in indexing a particular document. The role is a true syntactical device, and we can make up our own set of roles to solve the problems arising in our particular document collection. For example, to solve the "computer design" problem we need only two roles. Let 4 represent the role "object of action, patient, recipient," and let 2 represent the role "tool, agent, means of accomplishment." When we index the document on design of aircraft using computers, we assign descriptors and roles as follows:

DESIGN
AIRCRAFT (4)
COMPUTERS (2)

But when we search the collection for documents on design of computers we use the strategy

COMPUTERS (4) *and* DESIGN

Although the strategy matches the irrelevant document at the term level, it does not match it at the term-role level; the irrelevant citation is thus correctly rejected. The same simple role pair will also solve the "aluminum coating" problem: ALUMINUM (4) *and* COATING signifies "coating of aluminum," whereas ALUMINUM (2) *and* COATING signifies "coating with aluminum."

Systems of role indicators presently used in the United States have their origins in work carried out in the late fifties by Whaley [27] at the Linde Company; Perry et al. [20] at Western Reserve University (WRU); Andrews and Newman [2] at the U.S. Patent Office; and Costello and Wall [6] at Du Pont. A great impetus to the more general use of roles was given by the publication of the *Chemical Engineering Thesaurus* in 1961, and the inclusion of index entries, linked and roled, with articles published in the journals of the American Institute of Chemical Engineers. An even greater boost occurred when the Engineers Joint Council produced a set of role indicators, published its *Thesaurus of Engineering Terms,* and began sponsoring a series of courses on coordinate indexing using links and roles. The complete set of EJC role indicators is displayed in Table 25.

Although role indicators are capable of resolving various syntactic ambiguities, the practical application of these devices has caused great problems, has had extremely adverse effects in certain systems, and has added significantly to system operating costs. Several studies of the value of role indicators have been conducted, all with somewhat negative results.

An evaluation, in the prototype stage, of SHARP (Ships Analysis and Retrieval Project), a mechanized retrieval system designed to control the reports collection of the Bureau of Ships Technical Library, revealed certain problems in the application of EJC role indicators.[11, 14] The test was conducted after approximately 1,000 reports had been indexed into the system. Fifty requests based on reports known to exist in the test collection (i.e., source documents) were put to the system. Twelve of the 50 source documents were not retrieved in the test searches. Of these, 3 were lost due to problems in the application of the role indicators. Of the total of 46 known relevant documents that were missed in searching, 9 (or approximately 20 percent) were not retrieved because of role indicator problems. These were not straightforward cases of misapplication (i.e., pure human errors in which indexer or searcher used obviously inappropriate role combinations); such errors were classified as indexing failures or searching failures. The failures designated "role indicator failures" were those that appeared to be attributable entirely to the roles themselves; that is, situations in which both indexer and searcher used seemingly appropriate combinations of roles to express the precise interrelationship of concepts contained in the document or in the request. Relevant documents were missed because, although descriptors matched, role combinations chosen by indexer and searcher did not.

Sinnett [23] studied the use of another set of roles in the retrieval system of the Air Force Materials Labora-

TABLE 25 The EJC System of Roles

8	*8*

The primary topic of consideration is; the principal subject of discussion is; the subject reported is; the major topic under discussion is; there is a description of

1	*1*

Input; raw material; material of construction; reactant; base metal (for alloys); components to be combined; constituents to be combined; ingredients to be combined; material to be shaped; material to be formed; ore to be refined; sub-assemblies to be assembled; energy input (only in an energy conversion); data and types of data (only when inputs to mathematical processings); a material being corroded

2	*2*

Output; product, by-product, co-product; outcome, resultant; intermediate product; alloy produced; resulting material; resulting mixture or formulation; material manufactured; mixture manufactured; device shaped or formed; metal or substance refined; device, equipment, or apparatus made, assembled, built, fabricated, constructed, created; energy output (only in an energy conversion); data and types of data (only as mathematical processing outputs)

3	*3*

Undesirable component; waste; scrap; rejects (manufactured devices); contaminant; impurity, pollutant, adulterant, or poison in inputs, environments, and materials passively receiving actions; undesirable material present; unnecessary material present; undesirable product, by-product, co-product

4	*4*

Indicated, possible, intended present or later uses or applications. The use or application to which the term has been, is now, or will later be put. To be used as, in, on, for, or with; for use as, in, on, for, or with; used as, in, on, for, or with; for later use as, in, on, for, or with

5	*5*

Environment; medium; atmosphere; solvent; carrier (material); support (in a process or operation); vehicle (material); host; absorbent, adsorbent

6	*6*

Cause; independent or controlled variable; influencing factor; "X" as a factor affecting or influencing "Y"; the "X" in "Y is a function of X"

7	*7*

Effect; dependent variable; influenced factor; "Y" as a factor affected or influenced by "X"; the "Y" in "Y is a function of X"

9	*9*

Passively receiving an operation or process with no change in identity, composition, configuration, molecular structure, physical state, or physical form; possession such as when preceded by the preposition *of, in,* or *on* meaning possession; location such as when preceded by the prepositions *in, on, at, to,* or *from* meaning location; used with months and years when they locate information (not bibliographic data) on a time continuum

10	*10*

Means to accomplish primary topic of consideration or other objective

0	*0*

Bibliographic data, personal names of authors, corporate authors and sources, type of documents, dates of publication, names of journals and other publications, other source-identifying data, and adjectives

SOURCE: EJC *Thesaurus of Engineering Terms*

tory, Wright-Patterson Air Force Base. By analysis of the results of 22 searches, Sinnett determined that the use of roles alone reduced recall by 4.7 percent, yet improved precision by only 2.8 percent. Used in conjunction with links, roles were found to reduce recall by 5.2 percent, yet improved precision by only 2 percent.

Van Oot et al.,[26] at the Textile Fibers and Film Departments at Du Pont, also carried out some tests on role indicators. His findings corroborated those obtained at the Bureau of Ships, namely, that the lack of clearcut mutual exclusiveness in role definitions caused relevant documents to be missed. Roles must be mutually exclusive if they are to work reasonably well.

Van Oot concluded that "the lack of discrimination caused by overlapping role definitions was largely responsible . . . for the blocking of relevant information." However, the problems occurred largely with nonchemical terms and were not so apparent with chemical term-role combinations.

Hyslop,[10] at the American Society for Metals (ASM), conducted a survey of the use made of WRU roles in 150 computer searches for ASM subscribers. The results showed a heavy preponderance in the use of certain role indicators, a correspondingly light use of others, and the complete absence of role indicators in a large number of searches.

Of the 150 searches, 82, or 54.7 percent, were formulated without any use of role indicators. (In the Cranfield tests of the WRU index,[1] only 27 percent of the WRU search formulations involved the use of roles). Moreover, of the 12 role indicators used in these 150 searches, four of the roles accounted for 82 percent of the usage. These roles were: KEJ, material processed, used 88 times; KUJ, major component, used 57 times; KOV, property given for, used 32 times; and KWJ, product, used 26 times. The role KAH, condition, was used four times; KAP, property influenced, three times; and KWV, property given, only once.

Mrs. Hyslop conjectured that one of the reasons why roles were not used in more searches was because searchers were afraid of their probable effect on recall. In other words, they had little confidence in the possibility of consistent application of these roles. That four role indicators did the "lion's share" of the work suggests that these four are probably the most unambiguous and generally applicable. "Search programmers . . . were hesitant to specify those role indicators which carry precise shades of meaning, since they could not be confident that the original analysis of the document would parallel the search requirement when translated into a precise computer program." She suggests that the concentration on four role indicators might reflect some unfortunate experiences in attempting to formulate precise searching strategies using a larger variety of roles.

Jessica Melton,[16] at Western Reserve University, conducted an experiment on searching a file of 768 natural-language abstracts on metallurgy from *Chemical Abstracts*. These abstracts were reduced to tree structures by a simplified automatic grammatical analysis. Each of 12 searches was carried out twice, once using the structured representation and once using term co-occurrence only. Results suggested that syntax was of negligible importance in retrieval.

Blagden[3] analyzed a keyword system at the Zinc and Lead Development Association with a view to determining whether the addition of roles and links

would be justified in terms of the amount of noise (irrelevancy) eliminated. His results indicated that false coordinations and incorrect term relationships were not the major cause of precision failures. The introduction of links would be likely to reduce irrelevancy by about 20 percent and the addition of roles by about 10 percent.

More recently, Mullison et al.[18] have compared indexing with keywords alone against indexing with keywords plus roles. Their findings confirm those of earlier investigators: the roles lead to reduced consistency, allow higher precision, but cause lower recall. Inexperienced indexers took 30 percent longer to index with roles than without them.

Why do role indicators of the EJC type cause problems in the searching of information retrieval systems?

Analysis of recall failures in the Bureau of Ships evaluation[11] demonstrated two prime reasons why role indicators of indexer and searcher frequently failed to match:

1. When roles are used, the omission of a term in the indexing of a document may be more serious than the simple omission of a term from indexing without syntax. Consider the following two index term profiles for the same document:

(A)	(B)
Evaluation Tests (8)	Evaluation Tests (8)
Power Equipment (9)	Power Equipment (9)
Destroyers (4)	Destroyers (4)
Operation (7)	Operation (7)
Transients (6)	Starting (6)
Electric Potential (6)	Transients (7) and (6)
Electronic Equipment (9)	Electric Potential (7) and (6)
	Electrical Equipment (9)

The report describes transient and steady-state voltage dip tests conducted aboard a destroyer. In Profile A the term STARTING does not appear, so TRANSIENTS and ELECTRIC POTENTIAL appear only in Role 6, as factors influencing the operation (thus OPERATION in Role 7, as the thing influenced) of electronic equipment on the destroyer. Profile B is similar to Profile A except that the additional term STARTING is used. STARTING must appear in Role 6, and the terms TRANSIENTS and ELECTRIC POTENTIAL in Role 7, because the starting operation is the cause of these phenomena. However, in a separate link, TRANSIENTS and ELECTRIC POTENTIAL must also appear in Role 6 to show that these phenomena affect the operation of the electronic equipment. Thus it can be seen that the simple omission (or, conversely, addition) of a single term in the indexing of a document, or of a request, can have

significant effect on the entire descriptor-link-role structure.

2. A document relevant to a request will normally be indexed by terms additional to those used in the search formulation for that request. When we search, we are faced with the problem that the terms by which we search (i.e., terms for concepts demanded or implied in the request) are likely to be only a few of the terms actually used to index relevant documents into the system. We cannot know what the other terms are. Yet these other terms will be related to the terms upon which we search and may in fact determine the role indicators applied to the terms in which we are interested. Therefore, when we search, we must consider not only the terms of the request, the synonyms, and the terms related to the request terms in a hierarchical or other relationship, but we must also take into account that our search terms will form only part of some complete interrelationship of terms used in the indexing of documents. Their function in the indexing (i.e., their roles) may be governed by other terms about which we know nothing. In other words, we may often find ourselves trying to guess what possible roles our search terms could have appeared in, although these roles may have nothing particularly to do with the relationships of terms demanded in the request. In fact, in formulating searching strategies, too frequently we must ask for terms in every possible role (i.e., we must drop roles completely).

The usefulness of, and necessity for, role indicators may vary substantially with the subject field. The studies of Montague [17] and Van Oot [26] indicate that certain roles do have great value in the "tagging" of terms describing chemicals in dynamic reactions or processes. Continued experience at Du Pont has consistently borne this out. However, in many of the applied fields of technology and engineering, once a document has been analyzed conceptually and partitioned into themes, each theme being expressed by a group of descriptors joined by a link letter, little possible ambiguity remains. Sinnett, [23] for example, firmly recommended that role indicators be discontinued in the retrieval system being developed at the Air Force Materials Laboratory (AFML). Instead, he suggested that increased emphasis be placed on the use of stylized statements in the application of links to indexing. Roles were subsequently dropped at AFML.

Similarly, in the Cranfield Project, [5] it was found that little possible ambiguity existed in the index term profiles of aerodynamics documents once the terms had been marshalled into suitable links or themes.

Barbara Montague's [17] investigations also suggest that roles may be effective in certain subject fields but not in others. She points out that, in formulating a search strategy, one is frequently forced to search terms in several roles to ensure completeness of retrieval because some concepts can be indexed in more than one role. However, if role indicators are to be really effective, they should be capable of precise and unambiguous application; that is, in formulating a search one should need to specify only a single role for each term.

She carried out a number of searches in which a single "best" role was assigned to each term. She then compared these results with a situation in which normal search strategy using alternative role combinations was employed. For chemical questions, recall dropped only 4 percent, from 83 to 79 percent, while precision increased from 34 to 36 percent. For nonchemical questions, however, recall dropped from 83 to 31 percent, while precision improved from 7 to 9 percent. From this she concluded that, when used with a precise and reasonably unambiguous language such as chemistry, roles could be mutually exclusive and rigidly applied. However, redundant searching by merging of several selected term-roles is required to handle the less precise, general nonchemical information. These findings essentially confirm those of Van Oot. [26]

In reviewing the rather negative results of their studies on roles, Mullison et al. [18] suggest that the full value of roles will emerge as a file becomes larger.

Without empirical evidence to the contrary, it would be reasonable to assume that role indicators might become necessary, in order to increase specificity and thus improve precision, when a retrieval system becomes extremely large. However, results from the MEDLARS evaluation, conducted at a time when the data base included half-a-million citations, the great majority of which were indexed without any syntactic devices (subheadings were added to MEDLARS only in 1966), show that even an extremely large mechanized retrieval system can successfully restrict class definition largely by the principle of class intersection without the need for further refinements to specify the precise relationships between classes. [13]

The power of simple class intersection was also stressed by Melton [16] in the previously cited investigation on natural-language abstracts: "the more words there are in a question, the more clear their relationships are to one another if they are to be combined in a way to make sense." This has further been corroborated by Cleverdon's [4] findings in the latest Cranfield study: "the use of precision devices such as interfixing and partitioning was not as effective as the basic precision device of coordination."

Class intersection in a post-coordinate system is a very effective device for resolving syntactic ambiguities. Many possible ambiguous relationships are really only theoretical ones. If we intersect the terms LAMB, EXPORT, and AUSTRALIA, we could theoretically retrieve items on export of lamb to Australia; but, there is an infinitely higher probability of retrieving what we are seeking, namely, export of lamb from Australia.

In the MEDLARS evaluation it was found that false coordinations contributed to only 11 percent of all the precision failures, and incorrect term relationships to only 7 percent. These figures are based on an analysis of reasons for precision failures in 278 actual MEDLARS searches. Although some false coordinations occurred in 39 percent of these searches, and incorrect term relationships in 30 percent, the total number of failures attributable to these causes was quite small in relation to the total number of precision failures.

Role indicators essentially function to increase the specificity of an index language. Thus, the ability to attach roles to an index term, say ALUMINUM, increases the size and specificity of the vocabulary by allowing the creation of new class labels, such as "aluminum as a raw material," "aluminum as a catalyst," "aluminum as an undesirable element," and "aluminum as a finished product." Therefore, the types of precision failures that can be avoided by the use of role indicators can usually be avoided by increasing the specificity of the vocabulary in other ways. Most of the precision failures occurring in MEDLARS that could be corrected by role indicators could be prevented by increased specificity in *Medical Subject Headings.* For example, the coordination of the terms TOXINS and FISH, in a search on toxins produced by fish, retrieved a number of irrelevant articles on bacterial toxins affecting fish. While this type of unwanted retrieval could be prevented by role indicators (fish as pro-ducer, fish as host or target), it could equally well be prevented by the use of the more specific subject headings ANIMAL TOXINS (or ZOOTOXINS) and BACTERIAL TOXINS. If role indicators were used in MEDLARS, the type of precision failure encountered could be obviated by a small number of broad, basic indicators; for example, to distinguish "agent" from "patient," and to indicate sequence of events (as a disease following rather than preceding a particular form of therapy). Likewise, the roles found useful at Du Pont are broad, basic roles (e.g., "reactant" and "product").

SUBHEADINGS

Instead of using role indicators to solve the problems of incorrect term relationships, it is perfectly possible to achieve the same results by the use of subheadings. This is the route that has been taken by the National Library of Medicine, which introduced subheadings into MEDLARS in 1966. Although introduced primarily to facilitate use of *Index Medicus* and other printed indexes, these subheadings have proven extremely valuable in retrospective machine searching because they introduce a further element of pre-coordination into the vocabulary. There are now 60 topical subheadings in the MEDLARS index language. A complete list of these subheadings, as used in January 1970, is given in Table 26. If used carefully, these subheadings will act as links and as role indicators simultaneously. Consider a search on the subject of oral hypoglycemic agents in the treatment of diabetes mellitus. One of the search combinations will be DIABETES MELLITUS and TOLBUTAMIDE. Prior to the introduction of subheadings, this combination would retrieve certain irrelevant items (e.g., articles on the tolbutamide tolerance test) having nothing to do

TABLE 26 Topical Subheadings in MEDLARS Index Language (January 1970)

Abnormalities	Classification	Familial & Genetic	Nursing	Rehabilitation
Administration & Dosage	Complications	Growth & Development	Occurrence	Secretion
Adverse Effects	Congenital	History	Pathogenicity	Standards
Analysis	Cytology	Immunology	Pathology	Supply & Distribution
Anatomy & Histology	Diagnosis	Injuries	Pharmacodynamics	Surgery
Antagonists & Inhibitors	Diagnostic Use	Innervation	Physiology	Therapeutic Use
Biosynthesis	Drug Effects	Instrumentation	Physiopathology	Therapy
Blood	Drug Therapy	Isolation & Purification	Poisoning	Toxicity
Blood Supply	Education	Manpower	Prevention & Control	Transplantation
Cerebrospinal Fluid	Embryology	Metabolism	Radiation Effects	Urine
Chem Synthesis	Enzymology	Microbiology	Radiography	Utilization
Chemically Induced	Etiology	Mortality	Radiotherapy	Veterinary

SOURCE: *Medical Subject Headings*

with therapy. This type of unwanted retrieval can now be avoided by the intersection of DIABETES MELLITUS/DRUG THERAPY and TOLBUTAMIDE/THERAPEUTIC USE. The subheadings both tie the terms together (i.e., act as links) and also indicate the relationship between these terms (i.e., act as role indicators). Subheadings allow us to make the important distinction between drug X leading to disease Y and drug X being used therapeutically in the treatment of disease Y. The former relationship is expressed by

Drug X/ADVERSE EFFECTS
Disease Y/CHEMICALLY INDUCED

while the latter is represented by

Drug X/THERAPEUTIC USE
Disease Y/DRUG THERAPY.

Although subheadings have not been tested as rigorously as role indicators, they probably present some of the same problems. There is little doubt that use of subheadings will reduce indexing consistency. If two analysts index a particular set of documents, there will be greater consistency between them when they index with descriptors only than when they index with descriptors plus subheadings; that is, they will agree more on the descriptors than they will on the relationships obtaining between these descriptors. Nevertheless, subheadings have proved extremely valuable in MEDLARS, and they provide a convenient and economic way of greatly increasing the size of the specifier vocabulary. A single subheading, say TRANSPLANTATION, can be used with several descriptors in the vocabulary, and it eliminates the need for including pre-coordinate terms combining the transplantation concept with the tissue involved (e.g., HEART TRANSPLANTATION, KIDNEY TRANSPLANTATION). Because of their natural-language basis, subheadings may well present fewer problems of interpretation than do conventional role indicators.

OTHER RELATIONAL INDICATORS

A very elementary relational indicator, related to the role, was described by Johnson,[12] who wanted to distinguish a term describing a "thing itself" (noun form) from the same term used adjectivally (e.g., "water" as a subject of study from "water" in "water pumps" or "water wheels"). He does this very simply by using a hyphen to distinguish the adjectival form, as WATER-. Of course, this device increases the size of the vocabulary (we need a term WATER and another WATER-) but so do role indicators and subheadings.

Relational indicators can be used in pre-coordinate as well as in post-coordinate systems. Of course pre-coordinate systems are able to display relationships by means of context, sequence, and punctuation. When we see the subject heading COMPUTER DESIGN we tend to think immediately of "design of computers" rather than of "design by means of computers." Likewise, in the Coates-type of index entry

RETINA, DETACHMENT, SURGERY, CHOROIDITIS

the sequence of words tells us, more or less, the complex relationship involved: choroiditis occurs as a complication following surgery to correct a retinal detachment. The same is true of printed subject indexes, of the *Chemical Abstracts* type, in which sequence, punctuation, and syntactic words (prepositions particularly) are used to indicate semantic relationships (Figure 12).

The context in which a term appears in a classification schedule also indicates the role of the term. For example, the term ARGON in the welding schedule appears in the role of protective atmosphere; in another position, it may play a completely different role, such as an undesirable element.

Some designers of index languages for pre-coordinate systems have built in explicit relational indicators. A good example is the *Symbolic Shorthand System* of Hans Selye,[22] which had its origins as far back as 1926. Selye uses a limited set of symbols to represent possible relations between his subject codes, as in the following:

Notation	Meaning
BMR ← ACTH	Basal metabolic rate affected by ACTH. The arrow indicates direction of action: BMR is target and ACTH is agent.
GTH (FSH + LH)	Gonadotrophic hormone is composed of follicle-stimulating hormone and luteinizing hormone. The parentheses are used to show the *component* relationship.
Glu < B	Blood sugar. The symbol < indicates that the sugar is contained in the blood.
Glu < B(:Ur) ← Con	Effect of cortisone on the sugar content of the blood compared with its effect on the sugar content of the urine. The colon, used in parentheses, indicates a comparison. All earlier elements are shown, by the arrow, to be affected by cortisone.

Ranganathan incorporated relational indicators into his *Colon Classification*. The colon itself merely connects two or more notational elements but does not explicitly specify the type of relationship involved. In a sense it is more akin to a link than to a role. However, Ranganathan also described the use of various other punctuation marks which, when appearing between notational elements, would indicate the precise relationship obtaining. These *phase indicators* are capable of expressing such relationships as bias, comparison, and influence.

Probably the most elaborate set of relational indicators is that devised by Farradane. It was first described in 1950 [8] but has since been developed much further.[7] Farradane's system emphasizes the relations between terms. The sets of relationships he devised are drawn from modern work on the experimental psychology of thinking. They are based originally on the work of Piaget, Vinacke, Nathan Isaacs, and others, and have been reinforced by the work of Guilford on the "structure of intellect." Nine explicit relations exist in Farradane's scheme, each relation being represented by an "operator." The complete set of these operators is given in Table 27. The scheme represents stages in discrimination drawn from child psychology; i.e., the stages through which a child develops in discriminating in time and space. There are two sets of gradation: gradations in time and gradations in space. The first "time" stage is simple co-occurrence of ideas without reference to time; the second is temporary association between ideas; and the third is the fixed (permanent) co-occurrence of ideas. The stages of "space" discrimination are: simple concurrence (concepts hard to distinguish), convergence (concepts having much in common), and divergence (concepts that can be completely distinguished).

Using Farradane's system we build up indexing statements by joining terms ("isolates") together by means of these operators. An indexing statement, consisting of terms related by means of operators, is called an "analet." Some simple examples are:

Birds /* Migration
Iron Ore /— Smelting

and a more complex one:

Sugar [/— Hydrolysis /; Acid] /: Glucose

which represents sugar acted upon by hydrolysis, using acid, to yield glucose. Two-dimensional display is used where necessary, as:

Beet /— Storing
/;   The storage of washed beets.
Washing

Molasses /(Glutamic Acid
/—   Effect of purification on the glutamic
Purifying   acid content of molasses.

Farradane's scheme is interesting but somewhat impractical. It is an example of a system of classification derived as an intellectual exercise with little real justification from a practical point of view. It is now well established that it is possible to operate extremely large information retrieval systems (in excess of a million items) effectively with syntax very much simpler than that proposed by Farradane. The truth of the matter is that, for information retrieval applications, we just do not need the capability of express-

TABLE 27 Farradane's System of Relations

		Increasing Association (Mental time)		
		Cognition (Awareness)	Memory (Temporary memory)	Evaluation (Fixed memory)
Increasing Clarity of Perception	Recognition (Concurrent)	(Concurrence) / θ	Self-activity / *	Association / :
	Convergent Thinking (Not-distinct)	Equivalence / =	Dimensional (time, space, state) / +	Appurtenance / (
	Divergent Thinking (Distinct)	Distinctness /)	Reaction / —	Functional dependence (causation) / ;

SOURCE: J. Farradane.[7]

ing the fine shades of meaning that Farradane's operators are designed to give us. In terms of cost-effectiveness it is simply impossible to justify this type of approach for most applications.

Note that we stressed "for most applications." There are certain indexing and retrieval situations in which it is essential to express highly complex relationships. One such situation is that of patent searching. Over the years, the U.S. Patent Office has conducted considerable research on methods of encoding patent literature. An essential element in many patents, particularly those in the mechanical and electrical arts, is a diagram—of a mechanism, a container, a circuit, or whatever. From such a diagram a subject specialist can see at a glance the precise relationships between the various components and parts. These precise relationships are extremely difficult to code in any indexing scheme. Andrews and Newman [2] developed various schemes of relational indicators in an attempt to tackle some of these problems. For example, temporal relations are expressed in the following scheme:

(1) Syncwith-Syncwith: Simultaneous, of equal length
(2) Syncstart-Syncbegin: Unequal, simultaneous start
(3) Syncstop-Syncend: Unequal, simultaneous end
(4) During-While: Shorter occurs once during longer
(5) Recurper-While: Shorter recurs during longer
(6) Aforlap-Aftlap: Overlapping periods
(7) Timafor-Timaft: Sequence, not overlapping
(8) Timnear-Timnear: No sequence expressed

Spatial relationships are expressed in the following scheme:

(1) Sepfrom: Nothing in common
(2) Intersec: Portions common and noncommon
(3) Surtact-Intact: Large surrounds smaller and is in contact with it
(4) Coinc: Coincident
(5) Compor: Common portions
(6) Enclos-embed: Larger encloses smaller, no common border
(7) Combor: Common border
(8) Extact: External contact

It is possible to represent quite complex mechanical and electrical concepts with relational indicators of this type.

WEIGHTING

The final precision device we need to consider is that of term weighting. Most indexing involves a binary decision: a term is or is not assigned to a document. Instead of this binary decision, we can weight terms to indicate their relative importance in representing the subject matter of the document. Let us, say, use a three-point scale, as in this illustration:

A— 3
B— 3
C— 2
D— 2
E— 2
F— 2
G— 1
H— 1

The document is primarily about A and B, and these terms receive the highest available weight, 3. C, D, E, and F are treated in less detail and receive a weight of 2. G and H are dealt with rather peripherally and receive the lowest weight. Weighted indexing gives us flexibility to vary our search strategies in order to seek maximum recall or maximum precision. Suppose we are looking for documents on viral encephalitis but are only interested in documents in which encephalitis is discussed in detail. We can restrict our search by asking for retrieval only of documents in which the viral encephalitis term has a weight of 3 (i.e., documents whose central subject matter is viral encephalitis). By this device we can avoid retrieval of items which make only peripheral mention of encephalitis. Suppose, however, that we are interested in all cases of encephalitis as a sequel of chicken pox. We want all references to the association between the two diseases. Here, we ignore the weights. It is a high recall situation and we ask, essentially, for retrieval of any document that bears the necessary terms, whatever weight they have been given.

With weighted indexing we can also use a "threshold" search strategy. For example, we can retrieve any documents indexed under A and B and C, but only when the combined weights of these terms is equal to or exceeds 7. Such a strategy ensures that at least one of the search terms appears at maximum weight and, in fact, it will not retrieve any item in which the three terms appear at values less than 3—2—2.

An important advantage of weighted indexing is that it allows the output of a search to be ranked in order of degree of match between document indexing and search requirement. Hopefully this degree of match will also reflect the probable relevance of the document to the request. Consider a search for documents indexed under A and B and C. In a computer-based system it is possible to conduct this search and to receive a printout ranked according to degree of match. The following scale will apply:

1. Documents with a weight of 9 (all three search terms have top weight)

2. Documents with a weight of 8 (one of the three search terms has a weight of 2)

3. Documents with a weight of 7,

and so on.

The documents represented at the top of such a list should be those most likely to be relevant to our interests.

Most retrieval systems have some form of term weighting, albeit rather unsophisticated. The sequence in which we combine notations in an analytico-synthetic classification is in a sense a form of weighting, with the top weight being given to the facet cited first. Similarly, the sequence in which we build up complex subject headings reflects a weighting of a sort.

In MEDLARS there is a very simple two-level weighting. The terms assigned to a document, representing the major aspects of that document, are starred by the indexer. These are then known as *print* or *Index Medicus* terms, because they are the terms under which a reference to the document is made in the printed *Index Medicus*. The remaining terms assigned by the indexer are "nonprint": no citations appear under these terms in *Index Medicus*; they are used only for retrospective search purposes.

Some investigators have proposed very elaborate weighting schemes. Maron et al.,[15] for example, base their "probabilistic indexing" on an eight-point weighting method. This is likely to be too refined for practical application. How do you distinguish between a term with value 7 and one with value 6?

The weighting of index terms to indicate the relative importance of these terms in representing subject matter of a document is completely different from the use of term weighting in place of Boolean algebra in the construction of search strategies. If we use weighted term searching, as described by Sommar and Dennis,[24] we can avoid Boolean algebraic expressions. For example,

A *and* B *and* C

is replaced by

A—3
B—2   Minimum retrieval threshold—5
C—1

This means that we will accept a document indexed under A *and* B *and* C and also one indexed under A *and* B alone, but we will not accept A *and* C or C *and* B. Weighted term searching of this type can be used to simulate any Boolean search equation involving logical sums, products, or negations. No weighting of terms at the time of indexing is required in this application. This technique allows us to weight terms in accordance with their importance to a particular request

(and will thus provide a corresponding ranked output) rather than on the basis of their importance to particular documents.

Before we finally leave the subject of index-language devices, there are two further points that are well worth making:

1. A computer-based system gives us great flexibility to use or ignore index-language devices for individual searches as we see fit. For example, we can allow indexers to use all synonyms of a particular term, whichever they happen to come across in the text at hand. For search purposes we can lump them all together but still maintain their separate identities. Thus, all possible trade names for acetaminophen can be mapped to the descriptor ACETAMINOPHEN to facilitate search, but can still retain their separate identities on the machine records. Normally we will want to search for all brands of acetaminophen, and the synonym control allows us to do this very conveniently. In other, more rare, situations we may wish to search for a particular brand only, say *Panadol*. This, too, we can do when the need arises, as long as we have allowed our indexers to assign specific trade names and have mapped these to the appropriate class term by machine.

Similarly, in computer-based natural-language systems, we can search on word roots or we can search on complete words, whichever appears to be most suitable for a particular search. We can also use links or ignore them, use roles or ignore them, and use or ignore term weightings. The computer gives us great flexibility in this area, which is virtually impossible to equal in manual systems.

2. Although we have discussed "recall devices" and "precision devices," the difference between the two groups is not as clear-cut as it may appear. Because searching involves a compromise between recall and precision, in the long run, the addition of a precision device may actually improve the recall performance of a system, and vice versa. Consider an index language that cannot precisely express the concept A_{11}. The searcher tries related notions A_{12} and A_{13}, but does not generalize to A because this is likely to produce too much irrelevancy. However, generalization is in fact necessary to obtain adequate recall. If it were possible (by more specific terms, by role indicators, or by some other "precision" device) to specify A_{11} exactly, recall would obviously improve in this search.

Finally, the ASLIB Cranfield Project, under the direction of Cleverdon, has undertaken a comprehensive evaluation of index languages and index-language devices and the effect of these on retrieval system performance. The results of these studies are highly

relevant to the subject of natural-language searching so we will defer their consideration until the next chapter.

REFERENCES

1. Aitchison, J. and Cleverdon, C. *A Report on a Test of the Index of Metallurgical Literature of Western Reserve University.* Cranfield, England: College of Aeronautics, ASLIB Cranfield Research Project, 1963.

2. Andrews, D. C. and Newman, S. M. *Storage and Retrieval of Contents of Technical Literature—Nonchemical Information.* Washington, D.C.: Office of Research and Development, U.S. Patent Office, 1956. *First Supplementary Report,* by S. M. Newman, June 1957.

3. Blagden, J. F. "How Much Noise in a Role-Free and Link-Free Coordinate Indexing System?" *Journal of Documentation* 22 (1966): 203-209.

4. Cleverdon, C. and Keen, M. *Factors Determining the Performance of Indexing Systems. Vol. 2, Test Results.* Cranfield, England: College of Aeronautics, ASLIB Cranfield Research Project, 1966.

5. Cleverdon, C. et al. *Factors Determining the Performance of Indexing Systems. Vol. 1, Design.* Cranfield, England: College of Aeronautics, ASLIB Cranfield Research Project, 1966.

6. Costello, J. C. and Wall, E. *Recent Improvements in Techniques for Storing and Retrieving Information.* Wilmington, Del.: E. I. Du Pont de Nemours & Co., 1959.

7. Farradane, J. "Concept Organization for Information Retrieval." *Information Storage and Retrieval* 3 (1967): 297-314.

8. Farradane, J. "Scientific Theory of Classification and Indexing and Its Practical Applications." *Journal of Documentation* 6 (1950): 83-99.

9. Gardin, J. C. *Syntol.* New Brunswick, N. J.: Rutgers, the State University, 1965.

10. Hyslop, M. R. "Role Indicators and Their Use in Information Searching—Relationship of ASM and EJC Systems." *Proceedings of the American Documentation Institute* 1 (1964): 99-107.

11. Johanningsmeier, W. J. and Lancaster, F. W. *Project SHARP (Ships Analysis and Retrieval Project) Information Storage and Retrieval System: Evaluation of Indexing Procedures and Retrieval Effectiveness.* Washington, D.C.: Bureau of Ships, 1964. (NAVSHIPS 250-210-3).

12. Johnson, A. "Experience in the Use of Unit Concept Coordinate Indexing Applied to Technical Reports." *Journal of Documentation* 15 (1959): 146-155.

13. Lancaster, F. W. *Evaluation of the MEDLARS Demand Search Service.* Bethesda, Md.: National Library of Medicine, 1968.

14. Lancaster, F. W. "Some Observations on the Performance of EJC Role Indicators in a Mechanized Retrieval System." *Special Libraries* 55 (1964): 696-701.

15. Maron, M. E. et al. *Probabilistic Indexing—A Statistical Technique for Document Identification and Retrieval.* Los Angeles: Thompson Ramo Wooldridge, Inc., 1959.

16. Melton, J. S. "Automatic Language Processing for Information Retrieval: Some Questions." *Proceedings of the American Documentation Institute* 3 (1966): 255-263.

17. Montague, B. A. "Testing, Comparison and Evaluation of Recall, Relevance and Cost of Coordinate Indexing with Links and Roles." *Proceedings of the American Documentation Institute* 1 (1964): 357-367.

18. Mullison, W. R. et al. "Comparing Indexing Efficiency, Effectiveness and Consistency With or Without the Use of Roles." *Proceedings of the American Society for Information Science* 6 (1969): 301-311.

19. Mulvihill, J. G. and Brenner, E. H. "Faceted Organization of a Thesaurus Vocabulary." *Proceedings of the American Documentation Institute* 3 (1966): 175-183.

20. Perry, J. W. et al. *Machine Literature Searching.* New York: Interscience Publishers, 1956.

21. Salton, G. *Automatic Information Organization and Retrieval.* New York: McGraw-Hill, 1968.

22. Selye, H. *Symbolic Shorthand System.* New Brunswick, N. J.: Rutgers, the State University, 1966.

23. Sinnett, J. D. *An Evaluation of Links and Roles Used in Information Retrieval.* Dayton, Ohio: Air Force Materials Laboratory, Wright-Patterson Air Force Base, 1964. AD 432 198.

24. Sommar, H. G. and Dennis, D. E. "A New Method of Weighted Term Searching With a Highly Structured Thesaurus." *Proceedings of the American Society for Information Science* 6 (1969): 193-198.

25. Sparck Jones, K. *Synonymy and Semantic Classification.* Cambridge, England: Cambridge Language Research Unit, 1964. M.L. 170.

26. Van Oot, J. G. et al. "Links and Roles in Coordinate Indexing and Searching: An Economic Study of Their Use, and An Evaluation of Their Effect on Relevance and Recall." *Journal of Chemical Documentation* 6 (1966): 95-101.

27. Whaley, F. R. "A Deep Index for Internal Technical Reports." In *Information Systems in Documentation. Vol. 2, Advances in Documentation and Library Science.* Edited by J. H. Shera et al. New York: Interscience Publishers, 1957, 352-383.

16 *Searching Natural-Language Data Bases*

The computer offers possibilities in information retrieval that were completely impracticable less than twenty years ago. One possibility is to reduce the entire text of a document collection (or at least document abstracts), word by word, to machine-readable form, and then to conduct various computer manipulations, including searches, of this data base. This type of searching is frequently referred to as "natural-language searching" or "free-text searching." It does not involve the use of a controlled vocabulary, at least at the input stage.

It is, of course, costly to reduce a corpus of documents *ab initio* to machine-readable form. If a special keyboarding operation (punched cards or paper tape, for example) is needed to produce the corpus, it is doubtful whether the cost of creating the data base is economically competitive with human indexing. However, it is frequently possible to obtain a searchable data base as a by-product of some other operation. For example, in the production of an abstracting publication, the abstracts need to be keyboarded at some time to allow them to appear in printed form. A machine-readable data base, say on paper tape, can be generated simultaneously with the initial keyboarding operation. Perhaps the machine-readable data base will itself be used in the printing operation; e.g., as input to photocomposition procedures. The technical reports of an industrial organization also have to be typed at some stage. A machine-readable data base of these reports, or abstracts of them, can

be obtained as a by-product of the typing operation; or, if a special type face is used, the abstract can be put into machine-readable form by means of an optical character reader. Some other useful data bases can also be captured readily in machine-readable form; for example, teletype messages, which are extremely valuable in defense, intelligence, and news environments. Natural-language search systems are attractive if we can obtain the initial data base inexpensively. They are less attractive, economically at least, if we must charge the full cost of data base preparation to the retrieval system itself.

There are several natural-language searching systems in operation. Some of the early experimental work was conducted by Swanson.[23, 24] The first operating system of any real note was established in the legal field at the Health Law Center, University of Pittsburgh, in 1959.[10, 11, 12] Since 1959, large corpora of legal text have been put into machine-readable form, including the complete statutes of many states, health statutes of all states, the United States Code, the Internal Revenue Code and Regulations, and the decisions of the U.S. Court of Appeals and the U.S. Supreme Court. The Pittsburgh system was subsequently adopted by the Department of Defense, where it became known as Project LITE (Legal Information Through Electronics). The legal retrieval activities of the Health Law Center were later taken over by a commercial organization, Aspen Systems Corporation, formed to meet the needs of attorneys,

Vocabulary Listing

DOCUMENT NUMBER
SENTENCE NUMBER
WORD POSITION
LINE TYPE
WORD-LOCATOR

ABANDONMENT

```
00003 007 059 3    00003 008 073 3    00001 022 118 3    00001 022 129 3    00001 025 020 3    00003 002 003 K    00003 003 080 3
00007 011 023 3    01113 011 062 3    00005 005 002 3    00007 006 005 3    00007 007 039 3    00007 007 052 3    00007 008 002 3
02450 003 055 3    03169 007 007 3    01147 004 042 3    0125C C04 043 3    02442 005 023 3    02448 004 023 3    0245C C02 003 K
03211 007 007 3    03213 003 010 3    03174 002 003 K    03192 002 010 2    03193 003 013 3    03205 006 009 3    03208 003 010 3
04689 002 006 2    04689 002 010 K    03215 006 002 3    03215 C12 009 3    03224 009 003 3    03224 010 033 3    04576 010 003 3
05055 002 003 K    05055 003 128 3    04689 003 070 3    04685 004 017 3    04689 004 071 3    04689 004 084 3    04689 004 135 3
08345 005 004 3    09196 032 013 K    05566 004 000 3    06192 004 008 3    07023 002 008 K    07745 003 079 3    08345 002 007 K
14704 002 006 2    14782 002 004 2    09244 004 014 3    10348 002 003 K    12066 002 003 K    13178 002 004 2    13193 008 005 3
15902 056 002 3    15902 057 005 3    14782 003 061 3    14782 003 122 3    14785 004 013 3    14795 002 007 K    14963 003 006 3
18289 005 013 3    16352 005 021 3    1672E 002 003 K    17678 C03 071 3    17818 002 003 K    18289 003 016 3    18289 004 011 3
18994 005 042 3    18995 014 003 3    1843C 005 017 3    18738 C05 018 3    18781 002 005 K    18781 004 017 3    18994 C03 004 3
           078 3   22872 005 017 3    19655 005 113 3    21378 C04 109 3    21672 002 006 K    21672 C03 027 3    2211C C02 003 K
                   25245 002 013 K    25163 002 005 K    25163 C05 035 3    25163 006 005 3    25168 C05 043 3    25194 021 165 3
           033 006 013 3    25245 004 003 3    25263 C03 076 3    25890 004 020 3    26629 002 003 K    26630 009 067 3
           05 437 3    27043 003 109 3    27056 C03 047 3    27304 002 003 K    27304 003 037 3    27304 003 061 3
           078 3   27410 002 003 K    27532 C03 072 3    27567 005 079 3    28253 C04 020 3    28253 006 005 3
           3        31254 015 026 3    31850 002 003 K    31850         32098 004 017 3
           3        03706 003 088 3    08258 003 042 3           028 3    08401 017 0
```

FIGURE 54 Concordance created by the Pittsburgh system.

government agencies, industry, and other potential users of legal text.

The Pittsburgh system [27] works as follows. The entire text of the legal corpus is put into machine-readable form, each section of a statute being regarded as a separate document and given a unique document number. The computer reads each word of each section and gives it a "word locator." This is a four-part number identifying the document in which the word appears, the sentence in which it is found, its word position within the sentence, and the type of line in which it occurs (i.e., citation, scope note, text, or chapter name).

The computer gathers together all the word locators (addresses) associated with each unique word and stores them with the word. The words are then sorted into alphabetical sequence. The result is a conventional inverted file in which each searchable term has a set of document addresses associated with it. In a sense, the search file thus created is a complete concordance to the corpus at hand. Figure 54 shows a sample machine printout from such a concordance under the term ABANDONMENT. Note how the word locators under this term indicate document number, sentence number, word position, and line type. As a by-product of the creation of the search file the computer prints a word-frequency list: an alphabetical list of all the words in the corpus, showing against each the number of times it appears in the statutes and the number of different sections in which it is used (Figure 55). The word-frequency list is a useful search aid since it enables the searcher, to a certain extent, to forecast the probable volume of material his search will retrieve, allowing him to tailor his strategy accordingly.

We search a free-text data base of this type by con-

Word Frequency List

TOTAL OCCURRENCES
DIFFERENT SECTIONS

56-53 ABANDON	7-5 ABRIDGED	4-4 ACCELERATED	1453-844 ACCOUNTS
255-150 ABANDONED	1-1 ABRIDGMENT	3-3 ACCELERATING	1-1 ACCOUTREMENT
16-13 ABANDONING	6-5 ABROAD	12-11 ACCELERATION	24-15 ACCOUTREMENTS
11-11 ABANDONMENT	11-11 ABROGATE	662-552 ACCEPT	2-2 ACCREDIT
8-7 ABANDONS	10-10 ABROGATED	5-5 ACCEPTABILITY	6-6 ACCREDITATION
14-14 ABATABLE	1-1 ABROGATING	67-57 ACCEPTABLE	104-61 ACCREDITED
123-92 ABATE	1-1 ABROGATION	513-349 ACCEPTANCE	6-4 ACCREDITING
134-86 ABATED	3-1 ABRUPT	22-8 ACCEPTANCES	1-1 ACCREDITMENT
250-173 ABATEMENT	8-7 ABSCOND	1-1 ACCEPTANT	1-1 ACCREDITS
124-124 ABATEMENTS	17-11 ABSCONDED	463-404 ACCEPTED	13-8 ACCRETIONS
1-1 ABATES	1-1 ABSCONDERS	120-105 ACCEPTING	10-7 ACCRUAL
29-26 ABATING	10-7 ABSCONDING	35-19 ACCEPTOR	158-139 ACCRUE
1-1 ABATTOIR	1-1 ABSCONDS	9-7 ACCEPTORS	416-327 ACCRUED
2-2 ABBREVIATED	682-471 ABSENCE	58-54 ACCEPTS	23-19 ACCRUES
44-21 ABBREVIATION	3-2 ABSENCES	279-196 ACCESS	229-179 ACCRUING
8-6 ABBREVIATIONS	250-190 ABSENT	1-1 ACCESSIBILITY	34-29 ACCUMULATE
1-1 ABDUCT	2-2 ABSENTED	97-81 ACCESSIBLE	344-165 ACCUMULATED
1-1 ABDUCTION	186-32 ABSENTEE	1-1 ACCESSIBLY	6-4 ACCUMULATING
1-1 ABERRATION	6-4 ABSENTEE-S	5-3 ACCESSIONS	88-51 ACCUMULATION
15-14 ABET	7-7 ABSENTEES	35-26 ACCESSORIES	39-36 ACCUMULATIONS
17-16 ABETS	8-7 ABSENTIA	32-24 ACCESSORY	89-71 ACCURACY
4-4 ABETTED	2-2 ABSENTING	408-212 ACCIDENT	192-174 ACCURATE
1-1 ABETTERS	1-1 ABSENTS	44-30 ACCIDENTAL	63-60 ACCURATELY
19-18 ABETTING	233-182 ABSOLUTE	8-8 ACCIDENTALLY	13-10 ACCUSATION
1-1 ABETTOR	436-391 ABSOLUTELY	78-63 ACCIDENTS	1-1 ACCUSATIONS
5-4 ABETTORS	1-1 ABSOLVING	57-53 ACCOMMODATE	4-2 ACCUSE
1-1 ABEYANCE	4-3 ABSORB	51-43 ACCOMMODATED	185-116 ACCUSED
51-48 ABIDE	3-3 ABSORBED	1-1 ACCOMMODATES	1-1 ACCUSES
1-1 ABIDING	1-1 ABSORBING	11-8 ACCOMMODAT	5-5 ACCUSING
4-4 ABILITIES	4-4 ABSORPTION	4-	6-5 ACCUSTOMED
ABILITY	ABSTAIN		1-1 ACE
			1-1

FIGURE 55 Word-frequency list produced by Pittsburgh system.

ceptualizing our information need and deciding which words, in which combinations, are most likely to occur in documents relevant to our interests. Suppose we are looking for statutes relevant to the rights of parents with respect to abandoned children up for adoption. This topic has four facets: parent, adoption, abandonment, and child. In reducing this requirement to word form we may produce the following as our search strategy:

1		2		3		4
CHILD		PARENT		ADOPT		ABANDON
CHILDREN	*and*	PARENTS	*and*	ADOPTION	*and*	ABANDONED
MINOR		FATHER		ADOPTING		ABANDONING
INFANT		MOTHER				ABANDONMENT
						ABANDONS

This is a conventional Boolean search strategy, which specifies that a document should only be retrieved if it contains at least one word from each of the four conceptual groups. The search is conducted by comparing the addresses under each word involved and selecting those documents containing at least one word from each group. These documents, or sections, are then printed out in their entirety. In the Pittsburgh system, the computer lists in the right margin of the printout those words in the text that match the search strategy and thus caused the document to be retrieved (Figure 56). It is customary in most natural-language systems to use a "stop list" to prevent processing the purely syntactical words (e.g., articles, prepositions, conjunctions) that do not in themselves indicate subject matter. These "common words," while retained in the machine-readable corpus to allow printout of complete texts, do not get into the inverted (concordance) files and thus are not searchable.

From the foregoing example it should be obvious that the success of a search in this type of system depends very heavily upon the quality of the search strategy; i.e., the degree to which the searcher is able to think of all possible words that might represent a

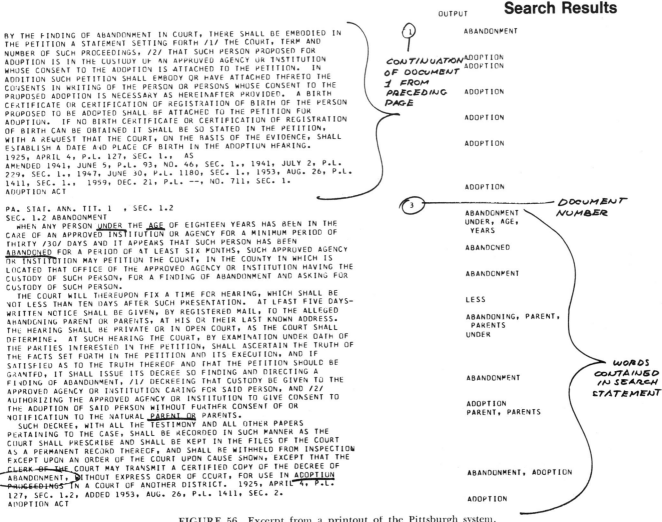

FIGURE 56 Excerpt from a printout of the Pittsburgh system.

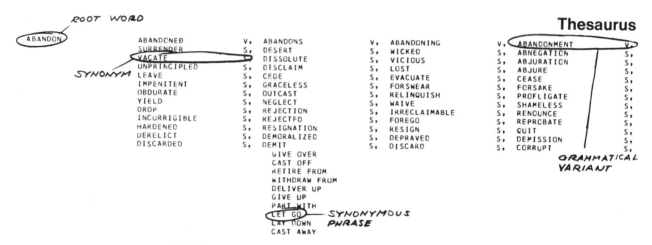

FIGURE 57　Sample "thesaurus" group from Pittsburgh system.

particular item of subject matter. In practice, it has been found that it is both unwise and inefficient to place this heavy burden on the individual searcher. Usually some type of "thesaurus" is constructed to bring related words together and thereby aid the searcher in the conduct of productive searches. Figure 57 shows a portion of such a thesaurus, as used in the Pittsburgh system. For the root word ABANDON a list is given of words and phrases considered synonymous or nearly synonymous, as well as grammatical variants of the word. Such a thesaurus differs from those discussed earlier, in that:

1. It is used solely as a searching tool and not at all in any indexing operation, and

2. It does not involve any actual vocabulary control; it is based entirely on words occurring in natural-language text, merely bringing these words together in relationships that may be useful in the construction of search strategies.

The Pittsburgh system also uses a supplementary searching tool. This is a KWIC (Keyword-in-Context) listing in which each substantive word becomes an entry point in a printed index. The index shows every occurrence of the word in the corpus. For each occurrence the keyword is shown embedded in approximately 70 characters of surrounding text (Figure 58), accompanied by the citation to the document in which this text appears. The computer program that

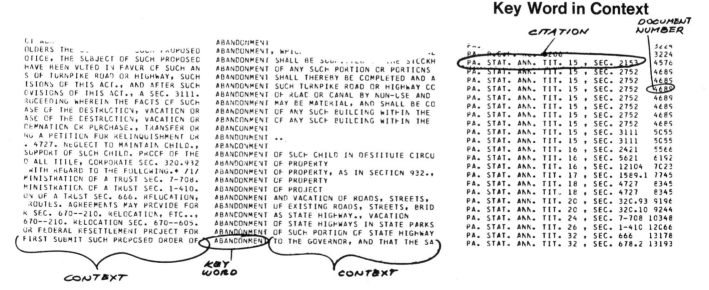

FIGURE 58　KWIC listing as used in the Pittsburgh system.

produces the KWIC index aligns the keyword in the center of the page to facilitate easy scanning.

Natural-language retrieval systems can be used for the purposes of selective dissemination (SDI) as well as for retrospective search. A system similar to that of Pittsburgh is in operation at the IBM Technical Information Retrieval Center,[16, 17] where both SDI and retrospective search facilities, based on text of abstracts, are offered.

Compared with conventional systems based on human indexing and a controlled vocabulary, natural-language searching offers the following advantages:

1. No information loss. The entire document may be stored and available for searching. In a conventional system the document is reduced to some form of representation or surrogate. In a natural-language system based only on abstracts, however, there will clearly be some loss.

2. No loss of specificity. Since there is no controlled vocabulary, the specific language of the documents themselves is used as the basis of searching. In a natural-language system there should be no search failures due to "lack of specificity" in the vocabulary.

3. There is no "vocabulary lag." A new term, e.g., laser, will get into the system as soon as it appears in the literature. The vocabulary of a natural-language system has full bibliographic warrant.

4. Human indexing error is eliminated.

5. The system may be "cost-effective" in that the intellectual burden is all placed on the output side. In a conventional system much of the intellectual effort is placed on the input side. Since the number of documents indexed annually is usually much greater than the number of searches conducted (and since many of the documents indexed may in fact never be used) it is sometimes economically attractive to place the intellectual load on the searching end of the operation.

The major disadvantages are:

1. Input costs are high unless the data base can be obtained as a by-product from some other operation.

2. A greater intellectual burden is placed upon the searcher.

3. False coordinations and incorrect term relationships are likely to be more prevalent than they are in controlled-vocabulary systems. Failures due to "exhaustive indexing" are also likely to occur in full-text systems.

Natural-language systems, of the Pittsburgh and IBM types, are not entirely without some of the index-language devices discussed in Chapter 15. As we have seen, certain natural-language systems make some attempt to control synonyms by means of a simple thesaurus used at output stage only. Word endings may also be controlled. In the Pittsburgh system grammatical variants are listed in the thesaurus, and the searcher uses all such variants in his strategy. A more common alternative is to incorporate a truncation device whereby we can search on a portion of a word only. For example, a search is conducted on ABANDON#, where the indicator # signifies that the searcher does not care which letters follow. The search will thus pull in ABANDON, ABANDONS, ABANDONING, ABANDONMENT, and ABANDONED. This is a powerful tool that gives the searcher great flexibility to search on word roots or complete words as the nature of the search dictates. Of course the searcher must be careful not to lose search precision through premature truncation. For example, a search on ANAL#, intended to retrieve documents on analysis and analytical procedures in medicine, might well retrieve items on inflammation of the anus!

Some systems permit left truncation as well as right truncation. If we search on the suffix MYCIN, for example, we can retrieve all references on a large group of antibiotics without the need to list them.[30]

There is no hierarchy in a natural-language system unless it is built into the searcher's thesaurus. However, the hierarchical structures of other thesauri can also be used as a guide in searching. This is one of the advantages of natural-language searching: we can use all kinds of term lists to help us think of words that might represent the subject of our inquiry. Moreover, we can incorporate indexed data bases, available from various sources in machine-readable form, into our natural-language base, treating the controlled indexing of other agencies as if it were natural language.

Some natural-language systems use statistical associations between terms as a means of creating term groupings that may be useful for retrieval purposes. We will discuss this at greater length later.

The syntax of a natural-language system is obtained by means of word combination and by the use of positional indicators. These substitute for links, roles, subheadings, and similar devices in more conventional systems. As previously mentioned, simple coordination (co-occurrence) is a very powerful tool in reducing ambiguity and establishing context. Co-occurrence can be strengthened by demanding that two words must co-occur in the same paragraph or the same sentence. It is possible to improve precision by demanding closer physical proximity of words in this way. Presumably, the closer two words appear to one another in a text the greater the probability of their being directly related. Taken to its logical extreme, we can demand that two words should appear in

immediate physical juxtaposition (i.e., we search on a two-word phrase). For example, by searching for BLACK COMEDY as an adjacent pair, we avoid retrieving items associating comedies with black actors.

Weighting can obviously be used in free-text systems by the simple expedient of demanding a certain minimum occurrence of a word in a text. For example, we can specify retrieval of any document containing a "child" word and also containing an "abandon" word but only where the latter concept occurs more than X times in the text.

A critical problem in natural-language systems is that of textual accuracy. A typographical error or a garbled word has little effect on conventional systems but may have a considerable effect on free-text searching. Word garbling is particularly prevalent and troublesome in systems processing texts of wire messages (e.g., teletype) for dissemination and retrieval.

Word co-occurrence, positional indicators, and weighting are effective devices in allowing retrieval, with reasonable precision, from natural-language data bases. The Pittsburgh system has operated successfully with no more sophisticated devices than these for more than ten years. Some investigators, however, attempt to impose rigorous syntactic control on a natural-language system by means of automatic syntactic analysis (sentence parsing) programs. Such a program will determine structural dependencies between words in a sentence, and will store a syntactic representation of the sentence, or at least a reduced syntactic structure, in the form of a tree or "abstract graph," each word being a node in the tree and the syntactic dependencies represented by branches. Salton [20] describes techniques for this type of syntactic analysis in some detail. Figure 59, taken from Salton, is an example of a modified dependency tree structure resulting from syntactic analysis.

Automatic syntactic analysis of this type will yield a machine-readable corpus capable of producing extremely high levels of search precision (but with concomitant loss in recall) because it allows us to specify the exact relationships obtaining between words in document text as well as words occurring in request statements. While syntactic analysis may be needed for so-called "fact retrieval" or "question-answering" systems (i.e., systems that attempt to provide a direct answer to a question rather than retrieving a piece of relevant text) of the type surveyed by Simmons,[22] it is unnecessary for the type of information retrieval discussed in this book (i.e., retrieval of documents, document representations, or even sections of text).

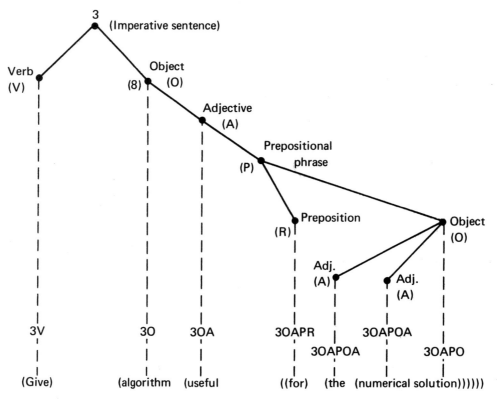

FIGURE 59 Example of a modified dependency tree structure produced by syntactic analysis.

Despite the accumulation of practical experience in operating natural-language systems with a minimum of syntax, and despite the fact that there is a quite evident move toward simplification in information retrieval, certain investigators, such as Moyne,[18] are still strongly advocating the use of "linguistic systems" based on transformational grammars, though they offer no objective justification for the cost and needless complexity of this approach.

The range of flexibility in natural-language searching is well illustrated by an examination of two such systems; one rather simple, and the other more sophisticated and complex. The first of these experimental systems is BROWSER, developed by Williams of IBM,[28, 29] and the second is the SMART system developed by Salton,[20] first at Harvard and now at Cornell.

BROWSER

The BROWSER system (Browsing On-line with Selective Retrieval) processes and searches abstracts. The input programs first delete all "common words" (noncontent-bearing) from an abstract and then match the residue against a humanly prepared dictionary of word roots ("rootwords"). Approximately 1,800 of these rootwords were derived from a file of 17,000 patent abstracts. When a root in an abstract matches a root in the dictionary, the document number is posted to that rootword in a conventional inverted search file. The rootword dictionary carries statistics on the total number of occurrences of each rootword in the corpus. It also carries an "information value" (I-value) for each rootword, which is inversely proportional to the number of occurrences of the rootword in the corpus.

The root TREMOR occurs only once in a particular corpus and achieves an I-value of 12.98, whereas TUBE occurs 293 times and achieves an I-value of 4.79. A high I-value is presumed to equate with *potency* for retrieval. The value is really a weighting in negative powers of 2. A value of 1.0 indicates a term that occurs in exactly one-half of the abstracts, a value of 2.0 indicates a term that occurs in one-quarter of the abstracts, and so on.

Searching in BROWSER is conducted on natural-language request statements rather than Boolean algebraic expressions. Words occurring in the request are automatically checked against the term dictionary and those recognized are arranged in descending order of I-value. The inverted term file is then searched and each document abstract in the file is given a value in relation to the request, the value being the sum of the I-values of all matching terms. In other words, the system produces a ranked output, with the abstracts most closely matching the request appearing at the top of the list. BROWSER is intended primarily for on-line, interactive implementation, to allow modification of request statements in the light of items retrieved during a search. The system is unusual in that it contains essentially no syntax; not even positional indicators are used. Tests appear to indicate that the system can operate effectively without them.

SMART

The SMART system is similar to BROWSER in that it operates on the natural language of abstracts and the natural language of request statements. However, it is much more sophisticated than BROWSER in its text processing and in its search options. Salton's document-processing procedures are applied to all words in an abstract except the "common words," which are recognized by means of a stop list. A stem-suffix cutoff program is used to reduce all words to their root form. Each word root in an abstract is then given a weight, using frequency and other criteria. A particular abstract may contain the word WELDING only once, but it may contain the root WELD several times. The root will thus be given a high weight in this abstract even though no single "welding" word occurs more than once. The word-stem list in SMART is known as a "Null thesaurus."

Each word stem is looked up in a "synonym dictionary," which is a simple machine-stored thesaurus. One or more so-called "concept numbers" are assigned to the abstract as a result of this match. The thesauri in SMART are humanly prepared. Table 28 shows an excerpt from a typical SMART thesaurus.[15] At the right of the table appear three thesaurus classes, 344, 345, and 346, and the words or roots that belong in these classes. The root (stem) METEOROLOG in an abstract, for example, will cause assignment of the concept code 345. This may subsequently allow the abstract to be retrieved in response to a request in which WEATHER, ATMOSPHERE, or WIND occurs. Homographs are distinguished by the fact that they appear in different thesaurus groups. The word WIND as a noun appears in group 345, where it is associated with other meteorological terms. As a verb it appears in group 233, along with such words as WINDING, WIRE-WOUND, and SOLENOID. Because the word WIND appearing in a document or a request may be ambiguous to the computer programs, categories 233 and 345 will both be assigned whenever the word appears. However, the assigned stem weight will be divided between

TABLE 28 Classes and Roots in SMART Thesaurus

Alphabetic Order			Numeric Order	
Word	Concept Code	Syntax Code	Concept Code	Word
Wide	438	001 043 040	344	obstacle
Will	32032	009 070 043 044 049		target
Wind	345 233	070 043	345	atmosphere
				meteorolog
Winding	233	070 136 137		weather
Wipe	403	043 070		wind
Wire	232 105	070 043	346	aircraft
				airplane
Wire-wound	233	001		bomber
				craft
				helicopter
				missile
				plane

SOURCE: M. E. Lesk and G. Salton.[14]

the two groups. In effect, this means that ambiguous words receive lower weight than unambiguous ones. Note that the "common word" WILL appears in the thesaurus but is given a high concept number (32032), which means that it is not used for concept identification.

Salton prepares a special thesaurus for each subject field in which he has an experimental collection. The following principles are followed:

1. No very rare concepts should be included in the thesaurus since they could not be expected to produce many matches between documents and search requests.

2. Very common high-frequency terms should also be excluded from the dictionary, since they produce too many matches for effective retrieval. (Individual high-frequency terms may be replaced by much more specific compound or hyphenated terms; for example, terms such as "computer" or "control" might well be eliminated in favor of a term such as "computer control," since the former are clearly ambiguous in many contexts whereas the latter is much more specific.)

3. Nonsignificant words should be studied carefully before they are included in the list of words to be eliminated (for example, a term such as "hand" should be included in a thesaurus dealing with biology, but it should not be included if its high-frequency count is due to expressions such as "on the other hand").

4. Ambiguous terms should be coded only for the senses that are likely to be present in the document collections to be treated. (For example, at least two category numbers must be shown for the term "field," corresponding on the one hand to the notion of subject area, and on the other hand to its technical sense in algebra; however, no category number need be shown to cover the notion of a patch of land if the dictionary deals with the mathematical sciences or related technical fields.)

5. Each concept class should include only terms of

roughly equal frequency so that the matching characteristics are approximately the same for each term within a category.

Salton usually employs machine-assisted procedures for the preparation of thesauri. The steps are roughly as follows:

1. A sample corpus of abstracts in the subject area to be treated is put into machine-readable form.

2. An automatic word frequency count is made. This results in a printout showing how many times each word has appeared in the entire corpus.

3. A keyword-in-context (KWIC) or keyword-out-of-context (KWOC) listing (Figure 60) is generated to show the various contexts in which each word is used.

4. The different senses in which each word is used is recognized by a human analyst through the examination of the KWIC listing. For example, SPECTRAL is found to have only one context (in the phrase SPECTRAL NORM) in a particular collection, whereas SQUARE has two (1, a rectangle of equal sides; 2, the power of two).

5. Words appearing in the corpus are grouped into thesaurus classes on the basis of a human decision as to their "semantic closeness," words with various senses being assigned to more than one thesaurus group.

In addition to the thesaurus, as described above, the SMART system incorporates various other devices to improve recall or precision. The thesaurus conceptual groups are arranged into hierarchies to facilitate the automatic broadening or narrowing of search strategies. The hierarchies generated are empirically derived and have been shown to be useful for retrieval purposes; they do not necessarily reflect true genus-species relations.

Another SMART procedure is "statistical phrase" recognition, which makes use of a preconstructed phrase dictionary consisting mainly of word pairs. A statistical phrase is assigned to a document on the basis of simple co-occurrence of thesaurus concepts. For example, if an abstract contains the concept "language" and also contains the concept "program," the statistical phrase "programming language" is assigned. A sample from a statistical phrase dictionary is shown in Table 29. Note that the phrase identified by the number 543 is assigned whenever the concept groups 544 and 608 are present in a document.

Another program option involves the syntactic analysis of sentences and the recognition of "syntactic phrases." A syntactic phrase is similar to a statistical phrase except that each word in the phrase must bear a specified syntactic relation with the other words in the phrase. Possible ambiguities can be resolved by this syntactic analysis. For example, at the level of the

KEYWORD	DOCUMENT
EXCESS REVERSE CURRENT IN GROWN GERMANIUM PN JUNCTION	0000000246
EXCESS STOCK IN A MULTIWAREHOUSE SYSTEM$....CONTROL OF	0000015771
EXCESS TELLURIUM$RTIES CF BISMUTH TELLURIDE CONTAINING	0000005985
EXCHANGE AND THE EFFECTS CF INNOVATION AND CHANGE$TION	0000003118
EXCHANGE ANISTROPHY IN AN IRON ALUMINUM ALLOY$.........	0000004320
EXCHANGE ANISTROPHY IN DISORDERED NI 3 MN$.............	0000004319
EXCHANGE BEHAVIOR AND SUBSEQUENT RESEARCH$ INFORMATION	0000003119
EXCHANGE CENTRALIZED ACCOUNTING SYSTEM$..MIDWEST STOCK	0000016549
EXCHANGE CENTRALIZED ACCCUNTING SYSTEM$..MIDWEST STOCK	0000007797
EXCHANGE ENERGY DENSITY IN COBALT FLUOSILICATE HEXAHYD	0000011728
EXCHANGE INTERACTION$CONTAINING THREE MAGNETIC IONS IN	0000011729
EXCHANGE INVARIENCE IN FLUID SYSTEMS$.................	0000009060
EXCHANGE MOLECULAR BEAMS$.......A NEW CONCEPT IN CHARGE	0000014063
EXCHANGE RESINS$..ION	0000001884
EXCHANGE RESONANCES IN GADOLINIUM IRON GARNET NEAR THE	0000004251
EXCHANGE STRUM LICUVILLE PROBLEM$ OC CURRENT FLOW HEAT	0000006583
EXCHANGE STURM LICUVILLE PROBLEM$ OC CURRENT FLOW HEAT	0000009268
EXCHANGE SYSTEM USING PARAMETRONS$L CROSSBAR TELEPHONE	0000001345
EXCHANGE SYSTEM USING PARAMETRONS$L CROSSBAR TELEPHONE	0000001620
EXCHANGE$.....................DOCUMENTS AND INFORMATION	0000003025
EXCHANGE$....................A SYSTEM FOR AUTOMATIC VALUE	0000006563
EXCHANGE$....................A SYSTEM FOR AUTOMATIC VALUE	0000009248
EXCHANGE$...........A SIMPLE MODEL FOR GAS SOLID ENERGY	0000013967
EXCHANGE$THE ROLE CF A PROFESSIONAL SOCIETY IN PROGRAM	0000007847
EXCHANGER UTILIZING PELTIER EFFECT SEMICONDUCTORS$HEAT	0000007617
EXCHANGES$.................RECENT ACTIVITIES IN FOREIGN	0000003000
EXCITABLE MEMBRANE$SE CF GAS ION PROCESSES IN MODELING	0000002677
EXCITATION COMPLEXES$...THE QUANTUM CHEMISTRY CF BOUND	0000005902
EXCITATION PARAMETRIQUE D UN RESONATEUR NON LINEAIRE E	0000001602
EXCITATION SPECTRA OF CRYSTALS$GLE PARTICLE ELECTRONIC	0000014256
EXCITATION SPECTRA OF DONORS IN SILICON$ STRESS ON THE	0000005914
EXCITATION USING BARRIER CAPACITANCE OF SEMI CONDUCTOR	0000001311
EXCITATION USING FERROELECTRIC MATERIALS$...PARAMETRIC	0000001335
EXCITATION USING VARIABLE CAPACITANCE OF FERROELECTRIC	0000001608
EXCITATION$ PARAMETRON USING TRANSVERSE MAGNETIC FIELD	0000001322
EXCITED BY QUENCHING INFRARED RADIATION$CTIVITY OF CDS	0000005941
EXCITED DIAMONDS$.............PHOTOCONDUCTIVITY OF U V	0000005943
EXCITED DIELECTRIC TUBE ANTENNA$RY ANALYSIS OF A HELIX	0000004336
EXCITED NETWORKS$............ANALYSIS OF PARAMETRICALLY	0000001605
EXCITED NON LINEAR CONTROLS$IMATE ANALYSIS CF RANDOMLY	0000005500
EXCITED NON LINEAR RESONATORS$CATION OF PARAMETRICALLY	0000001295
EXCITED STATES$CASE OF MULTIELECTRON CENTERS WITH MANY	0000005918
EXCITING POWER OF A PARAMETRON CORE AND ITS DEPENDENCY	0000001330
EXCITON COMPLEX IN CDS$E VIBRATIONAL SPECTRUM CF BOUND	0000005904
EXCITON COMPLEX IN GERMANIUM$IBRATIONAL SPECTRUM CF AN	0000005905
EXCITON EMISSION IN CDS CRYSTALS BY ELECTRIC FIELDS$OF	0000005928
EXCITON IN GERMANIUM$......ROTARY DISPERSION OF DIRECT	0000005924
EXCITON SERIES IN CU2O$ELC ZEEMAN EFFECT OF THE YELLOW	0000005926
EXCITON STATES IN SEMICONDUCTORS$TION TO THE THEORY OF	0000011965
EXCITON STATES NEAR THE EDGE IN THE DEPTH OF THE FUNDA	0000005938

FIGURE 60 Permuted keyword printout.

TABLE 29 Statistical Phrase Recognition (SMART)

Phrase Concept	Component Concepts					
543	544	608	—0	—0	—0	—0
282	280	281	—0	—0	—0	—0
282	306	?1	—0	—0	—0	—0
280	69	648	—0	—0	—0	—0
280	69	215	—0	—0	—0	—0
694	1285	1285	—0	—0	—0	—0
291	265	290	—0	—0	—0	—0
291	265	496	—0	—0	—0	—0
422	646	185	—0	—0	—0	—0
640	309	290	—0	—0	—0	—0
294	21	293	—0	—0	—0	—0
393	21	635	—0	—0	—0	—0
393	635	106	—0	—0	—0	—0
294	21	245	—0	—0	—0	—0
695	44	150	—0	—0	—0	—0
78	572	565	—0	—0	—0	—0
411	370	328	—0	—0	—0	—0
411	370	389	—0	—0	—0	—0
411	370	476	—0	—0	—0	—0
666	46	601	—0	—0	—0	—0
666	330	53	601	—0	—0	—0
666	347	46	—0	—0	—0	—0
666	347	290	—0	—0	—0	—0
666	347	601	—0	—0	—0	—0
666	357	290	—0	—0	—0	—0

SOURCE: Gerard Salton.[20]

statistical phrase, the word pair LINGUISTIC PROGRAM could lead to the assignment of the phrase PROGRAMMING LANGUAGES. If the syntactic analysis option is applied this ambiguity is avoided; the phrase PROGRAMMING LANGUAGES is only assigned to abstracts containing the necessary words in the correct syntactic relationship.

A further SMART option uses statistical associations between text words in order to generate classes of terms that are somehow related. The use of these kinds of co-occurrence statistics is discussed in more detail in the next chapter.

Searches are conducted in SMART on natural-language request statements. These request statements are processed essentially in the same way that documents are processed, including reduction to word stems, assignment of conceptual group numbers, and weighting of these groups. The natural-language request is processed against the file of document representations, and the search program looks for abstracts that most closely match the request statement. A "correlation coefficient" is derived to show the degree of similarity between the request statement and each document, and the entire collection is ranked in de-

creasing order of correlation coefficient. The result is a ranked output of document representations printed in order of this degree of match. In practice, some cutoff point or "threshold" is usually established to avoid printing out the entire set of document representations.

SMART is a very important experimental system because it offers many possible search options. A request can be processed against a document collection at any of several levels: simple word match, word stem match, statistical phrases, syntactic phrases, thesaurus groups, hierarchical groupings, or statistical associations. The searcher is thus given great flexibility in varying the search criteria in order to move in the direction of high recall or high precision. The system has built-in evaluation procedures whereby the results of one search option can be compared with the results of any alternative. Although many possible search options exist, Salton has generally found that he is able to achieve acceptable search results with the less sophisticated procedures (word stem match, thesaurus group match), and, in some instances at least, the more complex procedures have actually led to inferior overall performance.

It is intended that SMART be used with *iterative searches;* that is, the searcher will receive preliminary results from one search option, will evaluate these, and will indicate which of the retrieved items are relevant and which are not. When these relevance decisions are fed back into the system, the search programs automatically modify the weights of terms in the request statement in order to bring the statement closer to the profiles of the relevant documents in the collection, and thus to improve the quality of the second search.

Salton [19] has conducted a preliminary study comparing searches conducted in SMART with searches, for the same request, conducted in MEDLARS. The comparison is not clear-cut because of the problems of scale — it is difficult to know how SMART would have performed on a collection as large as that of MEDLARS. However, on a small experimental corpus, SMART appears to achieve results comparable to those that MEDLARS searches would attain in the same corpus. SMART tends to exert a normalizing influence on the search results; that is, the SMART search results tend not to equal the very best of the MEDLARS results, where the human search analyst has perfectly understood the request and has prepared a comprehensive search strategy. On the other hand, SMART avoids the worst MEDLARS results, in which the search analyst badly misinterprets the user's requirements and prepares an inadequate strategy. The net result is that SMART achieves recall and precision figures, averaged over a group of searches, that are

comparable to those achieved by MEDLARS searches on the same corpus.

The SMART system has many further ramifications that cannot be covered adequately here. I have concentrated on those aspects that are particularly relevant to the subject of vocabulary control. Further details can be obtained from Salton's own extensive writings.

TWO-LEVEL SEARCHING

In the last five years there has been an evident trend toward simplification in information retrieval. It has become more widely recognized that it is possible to operate systems effectively with a somewhat minimal level of vocabulary control. Generally speaking, syntactic analysis has proven to be unnecessary and unjustifiable in terms of cost-effectiveness. The same can be said of roles and other relational indicators. As an illustration of this trend, let us consider an actual case history involving a large information processing agency in the United States.

The Central Intelligence Agency has made a deliberate move away from a highly sophisticated system based on a large carefully controlled vocabulary (a classification scheme including various relational indicators). The present system, a very large machine-based operation, is now much less sophisticated. Three separate vocabulary components are involved in the indexing and retrieval operations:

1. A small controlled vocabulary of about 250 broad subject codes.
2. A list of codes representing geographic areas (area codes).
3. Keywords or phrases occurring in the titles or text of documents.

In indexing a document, the analyst assigns subject codes and area codes necessary to represent adequately the broad subject matter and the countries involved. The analyst also marks up the title of the document to indicate words or phrases that might be useful for retrieval purposes (let us just call them "keywords"). If the title is insufficiently descriptive the indexer will expand it by adding, parenthetically, additional descriptive words or phrases contained in the text of the document itself or otherwise illustrative of its content or type.

This indexing represents a significant economy over the previous indexing which employed the large carefully controlled vocabulary. The reasons are twofold:

1. The subject codes are sufficiently broad that a relatively unskilled indexer can assign them without much difficulty.

2. The subject codes are small enough in number that the indexer can retain most in his memory and avoid the necessity for constant look-up in a vocabulary listing.

In fact, several of the indexers have no more than a high school education. All indexing is done on the document itself; that is, the indexer writes subject codes and area codes on the face of the document, marks up the title to indicate keywords, and may add additional words to the title. No indexing forms need to be completed. The input typist works directly from the document itself. Indexing is fast. In fact, a good indexer may index a hundred or more items in a day.

Searching is conducted by trained search analysts on combinations of keywords, subject codes, and area codes. Although any one of these on its own is relatively crude, the joint use of a keyword (to give specificity) and a subject or area code (to give context) is an extremely powerful device. For example, the keyword PLANT means something entirely different when coordinated with the subject code for agriculture than when it is coordinated with the subject code for, say, metal industry. Likewise, the keyword STRIKE associated with the area code for Jordan will probably signify a strike force, whereas when it is coordinated with the area code for England it is more likely to signify a labor dispute. Moreover, the joint use of broad subject codes, area codes, and keywords is extremely effective in illustrating relationships, even when these relationships are not explicitly specified. For instance, area code Australia, area code England, and keyword LAMB are very likely to represent a document discussing some aspect of export of lamb from Australia to England.

Keywords are completely uncontrolled in this system. The indexer may assign any word or phrase he wishes. The searcher is supplied with various searching aids, including a complete list of keywords with an indication of the number of times each one has been used, and lists showing the number of times each keyword has co-occurred with each subject code, and vice versa. The result is a crude classification of keywords that is nevertheless extremely useful in searching. For example, under the broad code for metal industry will appear a complete list of metals-related keywords. This is an interesting example of one system operating effectively with a minimum of vocabulary control. In fact, the system works on a combination of a small controlled vocabulary of broad descriptors used in association with a very large uncontrolled vocabulary of natural-language expressions occurring in documents, particularly document titles.

A very similar approach (i.e., one using two-level searching — broad subject codes plus specific keywords or descriptors) has been described by Uhlmann [26] and by Holst.[9] The system is in the field of nuclear science and the thesaurus [1] used has three parts:

1. A group of broad subject categories, derived from those used by *Nuclear Science Abstracts,* with inter-category cross-references.

2. An alphabetical list of terms without any cross-reference structure.

3. An asssociation list showing statistics on co-occurrence (in indexing) of terms and categories. This is a searching aid.

In this system a document cannot be indexed by the terms alone. Terms must be accompanied by one or more of the subject categories, as:

Document	Category	Terms
"Influence of irradiation on the corrosion behavior of Zircaloy"	0905 RADIATION EFFECTS ON MATERIALS	CORROSION ZIRCALOY
"Influence of corrosion on radiation effects on Zircaloy"	0902 CORROSION	RADIATION EFFECTS ZIRCALOY

Note how the joint use of broad subject categories plus specific terms is capable of expressing quite complex relationships unambiguously and economically.

ASLIB CRANFIELD EVALUATION

It is now time to consider the implications of the second major series of investigations directed by Cleverdon at Cranfield, England, and generally referred to as "Cranfield II." [7] These studies were concerned with the composition and structure of index languages; in particular, they investigated the effects of various recall and precision devices on the performance of a retrieval system. The test collection included 1,400 research papers mainly in the field of aerodynamics, and 221 information requests based on the document collection. The requests were compiled by the authors of papers contained in the experimental corpus. By means of brute force procedures it was possible to determine, for each request, exactly which documents were relevant and which were not. This resulted in a complete request-document relevance matrix, and it allowed the investigators, using recall and precision ratios, to measure the effect of variations in the index language on the performance of searches conducted for each of the requests. Each document was indexed very exhaustively by the research team. Three levels of indexing were employed, as illustrated in Figure 61.

First, the document content was represented by simple Uniterms extracted from the text itself. Each term was weighted on a three-point scale: 1 representing a major aspect of the document; 2, a minor aspect; and 3, a very minor aspect. The Uniterms were then combined into "concepts," i.e., they were "interfixed." Finally, the "concepts" were combined into "themes." The themes and the concepts represent the two levels of linking (partitioning and interfixing) described in Chapter 15.

Many different index languages were created and tested on the basis of this initial indexing. One group of index languages consisted of single-word, natural-language vocabularies. They included single words with no control, with synonyms controlled, with quasi-synonyms controlled, with word endings controlled, and several combinations of these. The single words were also grouped into various single-word hierarchies. This was a rather artificial device, but it needed to be tested. It resulted in reducing the size of the vocabulary since groups of related terms, rather than single words, were searched. Two stages of hierarchical reduction were used.

Various index languages were also created on the basis of the "concepts" derived in indexing and on the basis of grouping in various ways to form "controlled vocabularies." Further index languages were derived on the basis of words used only in the titles of documents and words occurring in the document abstracts. For each request, a search was conducted in such a way that separate results could be derived for each of the 33 "systems" (each one having a different index language) being evaluated. The results were expressed in many different ways including conventional recall and precision plots, and also by means of "normalized recall," a measure borrowed from Salton. "Normalized recall" is really a single figure of merit which takes into account both the recall ratio and the precision ratio.

Vast quantities of data were accumulated in these Cranfield studies, and it is impossible to do justice to them here. The full reports require careful study by any serious student of index languages. Condensed versions have been prepared by Cleverdon,[4, 5] and the studies have been analyzed by Te Nuyl [25] and others. The gross overall results are displayed in Table 30. In general, the single-term index languages produced the best performance, the "controlled term" languages were second, and the "simple concept" languages were least satisfactory. There are many significant points of interest in this table. A very important one

B1590 Base Document A137	AUTHOR STONE, A. TITLE Effect of stage characteristics and matching on axial flow compressor performance REFERENCE *Trans. American Soc. of Mechanical Engineers*, 80, 1958, p. 1273	Indexer J.M.	Date 17-6-63

THEMES (partitioning)		CONCEPTS (Interfixing)		CONCEPTS (Interfixing)		TERMS & WEIGHTS		TERMS & WEIGHTS	
A	cd *effect of* a *use of* ef	a	Stage characteristics	t	Range of operations	Stage	1	Blade	3
B	———— b ————	b	Stage matching	u	Stage flow coefficient	Characteristic	1	Range	2
C	cdh	c	Axial flow compressor	v	Mass flow	Matching	1	Operations	2
D	cdi *effect of* j *with* k	d	Stage performance	w	Choking flow co-efficient	Axial	1	Mass	2
E	cdl *effect of* g	e	Test data	x	Surge line	Flow	1	Choking	2
F	cmp *effect of* n	f	Analysis	y	Change in slope	Compressor	1	Line	2
G	———————— vo	g	Mach number	z	Knee double valued performance curve	Performance	1	Slope	3
H	cmdq	h	Velocity distribution	aa	Unstalling hysteresis	Test	1	Knee	3
I	cmdr	i	Temperature co-efficient	bb	Inlet guide vane stagger	Data	1	Double	3
J	cmdt *effect of* sg	j	Flow co-efficient	cc	Uprating stage one	Analysis	1	Curve	3
K	cmu *effect of* g	k	Constant flow angle	dd	Uprating stage two	Mach	2	Unstalling	3
L	————————v	l	Cascade losses	ee	Blade stagger	Velocity	2	Hysteresis	3
M	cbv *effect of* w	m	Idealised compressor	ff	Stage loading	Distribution	3	Inlet	3
N	cbx *effect of* o	n	Total pressure ratio	gg	Annular area	Temperature	3	Guide	3
O	cbxy *effect of* o	o	Percentage of design speed			Coefficient	3	Vane	3
P	cbz *effect of* aa	p	Performance			Constant	3	Stagger	3
Q	cu *effect of* bb	q	Stalling point			Angle	3	Uprating	3
R	————————cc	r	Compression surges			Cascade	3	One	3
S	————————dd	s	Pitch line blade speed			Loss	3	Loading	3
T	cx *effect of* ee					Idealized	2	Annulus	3
U	————————ff					Total	3	Area	3
V	————————gg					Ratio	3	Number	2
W	————————vq					Percentage	2	Line	3
						Design	2	Valued	3
						Speed	2	Two	3
						Stalling	2	Pressure	2
						Point	2		
						Surge	2		
						Pitch	3		

FIGURE 61 Complete indexing record for document in Cranfield II corpus.

is the fact that the interfixing of uncontrolled single words into natural-language "concepts" has an unusually drastic effect on performance (the single-word, natural-language vocabulary appears in position 3, while the interfixed vocabulary of these words drops to the bottom in the rankings). The only improvement over uncontrolled single words was effected by the simple control of word endings and synonyms. Any further controls introduced led to reduced overall performance.

THE INSPEC STUDY

Another comparative study was undertaken by Aitchison et al.[2, 3] who evaluated five index languages from the viewpoint of their utility in the INSPEC program (Information Service in Physics, Electrotechnology and Control) of the Institution of Electrical Engineers. The languages were:

1. Titles of papers (uncontrolled natural language).

2. Titles and abstracts (uncontrolled natural language).

3. A hybrid system consisting of *Science Abstracts* subject headings plus free-text modifiers.

4. Free-language assigned terms.

5. Assigned terms from a controlled vocabulary.

The evaluation was conducted with a set of 542 documents and a group of 97 questions, for each of which certain of the documents in the corpus were known to be relevant.

The results of the study, in basic terms, are as follows:

Title. The highest precision but low recall because of low exhaustivity.

Abstract. High recall but low precision.

Hybrid. Good precision; not as good on recall because of low exhaustivity. Better overall than either titles or abstracts.

Free indexing. The best recall (high exhaustivity) and adequate precision.

TABLE 30 Overall Results of Cranfield Studies of Index Languages

Order	Normalized recall		Indexing language
1	65·82	I-3	Single terms. Word forms
2	65·23	I-2	Single terms. Synonyms
3	65·00	I-1	Single terms. Natural language
4	64·47	I-6	Single terms. Synonyms, word forms, quasi-synonyms
5	64·41	I-8	Single terms. Hierarchy, second stage
6	64·05	I-7	Single terms. Hierarchy, first stage
7 =	63·05	I-5	Single terms. Synonyms. Quasi-synonyms
7 =	63·05	II-11	Simple concepts. Hierarchical and alphabetical selection
9	62·88	II-10	Simple concepts. Alphabetical second stage selection
10 =	61·76	III-1	Controlled terms. Basic terms
10 =	61·76	III-2	Controlled terms. Narrower terms
12	61·17	I-9	Single terms. Hierarchy third stage
13	60·94	IV-3	Abstracts. Natural language
14	60·82	IV-4	Abstracts. Word forms
15	60·11	III-3	Controlled terms. Broader terms
16	59·76	IV-2	Titles. Word forms
17	59·70	III-4	Controlled terms. Related terms
18	59·58	III-5	Controlled terms. Narrower and broader terms
19	59·17	III-6	Controlled terms. Narrower, broader and related terms
20	58·94	IV-1	Titles. Natural language
21	57·41	II-15	Simple concepts. Complete combination
22	57·11	II-9	Simple concepts. Alphabetical first stage selection
23	55·88	II-13	Simple concepts. Complete species and superordinate
24	55·76	II-8	Simple concepts. Hierarchical selection
25	55·41	II-12	Simple concepts. Complete species
26	55·05	II-5	Simple concepts. Selected species and superordinate
27	53·88	II-7	Simple concepts. Selected co-ordinate and collateral
28	53·52	II-3	Simple concepts. Selected species
29	52·47	II-14	Simple concepts. Complete collateral
30	52·05	II-4	Simple concepts. Superordinate
31	51·82	II-6	Simple concepts. Selected co-ordinate
32	47·41	II-2	Simple concepts. Synonyms
33	44·64	II-1	Simple concepts. Natural language

SOURCE: C. Cleverdon et al.[7]

Controlled. The best overall results in terms of recall and precision.

The investigators reached the following conclusions:

1. In this evaluation, the controlled language is superior in performance to any of the other languages.

2. The free-language equivalent of this controlled language is in turn superior in performance to any of the remaining languages.

3. Of the free languages requiring no additional processing (i.e., the "natural" languages), the Title is not sufficiently rich in terms to ensure that most of the relevant items are retrieved, although it produces a low proportion of nonrelevant items.

4. The other "natural" language, the Abstract (i.e., the title and abstract), is over-rich in terms, and although it retrieves most of the relevant items it also produces a very high proportion of nonrelevant items.

5. The hybrid language has a comparatively low retrieval capability because, although a particular document may be represented by several subject headings with free modifiers, many of the terms are repeated in several of the strings so that the number of *distinct* index terms is comparatively few (i.e., overall exhaustivity is low).

6. The "indexing" of the controlled language and the free language is identical, since the former is a translation of the latter into a controlled language. It follows that the superiority of the controlled language must be attributable to the search strategies used. Analysis shows that the superiority stems from the facility provided by the controlled language for including in the formulation all the alternative words and concepts which may be used to express the question. This is a function of the thesaurus and, in particular, of its constant updating by addition of new entry terms to account for new terms as they occur in the

indexing of the documents. *A similar retrieval performance should be obtainable with free-language indexing with the use of a free-language thesaurus to which would be added, for use in subsequent searching, all the new terms as they occurred in the documents.*

The INSPEC investigators go on to make the following recommendations:

Although it ranked only second in performance in the test, it is recommended that a free-language indexing system, similar to Free-Index of the test, be developed for INSPEC and that a free-language thesaurus should be developed for use with it. This will ensure that most of the advantages of a controlled language are obtained in retrieval, by recording all new terms as they are input to the system and displaying their relations to other terms for use in search formulations. This will be equivalent to the constant addition of new lead-ins,* etc., which contributes so much to the effectiveness of a controlled language.

The free-language indexing is chosen in preference to the controlled language for two main reasons: the disadvantages of using a controlled language, and the greater retrieval effectiveness which is potentially obtainable with uncontrolled terms.† Since the terms selected from the document (added to where necessary by the indexer) are not changed on input to the data base when using an uncontrolled language, they will always be available for retrieval in whatever combination is required. With controlled terms the subsequent retrieval must be limited by the confounding of terms and the pre-coordination of the concepts which takes place in the translation into the controlled language.

The other disadvantages of a controlled language, which cause it not to be recommended for INSPEC, are:

(1) It requires the setting up and continuous development of the thesaurus for use in indexing: the up-dated thesaurus must be available to each indexer.

(2) It is extremely difficult if not impossible to ensure the required consistency in the use of the controlled terms by many indexers.

(3) The translation of the indexing concepts into controlled terms is an additional expense and causes a loss in precision.

(4) It reduces the possibility of obtaining indexed material from other organisations.

(5) The compilation of profiles and formulation of searches by the user without the interposition of information staff is made difficult with a controlled language. Similarly on-line retrieval in conversational mode is only possible either with the constraint on the searcher of using the controlled language or with the penalty of repeated translation to and from the controlled language by program.

The results of another study, reported by Hersey et al.,[8] appear at first sight to conflict with those of the INSPEC study. The study was conducted on a data base at the Science Information Exchange. On the basis

of a group of 39 real requests it was discovered that improved results in recall and precision were achieved when searching on subject codes as opposed to free-text words (the Data Central on-line search system was used). The failure, however, was not a failure inherent in natural-language searching systems as much as a failure in the searching strategies used. No type of thesaurus was provided to assist the searcher in the construction of effective natural-language strategies. The investigators concluded, in fact, that there are pros and cons to both approaches (with the text useful for specifics and the subject codes for broader conceptualizations), *and that a joint system might provide the best of both worlds* (the two-level search approach again!).

That natural-language searching, based on uncontrolled single words occurring in text, can be an effective method of implementing retrieval systems is supported by:

1. The results from Cranfield and INSPEC.
2. The results from SMART, which tend to indicate that the less sophisticated search options produce acceptable results.
3. Several years of operating experience with natural-language systems of the Pittsburgh type.

We now need to consider why natural-language searching appears to be so effective. The reasons, on reflection, are fairly obvious. The principal factor controlling the recall of a retrieval system is the exhaustivity of the indexing (i.e., the extent to which the breadth of subject matter in a document is covered in the indexing operation), and the principal factor controlling the precision of a retrieval system is the specificity of the index language.[14] Natural-language systems of the Pittsburgh type have the advantages of complete exhaustivity (since the entire text is stored) and complete specificity (since the language of the document is used intact with no artificial "class terms" imposed upon it). Consequently, given the ability to create effective search strategies, a natural-language system should have great flexibility in achieving high recall or high precision, as the circumstances dictate.

Cleverdon[6] has elaborated usefully on this point. He mentions two principal ways of creating a controlled vocabulary:

1. By grouping together, into classes, terms which can be considered sufficiently synonymous for retrieval purposes in a particular environment (e.g., DRIVEN, PROPELLED, LAUNCHED, PROJECTED, FIRED).
2. By grouping related specific terms under a more generic term (e.g., all specific lung diseases under LUNG DISEASE).

---

* That is, entry terms.
† Here the INSPEC investigators refer to the potential improvement possible with a search thesaurus.

TABLE 31   Natural-Language Indexing vs. Controlled-Vocabulary Indexing

	Pro	Con
Natural-language indexing (i.e., indexing by humans without a controlled vocabulary)	Requires lower level of knowledge and experience from indexers. Indexing is faster (no look-up) and therefore cheaper. Complete specificity is possible and this allows high search precision. The language of documents is likely to be user-oriented (bibliographic warrant).	An increased burden is placed upon the searcher. It is somewhat more difficult to obtain a high recall.
Controlled-vocabulary indexing	Leads to greater consistency in terminology. Reduces the burden on the searcher. Makes it somewhat easier to obtain a high recall.	Indexing is slower (requires look-up) and more expensive. Requires a relatively high level of knowledge and training on the part of the indexers. Full specificity is sacrificed. A large controlled vocabulary is costly to maintain.

In practice, most controlled vocabularies employ both grouping devices.

The point is essentially this. Without the application of computers to information retrieval, terms can be grouped together only by constructing a controlled vocabulary that indexers must use. Such a controlled vocabulary fixes, once and for all, the level of specificity possible and thus the precision capabilities of the system. If we decide to subsume all specific lung diseases under the generic LUNG DISEASES, we have lost forever the capability of precisely retrieving documents on pulmonary tuberculosis, emphysema, pneumonia, and other specific pulmonary diseases. In a computer-based system, however, we do not need to control the vocabulary *until we conduct the search.* This is a very important distinction. In a natural-language system we can retrieve on the specific lung disease terms when we need to. However, when a generic search on all lung diseases is desired, we can incorporate into our strategy the "conceptual group" of terms representing lung disease. This gives us great flexibility in searching, since any term class that is formed at the input stage (by control of synonyms, confounding of word endings, or establishing of hierarchies) can equally well be formed at the time of searching. *That is, we can develop a "controlled vocabulary" which is used only as a searching aid.* Furthermore, any existing thesaurus (Roget as well as information retrieval thesauri) is potentially of value as a searching aid in a natural-language system. So, of course, are dictionaries. We

should distinguish the two approaches to vocabulary control by calling one a *pre-controlled vocabulary* and the other a *post-controlled vocabulary.* The flexibility of being able to form classes at the time of searching (a flexibility that is lost when these classes are rigidly established by a controlled vocabulary) has led Cleverdon to state that "the performance with natural language can never be lower than with controlled language." The findings of these various studies, plus his own work on machine-aided indexing at the Defense Documentation Center, have led Klingbiel[13] to state that "highly structured controlled vocabularies are obsolete for indexing and retrieval" and that "the natural language of scientific prose is fully adequate for indexing and retrieval." Some of the more important pros and cons of natural-language indexing versus controlled-vocabulary indexing are summarized in Table 31.

Senko[21] has stated that full-text searching appears to be entirely feasible in the following situation:

1. Each document (or section which can be treated as a separate item) is normally less than two or three hundred words.

2. The entire data base is less than one million words.

3. The vocabulary of the documents and/or the queries is relatively constrained.

He suggests the following materials as probably suitable: statutes, some medical records, technical ab-

stracts, single classes of the patent art, magazine and newspaper articles, and criminal records. The major problem is not lack of suitable search programs but lack of machine-readable text. With the general trend toward on-line implementation of retrieval systems, natural-language searching is likely to increase in appeal and practicability.

Parenthetically, it is worth noting that more and more natural-language data bases are becoming available in machine-readable form. Usually these data bases are produced as part of a publishing operation, particularly the publication of abstracts. As a result of the availability of these data bases, a number of "scientific information dissemination centers" have been set up both in the United States and in Europe. These centers act as information retailers by purchasing or leasing tapes from the information wholesalers (e.g., *Chemical Abstracts, Biological Abstracts*) and providing services, especially dissemination services, on a subscription basis. These information centers base their operations very largely upon natural-language searching and are developing searching techniques of ever increasing sophistication. An example of a European center of this type is the United Kingdom Chemical Information Service, Nottingham University. An example of a United States center is the Computer Search Center, IIT Research Institute, Chicago.[30]

In conclusion, I would like to re-emphasize the fact that thesauri are not made redundant by natural-language systems. In fact, the searcher who most needs a thesaurus is the searcher in a natural-language system.

REFERENCES

1. AB Atomenergi. *Nuclear Science and Technology: A Documentation Thesaurus.* Experimental edition. Stockholm: April 1966. Report FTI–13.
2. Aitchison, T. M. and Tracy, J. M. *Comparative Evaluation of Index Languages.* Part 1. *Design.* London: Institution of Electrical Engineers, July 1969.
3. Aitchison, T. M. et al. *Comparative Evaluation of Index Languages.* Part 2. *Results.* London: Institution of Electrical Engineers, July 1970.
4. Cleverdon, C. "The Cranfield Tests on Index Language Devices." *ASLIB Proceedings* 19 (1967): 173-194.
5. Cleverdon, C. "The Efficiency of Index Languages." In *Communication in Science: Documentation and Automation.* Edited for Ciba Foundation by A. De Reuck and J. Knight. London: J & A Churchill Ltd., 1967, 84-93.
6. Cleverdon, C. *Search Techniques in Mechanized I. R. Systems.* Unpublished note, November 1969.
7. Cleverdon, C. et al. *Factors Determining the Performance of Indexing Systems.* 3 Vols. Cranfield, England: College of Aeronautics, ASLIB Cranfield Research Project, 1966.
8. Hersey, D. F. et al. "Comparison of On-Line Retrieval Using Free Text Words and Scientist Indexing." *Proceedings of the American Society for Information Science* 7 (1970): 265-268.
9. Holst, W. "Problemer ved Strukturering og Bruk av den Polytekniske Tesaurus." *Tidskrift för Dokumentation* 22 (1966): 69-74.
10. Horty, J. F. "Legal Research Using Electronic Techniques." *Proceedings of the Fifth Biennial A. A. L. L. Institute of Law Librarians.* 1961: 56-58.
11. Kehl, W. B. "Communication Between Computer and User in Information Searching." In *Information Retrieval Management.* Edited by L. H. Hattery and E. M. McCormick. Detroit: American Data Processing, Inc., 1962, 83-91.
12. Kehl, W. B. et al. "An Information Retrieval Language for Legal Studies." *Communications of the Association for Computing Machinery* 4 (1961): 380-389.
13. Klingbiel, P. H. *The Future of Indexing and Retrieval Vocabularies.* Alexandria, Va.: Defense Documentation Center, November 1970. AD 716 200.
14. Lancaster, F. W. *Information Retrieval Systems: Characteristics, Testing, and Evaluation.* New York: Wiley, 1968.
15. Lesk, M. E. and Salton, G. "Interactive Search and Retrieval Methods Using Automatic Information Displays." *Proceedings of the Spring Joint Computer Conference* 34 (1969): 435-446.
16. Magnino, J. J., Jr. *CIS—A Computerized Normal Text Current Awareness Technique.* Yorktown Heights, N. Y.: IBM, Thomas J. Watson Research Center, 1965. ITIRC–006.
17. Magnino, J. J., Jr. *IBM Technical Information Retrieval Center—Normal Text Techniques.* Yorktown Heights, N. Y.: IBM, Thomas J. Watson Research Center, 1965. ITIRC–002.
18. Moyne, J. A. "Information Retrieval and Natural Language." *Proceedings of the American Society for Information Science* 6 (1969): 259-263.
19. Salton, G. "A Comparison Between Manual and Automatic Indexing Methods." *American Documentation* 20 (1969): 61-71.
20. Salton, G. *Automatic Information Organization and Retrieval.* New York: McGraw-Hill, 1968.
21. Senko, M. E. "Information Retrieval and Application Areas: Impact and Feedback." *Proceedings of the Fourth Annual National Colloquium on Information Retrieval.* Edited by A. B. Tonik. Philadelphia, Pa.: International Information Incorporated, 1967, 177-184.
22. Simmons, R. F. "Answering English Questions by Computer; a Survey." *Communications of the Association for Computing Machinery* 8 (1965): 53-70.
23. Swanson, D. R. "Interrogating a Computer in Natural Language." Paper presented at the IFIPS Conference, Munich, 1962.
24. Swanson, D. R. "Searching Natural Language Text by Computer." *Science,* October 21, 1960, 1099-1104.
25. Te Nuyl, T. W. *Examination of the Validity of the Conclusions Arrived at in the ASLIB Cranfield Research Project.* Copenhagen: Danish Centre for Documentation, 1968. FID/CR Report No. 7.
26. Uhlmann, W. "A Thesaurus *Nuclear Science and Technology:* Principles of Design." *Teknisk-Vetenskaplig Forskning (TVF)* 38 (1967): 46-52.
27. University of Pittsburgh. *Searching Law by Computer: How it works.* Pittsburgh, 1968.

28. Williams, J. H., Jr. *BROWSER: An Automatic Indexing On-line Text Retrieval System. Annual Progress Report.* Gaithersburg, Md.: IBM, Federal Systems Division, 1969. AD 693 143.

29. Williams, J. H., Jr. and Perriens, M. P. *Automatic Full Text Indexing and Searching System.* Gaithersburg, Md.: IBM, Federal Systems Division, 1968.

30. Williams, M. E. *Experiences of IIT Research Institute in Operating a Computerized Retrieval System for Searching a Variety of Data Bases.* Paper presented at the Third Cranfield International Conference on Mechanized Information Storage and Retrieval Systems, July, 1971. Chicago: IIT Research Institute, 1971.

17 Creating Index Languages Automatically

In the systems discussed in Chapter 16 no indexing is involved.* The entire text of a document, or at least an abstract, is stored in machine-readable form, word by word, and is searched in its full-text form. The application of computers to information retrieval has introduced another interesting possibility, that of automatically reducing a document to an indexed representation. This process is known as *automatic indexing* or sometimes as *machine indexing*. An excellent and complete review of the subject has been prepared by Stevens,[27] and a valuable symposium appeared in 1965.[22] A more condensed review was published earlier by Lancaster.[15]

There are two major types of automatic indexing:

1. *Indexing by extraction.* Automatic extraction of words from a document to represent its subject matter.

2. *Indexing by assignment.* Automatic assignment of terms to a document from a controlled vocabulary based on characteristics of the vocabulary of the document.

Indexing by extraction is the easier process of the two, and experiments with this have met with moderate success. Automatic indexing by assignment is much more difficult and has met with little success. Fortunately it is not worth doing anyway, a point to which we will return later. All automatic indexing of either type has been experimental. I know of no system truly based on automatic indexing which can be regarded as an operating system.†

The procedures used in automatic indexing have been similar in all investigations conducted. The justification for automatic indexing is the perfectly reasonable assumption that the individual words occurring in a document are good indicators of its content (subject matter). Moreover, if we ignore the common (non-substantive) words that merely provide syntax, the more frequently a word occurs in a document the more likely it is to indicate its subject matter. If, for example, we discover a document in which the most frequently occurring words are "stall," "lift," "flutter," "delta," and "wing," we can make a number of reasonable assumptions:

1. That it belongs to the general class of documents dealing with aerodynamics.

2. That the five high-frequency keywords are reasonably good index terms to represent its content.

3. That other documents in which these five words all occur frequently will also be on the same topic.

Obviously, if we can make these assumptions, there is

---

* Although abstracting is involved in some of the systems and this may require more intellectual effort than indexing.

† I am excluding from consideration KWIC and KWOC indexes, which are automatically prepared but usually do no more than produce a permutation on words occurring in the titles of documents. Such indexes, while interesting and popular, have little relevance to the subject of vocabulary control.

a reasonable chance that a computer can be used to (a) extract from a document keywords that are adequate indicators of its subject, (b) assign documents to broad subject categories such as "aerodynamics," and (c) form classes of documents that, on the basis of words they contain, are "similar" in subject coverage.

STATISTICAL CRITERIA

The earliest proposals for automatic indexing were made by Luhn [17] and Baxendale [4] of IBM. Luhn relied primarily on statistical criteria for extraction of words from documents. The techniques suggested by Luhn, and elaborated on by later investigators, are somewhat as follows:

1. A document collection is put into machine-readable form.

2. Common words (pronouns, articles, conjunctions, conjunctive adverbs, copula and auxiliary verbs, quantitative adjectives) are eliminated from further processing by means of a "stop list." Typically, this will reduce the vocabulary of a document by about 50 percent. A good stop list is likely to contain about 150 words.

3. Substantive words occurring too frequently to be of value for retrieval purposes may also be eliminated by a stop list. Such a word might be "computer" in a data-processing collection.

4. The remaining text words are sorted into alphabetical order and the frequency of occurrence of each is recorded. The words are then ranked in frequency order.

5. Word pairs or triples occurring more than x times in the text, in immediate physical juxtaposition, may also be recorded and ranked by frequency.

6. The most frequently occurring words and/or word strings are selected to act as index terms for the document. Some cutoff point is established. For example, a certain fixed number of terms, or all terms occurring more than x times, are selected. The cutoff criterion for selection of strings will usually be less stringent than the criterion for selection of single words. The word "cooling," for example, may be regarded as nonsignificant if it occurs only twice in the text, while the pair "transpiration cooling" may be selected as being significant on two appearances only.

7. Finally, the set of selected words and word strings is stored with the document identification to represent its content and to provide a surrogate that can be searched in response to subject requests. A typical surrogate thus created may look something like this:

PATTERN RECOGNITION
PATTERN
RECOGNITION
CHARACTER
CHARACTERIZER
ARRAY
TEMPLATE
PROGRAM
MATRIX

RELATIVE FREQUENCY APPROACH

The foregoing procedures index a document collection by extraction of words from text, the extraction being based on the absolute frequency of occurrence of the words. Another possible approach, advocated by Bar-Hillel [2] and by Oswald et al.,[21] among others, uses similar procedures but bases these on relative frequency rather than absolute frequency. The relative frequency approach has much to commend it. The most significant words for indexing and search purposes are likely to be those that occur more frequently than one expects them to occur on the basis of statistics of word occurrence in running text. Suppose we analyze the text of, say, a thousand aerodynamics documents selected at random. As a result we discover how frequently each substantive word has occurred per ten thousand words of running text. We store this frequency-ordered vocabulary in machine-readable form and use it in the automatic indexing of a new set of documents. However, words are selected as being significant not on the basis of how frequently they occur in absolute terms but on the basis of whether or not they occur more frequently per ten thousand words of text than one expects them to from the statistics in the frequency-ordered vocabulary. Thus, the word "wing" may be rejected in several documents, even though it is the most frequently occurring word in these documents, because it does not occur more frequently than expected in any set of aerodynamics documents selected at random. On the other hand, several words in these same documents that occur much less frequently than "wing" are selected as being significant because they do occur more frequently than expected. Such words might include "buzz," "sweptback," and "vibration," none of which would have been selected by means of absolute frequency criteria.

The relative frequency approach gives low significance to normally rare words that occur infrequently in a document. It gives high significance to normally rare words used frequently in a particular document.

OTHER APPROACHES

Automatic extraction indexing implies the conduct of statistical analysis on the complete text of a document. However, it is expensive to process complete

texts even if we can capture them inexpensively in machine-readable form. Various investigators have therefore proposed that term extraction should be based on those portions of a document most likely to bear the most potent content indicators. Baxendale [4] recommended the machine analysis of only the first and last sentences of each paragraph because she determined experimentally that these are usually the most significant information-bearing sentences. Alternatively, she suggested that the words in prepositional phrases be considered prime candidates for selection, on the grounds that these phrases are more likely to yield significant content indicators than any other simple syntactical unit and that prepositions can easily be identified by a simple computer program.

Automatic extraction indexing, with the extracted terms linked and weighted, has been carried out experimentally by Artandi and Wolf [1] as part of Project MEDICO, which is concerned with the automatic indexing of biomedical literature in general and drug-related literature in particular. The extracted words are weighted to represent the frequency with which they occur for each 1,000 words of text. Links are assigned automatically on the basis of contextual contiguity: the co-occurrence of two words in a sentence is evidence that they "belong together" in some sense. The automatic weighting and linking procedures were evaluated against a human standard. In 194 term extractions, from 15 articles, there was approximately 71 percent (138/194) agreement between a human judge and the weighting algorithm on a three-level scale. In the same group of articles, 285 links were created automatically, and 222 of these were judged valid by the human standard (a 72 percent agreement rate). Automatic indexing based on full texts was compared with automatic indexing from abstracts only. The results tend to indicate that the abstracts alone would have yielded most of the key terms. Eighty-six percent of terms having a weight of 3, 46 percent of terms with a weight of 2, and 11 percent of terms having a weight of 1 in the full text analysis were also generated from the reduced text.

The subject of automatic indexing is relevant to this text simply because the extraction processes create a type of controlled vocabulary. It is a vocabulary constructed by the criterion of frequency of occurrence, either absolute frequency or relative frequency.

INDEXING BY ASSIGNMENT

Machine assignment of index terms from a pre-established list of terms can also be accomplished, although the experimental results of automatic assignment indexing have not been particularly encouraging. Suppose we have a controlled vocabulary of, say, a hundred descriptors, and we would like to have these assigned automatically to a document corpus available in machine-readable form. The key steps are essentially these:

1. For each of the descriptors, establish a list of words likely to occur in documents to which the descriptor should be assigned. This involves the creation of a natural-language "profile" of each descriptor. This can be done through a computer analysis of the texts of documents to which the descriptors have already been assigned by human indexers. The final descriptor "profile" will consist of "clue words" or "predictors" of the descriptor. These will usually be words that occur neither very frequently nor very infrequently in the corpus as a whole, because neither of these groups is likely to provide good predictors of particular descriptors.

2. A new corpus of documents in the subject field is acquired in machine-readable form and a statistical analysis is performed. The words appearing in the text of each document, with the words weighted to represent their frequency of occurrence, are matched against the profiles of the descriptors in the controlled vocabulary. The descriptor or descriptors whose profiles best match the text words are then assigned to the documents by machine.

Work in automatic assignment indexing has been conducted by various investigators, notably Borko [5, 6] and Maron. [18]

MACHINE-AIDED INDEXING

A variation of "automatic indexing" is "machine-aided indexing," so called because the indexing task is shared between man and machine. Usually, in machine-aided indexing the natural-language text is matched against a stored vocabulary of descriptors. When a perfect match occurs, and certain other conditions are met (e.g., frequency of occurrence or location of the term in a document), the descriptor is assigned automatically. Certain other terms or phrases in the text may, by various linguistic analyses, be identified as candidate descriptors and printed out for human decision and possible inclusion in the approved vocabulary. A sophisticated approach to machine-aided indexing has been presented by Klingbiel. [14]

AUTOMATIC FORMATION OF CLASSES

The ability to conduct word frequency counts by computer allows us to index automatically, at least

by extraction. It also allows us to do something else highly relevant to the subject of this book, namely, to group related terms together (i.e., to form term classes) on the basis of statistical characteristics of these terms. Clearly, if we can select index terms automatically, and if we can group these terms into classes, or at least establish useful relations between them, we have gone a long way toward creating an index language automatically.

Some of the most interesting work in automatic term classification has been conducted in England at the Cambridge Language Research Unit, first by Needham [19] and later by Jackson [12] and by Sparck Jones and Jackson.[25] Early work in this area was also conducted by Borko [5, 6] and by Dale and Dale.[7]

The basic assumption of this research is that the more frequently two or more substantive words tend to co-occur together in a collection of documents, the more likely they are to be related in some way, and the more likely they are to be substitutable for each other in searching operations. Carried to its logical extreme, if the terms A and B always co-occur together (A never occurs without B and vice versa), it obviously does not matter which one is used in the conduct of a search. There is a perfect correlation between the two terms and they are thus completely interchangeable. For example, the word "flip" and the word "flop" are likely to correlate perfectly in an electronics collection. The first step in automatic class-forming operations is usually the automatic construction, for a particular document collection, of a document-term matrix (Figure 62). In its simplest form, such a matrix merely indicates which terms appear in which documents. Ultimately, we need a matrix to show the frequency

with which each term occurs in each document. Such a matrix will allow either of two operations:

1. The automatic grouping of documents on the basis of the terms they contain.

2. The automatic grouping of terms on the basis of the documents containing them.

For the automatic grouping of terms a second matrix is derived by computer. This is a term-term matrix (Figure 63) which shows, for each term pair, how frequently the terms tend to co-occur together. The matrix expresses this tendency to co-occur by means of a *correlation coefficient,* a decimal number varying from +1.000 to −1.000. A perfect correlation is represented by +1.000; a zero correlation indicates no particular relationship between the occurrence of the two words in documents; and a negative correlation indicates that if word A occurs, then B is not likely to occur in the same document.

Various procedures can be applied by computer to the term-term matrix in order to isolate classes of related terms. Borko applied factor analysis to form term groups and thereby to establish an "empirical classification" of terms. Needham used vector analysis of the term similarity matrix to derive *clumps* of related terms. A group of terms forms a legitimate clump if the sum of the connections of any member to the other members exceeds the sum of its connections to nonmembers, and vice versa for nonmembers.

A clump of terms, formed on the basis of co-occurrence statistics, may well be a useful class of terms for searching operations. Such a class can be used in searches to improve recall. For example, the strategy A *and* B *and* C can be expanded to A *and* B *and* the clump of terms of which C is a member. What we are doing is substituting for C an entire class of terms that are presumed to be related in some way to C. A clump will usually reflect a fairly heterogeneous group of relationships. Some terms may be near-synonyms, others may be in genus-species relations, while yet others will be related in less specifiable ways (e.g., terms that might be "related terms" in a conventional thesaurus). An automatically derived class will not be as clearly defined as a humanly derived class but it still may be a useful class for search purposes. It may be used as a precision device as well as a recall device. For instance, we may search on A *and* B *and* C and get zero retrieval, and go on to substitute A *and* B *and* "C clump." This may be expected to yield greater search precision than A *and* B only.

In later work at Cambridge, reported by Sparck Jones,[24] alternatives to clumps were identified and tested, including *strings, cliques,* and *stars.* The sequence string, star, clique, and clump represents

Documents

	A	B	C	D	E	F	G	H	I
Heat	25	9	17	20	30	2	1	17	0
Liquid	9	6	0	2	4	0	8	21	9
Boiling	0	12	12	4	3	0	12	9	12
Nucleate	0	0	0	2	0	0	5	0	0
Steam	7	12	24	9	7	1	2	4	0
Boiler	7	8	4	10	12	16	8	25	2
Corrosion	12	4	0	0	10	12	20	0	0
Tube	8	3	4	2	12	7	16	6	0
Metal	15	12	7	0	9	20	8	0	5
Conduction	8	0	0	12	0	0	0	0	0

Terms

FIGURE 62   Part of a document/term matrix.

	Flutter	Lift	Drag	Delta	Wing	Aileron	Buzz	Flow	Inviscid
Flutter		0.6105	0.2756	0.0974	0.6902	0.3620	0.5525	0.9806	0.1762
Lift	0.6105		0.3891	0.1715	0.6824	0.1105	−0.1963	0.9548	−0.2187
Drag	0.2756	0.3891		0.0512	0.7123	−0.2271	−0.2754	0.7056	0.0034
Delta	0.0974	0.1715	0.0512		0.9802	0.3610	0.0652	0.7049	0.0021
Wing	0.6902	0.6824	0.7123	0.9802		0.4175	0.0962	0.8624	0.0921
Aileron	0.3620	0.1105	−0.2271	0.3610	0.4175		0.2408	0.5610	−0.3821
Buzz	0.5525	−0.1963	−0.2754	0.0652	0.0962	0.2408		0.4830	−0.6214
Flow	0.9806	0.9548	0.7056	0.7049	0.8624	0.5610	0.4830		0.1211
Inviscid	0.1762	−0.2187	0.0034	0.0021	0.0921	−0.3821	−0.6214	0.1211	

FIGURE 63 Part of a term/term matrix.

classes of increasing complexity. To form a string we take a specific element (A), find another (B) connected with it, then a third (C) connected with the second, and so on. To form a star, we take an individual element and then identify a number of other elements connected with it. A clique is a set of elements that are all connected with each other. The members of a clump are also connected with each other. However, the clump differs from the clique in that its members must not only be connected but they must be connected with each other more strongly than they are connected with nonmembers of the clump. Thus, the formation of a clump is dependent upon external connections as well as internal ones.

A closely related project is the research on *associative indexing*, or *associative retrieval*, first developed by Stiles,[28] and later elaborated by Spiegel,[26] and by Giuliano and Jones.[11, 12] An associative system works on terms in document profiles, which may be words occurring naturally in text or humanly assigned descriptors, and establishes an elaborate network of relationships among these terms based on the tendency of such terms to co-occur. In this syndetic network, the strengths of term association reflect the degree to which various terms tend to co-occur. The Stiles association factor is not based simply on the number of times two terms co-occur; rather, it is based on the discrepancy between the observed joint occurrence and the expected joint occurrence, assuming statistical independence.

Doyle [9, 10] proposed an association factor based on the simple equation $f(A+B-f)$, where f is the prevalence of co-occurrence of terms A and B in documents, A is the prevalence of occurrence of term A, and B is the prevalence of occurrence of term B.

Such an association network may be regarded as a form of index language mechanically derived. When stored in machine-readable form, this network can be used to elaborate automatically on an original set of search terms, in order to retrieve potentially relevant documents which may not contain (or be indexed under) any of the original search terms. Word stem associations can be used instead of single-word associations.

The steps involved in associative retrieval are best illustrated by an example. Consider a request for documents on the stability of laminar boundary layers, for which the original search terms (starting terms) are STABILITY, LAMINAR, BOUNDARY, and LAYER (Table 32). Given these starting terms, the search program consults its associative network and expands this group by adding "first generation" terms, which are terms statistically associated with the starting terms. These terms may be further elaborated to yield a set of "second generation" terms (i.e., terms statistically related to all starting terms and first generation terms). These elaborations lead to the expanded lists shown in Table 32. The second generation elaboration may yield terms that are synonymous with the starting terms, because it is the synonymous relationship that

TABLE 32 Associative Retrieval

Starting Terms	First Generation Terms (terms related, on the basis of co-occurrence, to all four starting terms)	Second Generation Terms (top-ranking terms from a list of other terms statistically related to starting terms and first generation terms)
Stability	Transition	Retardation
Laminar	Flow	Trip
Boundary	Control	Stabilization
Layer	Promoter	Turbulence

is not likely to be brought out by the first generation elaboration. Consider the group of terms represented below:

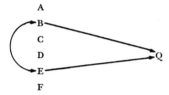

B is very closely related by co-occurrence statistics to Q, and E is also very closely related to Q. There is no tendency for B and E to co-occur. However, B and E are assumed to be related because of their common association with Q. The relationship between B and E may be that of true synonymy since true synonyms will rarely co-occur together in documents. For example, DELTA and TRIANGULAR are synonymous in the aerodynamic field but they are not likely to co-occur frequently in documents (if a writer talks of a "delta wing" he is unlikely to switch his terminology to "triangular wing" midway through his paper).

When the full elaboration has been made, the search program calculates the association factor between each term in the final list (first generation, second generation, starting terms) and each other term in the list. The sum of these association factors for a term, divided by the total number of terms in the final list, gives a weight which allows the arrangement of terms according to "probable relevance" to the original request. In searching the collection, documents are retrieved which have a sufficient number of these terms so that the sum of their weights is above some pre-established value. Obviously, it is possible to rank the output in order of "probable relevance." In the example in Table 32 it is possible that the terms TRANSITION and TURBULENCE prove to have the highest weight in relation to the request and thus permit retrieval of documents (hopefully relevant) on terms not among those that were used initially in searching. Investigations reported by Tague [29] indicate that related terms found

by associative procedures tend to be different from those found through use of a conventional thesaurus.

Dennis [8] has described procedures used in automatic indexing and in automatic derivation of word associations for a body of legal text. The significance of a word as a content indicator was determined not by pure frequency of occurrence but by the distribution pattern of its occurrence. The investigator assumes that words that behave in much the same way throughout the corpus are "noninforming" because they are nonselective, while those whose use distribution across the file is erratic or "skewed" should be "informing" words. A way to analyze the difference between the two types of behavior by computer would be to assume that noninforming words would exhibit a symmetrical (i.e., normal) distribution, while informing words would appear skewed, if normalized word frequency within documents were plotted against number of documents (Figure 64). Dennis uses a "coefficient of skewness" as a basis for selecting informing words. A word thus selected is always used as an index term, whether it appears in a document once or a hundred times.

"Association factors" or "between-word distances" are calculated from frequencies of word co-occurrence within paragraphs. An association is considered significant if two words co-occur more frequently than expected, assuming that the words occur independently in the statistical sense. The "between-word-distances" are used to create a machine-stored "word map," recording strengths of association, and to group together seemingly related words into clumps. A search request is handled in natural-language form without being formalized by Boolean logic. Words falling within the same clump are automatically placed in an *or* relationship while those falling in separate clumps are placed in an *and* relationship.

A problem occurring in certain associative retrieval systems and caused by contextual ambiguity is: a word may appear in several contexts and the automatic elaboration may substitute some terms that are not related semantically to the original search terms. Elaboration

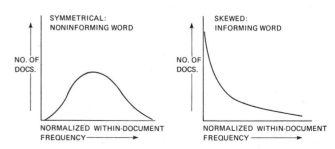

FIGURE 64 Distribution patterns of noninforming and informing words.

of the starting term EXPOSURE might pull in PHOTOG-RAPHY and NEGATIVE as related terms, when the actual context of the word in the request is that of climatic exposure, for which the related terms might include WEATHERING, AGING, and PAINT. Salisbury and Stiles [23] have shown how this may be avoided by the statistical grouping (clustering) of terms on the basis of co-occurrence statistics. The clusters formed by their "B-coefficient clustering procedure" tend to represent a single context in which a given term has been used. The "climatic" terms related to EXPOSURE will cluster together, while the photographic terms relating to EXPOSURE in another context will tend to form a second grouping. This clustering allows the automatic expansion of a set of request terms in a more precise way.

Vaswani and Cameron [30] also elaborate on simple statistical association factors to derive "similarity coefficients" between words. The similarity coefficient expresses the degree of similarity between two words (or word stems) on the basis of the words they tend to co-occur with. Thus, word J and word P have a strong similarity coefficient because both co-occur frequently with A, G, K, and R. This is equivalent to the "second generation" associations we mentioned before; words having a high similarity coefficient are likely to be synonymous or nearly synonymous.

As mentioned in Chapter 7, Doyle [9, 10] has proposed that a more useful application of data on statistical associations would be in the machine generation of exotic searching aids for subsequent human use. Such a man-machine combination would have the benefit of both statistical associations and "the highly individual cognitive associations which enable the human searcher to be selective in following statistically associative pathways." The data from a term-correlation matrix are used in the automatic compilation of a "semantic road map" displaying diagrammatically the strength of associations between terms (Figure 32). Doyle compares this map, which can be printed out or displayed on a computer console, to a microscope which allows the searcher to focus on smaller and smaller portions of the collection.

This is by no means a comprehensive study of automatic indexing and related techniques. It does, however, mention the principal procedures of relevance to the automatic generation of index languages. For further information, see the review by Stevens [27] and a useful short paper by Batty.[3]

Automatic extraction indexing, like full-text searching, has the advantage of using the specific language of the literature of a field; there is no reduction of precision caused by the superimposition of a controlled vocabulary of greater generality. However,

extraction indexing does involve some loss that is avoided in full-text searching. On the other hand, the reduced surrogate created by this system provides a search file that is smaller than the full-text search file and is therefore more economical to store and manipulate. The techniques of automatic formation of term classes, by clumping and other associative procedures, provide a type of syndetic structure to facilitate the conduct of productive searches. Lesk,[16] however, has found that associative procedures generally produce results inferior to those obtained through the use of a humanly constructed machine-stored thesaurus. He suggests that, in small collections at least, statistical associations are not useful for determining word meanings or relations, since the majority of the associated pairs depend on purely local meanings of the words and do not reflect their general meaning in technical text.

Machine *assignment* of descriptors, on the basis of the vocabulary of documents, is an inappropriate application of the computer because (a) such descriptors can be assigned more conveniently and accurately by humans, and (b) the specificity of the natural language of the document is sacrificed.

Although O'Connor [20] has very ably shown the problems involved in programming a computer to recognize concepts that are relatively easy for a human indexer to recognize, his findings are most pertinent to assignment indexing, and less so in relation to extraction indexing or full-text searching. The fact remains that natural-language systems have been shown to work, and natural-language searching appears to be an effective way of implementing a retrieval system for any document collection that can be acquired in machine-readable form at reasonable expense.

REFERENCES

1. Artandi, S. and Wolf, E. H. "The Effectiveness of Automatically Generated Weights and Links in Mechanical Indexing." *American Documentation* 20 (1969): 198-202.
2. Bar-Hillel, Y. "The Mechanization of Literature Searching." In *National Physical Laboratory: Proceedings of a Symposium on the Mechanization of Thought Processes* 2 (1959): 791-807. London: HMSO.
3. Batty, C. D. "The Automatic Generation of Index Languages." *Journal of Documentation* 25 (1969): 142-151.
4. Baxendale, P. B. "Machine-made Index for Technical Literature—an Experiment." *IBM Journal of Research and Development* 2 (1958): 354-361.
5. Borko, H. "Construction of an Empirically Based Mathematically Derived Classification System." *Proceedings of the Spring Joint Computer Conference* 21 (1962): 279-289.
6. Borko, H. and Bernick, M. "Automatic Document Classification." *Journal of the Association for Computing Machinery* 10 (1963): 151-162.

7. Dale, A. G. and Dale, N. "Clumping Techniques and Associative Retrieval." *Proceedings of the Symposium on Statistical Association Methods for Mechanized Documentation.* Edited by M. E. Stevens et al. Washington, D.C.: National Bureau of Standards, 1965, 230-235. NBS Miscellaneous Publication 269.

8. Dennis, S. F. "The Construction of a Thesaurus Automatically from a Sample of Text." *Proceedings of the Symposium on Statistical Association Methods for Mechanized Documentation.* Edited by M. E. Stevens et al. Washington, D.C.: National Bureau of Standards, 1965, 61-148. NBS Miscellaneous Publication 269.

9. Doyle, L. B. *Indexing and Abstracting by Association,* Part 1. Santa Monica, Calif.: System Development Corporation, 1962.

10. Doyle, L. B. "Semantic Road Maps for Literature Searchers." *Journal of the Association for Computing Machinery* 8 (1961): 553-578.

11. Giuliano, V. E. and Jones, P. E. "Linear Associative Information Retrieval." In *Vistas in Information Handling.* Vol. 1. Edited by P. W. Howerton and D. C. Weeks. Washington, D.C.: Spartan, 1963, 30-54.

12. Giuliano, V. E. and Jones, P. E. *Study and Test of a Methodology for Laboratory Evaluation of Message Retrieval Systems.* Cambridge, Mass.: Arthur D. Little, Inc., 1966.

13. Jackson, D. M. *The Construction of Retrieval Environments and Pseudo-Classifications Based on External Relevance.* Columbus, Ohio: Ohio State University, Computer and Information Science Research Center, 1969. Technical Report 69-3.

14. Klingbiel, P. H. *Machine-Aided Indexing.* Alexandria, Va.: Defense Documentation Center, June 1969. AD 696 200.

15. Lancaster, F. W. "Mechanized Document Control: A Review of Some Recent Research." *ASLIB Proceedings* 16 (1964): 132-152.

16. Lesk, M. W. "Word-Word Associations in Document Retrieval Systems." *American Documentation* 20 (1969): 27-38.

17. Luhn, H. P. "A Statistical Approach to Mechanized Encoding and Searching of Literary Information." *IBM Journal of Research and Development* 1 (1957): 309-317.

18. Maron, M. E. "Automatic Indexing: An Experimental Inquiry." *Journal of the Association for Computing Machinery* 8 (1961): 404-417.

19. Needham, R. M. *Research on Information Retrieval, Classification and Grouping, 1957-61.* Cambridge: Cambridge Language Research Unit, 1961. ML 149.

20. O'Connor, J. "Automatic Subject Recognition in Scientific Papers: An Empirical Study." *Journal of the Association for Computing Machinery* 12 (1965): 490-515.

21. Oswald, V. A., Jr. et al. *Automatic Indexing and Abstracting of the Contents of Documents.* Los Angeles: Planning Research Corporation, October 1959. RADC-TR-59-208.

22. *Proceedings of the Symposium on Statistical Association Methods for Mechanized Documentation.* Edited by M. E. Stevens et al. Washington, D.C.: National Bureau of Standards, 1965. NBS Miscellaneous Publication 269.

23. Salisbury, B. A., Jr. and Stiles, H. E. "The Use of the B-Coefficient in Information Retrieval." *Proceedings of the American Society for Information Science* 6 (1969): 265-268.

24. Sparck Jones, K. *Automatic Keyword Classification for Information Retrieval.* London: Butterworth, 1971.

25. Sparck Jones, K. and Jackson, D. M. "Current Approaches to Classification and Clump-finding at the Cambridge Language Research Unit." *Computer Journal* 10 (1967): 29-37.

26. Spiegel, J. et al. *Statistical Association Procedures for Message Content Analysis.* Bedford, Mass.: Mitre Corporation, October 1962.

27. Stevens, M. E. *Automatic Indexing: A State-of-the-Art Report.* Washington, D.C.: National Bureau of Standards, 1965. NBS Monograph 91. Reissued with additions in 1970.

28. Stiles, H. E. "Machine Retrieval Using the Association Factor." In *Machine Indexing, Progress and Problems.* Washington, D.C.: American University, 1961, 192-206.

29. Tague, J. "An Evaluation of Statistical Association Measures." *Proceedings of the American Documentation Institute* 3 (1966): 391-397.

30. Vaswani, P. K. T. and Cameron, J. B. *The National Physical Laboratory Experiments in Statistical Word Associations and Their Use in Document Indexing and Retrieval.* Teddington, England: National Physical Laboratory, 1970.

18 *Compatibility and Convertibility of Vocabularies*

Earlier in this book I stressed that, for maximum effectiveness, a controlled vocabulary must be carefully tailored to the requirements of a particular organization or user community. Each organization tends to have its own viewpoints, and it is unlikely that a general vocabulary such as TEST will completely satisfy the peculiar needs of an organization specializing in some subfield of science and technology. Adoption of a general scheme, *in toto,* will probably mean that the specialized organization has compromised between ease of vocabulary adoption and optimum utility for indexing and retrieval.

THE NEED FOR COMPATIBILITY

The fact that many specialized vocabularies do exist, however, causes problems when various agencies join together in cooperative ventures. Interagency or inter-institutional cooperation is increasing in the overall area of information retrieval, as the following evidence shows.

1. Networks of information centers are springing up in increasing numbers. Such networks may be geographically oriented, as in MEDLARS,[1] or subject-oriented, as in the ERIC system [25] or the neurological information network of the National Institute of Neurological Diseases and Stroke.[2]

2. Professional societies are tending to cooperate in joint information processing ventures, both na-tional and international in scope. An example of the former is the cooperative relationship between the American Society for Metals, Engineers Joint Council, and the Engineering Index.[20] An example of the latter is the cooperative arrangement between the American Institute of Physics and the Institution of Electrical Engineers in London.[17]

3. There are international cooperative undertakings at the government level or between governments and international agencies, such as the relationship between the U.S. Atomic Energy Commission and EURATOM.

4. A feasibility study has been conducted on a World Science Information System (UNISIST).[34]

5. The National Technical Information Service in the Department of Commerce processes reports of many other federal agencies, including the Department of Defense, the U.S. Atomic Energy Commission, and the National Aeronautics and Space Administration.

When two or more existing organizations undertake cooperative information processing activities they are faced with the problem of securing some compatibility or convertibility among the various vocabularies used. This problem, and possible approaches to its solution, will be considered in this chapter.

In a sense, the very existence of a controlled vocabulary implies a desire for compatibility—among the terms used by authors, indexers, and searchers,

and among the various centers in a complete system. Several professional societies (e.g., American Institute of Physics, American Institute of Chemical Engineers, and Engineers Joint Council) have initiated programs for "indexing at source" (i.e., the assignment of index terms derived from a standard list by the authors of articles, or possibly by a journal editor, and the publication of these terms along with the article to which they relate). Indexing at source implies the desire to achieve compatibility of terminology within an entire community.

Most of the research on vocabulary compatibility in the United States has been conducted at the government level. One concern was to develop procedures whereby the controlled vocabulary and indexing protocols of one agency would be compatible with, or convertible to, the controlled vocabulary and indexing protocols of another agency. This would allow switching of subject searches and would greatly simplify interagency processing of reports and the publication of government-wide indexes. Much of the earlier research on compatibility has been summarized by Henderson et al.[16]

COMMON SUBSUMPTION SCHEMES

The most extensive group of studies was conducted by the Datatrol Corporation[7, 14, 15, 21] and fully reported in 1962-1964. The Datatrol investigators took the 7,145 descriptors in the first edition of the *Thesaurus of ASTIA Descriptors* (1960) and, for each descriptor, attempted to find identical, synonymous or usefully equivalent counterparts in the third (1960) edition of the *Subject Headings Used by the USAEC Division of Technical Information*.[35] The objective was to develop a unidirectional list of equivalents.

The investigators identified three major levels of convertibility. Descriptor A from one vocabulary may be mapped to descriptor x in a second vocabulary if: (a) A and x are identical, (b) A and x are synonymous, or (c) A is a species of the genus x. Between the subject headings of AEC and the descriptors of ASTIA, eight degrees of convertibility were isolated:

1. Identical terminology in spelling and context.
2. Synonymous but not identical.
3. An AEC subheading is identical to, or synonymous with, an ASTIA descriptor.
4. An AEC subject heading plus subheading is synonymous with or generic to an ASTIA descriptor.
5. Two or more subject headings are required to cover one descriptor.
6. A subject heading is generic to (subsumes) a descriptor.

7. A descriptor subsumes a subject heading.
8. No equivalent in AEC for an ASTIA descriptor.

Of the ASTIA descriptors, 23.8 percent had an exact equivalent in AEC, 38.1 percent were subsumed by more general AEC subject headings, 7.4 percent were more general than AEC subject headings, and 10.9 percent had no equivalent in the AEC vocabulary. The investigators concluded that a useful dictionary of equivalents could be produced and, in fact, published a preliminary table of such equivalents.

A separate but related study was conducted by Painter,[29] who also worked with the vocabularies of AEC and ASTIA. She examined 200 documents and how they had been indexed by both agencies. To this group of documents AEC had assigned 640 subject headings and ASTIA had assigned 2,217 descriptors. Over the 2,857 term assignments, 30 percent "similarity" was discovered in the indexing of the two agencies. This similarity was defined by the ratio

$$\frac{\text{Terms for which equivalency exists in the two vocabularies}}{\text{Total of distinct ASTIA terms used in indexing + total of distinct AEC terms used in indexing}}$$

Painter identified several key problems involved in mapping from one vocabulary to another, including the situation in which a term in one vocabulary subsumes two or more terms in the second vocabulary. She pointed out further that machine conversion from one vocabulary to another would be adversely affected by the generally poor rates of consistency among indexers in term assignment.

As a result of their studies, the Datatrol investigators recommended that, if a central clearinghouse were to accept the original indexing of several agencies and integrate these sources into a composite announcement publication, it would be necessary to devise a "common subsumption scheme" which would be superimposed upon the vocabularies of the various agencies. As proposed by Hammond,[13] indexers at each agency would assign terms from the common subsumption scheme as well as from the agency vocabulary. Hammond suggested that the entire process could then be carried much further automatically. For each category in the subsumption scheme an "association profile" could be developed. The association profile of a category would be composed of descriptors used in association with the category heading in indexing. A profile for a particular category would actually consist of several profiles, one for each agency participating in the scheme, and each profile would show the strength of association between the category heading and each descriptor. Table 33 shows term profiles for the general category "guidance" and the general cate-

TABLE 33 Term Profiles from DDC and NASA

Total usage frequency of parent term
  Total usage frequency of associated term
    Total co-occurrence with parent term
      Association factor (× 100)

TERM PROFILES NASA

442 GUIDANCE

13	7	529	Aboard
57	16	550	Abort
130	30	594	Apollo*Project
60	16	544	Autopilot
1101	70	513	Computer
2059	141	599	Control*/Noun/
824	71	560	Controls,*Control*Systems
126	21	518	Gyroscope
285	52	623	Inertia
410	47	556	Landing*/Noun/
489	54	565	Launch*/Noun/
119	25	564	Maneuver
61	14	513	Matching
49	33	720	Midcourse
640	55	533	Missile*/Noun/
340	40	542	Mission
356	132	798	Navigation
933	80	572	Orbit*/Noun/
22	8	502	Pershing*Missile
61	14	513	Platform
838	63	528	Propulsion*/Noun/
800	55	500	Reentry
163	35	602	Rendezvous
8	6	546	Sextant
52	21	619	Space*Navigation
979	107	635	Spacecraft*/Noun/
15	7	514	Spacecraft*Navigation
2681	139	552	System
302	34	520	Target
51	14	533	Telecommunications
86	22	573	Terminal
30	10	518	Tracker
545	50	532	Tracking*/Noun/
761	115	683	Trajectory*/Noun/

DDC

403 GUIDANCE

250	28	628	Astronautics
136	21	632	Automatic Pilots
207	16	527	Booster Motors
14	9	689	Celestial Guidance
125	18	608	Command & Control Systems
762	34	541	Communication Systems
670	32	543	Control
1564	120	735	Control Systems
69	14	618	Doppler Navigation
1188	58	607	Errors
345	29	599	Flight Paths
32	11	647	Guided Missile Computers
285	31	635	Guided Missile Trajectories
2476	156	740	Guided Missiles
242	23	589	Gyroscopes
42	16	698	Homing Devices
115	39	779	Inertial Guidance
80	12	569	Inertial Navigation
44	7	515	Interception
242	25	607	Landings
81	11	549	Launching Sites
12	7	650	Light Homing
228	28	638	Lunar Probes
172	26	652	Manned
348	21	527	Moon
298	36	662	Navigation
79	15	618	Navigation Computers
861	85	728	Orbital Trajectories

DDC—Continued

137	17	586	Planets
277	23	574	Propulsion
12	6	616	Radar Homing
523	26	526	Reentry Vehicles
59	22	729	Rendezvous Spacecraft
18	5	534	Retro Rockets
1782	67	589	Satellites (Artificial)
800	74	707	Space Flight
170	56	813	Space Navigation
303	27	598	Space Probes
901	82	715	Spacecraft
99	10	506	Stabilization Systems
23	8	612	Star Trackers
1025	67	657	Surface to Surface
4	4	637	Terminal Guidance

TERM PROFILES NASA

356 NAVIGATION

39	18	639	Aid
104	20	555	Air*Traffic
42	23	683	Airspace
130	30	618	Apollo*Project
21	7	500	Avoidance
15	7	536	Circumlunar
665	47	520	Communication
18	9	572	Compass
1101	73	557	Computer
16	8	559	Doppler*Navigation
959	58	519	Flight*/Noun/
442	132	798	Guidance*/Noun/
10	7	579	Gyrocompass
126	23	564	Gyroscope
285	34	554	Inertia
119	17	503	Maneuver
49	17	603	Midcourse
340	31	511	Mission
933	54	505	Orbit*/Noun/
61	12	503	Platform
83	57	800	Proportion
838	63	559	Propulsion*/Noun/
163	21	513	Rendezvous
8	5	527	Self-Contained
8	6	568	Sextant
52	27	694	Space*Navigation
979	64	541	Spacecraft*/Noun/
15	7	536	Spacecraft*Navigation
2681	112	530	System
30	11	562	Tracker
545	45	536	Tracking*/Noun/
761	48	505	Trajectory*/Noun/

DDC

298 NAVIGATION

203	18	588	Air Traffic Control Systems
1156	34	526	Airborne
218	19	592	Airplane Landings
57	11	618	All-Weather Aviation
136	17	619	Automatic Pilots
53	14	677	Beacon Lights
25	5	531	Bombing
50	10	611	Buoys
50	7	533	Celestial Navigation
39	12	676	Compasses
7	3	543	Course Indicators
204	13	517	Direction Finding
643	33	591	Display Systems
69	9	555	Doppler Navigation

gory "navigation" based on the vocabularies of DDC and NASA. The statistics appearing in this table can best be explained by the following example. The category heading GUIDANCE was used 442 times in the sample taken from NASA. The descriptor TARGET was used 302 times in the same sample. GUIDANCE and TARGET co-occur 34 times in the corpus. The calculated "association factor" ($\times$ 100) is 520. Hammond's intention in developing these profiles was to allow the automatic transfer of search strategies from one system to another, using the subsumption scheme to effect the transfer. For example, a "guidance" search could be conducted in the NASA system, in an associative retrieval mode (see Chapter 17), using the NASA association profile displayed in Table 33. The search could then be switched to the DDC system where it would be conducted, again in the associative mode, using the association profile derived through DDC indexing.

In 1964, Datatrol presented a hierarchical superstructure to be superimposed upon the individual vocabularies of the cooperating agencies. It was developed as a result of the study and analysis of the use of index terms, including frequency, by AEC, DDC, NASA, and the Office of Technical Services.[15] Out of this evolved an officially accepted subsumption scheme, the *COSATI Subject Category List.*[6] The COSATI list has a two-level arrangement consisting of 22 major subject "fields" subdivided into 178 "groups." The first-level breakdown is presented in Table 34. The list is intended to provide an overall scheme of subject arrangement for use in government announcement and distribution activities related to technical reports; it also has application in management reporting. It is used in the arrangement of *Government Reports Announcements* issued by the National Technical Information Service, and provides one of several possible bases used in the selective dissemination of microfiche (SDM) by the same agency. In scientific and technical thesauri issued by agencies of the U.S. Government, it is now customary to present a display of descriptors arranged alphabetically under broad subject categories, using the COSATI list as the basis of the arrangement.

CONVERSION FROM ONE VOCABULARY TO ANOTHER

Now that libraries and information centers have greater access to computing equipment, an increasing number of organizations are offering (or planning to offer) bibliographic data bases in machine-readable form. Table 35 lists 34 government and other organi-

TABLE 34　COSATI Fields

01	Aeronautics
02	Agriculture
03	Astronomy and Astrophysics
04	Atmospheric Sciences
05	Behavioral and Social Sciences
06	Biological and Medical Sciences
07	Chemistry
08	Earth Sciences and Oceanography
09	Electronics and Electrical Engineering
10	Energy Conversion (Non-propulsive)
11	Materials
12	Mathematical Sciences
13	Mechanical, Industrial, Civil, and Marine Engineering
14	Methods and Equipment
15	Military Sciences
16	Missile Technology
17	Navigation, Communications, Detection, and Countermeasures
18	Nuclear Science and Technology
19	Ordnance
20	Physics
21	Propulsion and Fuels
22	Space Technology

SOURCE: COSATI.[6]

zations that in 1970 regularly supplied bibliographic records in machine-readable form. The list, which was published in a report from the Auerbach Corporation as part of a study conducted for the National Agricultural Library,[22] is probably incomplete. The Auerbach investigators point out that none of these tape services existed before 1963, and they project that as many as 100 could be available by 1975. A more detailed description of many of these data bases is provided by Carroll.[3]

The availability of bibliographic data bases in machine-readable form provides the possibility that any information center may integrate portions of these external data bases into its own processing activities. Unfortunately, there are a number of basic intellectual and technical problems involved in combining machine-readable data from multiple sources (and in multiple formats) into a central data bank. Not the least of these problems is that of diverse vocabularies.

The previously mentioned Auerbach study was an investigation of how the National Agricultural Library (NAL) could best exploit a group of data bases—relevant to NAL interests—that are available in machine-readable form. The nine data bases of interest are those generated by the following organizations:

Biosciences Information Service of Biological Abstracts (BIOSIS)
U.S. Atomic Energy Commission

National Technical Information Service
Engineering Index, Inc.
Library of Congress Machine-Readable Catalog Service (MARC)
National Library of Medicine (MEDLARS)
Institute for Scientific Information
CCM Information Services (PANDEX)
Chemical Abstracts Service

Five possible modes were recognized by which data contained in these data bases could be utilized by NAL:

1. *Combined mode.* NAL converts extracted portions of other data bases to a common file structure (separate from NAL's own data base), to a common computer medium, and to a common format. The vocabularies are not converted, however. The various data bases are searched by NAL software and hardware, but the use of different terminologies is necessary.

2. *Separate mode.* Extracted portions of external data bases are converted to a common computer medium at a single location. Each data base must be searched by using its own software and indexing terminology.

3. *Remote on-line.* NAL searches a data base from another organization remotely, via on-line terminals, using the system's own terminology, software, and hardware.

4. *Remote off-line.* NAL uses the facilities of the various information centers in off-line mode using mail, TWX, and telephone in transmission of requests and search results.

5. *Integrated mode.* NAL converts portions of data bases not only to its own file structure, computer medium, and format, but also to its own indexing terminology, thereby permitting the merging of all sources into a master bibliographic data base used for searching and/or announcement.

The remote on-line alternative was dropped from consideration because, in 1968, the services in question were not providing facilities for remote on-line interrogation. The separate mode was rejected because the maintenance of separate files for various data bases would be both difficult and costly, since it would involve not only maintenance of varied software, search strategies, file structures, and vocabularies, but also heavy investment in the sophisticated programming required in using diverse systems.

Although the integrated mode involves vocabulary conversion processes which may be both difficult and expensive, it would certainly be most acceptable from the viewpoints of centralized control and ease of exploitation in searching and announcement activities.

The potential promise of this mode led to an investigation, reported by Wall and Barnes,[37] on the compatibility or convertibility of the various vocabularies used in data bases of most immediate interest to the National Agricultural Library. The major objectives of this study were:

1. To develop procedures whereby machine-readable indexing records from another information center can be converted, with as little intellectual effort as possible, to indexing records compatible with NAL's own data base and with the NAL vocabulary, the *Agricultural/Biological Vocabulary.*[27]

2. To develop a technique whereby the degree of convertibility possible between two vocabularies can be measured quantitatively.

A term conversion algorithm was developed and tested in the conversion of samples from eleven source vocabularies to the *Agricultural/Biological Vocabulary* (ABV). The algorithm minimizes human intervention in the conversion process but does involve a number of intellectual decision points. The eleven source vocabularies, ranked by ease of convertibility to ABV, are:

Medical Subject Headings
Engineering Index Subject Headings (for electronics and plastics)
Thesaurus of Engineering and Scientific Terms
Chemical Abstracts Search Guide
Engineering Index Subject Headings (subjects other than electronics and plastics)
U.S. Government Research and Development Reports Indexes *
Nuclear Science Abstracts (subject headings)
Subject Indexes of the Institute for Scientific Information
Subject Indexes of BIOSIS
PANDEX Subject Index
Library of Congress *Subject Headings*

The conversion algorithm will identify exact matches, some variant spellings, and some variations in word form. Under certain conditions it will also effect automatic mapping on the bases of cross-references and the hierarchical structure of the vocabularies. Some examples of the types of automatic mapping that are possible are given below:

1. *Exact match:* CALORIMETRY *to* CALORIMETRY
2. *Variant spelling:* ELECTRO OSMOSIS *to* ELECTRO-OSMOSIS
   HAEMOGLOBIN *to* HEMOGLOBIN

* Now known as *Government Reports Announcements Indexes.*

TABLE 35 Roster of Organizations Regularly Distributing Bibliographic Records in Machine-Readable Form (Magnetic Tape)

Organization	Records
American Geological Institute/Geological Society of America	*Bibliography and Index of Geology*
American Institute of Aeronautics and Astronautics	*International Aerospace Abstracts*
American Petroleum Institute	*Abstracts of Refining Literature* *Abstracts of Refining Patents*
American Psychological Association	*Psychological Abstracts*
American Society of Mechanical Engineers	*Applied Mechanics Reviews*
American Society for Metals	*Metals Abstracts*
Armed Forces Pest Control Board	Military Entomology Information Service Bibliographic Information
Atomic Energy Commission	*Nuclear Science Abstracts*
Automation Instrument Data Service Ltd. (London)	Product Specifications for Electronics, Instrumentation and Automation
BioSciences Information Service	*BA Previews*
R. R. Bowker Company	*Publishers' Weekly* *Forthcoming Books* *Paperbound Books in Print* *Subject Guide to Books in Print* *Children's Books for Schools and Libraries*
CCM Information Sciences, Inc.	PANDEX Weekly Tape Service
Chemical Abstracts Service	*Chemical Abstracts Condensates* *Basic Journal Abstracts* *Chemical—Biological Activities* *Chemical Titles* *Polymer Science and Technology*—P(atents) or J(ournals) *Patent Concordance*
Clearinghouse for Federal Scientific and Technical Information	*U.S. Government Research and Development Reports* and *Index*
Defense Documentation Center	*Technical Abstract Bulletin*
Derwent Publications, Ltd.	*Farmdoc* *Plasdoc* *Ringdoc*
Educational Resources Information Center (ERIC)	*Research in Education*
Engineering Index, Inc.	COMPENDEX (Computerized Engineering Index)
Paul de Haen, Inc.	De Haen Drug Information Services *Uniterm Index to U.S. Chemical Patents*
IFI/Plenum Data Corporation	*ISI Source Data Tapes*
Institute for Scientific Information	*ISI Citation Tapes* *Index Chemicus Registry System* *Automatic Subject Citations Alert* (ASCA)
Institute of Textile Technology	Keyterm Index to Abstracts in the *Textile Technology Digest*
Library of Congress	MARC Tapes
M.I.T. Libraries (Project TIP)	*The Current Journal Literature of Physics*
National Aeronautics and Space Administration	*Scientific and Technical Aerospace Reports*
National Agricultural Library	*Bibliography of Agriculture* Subject and Corporate Author Indexes *Pesticides Documentation Bulletin* Citations *International Tree Disease Register* *Herbicides Data File*

TABLE 35 Roster of Organizations Regularly Distributing Bibliographic Records in Machine-Readable Form (Magnetic Tape)—*Continued*

Organization	Records
National Library of Medicine	*Index Medicus* *NLM Current Catalog*
Preston Technical Abstracts Co.	Computer Tape for Searching the Gas Chromatographic Literature Nuclear Magnetic Resonance Literature Retrieval System
Project URBANDOC, Library, City University of New York	Bibliographic Records Related to Urban Planning and Renewal
Share Research Corporation	Abstracts of U.S. Government Report Literature (NASA, AEC, DoD, etc.) Citation to Journal Literature
State University of New York at Buffalo, Technical Information Dissemination Bureau	Bibliographic information on U.S. Government Reports
U.S. Geological Survey	*Abstracts of North American Geology*
University of Michigan	VELA Seismic Information Analysis Center Citations
University of Tulsa	*Petroleum Abstracts* (Exploration/Development/Production Literature and Patents)

SOURCE: H. B. Landau.[22]

3. *Word forms:* ELECTRIC MOTORS *to* ELECTRICAL MOTORS
4. *Inversions:* DISEASES, HUMAN *to* HUMAN DISEASES
5. *Via cross-references:* ABATTOIRS *to* SLAUGHTERHOUSES

(where the target vocabulary contains a reference ABATTOIRS *use* SLAUGHTERHOUSES)

6. *Via hierarchy:* CAROTID SINUS *to* ARTERIES

(where the hierarchy in the source vocabulary indicates that CAROTID SINUS is immediately subordinate to ARTERIES).

This algorithm will not do all the conversion automatically, but it will reduce the number of human intellectual mapping decisions needed. The degree to which a source vocabulary will map automatically to a target vocabulary will depend on:

1. The degree of overlap in the subject matter of the two vocabularies.

2. The degree of vocabulary control. Two controlled vocabularies are likely to be more compatible than a controlled and an uncontrolled vocabulary.

3. The degree of hierarchical and cross-reference structure. The more structure in the vocabularies, the more easily they will map.

4. The degree of pre-coordination. Two vocabularies are not likely to map easily to each other if one is highly pre-coordinate and the other is not.

In testing the algorithm it was found that 76 percent

of a sample of terms from *Medical Subject Headings* could be mapped automatically to ABV terms, because MeSH is a structured, controlled vocabulary somewhat similar in format to ABV and with considerable subject matter overlap. Only 11 percent success was achieved in mapping PANDEX terms, which are largely uncontrolled, and even less success was achieved in converting Library of Congress subject headings to ABV, primarily because these subject headings were much more pre-coordinate than the terms in the agricultural vocabulary.

Oddly enough, according to Wall and Barnes, one of the greatest obstacles to vocabulary conversion is the difficulty of equating singular and plural forms of a word automatically. In English, many plurals are formed by the addition of a final *s*, but other plurals are formed by a change of suffix, as *y* to *ies*, *a* to *ae*, *um* to *a*, *a* to *i*, and *a* to *ata*. The automatic determination of term equivalence is difficult in these cases; there is a danger that a too-general rule will cause terms to be regarded as equivalent when no equivalence really exists.

FACTORS PROMOTING COMPATIBILITY

Vocabulary compatibility in the United States has been greatly enhanced by:

1. The deliberate attempt by various government agencies to model their vocabularies on pre-existing

thesauri. The Bureau of Ships thesaurus is modeled on and compatible with the DDC thesaurus, as is the thesaurus of the Federal Aviation Administration. Such compatibility is due partly to personnel mobility within the Federal Government.

2. The gradual emergence of thesaurus rules, guidelines, and conventions through the accumulation of experience by the EJC, DDC and TEST (LEX) projects. The LEX conventions are essentially those officially adopted by COSATI.

3. The use of standard software packages in thesaurus construction has led to compatibility of formats for storage of thesaurus data in machine-readable (magnetic tape) form. Identical or highly similar computer programs have been used in the construction of the *NASA Thesaurus*, the *Urban Thesaurus*, and thesauri developed at Fort Detrick, the Department of State, and the Johnson's Wax Company. The form of the LEX tape layout, as presented by Hammond,[12] is shown in Table 19.

4. The *Thesaurus of Engineering and Scientific Terms* has been widely distributed and has had considerable influence. As of 1969, 4,500 copies had been sold by the Engineers Joint Council, and sales were still holding at a rate of about 150 per month. In addition, several thousand more had probably been distributed by the Defense Documentation Center to authorized DDC users. Table 36, taken from a paper by Speight,[32] shows the distribution of TEST in the United States by the type of organization acquiring the publication. About one third of all copies sold by EJC have been sent outside the United States.

MICROTHESAURI

Within a formal network of information centers there is certainly a need to develop compatibility of subject vocabularies. Ideally, all centers would use an identical vocabulary. However, the network may be such that it includes a variety of information centers, some

TABLE 36 Distribution of the TEST Thesaurus in the United States

	Percentage
Government, Federal, State, Local	11.5
Companies	51.4
Bookstores	10.4
Universities	12.5
Individuals	3.8
Professional societies, nonprofit institutions, etc.	10.4
Total	100.0

SOURCE: F. Y. Speight.[32]

highly specialized and some more general in subject coverage. The solution to this problem might be the development of a general thesaurus to cover the broad subject matter of the network as a whole, together with a number of *microthesauri* for use in the more specialized centers. A microthesaurus is a specialized thesaurus that is so constructed that it fits exactly into the hierarchical structure and terminological conventions of a more general thesaurus. In essence, a microthesaurus provides a vocabulary of terms in some specialized subject area at lower levels of the hierarchy than the terms in the general thesaurus. The first microthesauri appear to have been those developed by ASTIA, of which there were eleven in 1963, covering such subject areas as biological warfare, bionics, and refractory metals.

Sometimes, in the development of a network, it may be necessary to integrate pre-existing vocabularies to make them compatible or convertible. Hammond[12] has briefly described procedures for integrating two thesauri and making one a "satellite thesaurus" of the other. The case history involves the integration of the *Fort Detrick Thesaurus*, containing approximately 6,000 terms, with the *Thesaurus of Engineering and Scientific Terms*. The steps involved in the integration were as follows:

1. Detrick terms were keypunched and matched against the machine-readable TEST. All matching terms from TEST were "pulled" along with their associated cross-references. The embryo thesaurus thus created included two types of terms:

(a) Terms that exactly matched in the two thesauri, with TEST cross-references attached.

(b) TEST terms that were cross-referenced to other Detrick terms.

2. Only 1,100 of the 6,000 Fort Detrick terms could not be converted directly to TEST terms. These were mostly project names and nomenclature of the type intentionally omitted from TEST. It was then necessary to develop cross-references among the Detrick terms not listed in TEST and between these terms and the TEST terms. Cross-references were established only for synonyms (*use*), immediate broader terms (BT), and related terms (RT).

3. A computer pass generated reciprocal cross-references and filled out the intermediate generic (BT-NT) structure from the immediate BT relationship established intellectually.

The result of these activities was a satellite thesaurus fully compatible with TEST and capable of being manipulated by TEST maintenance and updating programs.

In another example of a satellite-parent thesaurus

relationship, the highly specialized thesaurus of the Parkinson's Disease Information Center, Columbia University, was mapped by human intellectual effort to the more general *Medical Subject Headings*. In this activity it was frequently necessary to map a highly specific term from the *Parkinsonism Thesaurus* to a much more general term in MeSH. For example:

NUCLEUS DENTATUS to CEREBELLUM
NUCLEUS DORSALIS CORPORIS TRAPEZOIDEI to PONS
NUCLEUS DORSOLATERALIS to OCULOMOTOR NERVE

A similar relationship exists between MeSH and the *Thesaurus of Rheumatology*.[30] The latter is designed for indexing the literature of rheumatology, but it also provides mapping instructions to MeSH (e.g., LUMBO-SACROILIAC STRAIN *use* SACROILIAC JOINT *and* BACKACHE) to facilitate the conduct of rheumatology searches in *Index Medicus* and in MEDLARS. The *Thesaurus for the Visual Sciences*,[8, 9] produced by the Vision Information Center, was also constructed in such a way that it fits within the general framework of MeSH. When a specialized thesaurus is mapped in this way to a more general one, the indexing of the specialized center may be automatically converted to the language and protocols of the higher vocabulary. Consider a typical network configuration comprising a general information center with a series of satellite subject-oriented centers. A general network thesaurus exists in machine-readable form, and the specialized thesauri of the network centers have been mapped intellectually to the general network thesaurus. Each center indexes for its own purposes and maintains its own retrieval and dissemination activities. In addition, all the indexing records generated by each center are submitted, in machine-readable form, to the network center. Here they may be matched by computer against the network thesaurus and automatically converted to the terms of this thesaurus (e.g., NUCLEUS DENTATUS is replaced by CEREBELLUM) for publication in a general printed index. A composite search file, including inputs from all network centers, but allowing searches to be conducted on all specific terms, may also be created. The configuration has the following characteristics:

1. Each center indexes for its own specialized purposes, and with its own vocabulary, as it did before it became a node in the network.

2. A network-wide information center, with a network-wide vocabulary, is able to accept inputs from the satellite centers and integrate them into a common data base without further intellectual processing.

3. Network-wide publication, dissemination, and retrieval operations can be conducted.

4. Switching of searches from center to center can be effected automatically or semi-automatically.

5. No duplicate indexing is involved. Each center indexes for its own purposes as it did before the network was established.

Obviously, we can convert automatically only from a special vocabulary to a general one; we cannot accomplish the reverse. For example, the specific terms NUCLEUS DENTATUS, NUCLEUS EMBOLIFORMIS, and NUCLEUS FASTIGII can all be converted automatically to CEREBELLUM. We cannot, however, take the general term CEREBELLUM and convert it automatically to the specific terms without the intervention of human intellectual effort. The use of a polytechnical thesaurus with a number of specialized microthesauri (satellite thesauri), plus multilingual processing, has been described by Holst.[18]

Another example of cooperation involving vocabulary sharing has been documented by Hyslop.[19, 20] It involves a cooperative program for information retrieval developed by the American Society for Metals and Engineering Index, Inc., covering the fields of metallurgy, plastics, and electrical and electronics engineering. The objective was to attain interchangeability of vocabulary structure and processing methods rather than a common vocabulary. The structure of the EJC *Thesaurus of Engineering Terms* was followed, and joint programs for computer manipulation and processing of the vocabulary structure, for both published indexes and machine-based retrospective searching, were developed.

THE INTERMEDIATE LEXICON

There is a further possibility for developing vocabulary compatibility among various information centers. This involves the method of "indirect concordance" between indexing systems by means of an "intermediate lexicon." The intermediate lexicon is not a vocabulary tool used by a particular information center but a conversion or switching mechanism. According to Coates,[4, 5] such a lexicon is "a tool or piece of software whereby indexing terms or notations applied to a given document entry under any one indexing system may be converted to their conceptual equivalents in any other indexing system, by clerical means and with the minimum of intellectual effort." Each information center within a network constructs a concordance between its own vocabulary and the intermediate lexicon. This is clearly more economical than the construction of separate direct concordances between every vocabulary. Communication between any two centers,

for the purpose of bibliographic exchange, will be effected via the intermediate lexicon. The intermediate lexicon will facilitate the exploitation by one information center, with its own vocabulary and indexing protocols, of bibliographic data bases prepared by other centers with different vocabularies and protocols. A multiplicity of different vocabularies can be accommodated by the intermediate lexicon. The concept of the intermediate lexicon, for interconversion between indexing systems, is similar to the concept of a common subsumption scheme. Coates,[4, 5] Gardin,[11] and Levy [23] have described preliminary steps taken to develop such a tool to permit interconversion between alphabetical and classified descriptor lists used for indexing literature in the field of documentation and library science. According to Fuellhart and Weeks,[10] in 1968 there were some thirty vocabularies in use in this field.

One of the most detailed studies of the problems of vocabulary reconciliation has been contributed by Neville,[28] who is concerned with the reconciliation of several independently created systems covering the same subject area. With the eventual goal of being able to exchange abstracts among various organizations profitably, Neville predicated his plan on the following assumptions:

1. That each descriptor in each vocabulary represents a "concept."

2. If concepts can be identified, it is possible to recognize conceptual equivalents in the terms of the various vocabularies.

3. If each concept is identified by a unique code number in a "supra-thesaurus," it becomes possible to convert each vocabulary to the common coding system and thereby translate from any vocabulary into equivalent terms in any other.

This is the intermediate lexicon approach again. It requires the creation of a joint series of code numbers for the concepts treated in several thesauri. Neville's procedures for reconciliation may involve the extensive addition of cross-references in each thesaurus.

Some additional descriptors may also need to be added, but these are kept to a minimum; no existing descriptors are altered or deleted, however. Suppose we want to reconcile four thesauri, A, B, C, and D. The process works as follows. Taking A as the "source thesaurus," each descriptor in A is given a unique code, and equivalent descriptors in B, C, and D are identified and given an identical code. Thesaurus B then becomes the source thesaurus, and new descriptors (i.e., those not already treated through thesaurus A) are given codes and reconciled with the other thesauri. The remaining vocabularies, C and D, are handled similarly. Presumably one takes the largest thesaurus as source first. As one moves to the smaller thesauri successively, the amount of new reconciliation needed will be progressively reduced.

Some of the more important types of reconciliation recognized by Neville are as follows:

1. Exact correspondence, including singular/plural variance and foreign-language equivalency (Table 37).

2. Synonymy. Synonymous descriptors are equated by being given the same code number, but additional synonymous expressions may need to be added to certain of the thesauri (e.g., in Table 38 the reference from *buried structures* has been added to Thesaurus B).

3. The source thesaurus contains a descriptor which does not appear in any form in another thesaurus. Three actions are possible:

(a) The descriptor is added to the other thesaurus. (Table 39).

(b) The descriptor is mapped to a broader term in the other thesaurus (e.g., SNOWDRIFTS to SNOW, Table 40). A new reference may need to be added to Thesaurus C. In this example, SNOW and SNOWDRIFTS receive different code numbers. If organization C *receives* an abstract marked 0300 or 0301, it can automatically convert to the descriptor SNOW. If C *issues* an abstract relevant to snowdrifts, it must assign SNOW for its own use plus the code 0301 to allow joint

TABLE 37 Vocabulary Reconciliation: Exact Correspondence

	Source thesaurus	Thesaurus B	Thesaurus C
Original entries	AIRFIELDS	AIRFIELD	FLUGPLÄTZE
Reconciled entries	AIRFIELDS (0101)	AIRFIELD (0101)	FLUGPLÄTZE (0101)
Keys to code numbers	0101 = AIRFIELDS	0101 = AIRFIELD	0101 = FLUGPLÄTZE

SOURCE: H. H. Neville.[28]

TABLE 38   Vocabulary Reconciliation: Synonymy

	Source thesaurus	Thesaurus B

Original entries	UNDERGROUND STRUCTURES
	buried structures, use
	   UNDERGROUND STRUCTURES
		SUBSURFACE STRUCTURES
		underground structures, use
		   SUBSURFACE STRUCTURES

Reconciled entries	UNDERGROUND STRUCTURES (0201)
	buried structures, use
	   UNDERGROUND STRUCTURES
	subsurface structures, use
	   UNDERGROUND STRUCTURES
		SUBSURFACE STRUCTURES (0201)
		underground structures, use
		   SUBSURFACE STRUCTURES
		buried structures, use
		   SUBSURFACE STRUCTURES

Keys to code numbers	0201 = UNDERGROUND STRUCTURES	0201 = SUBSURFACE STRUCTURES

SOURCE: H. H. Neville.[28]

processing. A similar situation exists if the source thesaurus contains terms in both noun and adjectival form but the target thesaurus does not (Table 41).

(c) If the descriptor of the source thesaurus is not wanted in the other thesaurus, it should be added as a "subsidiary entry." This solution should be avoided in favor of (a) or (b) wherever possible. This implies that organization D (Table 42) must manually assign this descriptor if interagency processing is to be effected. However, it is likely that the organization will never issue any abstracts on this topic, so the situation may never arise. It is more likely to receive abstracts on the subject from other agencies, in which case the descriptor may be ignored.

4. One thesaurus combines antonyms in a single term. Here the single descriptors will need to be cross-referenced to the combined term. Individual descriptors will need to retain their unique codes (Table 43).

5. The source thesaurus uses a pre-coordinate term while the target thesaurus uses separate descriptors. In this case the pre-coordinate term must be cross-referenced in the target thesaurus to the appropriate combination of descriptors (Table 44 and Table 45).

Semantically factored terms may be treated in the same way (Table 46).

6. The source thesaurus distinguishes homographs and another thesaurus does not. This is best solved by having the other thesaurus introduce such a distinction; e.g., TANKS (COMBAT VEHICLES) and TANKS (CONTAINERS).

7. The source thesaurus contains general modifiers that have no direct equivalents in another thesaurus. In this situation Neville recommends that the general modifier (e.g., HIGH) not be allowed to exist alone in the joint system. Instead, the organization using the source thesaurus should list all the commonly used combinations of the modifier with other descriptors. These *combinations* will be used as terms in the supra-thesaurus, they will be coded, and their equivalents will be sought in the other vocabularies (Table 47).

8. The source thesaurus contains a descriptor less explicit than an equivalent descriptor in another vocabulary. For example, it uses ADDITIVES when "cement additives" is meant, presumably because "cement" is implied in the context of the thesaurus itself. This situation requires the inclusion of an appropriate *use*

TABLE 39   Vocabulary Reconciliation: Descriptor Added to Target Thesaurus

	Source thesaurus	Thesaurus B
Original entries	SNOWDRIFTS	—
Reconciled entries	SNOWDRIFTS (0301)	SNOWDRIFTS (0301)
Keys to code numbers	0301 = SNOWDRIFTS	0301 = SNOWDRIFTS

SOURCE: H. H. Neville.[28]

TABLE 40   Vocabulary Reconciliation: Descriptor Mapped to Broader Term in Target Thesaurus

	Source thesaurus	Thesaurus C
Original entries	SNOW SNOWDRIFTS	SNOW
Reconciled entries	SNOW (0300) SNOWDRIFTS (0301)	SNOW (0300) snowdrifts (0301), use SNOW
Keys to code numbers	0300 = SNOW 0301 = SNOWDRIFTS	0300 = SNOW 0301 = snowdrifts

SOURCE: H. H. Neville.[28]

TABLE 41 Vocabulary Reconciliation: Descriptor Mapped to Broader Term in Target Thesaurus *

	Source thesaurus	Thesaurus B
Original entries	ALUMINIUM ALUMINIUM STRUCTURES	ALUMINIUM
Reconciled entries	ALUMINIUM (material) (0701) ALUMINIUM STRUCTURES (0702)	ALUMINIUM (material 0701) (structures 0702)
Keys to code numbers	0701 = ALUMINIUM (material) 0702 = ALUMINIUM STRUCTURES	0701 = ALUMINIUM (material) 0702 = ALUMINIUM (structures)

SOURCE: H. H. Neville.[28]
* Source thesaurus contains terms in both noun and adjectival form but target thesaurus does not.

TABLE 42 Vocabulary Reconciliation: Source Descriptor not Wanted in Target Thesaurus

	Source thesaurus	Thesaurus D
Original entries	SNOWDRIFTS	—
Reconciled entries	SNOWDRIFTS (0301)	snowdrifts(0301)
Keys to code numbers	0301 = SNOWDRIFTS	0301 = snowdrifts

SOURCE: H. H. Neville.[28]

TABLE 43 Vocabulary Reconciliation: Single Descriptors and Combined Terms (antonyms)

	Source thesaurus	Thesaurus B
Original entries	CONTRACTION EXPANSION	contraction, use EXPANSION/ CONTRACTION EXPANSION/ CONTRACTION
Reconciled entries	CONTRACTION (0402) EXPANSION (0403)	contraction (0402), use EXPANSION/ CONTRACTION expansion (0403), use EXPANSION/ CONTRACTION EXPANSION/ CONTRACTION
Keys to code numbers	0402 = CONTRACTION 0403 = EXPANSION	0402 = contraction 0403 = expansion

SOURCE: H. H. Neville.[28]

TABLE 44 Vocabulary Reconciliation: Pre-coordinate Terms and Separate Descriptors

	Source thesaurus	Thesaurus B
Original entries	FROST PENETRATION	frost penetration, use FROST + PENETRATION
Reconciled entries	FROST PENETATION (0501)	frost penetration (0501), use FROST + PENETRATION
Keys to code numbers	0501 = FROST PENETRATION	0501 = frost penetration

SOURCE: H. H. Neville.[28]

TABLE 45 Vocabulary Reconciliation: Pre-coordinate Terms and Separate Descriptors

	Source thesaurus	Thesaurus B
Original entries	STIFFNESS METHODS	stiffness methods, use STRUCTURAL ANALYSIS + DISPLACEMENT
Reconciled entries	STIFFNESS METHODS (0502)	stiffness methods (0502), use STRUCTURAL ANALYSIS + DISPLACEMENT
Keys to code numbers	0502 = STIFFNESS METHODS	0502 = stiffness methods

SOURCE: H. H. Neville.[28]

TABLE 46 Vocabulary Reconciliation: Semantically Factored Terms

	Source thesaurus	Thesaurus B
Original entries	THERMOMETER	thermometer, use TEMPERATURE + MEASUREMENT INSTRUMENT
Reconciled entries	THERMOMETER (0503)	thermometer (0503), use TEMPERATURE + MEASUREMENT INSTRUMENT
Keys to code numbers	0503 = THERMOMETER	0503 = thermometer

SOURCE: H. H. Neville.[28]

TABLE 47 Vocabulary Reconciliation: Modifiers with no Direct Equivalents

	Source thesaurus	Thesaurus B
Original entries	HIGH	—
Reconciled entries	HIGH (—) (HIGH + TEMPERATURE 0801) (HIGH + BUILDINGS 0802) (HIGH + STRENGTH 0803) high temperature (0801), use HIGH + TEMPERATURE high buildings (0802), use HIGH + BUILDINGS high strength (0803), use HIGH + STRENGTH multi-storey buildings (0802), use HIGH + BUILDINGS	HIGH TEMPERATURE (0801) MULTI-STOREY BUILDINGS (0802) HIGH-STRENGTH (0803) high buildings, use MULTI-STOREY BUILDINGS
Keys to code numbers	0801 = high temperature 0802 = high buildings 0803 = high-strength	0801 = HIGH TEMPERATURE 0802 = MULTI-STOREY BUILDINGS 0803 = HIGH-STRENGTH

SOURCE: H. H. Neville.[28]

reference in the source thesaurus and the equating of the two descriptors in the coding scheme (Table 48).

9. The source thesaurus contains a number of related terms with very fine shades of meaning. These distinctions are not wanted in the joint system. In this case it is recommended that, even though these distinctions are maintained in the source thesaurus, all the nearly synonymous terms be referred to the same code in the supra-thesaurus (Table 49).

The intermediate lexicon approach, as exemplified by Neville, differs from the Wall method previously described. Wall seeks an algorithm for *automatic* conversion of one vocabulary directly to another. In the intermediate lexicon approach we create the common supra-thesaurus by human intellectual process-

ing. Subsequent conversion, via the lexicon, may then be automatic although, as in Neville's examples, some additional human assignment may be needed to cover certain problem descriptors that have no direct equivalents in other vocabularies.

INTERNATIONAL COMPATIBILITY

Before leaving the subject of vocabulary compatibility we should consider the implications of increasing international cooperation in information retrieval and dissemination. Where an international relationship exists between information centers, as in an international network, each participating center could, of course, adopt a common language for indexing and

TABLE 48 Vocabulary Reconciliation: Source Thesaurus Less Explicit than Target Thesaurus

	Source thesaurus	Thesaurus B
Original entries	ADDITIVES	CEMENT ADDITIVES
Reconciled entries	ADDITIVES (cement)(0804) cement additives, use ADDITIVES	CEMENT ADDITIVES
Keys to code numbers	0804 = ADDITIVES (cement)	0804 = CEMENT ADDITIVES

SOURCE: H. H. Neville.[28]

TABLE 49 Vocabulary Reconciliation: Coding of Related Terms

	Source thesaurus	Thesaurus B
Original entries	SLOPE	INCLINATION
	GRADIENTS	slope, use INCLINATION
	PITCH (INCLINATION)	gradient, use INCLINATION
	inclination, use PITCH	pitch, use INCLINATION
Reconciled entries	SLOPE (0901)	INCLINATION (0901)
	GRADIENTS (0901)	slope, use INCLINATION
	PITCH (INCLINATION) (0901)	gradient, use INCLINATION
	inclination, use PITCH	pitch, use INCLINATION
Keys to code numbers	0901=SLOPE, GRADIENT, PITCH (INCLINATION)	0901 = INCLINATION

SOURCE: H. H. Neville.[28]

searching operations. This is the case in MEDLARS, an international system in which the English-language *Medical Subject Headings* is used throughout the network. Obviously, this type of system requires that all indexers and searchers in any participating center must have a good command of the English language and must understand medical English in particular.

An alternative is to have a multilingual thesaurus, such as the one developed by the French Road Research Laboratory for use by the road research laboratories of OECD member countries.[36] This thesaurus is novel in that it uses arrowgraphs to display term relationships, and a superimposable grid to show term equivalents in various languages. The draft of a set of guidelines for construction of multilingual thesauri was issued by UNESCO in July 1970.[33] For international operations, of course, a strong case can be made for the adoption of a classification scheme since class numbers from such a vocabulary are not language-dependent. The *Universal Decimal Classification* (UDC) has the great advantage of being available in several languages and widely adopted in many countries. Lloyd[24] has recognized that existing information centers in an international network would be reluctant to abandon thesauri already in use. He urges that consideration be given to the use of the UDC as a standard switching language (an intermediate lexicon, in effect) with which each vocabulary can establish a single concordance.

It is interesting to note that Salton[31] has considered the possibilities of multilingual processing with the SMART system. SMART procedures may be extended to foreign-language documents by the use of a multilingual thesaurus. Experiments indicate that cross-language processing (e.g., German queries against English documents, or vice versa) is almost as effective as processing within a single language. Moreover, a

simple translation of thesaurus categories appears to produce a content analysis that is equally effective in English or German.

Muench[26] has described the use of a computer to produce a bilingual (English/Spanish) index to six biomedical vocabularies: MeSH, the Cunningham Classification, the Boston Medical Classification, the National Library of Medicine Classification, and the medical portions of the Library of Congress and Dewey Decimal classifications. The index was compiled by first supplying the appropriate classification numbers (from all five schemes) to MeSH and to an existing Spanish translation of MeSH. These data were then put into machine-readable form, sorted, and printed alphabetically by subject headings (both in English and Spanish) and sequentially by classification number for each of the schemes, thus producing a cross-reference index to the various vocabularies and at least a rough Spanish translation for all the schemes. Such a composite index will facilitate the following activities, among others: (a) translation from one scheme to another (e.g., from classification numbers on Library of Congress printed cards to equivalent numbers from another scheme); (b) merging of one collection with another, where different classifications are used for each one; (c) use of *Index Medicus* and other MEDLARS products in Spanish-speaking countries; (d) production of a Spanish version of *Index Medicus* or other printed products of MEDLARS; (e) unmodified incorporation into MEDLARS of index records prepared by Spanish indexers using the Spanish version of MeSH.

In summary, given a group of independent information centers wishing to facilitate the interagency processing of documents for retrieval or dissemination, three obvious solutions to the vocabulary control problem exist:

1. Complete adoption of a common vocabulary by all centers.

2. Adoption of a common structure (master thesaurus) and the development of various microthesauri within this structure. The master thesaurus would be used for interagency processing. This mode of operation is exemplified by the relation between *Medical Subject Headings* and various specialized thesauri in the biomedical field.

3. The construction of an intermediate lexicon or concordance.

The first alternative is obviously the most simple and most desirable to implement. However, it may be difficult to construct a vocabulary that all centers will accept. Too many compromises (e.g., accepting less than complete specificity) may be required. Moreover, this approach is viable only if the centers do not already possess controlled vocabularies which they would be reluctant to abandon. The same is true of the second alternative. The intermediate lexicon is probably the best solution where existing vocabularies have been in use for some time and cannot readily be altered.*

Although we tend to associate the concept of vocabulary control with the concept of compatibility, this association is misleading in the context of intersystem compatibility. Two controlled vocabularies are compatible only if we deliberately make them so by one of the techniques discussed in this chapter. Natural-language systems, however, are completely compatible in this respect, and it is a comparatively simple task to integrate a number of natural-language systems. It is also easy to integrate a controlled vocabulary system into a natural-language system (simply by treating the controlled terms as though they were free-text terms), although it is much more difficult to work in the reverse direction (integrating a natural-language system into a controlled vocabulary) because intellectual mappings must be made between the natural-language expressions and the controlled vocabulary terms.

* In fact, a fourth possibility exists. Conceivably, we could derive algorithms, as described by Wall and Barnes, to map automatically from one vocabulary to another.

REFERENCES

1. Austin, C. J. *MEDLARS, 1963-1967.* Bethesda, Md.: National Library of Medicine, 1968.
2. Bering, E. A., Jr. and Caponio, J. F. *NINDS Neurological Information Network. Annual Progress Report.* Bethesda, Md.: National Institute of Neurological Diseases and Stroke, 1969.
3. Carroll, K. D. *Survey of Scientific-Technical Tape Services.* New York: American Institute of Physics, 1970.
4. Coates, E. J. "Library Science and Documentation Literature: a New Development in International Cooperation." *Library Association Record* 70 (1968): 178-179.
5. Coates, E. J. "Switching Languages for Indexing." *Journal of Documentation* 26 (1970): 102-110.
6. COSATI. *COSATI Subject Category List.* Washington, D.C., 1964. AD 612 200.
7. Datatrol Corporation. *Common Vocabulary Approaches for Government Scientific and Technical Information Systems.* Silver Spring, Md., 1963.
8. Eichhorn, M. M. and Reinecke, R. D. "Development and Implementation of a Thesaurus for the Visual Sciences." *Journal of Chemical Documentation* 9 (1969): 114-118.
9. Eichhorn, M. M. et al., eds. *Thesaurus for the Visual Sciences.* Boston: Harvard Medical School, Vision Information Center, 1969.
10. Fuellhart, P. O. and Weeks, D. C. *Compilation and Analysis of Lexical Resources in Information Science.* Washington, D.C.: George Washington University, Biological Sciences Communication Project, 1968.
11. Gardin, N. "The Intermediate Lexicon." *UNESCO Bulletin for Libraries* 23 (1969): 58-63.
12. Hammond, W. "Satellite Thesaurus Construction." In *The Thesaurus in Action: Background Information for a Thesaurus Workshop at the 32nd Annual Convention of the American Society for Information Science.* San Francisco, Calif., October 1969: 14-20. AD 694 590.
13. Hammond, W. "Statistical Association Methods for Simultaneous Searching of Multiple Document Collections." *Proceedings of the Symposium on Statistical Association Methods for Mechanized Documentation.* Edited by M. E. Stevens et al., Washington, D.C.: National Bureau of Standards, 1965, 237-243. NBS Miscellaneous Publication 269.
14. Hammond, W. and Rosenborg, S. *Experimental Study of Convertibility Between Large Technical Indexing Vocabularies.* Silver Spring, Md.: Datatrol Corporation, 1962.
15. Hammond, W. and Rosenborg, S. *Indexing Terms of Announcement Publications for Government Scientific and Technical Research Reports: A Composite Vocabulary.* 2 vols. Silver Spring, Md.: Datatrol Corporation, 1964.
16. Henderson, M. M. et al. *Cooperation, Convertibility, and Compatibility Among Information Systems: a Literature Review.* Washington, D.C.: National Bureau of Standards, 1966. NBS Miscellaneous Publication No. 276.
17. Herschman, A. *A Program for a National Information System for Physics, 1970-1972.* New York: American Institute of Physics, 1969.
18. Holst, W. "A User-Oriented Information System, Operational on a Regional Basis Within the Scandinavian Countries." *Information Storage and Retrieval* 6 (1970): 101-125.
19. Hyslop, M. R. "Joint Development of a Common Information System by Two Organizations Working in Different Disciplines." *Bulletin de l'Association Internationale des Documentalistes et Techniciens de l'Information* 5 (1966): 89-97.
20. Hyslop, M. R. "Sharing Vocabulary Control." *Special Libraries* 56 (1965): 708-714.
21. Jaster, J. J. *Subsumption Scheme for Dictionary of Indexing Equivalents.* Silver Spring, Md.: Datatrol Corporation, 1963.
22. Landau, H. B. *Research Study into the Effective Utilization of Machine-Readable Bibliographic Data Bases.* Final Report. Philadelphia, Pa.: Auerbach Corporation, 1969.

23. Levy, F. G. "Compatibility Between Classifications and The-sauri: First Evaluation of a Study in the Field of Informa-tion Storage and Retrieval." *Proceedings of the 33rd Con-ference of FID.* Tokyo, 1967. Paper IIIg2.

24. Lloyd, G. A. "The UDC in its International Aspects." *ASLIB Proceedings* 21 (1969): 204-208.

25. Marron, H. "ERIC . . . a National Network to Disseminate Educational Information." *Special Libraries* 59 (1968): 775-782.

26. Muench, E. V. "A Computerized English-Spanish Correla-tion Index to Five Biomedical Library Classification Schemes Based on MeSH." *Bulletin of the Medical Library Asso-ciation* 59 (1971): 404-411.

27. National Agricultural Library. *Agricultural/Biological Vocabulary.* 2 vols. Washington, D.C., 1967.

28. Neville, H. H. "Feasibility Study of a Scheme for Recon-ciling Thesauri Covering a Common Subject." *Journal of Documentation* 26 (1970): 313-336.

29. Painter, A. F. *An Analysis of Duplication and Consistency of Subject Indexing Involved in Report Handling at the Office of Technical Services.* Washington, D.C.: Depart-ment of Commerce, Office of Technical Services, 1963. PB 181 501.

30. Ruhl, M. J. and Sokoloff, L. *"A Thesaurus of Rheuma-tology."* In *Arthritis and Rheumatism* 8 (February 1965).

31. Salton, G. "Automatic Processing of Foreign Language Documents." *Journal of the American Society for Informa-tion Science* 21 (1970): 187-194.

32. Speight, F. Y. "Plans for Updating the *Thesaurus of En-gineering and Scientific Terms.*" In *The Thesaurus in Action: Background Information for a Thesaurus Work-shop at the 32nd Annual Convention of the American So-ciety for Information Science.* October 1969, San Francisco, Calif., 33-38. AD 694 590.

33. UNESCO. *Guidelines for the Establishment and Develop-ment of Multilingual Scientific and Technical Thesauri for Information Retrieval.* First Draft. Paris, July 1970.

34. UNESCO. *Joint UNESCO-ICSU Study on the Feasibility of a World Science Information System (UNISIST).* Final Report. Paris, 1970.

35. U.S. Atomic Energy Commission. *Subject Headings Used by the USAEC Division of Technical Information.* 6th ed. Washington, D.C., 1966. TID-5001.

36. Van Dijk, M. "Un Thésaurus Multilingue au Service de la Coopération Internationale." *Bulletin de l'Association In-ternationale des Documentalistes et Techniciens de l'Infor-mation* 5 (1966): 85-87.

37. Wall, E. and Barnes, J. *Intersystem Compatibility and Convertibility of Subject Vocabularies.* Philadelphia, Pa.: Auerbach Corporation, 1969.

19 *Some Further Controlled Vocabularies*

In this chapter, I want to discuss briefly some further controlled vocabularies which, while not widely used, are of interest because of the principles on which they are based, the influence they have had, or the lessons that may be learned from them. Specifically, I want to discuss the Mooers descriptor system, the *Symbolic Shorthand System* of Hans Selye, and the semantic code developed at Western Reserve University.

MOOERS

Calvin Mooers' Zator System is very interesting for a number of reasons. It was one of the earliest post-coordinate retrieval systems; it was pioneering in its application of edge-notched cards to information retrieval problems; and it introduced an ingenious system for random superimposed coding. It is the Mooers vocabulary concept that interests us here.

Mooers [4] was a strong advocate of small very carefully controlled vocabularies. He introduced the expression "descriptor" into the literature of information retrieval. The word has since become debased by very loose usage,* and now it tends to be used to indicate any term applied in indexing a document. Mooers, however, maintained a very strict interpretation of the word "descriptor." According to Mooers, a descriptor consists of two parts: a label and a verbal

* I am among the guilty!

or written definition. In creating a controlled vocabulary we isolate concepts that are likely to be useful for retrieval purposes and give each concept a separate label. "Lubrication" may be one label that we choose. It is important to recognize that, when we assign the label "lubrication" to one or more documents, we are creating a unique class of documents. It is also important to recognize the exact composition of this class. Clearly, it is not a class of "lubrication"; nor is it a class of "documents on lubrication"; it is simply a class of documents to which the label "lubrication" has been assigned. However, there should be a very close similarity between the class of documents "on lubrication" and the class of documents to which the label "lubrication" has been assigned.

With this interpretation, it becomes obvious that the label itself is relatively unimportant. Much more important is our definition of what is to be contained within a particular class (i.e., its scope). Having defined the scope of a class we can assign any label to it, as long as we use it consistently. Mooers was careful to point out that, even though we use an English word such as "lubrication" as a descriptor, we need not rely on the dictionary definition of this word as an indication of its scope. In fact it is better not to do so. Each organization has its own special viewpoint in relation to a topic, and it is this viewpoint that should be written into the definition of the scope of the class. For example, a definition associated with the label "lubrication" might be: "Deals with all methods for

diminishing the sliding or contact friction between two opposed moving surfaces." It does not matter in the least whether or not our definition is the one popularly adopted. The important thing is that, within our information system, this is the definition that we are using, and using consistently. The label is entirely separate from the definition. For convenience we tend to use English-language words as labels, but this is by no means essential. Although Mooers did not claim this, we should regard the label as merely a unique character string. As long as the same string is used consistently as the label for a defined class, it does not matter what this string is. For example, it would not interfere with retrieval if we used the string CATS as the label for the class of documents discussing canine animals, and the string DOGS as the label for the class of documents dealing with felines, as long as the composition of each class is well defined and the labels are used consistently. Likewise, a label could equally well be a "semantically empty" string such as XXYP. The distinction between the definition of a document class and the label assigned to it is an extremely important one. Mooers maintained this important distinction and recognized that it is the definition (i.e., scope) of a class that governs retrieval performance rather than what we call the class (i.e., label it). Unfortunately this simple point still appears to elude many people.

Mooers believed that a complete vocabulary of descriptors for a specialized subject area usually should not exceed 250–350. Only in very special cases will it grow to more than a thousand. Descriptors are relatively broad in scope because they are to be used in conjunction with other descriptors to form a "delineating set" describing a document or a request. Identifiers may also be used for proper names of various sorts. The Mooers descriptor sets have very definite literary warrant. Most of the Mooers Zator Systems were established in industrial organizations and were used for retrieval of the high-value internal reports of these agencies. The descriptor vocabulary is established in the following way. A working group consisting of about three members of the organization is formed, at the highest scientific level possible. This group works from a sample of the documents to be included in the system. They examine each document in the sample and ask themselves the questions "why do we need this document and what use do we have for it?" The answer might be "because it deals with lubrication." "Lubrication" thus becomes a "presumptive descriptor" in the vocabulary. Gradually the descriptor vocabulary is built up from the documents themselves, the chosen descriptors being those which, by group consensus, are likely to be needed for indexing and searching purposes. In one experience, at Allied Research Associates, Mooers[2] found that 80 percent of all the descriptors in the final schedule had been decided upon by the time fifty representative reports had been examined.

Some examples of Mooers descriptors, comprising both labels and definitions are presented in Table 50. Note the inclusion of conventional *use* references from nondescriptors (n.d.,) to descriptors, including one-to-many mappings. Because there are few descriptors in a Mooers system, they are relatively easy to remember. Moreover, their breadth of scope makes them relatively easy to assign unequivocally. Descriptors with finely drawn distinctions between them are avoided. According to Mooers, precision is not sacrificed, however, because specific ideas can be represented by combinations of broad descriptors.

The final list of descriptors is printed on a large sheet of paper, with related descriptors grouped together systematically. Table 51 shows a sample from such a descriptor schedule. In indexing a document the analyst essentially considers every descriptor in the schedule as potentially applicable. He asks himself

TABLE 50   Mooers' Descriptors

Stability
  In aeronautical engineering, pertains to the study of aircraft stability as used in conjunction with Static, Dynamic, Lateral, Longitudinal. Also refers to instability, such as buckling or other structural instabilities. Use with Derivatives in stability and control studies. For Lateral-longitudinal Stability Coupling (n.d.) use Stability plus Lateral plus Longitudinal plus Interference.
Stall and Buffet
  Stall pertains to the condition of partially or wholly separated flow on air-foils at high angles of attack. Buffet is the disturbance due to periodic boundary layer separation on a surface or the motion of a surface in a fluctuating wake.
Static
  With Stability, pertains to static stability studies.
Statistical Mechanics (n.d.)
  Use Thermodynamics
Statistics (n.d.)
  Use Probability.
Stick Force (n.d.)
  Use Control plus Biology.
Strain Gage (n.d.)
  Use Stress and Strain plus Instrumentation.
Stress and Strain
  Any process involving the loading and deflection of structures, e.g., bending of beams, deflections of plates, theoretical elasticity studies, elastic behavior. Use also for Torsion (n.d.). With Instrumentation it means Strain Gage (n.d.).

SOURCE: E. W. Brenner and C. N. Mooers.[2]

TABLE 51   Mooers' Indexing Sheet

What material was studied?	Is the process dynamic (rather than static)?	Are there specific aerodynamic loads?	Is structural strength and elasticity involved?
Metals	Vibrations	Lift	Stress and strain
Gases	Transient response	Drag	Plasticity
Plastics	Impact	Moment	Failure
Aluminum	Stability	Gust	Ultimate properties
Magnesium	Velocity	Pressure	Material properties
Titanium		Center of application	Aeroelasticity
Air		e.g., aerodynamic center, center of pressure, etc.	Flutter
What is the type of fluid flow?	**Is it a stability and control problem?**	**Or is there another aerodynamics problem?**	**Is a thermal process involved?**
Fluid flow	Stability	Boundary layer	Thermodynamics
Internal flow	Control	Aeroelasticity	Thermodynamic constants
Subsonic	Static	Flutter	Combustion
Transonic	Dynamic-Trans. resp.	Downwash	Heat transfer
Supersonic	Longitudinal	Stall and buffet	Cooling
Hypersonic	Lateral	Interference	Convection
Laminar	Derivatives	Hydraulics	Conduction
Turbulence	Damping	Trajectory	Thermal
Slip flow	Weight and balance	Droplets	Radiation
Compressibility	e.g., center of	Modifying technique	Aerodynamic heating
Viscosity	gravity, moments of	Performance	
Vortices	inertia, etc.		
Shock waves			
Finite span			

SOURCE: E. W. Brenner and C. N. Mooers.[2]

the questions posed by the descriptor list itself. If, for example, the answer to "are there specific aerodynamic loads?" is "yes" (i.e., the document at hand discusses specific loads), the analyst must account for this by assigning the most appropriate aerodynamic load descriptor or descriptors. The descriptor list, presented in this way, greatly simplifies the indexing process because it takes some of the intellectual burden from the indexer. He is relieved of the task of visualizing all possible uses of a document. The potential uses of interest to the organization are represented by the list of "leading" questions, which has been carefully compiled by senior scientific personnel. The indexer merely follows the leads given in this list.

THE SYMBOLIC SHORTHAND SYSTEM

The *Symbolic Shorthand System* (SSS) *for Physiology and Medicine* was developed by the famous endocrinologist Hans Selye,[6,7] and it had its origins as far back as 1926. The system has been applied to the indexing of an extremely large collection (approaching a million

items) on stress, calciphylaxis, and endocrinology at the Institut de Médicine et de Chirurgie expérimentales, Université de Montréal.

SSS is a classification scheme comprising 20 main classes. It is organized principally on the basis of body system. Thus, Class 5 is Renal System and Urinary Passages. Class 6 is Respiratory System. Within each body system, a faceted organization is apparent. Thus, the class Gastrointestinal System is subdivided according to the following facets:

Structure (i.e., parts of the system)
Interventions (i.e., human interventions such as surgery)
Function (i.e., natural functions of the system)
Specific Products (e.g., juices, hormones, secretions)
Diseases

This facet sequence is maintained in the organization of each body system. The SSS is partly enumerative. It lists or enumerates labels for fairly simple or elemental subjects upon which literature is known to exist. It is also partly synthetic: rules prescribe how the Symbolic Shorthand Symbols for elemental subjects

may be synthesized in order to express extremely complex subjects. For example, the Symbolic Shorthand symbol for the adrenal gland is Adr; for psyche it is Psy. We can synthesize these, thus:

$$\text{Adr} \leftarrow \text{Psy}$$

in order to express the subject "effect of psychic stimuli on adrenal structure."

The synthetic principle can be used to express subject matter of any degree of complexity, as shown by the following:

Adr   Adrenal gland
Hyp-x   Hypophysectomy
ACTH   Adrenocorticotrophic hormone
TX   Thyroxin
Adr ← Hyp-x + ACTH + TX   Effect on the adrenal of hypophysectomy in conjunction with adrenocorticotrophic hormone and thyroxin.

The classification is predictive. When, for example, the very first piece of literature on the subject "use of oxytocin and progesterone to induce uterine contractions" appeared, it was possible to index this document precisely by the use of the synthetic principle, as: U-c ← OX + PROG. The *Symbolic Shorthand System* is, in fact, an example of an analytico-synthetic classification.

Selye uses the SSS pre-coordinately, creating a specific index entry by coordinating classes at the time of indexing, as in the example Adr ← Hyp-x + ACTH + TX. However, the system could also be applied post-coordinately. For example, we could use each of the notations Adr, Hyp-x, ACTH, and TX as headings on peek-a-boo cards, retrieving items on the subject complex by manipulation of these cards at the time of searching.

We can recognize the component vocabularies of SSS when we come to index a group of documents by means of this language. Suppose we are indexing a group of items on various aspects of the retina. The very first document that comes to hand is a general article on all aspects of the retina. We consult Selye's code book and discover that there is a specifier "retina" which is represented by the descriptor Retina. The next article deals with the surgical procedure of retinal attachment. It is not possible to define this document class uniquely in SSS, so we subsume it under the more general class "retinal surgery," represented by the descriptor Retina-Su. We must, of course, include the term "retinal attachment" in our entry vocabulary so that we have a record of where this class has been put. "Retinal surgery," itself, is a specifier, uniquely defining a class.

An article on retinal diseases appears next for indexing, and is assigned the index term "retinal diseases," represented by the descriptor Retina. Similarly, the subject matter of the next document, "retinal hemorrhage," is capable of unique definition, the descriptor used being Retina (B↓). We cannot express the notion of "retinitis" precisely, so must be content with subsuming this class under the more general class "retinal diseases," recording this in our entry vocabulary. The last two documents in the group deal with aspects of the retina for which specifiers are available: Oc-Ar-Scl is the descriptor used for "arteriosclerotic retinopathy," and Retina (IN↓), the descriptor for "diabetic retinopathy."

The entry vocabulary generated by this group of documents will be as follows:

	Entry Terms		*Descriptors*
(Specifier)	Retina	*use*	Retina
	Retinal attachment	*use*	Retina-Su
(Specifier)	Retinal diseases	*use*	Retina
(Specifier)	Retinal hemorrhage	*use*	Retina (B↓)
(Specifier)	Retinal surgery	*use*	Retina-Su
	Retinitis	*use*	Retina
(Specifier)	Retinopathy, arteriosclerotic	*use*	Oc-Ar-Scl
(Specifier)	Retinopathy, diabetic	*use*	Retina (IN↓)

The *Symbolic Shorthand System* has a vocabulary of approximately 1,800 descriptors. However, it is capable of uniquely defining many more than 1,800 classes. In fact, the number of unique document classes that can be defined by notational synthesis is almost unlimited. At the present time, Selye's vocabulary comprises over 15,000 specifiers. In other words, more than 15,000 unique document classes are defined in his present search file, covering close to a million documents.

Consider now the index language devices of the *Symbolic Shorthand System*. It is obviously possible to control synonyms, as it is in any classification scheme, by referring from the several term variants to a single descriptor. Thus, Selye regards "hashishism" and "marihuana addiction" as synonymous, referring both terms in his entry vocabulary to the descriptor Psy-Hashish.

Word forms are rather ingeniously controlled within SSS. For example, the code symbol Int is used throughout the scheme to express the subject matter "intestines" or "intestinal." Thus, Int represents "in-

testines" in general, Int-c "intestinal contraction," and Int-itis "enteritis."

There is, of course, hierarchical linkage in the vocabulary, although the links are rather short, as exemplified by the following:

GI   Gastrointestinal system
    (Specific products)
      GI-E   Crude gastrointestinal extract
      Du-E   Duodenal crude extract

There is even a device in Selye's system which allows a form of clumping or clustering of document classes, although not on the basis of statistical associations. As an endocrinologist, Selye is very much interested in the effects of biological materials on various parts of the body. He would, for example, be interested in the effects of ACTH or of 11-Desoxycorticosterone on the nervous system and its parts. A document on the effect of ACTH on the hypothalamus would be coded Hypt ← ACTH, while a document on its effect on the tuber cinereum would be under Tuber ← ACTH. These classes would be separated by many other document classes if the order of precedence in filing were strictly enforced. Although the effects of these substances on specific organs are precisely coded, Selye allows a modification of his order of precedence (citation order) in order to bring together in his search file all articles relating to the effect of a particular agent upon a particular body system and its parts. Thus, the order adopted would be as follows:

$$\left.\begin{array}{l} \text{Cer} \leftarrow \text{ACTH} \\ \text{Hypt} \leftarrow \text{ACTH} \\ \text{Tuber} \leftarrow \text{ACTH} \end{array}\right\} \begin{array}{l}\text{effects of ACTH on various parts}\\ \text{of the nervous system}\end{array}$$

$$\left.\begin{array}{l} \text{Hypt} \leftarrow \text{DOC} \\ \text{Tuber} \leftarrow \text{DOC} \end{array}\right\} \begin{array}{l}\text{effects of 11-Desoxycorticosterone}\\ \text{on various parts of the nervous}\\ \text{system}\end{array}$$

This arrangement is more useful, for Selye's purposes, than an arrangement following his strict order of precedence, which would bring together studies of all agents affecting a particular organ, but disperse studies on effects of particular agents, as follows:

Cer← DOC   effects of various agents on the brain

Hypt ← ACTH
Hypt ← DOC   effects of various agents on the hypothalamus

Tuber ← ACTH
Tuber ← DOC   effects of various agents on the tuber cinereum

Turning now to the precision devices of the *Symbolic Shorthand System,* we already know that it employs coordination, both enumerative and synthetic.

GI-Tu, gastrointestinal tumors, is an example of enumerative coordination (i.e., the intersection of the class "gastrointestinal system" and the class "tumor" is pre-established in the schedules of the classification). However, the intersection of the class "liver" and the class "vessels" (i.e., "hepatic vessels") is not pre-established in the schedules. We must create this coordination by synthesis of the separate symbols, as Hep-Vs.

The two levels of linking (i.e., partitioning and interfixing) are apparent in the way Selye's system is used. A document dealing with the effect of heat on the adrenals and the effect of lack of oxygen on the thyroid would be partitioned into its two separate themes, each one being translated into a separate indexing statement:

$$\text{Adr} \leftarrow \text{Temp} \uparrow$$
$$\text{Tr} \leftarrow O_2 \downarrow$$

Thus, false coordinations between "adrenals" and "oxygen," and between "thyroid" and "heat," are avoided.

Selye also uses various punctuation marks to interfix within themes. The indexing statement

$$\text{R} \leftarrow (\text{'B/Rb} \leftarrow \text{R/Duck'})/\text{Rat}$$

precisely expresses the subject matter "injection of renal substance of duck into a rabbit's blood, and injection of serum thus formed into rats, thus producing renal changes." The oblique stroke (B/Rb and R/Duck) is used as an interfixing device to show that the blood belongs to the rabbit and the renal substance to the duck.

Selye also makes wide use of role or relational indicators within his language, as can be seen from the following sample indexing statements:

BMR ← ACTH   ("basal metabolic rate" in role of patient or target, ACTH in role of agent)

GTH (FSH+LH)   ("follicle‑stimulating hormone" and "luteinizing hormone" in the role of components in relation to "gonadotropic hormone")

Glu<B   ("sugar" in the role of component in relation to "blood")

Glu<B(:Ur) ← CON   (comparison role: effect of cortisone on sugar content of blood compared with sugar content of urine).

The *Symbolic Shorthand System* also incorporates a form of weighting. The strict order of precedence (con-

trolling the sequence in which descriptors are synthesized) is a method of weighting that gives precedence to concepts that Selye considers of prime importance to his own interests or to the interests of endocrinology.

Selye is an eminent authority on the subjects of endocrinology and stress, not a specialist in documentation. Yet the index language that he developed to meet the requirements of a particular user group, without being influenced by theoretical considerations and without studies of the literature on information retrieval (in fact, SSS predates most of this literature), incorporates, in one form or another, all of the recall and precision devices discussed in Chapters 14 and 15.

In the foregoing discussion we have shown how an index language may be dissected into its component vocabularies and its various ancillary devices. Any index language may be so analyzed, an exercise which is extremely useful if we wish to understand it fully and appreciate its true capabilities.

THE SEMANTIC CODE

The semantic code was developed at the Center for Documentation and Communication Research, Western Reserve University (now Case Western Reserve University). It was applied to a machine-based retrieval system in the field of metals, designed and operated by Western Reserve for the American Society for Metals. The system has been described in great detail by Perry and Kent,[5] and in more condensed form by Kent and Perry [3] and by Vickery.[8] It has been analyzed and evaluated by Aitchison and Cleverdon.[1]

The document surrogate in the Western Reserve system is a "telegraphic abstract." Telegraphic abstracts are prepared in standardized format, according to a set of rules, to eliminate variations and complexities of English sentence structure. Subject analysis forms are specially designed to assist the indexer in recording important aspects of subject matter in the form of telegraphic abstracts. The terms in the telegraphic abstract are encoded by means of a "semantic code dictionary." The basis of the semantic code is a semantic "stem." The stems (there are about 250 in the system) represent relatively broad concepts. Each stem is given a four-digit code consisting of three characters with a space for interpolation of a fourth character, as in the following examples:

C–TL   Catalyst
C–TR   Container
C–TT   Cutting and drilling
D–DD   Damage
D–FL   Deflection

Individual terms are built up by inserting a one-letter "infix" into the semantic stem and possibly by appending a numerical suffix. For example, DADD is used to represent both "wound" and "decay," where D–DD is the semantic stem for "damage" and the infix A merely stands for "is a." In other words, a "wound" is a type of damage. A numerical suffix is added merely to distinguish terms having identical stems and infix structure; the suffix in itself has no semantic significance.

The full list of infixes is presented in Table 52. The use of infixes with a stem allows the expression of various shades of meaning. For example, "bag" and "barrel" are both represented by CATR, where the infix A indicates that these are *types of* container. "Side wall," on the other hand, is represented by CITR, where the infix I indicates *part of* container. An individual complex concept may be built up from several "semantic factors." For example, the topic "telephone" is expressed by

DWCM.LQCT.MACH.TURN.001

where

D–CM represents Information
L–CT represents Electricity
M–CH represents Device
T–RN represents Transmission

and 001 is the unique suffix that distinguishes this term from others (e.g., Telegraph) having the same semantic factors. A maximum of four semantic codes may be combined to form a code for a specific concept.

Terms in a telegraphic abstract are syntactically related by means of role indicators. A list of these is

TABLE 52 Semantic Infixes in the Western Reserve System

A	is a
E	is made of
I	is part of
O	is made up of several
Q	makes use of, is produced, by means of
U	is used for, produces (frequently used for verbs ending in *ing*)
V	acts upon
W	brings about, affected by, is acted upon by (frequently used for verbs ending in *ed*)
X	is characterized by the absence of
Y	is connected with, characterized by, characteristically
Z	resembles, but is not
P	is characterized by an increase of
M	is characterized by a decrease of

SOURCE: J. W. Perry and A. Kent.[5]

given in Table 53. An example of the application of roles is:

KOV.KEJ	crystal
, KOV. KEJ. KUJ.	metal
, KOV. KEJ. KUJ.	alloy
, KOV. KEJ. KUJ.	beryllium
, KWV	hexagonal close packed
, KWV	elastic

which indicates that metal alloy crystals, specifically beryllium, are being processed in some way, and that they have the properties of being "hexagonal close packed" and "elastic." Note the use of "companion roles" in this system. KOV and KWV are companion or paired roles. When one of these is assigned to a particular term we expect to find the companion assigned to a second term, to tie the terms together and indicate their exact relationship. Thus, "crystal," by the role KOV, is shown to have a property given for it. These given properties are "elastic" and "hexagonal close packed" as indicated by the role KWV.

In addition to role indicators the system uses a highly elaborate method of linking terms (and roles) in the telegraphic abstracts. This linking is achieved by various levels of "punctuation":

1. *Subphrase.* A term with one or more role indicators attached.

2. *Phrase.* This is a set of closely related terms in a particular relationship. A finite number of phrase patterns is recognized. For example:

KAM (process)
KQJ (means of process)
KAH (condition of process)

3. *Sentence.* This is comprised of phrases and is also built up in standard patterns. For example, a

sentence may cover a product and its manufacture, or a material tested and the properties determined for it.

4. *Paragraph.* This is a set of sentences, and it may be co-extensive with the abstract itself. It can also be used to distinguish completely different topics within a single telegraphic abstract. A complete telegraphic abstract as it would be recorded on magnetic tape, and showing punctuation, roles, and semantic factors, is illustrated in Figure 65.

In conducting a search in this system, the request statement is converted to a strategy comprised of semantic factors and role indicators. Various "levels," corresponding to the punctuation of the telegraphic abstracts, can be used to restrict criteria to terms occurring within certain units. For example, search level 4 asks merely that a particular term be associated with a particular role indicator. This corresponds to the subphrase in punctuation of the telegraphic abstract.

The Western Reserve system is highly ingenious and is capable of expressing very fine shades of meaning. It has great flexibility. We can search with great precision using punctuation, roles, and specific semantic factors. Alternatively, we can search with relative broadness (for high recall) by ignoring these devices and by using the structure of the semantic code as a means of generalization (e.g., we can use the general concept D–DD for "damage" wherever it occurs as a component in a complex code).

Unfortunately the system is too ingenious for the intended application. It is complicated to apply, and both indexing and search formulation are time-consuming and expensive operations. Subsequent experience has taught us that, for reference retrieval purposes, we just do not need the level of sophistication built into the Western Reserve system. The system was too complex and expensive to be economically viable, and it was eventually abandoned by the American Society for Metals in favor of a simpler, more cost-effective approach.

TABLE 53 Role Indicators of the Western Reserve System

KEJ	material processed
KUJ	major component
KIJ	minor component
KOV	property given for
KWV	property given
KAM	process
KQJ	means of process
KAH	condition of process
KUP	property affected or determined by process
KAP	property affected by KAL
KAL	factor influencing KAP
KWJ	product

SOURCE: J. W. Perry and A. Kent.[5]

Abstract as Recorded on Tape

KOV.KEJ.CARS.001.,KOV.KEJ.KUJ.MATL.001.,KOV.KEJ.KUJ.LALL.001.,KOV.KEJ.KUJ.MATL.4.☐BQE.,KWV.CWRS.RANG.13X.008.,KWV.PAPR.6X.RAPR.150X.019.,KWV.LAMN.PWPH.4X.PYPR.001.,KWV.GAPR.037.*,KWV.PYPR.019.,-KAM.LWLL.PASS.001.,KAM.DAFL.002.,KAH.DYFL.6X.PAPR.002.*,KAH.TYHR.001.,KAM.CULC.002.*,KAM.TYHR.001.,KAM.CULC.MWLC.PWPH.PASS.4X.001.,-KUP.KAP.PAPR.6X.RAPR.150X.019.*,KUP.KAP.CARS.001.*,KUP.KAP.CWNG.001.,KUP.KAL.DYFL.6X.PAPR.002.*,KUP.KAL.GAPR.PURD.2X.001.,KUP,KAL.DYFL.6X.PAPR.002.*,KUP.KAL.CYNG.MWTN.004.,KUP.KAL.DYFL.6X.PAPR.002.*,KUP.KAL.LYCT.004.,KUP.KAL.DYFL.6X.PAPR.002.*,KUP.KAL.CANG.009.,KUP.KAL.BWMM.3X.PAPR.001.*,KUP.KAL.PYPH.006.,KUP.KAL.RANG.013.*,KUP.KAL.GARP.RQNG.001.

FIGURE 65 Telegraphic abstract as recorded on tape.

REFERENCES

1. Aitchison, J. and Cleverdon, C. *A Report on a Test of the Index of Metallurgical Literature of Western Reserve University*. Cranfield, England: College of Aeronautics, ASLIB Cranfield Research Project, 1963.

2. Brenner, C. W. and Mooers, C. N. "A Case History of a Zatocoding Information Retrieval System." In *Punched Cards: Their Applications to Science and Industry*. 2nd ed. Edited by R. S. Casey et al. New York: Reinhold, 1958, 340-356.

3. Kent, A. and Perry, J. W. "Searching Metallurgical Literature." In *Punched Cards: Their Applications to Science and Industry*. 2nd ed., Edited by R. S. Casey et al. New York: Reinhold, 1958, 248-260.

4. Mooers, C. N. "The Indexing Language of an Information Retrieval System." In *Information Retrieval Today*. Edited by W. Simonton. Minneapolis, Minn.: University of Minnesota, 1963, 21-36.

5. Perry, J. W. and Kent, A. *Tools for Machine Literature Searching*. New York: Interscience Publishers, Inc., 1958.

6. Selye, H. *Symbolic Shorthand System*. New Brunswick, N. J.: Rutgers, the State University, Graduate School of Library Service, 1966.

7. Selye, H. and Ember, G. *Symbolic Shorthand System for Physiology and Medicine*. 4th ed. Montreal: Université de Montréal, 1964.

8. Vickery, B. C. "The Structure of Semantic Coding." *American Documentation* 10 (1959): 234-241.

20 *The Role of the Controlled Vocabulary in Indexing and Searching Operations*

In this chapter we return to a topic discussed briefly in Chapter 1, namely, the function of the controlled vocabulary. An index language exists primarily to serve the following purposes:

1. To allow an indexer to represent the subject matter of documents in a consistent way.

2. To bring the vocabulary used by the searcher into coincidence with the vocabulary used by the indexer.

3. To provide means whereby a searcher can modulate a search strategy in order to achieve high recall or high precision as varying circumstances demand.

ROLE OF THE VOCABULARY IN INDEXING

First let us consider the role of the controlled vocabulary in the indexing process. It is necessary to recognize that subject indexing entails two distinct steps:

1. Analysis of subject content (i.e., "conceptual analysis" or "content analysis").

2. Translation of this conceptual analysis into terms or codes selected from a controlled list.

Content analysis involves deciding what a document is "about" (i.e., its subject matter) and, even more importantly, deciding who is likely to make use of it and for what purpose (i.e., anticipating requests for which this document might provide a relevant re-

sponse). The process of conceptual analysis is intellectually distinct from the process of translation, even though the activities may virtually occur simultaneously. The conceptual analysis is not, or at least should not be, influenced by the system vocabulary.

At the time of indexing, various errors or defects can occur which will have a deleterious effect on the performance of the retrieval system when searches are conducted. Essentially, there are five types of problems that may occur:

1. *Conceptual analysis failure.* The indexer fails to understand the subject matter of the document and misinterprets its content in his conceptual analysis.

2. *Translation failure.* The indexer recognizes what the document is about but chooses the wrong vocabulary term or terms to express it.

3. *Error of omission.* The indexer omits an important aspect of the document in his conceptual analysis.

4. *Lack of specificity in the vocabulary.* The indexer recognizes what a document is specifically about in his conceptual analysis but is forced to index it more generally because of lack of specific terms in the system vocabulary.

5. *Lack of specificity in indexing.* The indexer uses vocabulary terms that are general in relation to the precise subject matter discussed in a document even though more specific terms are available in the vocabulary.

185

Strictly speaking, only the fourth problem is directly caused by limitations of the vocabulary. However, the controlled vocabulary may contribute, at least indirectly, to some of the indexing failures, and it is worth considering them in this light.

Errors 1 and 2 above, although theoretically distinct, are in practice impossible to distinguish. If we find that an indexer has assigned the term x to a document when the "correct" term is actually y, we do not know exactly why this occurred. Is it because the indexer failed to understand the subject of the document, or because he failed to understand the distinction between x and y? For example, we find that a document dealing with premature rupture of the fetal membranes has been indexed under ABRUPTIO PLACENTAE. Did this error occur because the indexer interpreted the document as being about separation of the placenta, or because he erroneously thought that ABRUPTIO PLACENTAE means premature rupture of the membranes? It is an academic point really, since the end result is the same, namely, the assignment of an incorrect term. This type of error can result in either a recall failure or a precision failure, depending on the type of search conducted. If x is assigned when y should be, the document will be incorrectly retrieved in a search on x (precision failure) and missed in a search on y (recall failure).

The controlled vocabulary does not contribute directly to these failures. They are probably due either to lack of subject knowledge or to pure carelessness. Nevertheless, the controlled vocabulary may help to minimize failures of this kind. Presumably, careful term definition and adequate cross-referencing are most likely to reduce problems of incorrect term assignment. This is particularly true if descriptors which are somewhat related are carefully distinguished by scope notes. For example:

COILS

(Compact windings of conductors to form inductors. For coils producing magnetic fields for the conversion of electrical into mechanical energy see SOLENOIDS.)

Related term references should also help the indexer to select the most appropriate term to represent a topic. For example, he thinks first of ELECTROMAGNETIC PUMPS but is led on by the vocabulary (RT or *see also*) to LIQUID METAL PUMPS which he recognizes as being more appropriate to describe the subject matter dealt with. The entry vocabulary will also play an important part in guiding the indexer to the most appropriate descriptors. In fact, the richer the entry vocabulary, the less subject knowledge the indexer requires. This was discussed in Chapter 14.

In actual practice, indexing errors involving incorrect term assignment are relatively rare. The complete omission of an important aspect by the indexer is much more likely to occur. In the evaluation of MEDLARS performance [8] it was found that 10 percent of all the recall failures were due to the omission of an important term in indexing. Most of these omissions were caused by pure carelessness, and the system vocabulary will have no influence on them. Some omissions may occur, however, as a direct result of an inadequate entry vocabulary. They happen simply because the indexer does not know how a particular topic is to be indexed: there is no descriptor for this topic in the system, and the entry vocabulary fails to indicate how it should be indexed. For example, one aspect of a medical article deals with the topic of "equational division." There is no "equational division" descriptor in the system vocabulary, and the indexer does not know how to deal with the subject. He therefore takes the easy way out and omits it entirely. An adequate entry vocabulary might have avoided this omission by providing an appropriate instruction to the indexer, as:

Equational Division *use* MEIOSIS

A full entry vocabulary will not, of course, eliminate all errors of indexer omission, but it may reduce these errors very considerably.

In studying causes of failure in a retrieval system it is important to distinguish lack of specificity in the vocabulary from lack of specificity in indexing. The former implies that no specific term is available in the system to describe some precise concept, and the indexer is thus forced to use a more general term. Lack of vocabulary specificity is likely to be a significant cause of precision failures in all retrieval systems employing a controlled vocabulary. It was responsible for 18 percent of the precision failures discovered in the MEDLARS evaluation. The effect of vocabulary specificity on system performance was discussed in some detail in Chapter 13.

Lack of specificity in indexing is another matter. In this situation an appropriate specific term is available in the vocabulary but the indexer, for some reason, uses a more general term; e.g., he assigns POLYSACCHARIDES to a document that deals specifically with lipopolysaccharides, even though the precise term exists in the vocabulary. This type of error is relatively rare, and it is usually an error of carelessness on the part of the indexer. However, the index language will contribute to these errors if it fails to present the true hierarchical structure of the vocabulary. If the indexer looks under the term POLYSACCHARIDES he must be led to the more specific term

LIPOPOLYSACCHARIDES by a cross-reference (NT, *see also*, or *see also specific*), a graphic display, or a classified arrangement. If the vocabulary fails to do this it is obviously contributing to nonspecific indexing.

Some interesting studies on the role of the controlled vocabulary in the indexing operation were reported by Slamecka [11, 12] and by Slamecka and Jacoby.[13] Slamecka points out that controlled vocabularies serve one or the other, or both, of the following functions:

1. *Prescription.* They prescribe terms to be assigned.
2. *Suggestion.* They suggest terms to be considered instead of, or in addition to, terms thought of by indexers without their aid.

Most controlled vocabularies are partly prescriptive and partly suggestive. The *see* or *use* reference is a prescriptive indicator: the indexer must use the term referred to. The RT and *see also* references (and, to a certain extent, the BT and NT references) are suggestive: the indexer's attention is drawn to other terms that may be more appropriate than the one he has first considered. Prescription can be mechanized; that is, given any "referred from" term assigned by an indexer, a computer program can substitute the correct "referred to" term. Suggestion cannot be mechanized, at least not completely.

Slamecka tested the effect of a controlled vocabulary on the indexing process according to the following procedures. The test collection consisted of 75 chemical patents. These patents were indexed in four different ways:

1. By using uncontrolled Uniterms. This was the "base zero" against which the other procedures were evaluated.
2. By use of a classification scheme, the *Manual of Classification* of the U.S. Patent Office.
3. By use of an alphabetical subject authority list, the *Chemical Patents Code List* of Documentation Incorporated.
4. By use of the *Chemical Engineering Thesaurus* of the American Institute of Chemical Engineers.

From the entire corpus, three groups of 25 patents were established randomly. Each group was indexed using one of the three controlled vocabularies. The group was indexed three times, using three experienced indexers. The patents had previously been indexed by the Uniterm method. It was required that the title and claims of the patent ("bounded" section) be indexed; the remainder of the patent ("unbounded") was to be indexed according to the best judgment of the individual indexer. The indexing instructions are shown in Table 54.

TABLE 54 Indexing Instructions for Consistency Test

Phase II Tests are designed to measure the consistency of term assignment among indexers using various indexing aids. During the tests, the indexers should not communicate with each other regarding the indexing of any document.

The first test (of three scheduled) will utilize the Documentation Incorporated Chemical Patents Coding Manual.

Each indexer will index a total of 50 chemical patents according to the familiar rules of coordinate indexing, and will record freely assigned terms on the tracing card. Simultaneously, or subsequently, the indexer will consult the indexing tools for *each* term on the tracing card.

The indexing tool is to be used as an aid, i.e., indexers are free to adopt or reject any of the terms contained in the Manual. They will indicate, next to each term on the tracing card, one of the following alternatives:

(a) Original term, also found in the aid, was retained;
(b) Original term, not found in the aid, was retained;
(c) Original term was rejected upon inspection of the aid (irrespective of whether the term was found in the aid), and no new term selected;
(d) Term adopted from the aid instead of a term assigned originally;
(e) Additional term adopted from the aid.

The title and all claims of each patent must be indexed. The remainder of the patent should be indexed according to the judgment of each indexer of what is appropriate to describe the document.

SOURCE: V. Slamecka and J. Jacoby.[13]

First the indexer was to record his "conceptual analysis" of the patent in his own terms. Then he was to translate this conceptual analysis into controlled vocabulary terms, indicating which of his original terms he retained, which he failed to find in the controlled vocabulary, which he rejected on seeing the controlled vocabulary, and which terms he added as a result of seeing the controlled vocabulary. The average number of terms assigned per patent as a result of this exercise is shown below:

	Total Assigned	Bounded	Unbounded
Uniterm	37.8	13.4	24.4
Thesaurus	46.4	18.7	27.7
Alphabetical Authority	50.5	19.3	31.2
Classification	43.4	16.1	27.3

Indexing consistency was measured by determining the percentage of matching terms used by any pair of indexers. The results were as follows:

	Uniterm	Thesau- rus	Alpha- betical	Classifi- cation
Bounded section	9.5 *	8.2	41.2	40.6
Unbounded	8.8	8.4	35.2	34.3

* Percentage of matching terms used by any pair of indexers.

There was no significant difference in indexing consistency between use of the uncontrolled Uniterms and use of the thesaurus. But consistency was improved considerably by the alphabetical authority list and by the classification scheme. The investigators conclude that this discrepancy is due to the fact that these two vocabularies are primarily prescriptive and thus impose standardization, while the *Chemical Engineering Thesaurus* is largely suggestive. The suggestive power of the Patent Office classification is relatively low; it suggests only a small number of generically related terms. The *Chemical Patents Code List* is virtually all prescriptive, involving invariable instructions (*see, also post on*) and no variable ones. The thesaurus, however, presents rich associations and considerable freedom in term assignment. It is least prescriptive and authoritative. It offers greater choice among terms, allowing finer shades of meaning, and thus makes indexer consistency more difficult to attain.

The general conclusions of the investigators, in relation to the effect of a controlled vocabulary on the indexing process, are:

Inter-indexer consistency improves significantly with the use of prescriptive indexing aids containing a minimum of variable semantic relationships among terms. The use of indexing aids which enlarge the indexer's semantic freedom of term choice is detrimental to indexing reliability. Quality of indexing is best improved by vocabularies which formalize relationships so as to uniformly and invariably prescribe the choice of indexing terms.*

In a study of indexing aids, Korotkin et al.[7] investigated the use made of thesauri by 46 different information centers. They discovered that the tools were used prescriptively by 78 percent of the centers, and that they were used to suggest terms by 17 percent of the centers. Only 5 percent of the centers used a thesaurus both to prescribe and to suggest.

ROLE OF THE VOCABULARY IN SEARCHING

The vocabulary also has prescriptive and suggestive roles to play in the search process. It prescribes the language that the searcher must use by directing him

* Indexing consistency, it should be noted, does not necessarily equate directly with indexing quality.

from nonaccepted to accepted terms. The entry vocabulary bears the burden of this activity. This prescriptive function brings the vocabulary of the searcher into coincidence with the vocabulary of the indexer. Looked at in a different light, the controlled vocabulary must relate its own terminology to variant expressions occurring in the literature and in requests made to the system.

The suggestive role in searching is played by the organization of the vocabulary: its faceted structure, its hierarchy, and its network of cross-references. It must help the searcher to construct the best possible strategy in terms of the system user's needs (high recall, high precision, or some compromise between the two). In particular, it should prevent a searcher from missing relevant documents through failure to bring together semantically related terms. In the evaluation of MEDLARS it was found that 21.5 percent of all the recall failures could be attributed to the search analyst's inability to think of all possible approaches to retrieval. In some cases we can say that the searcher lacked ingenuity or perseverance in the construction of his strategy; but in other instances the vocabulary itself was at fault because it did not provide enough assistance to the searcher. For example, in a search on the topic of "oral manifestations of neutropenia," the searcher coordinates the neutropenia term AGRANULOCYTOSIS with the term ORAL MANIFESTATIONS and also with anatomy terms relating to the oral cavity (such as MOUTH, LIP, and GINGIVA). This strategy retrieves some of the relevant literature but not all of it. Some relevant items deal with specific oral manifestations and have been indexed with the appropriate specific terms (e.g., STOMATITIS, GINGIVITIS). The searcher has missed an important approach to retrieval (namely, the coordination of AGRANULOCYTOSIS with specific terms relating to possible oral manifestations). We place the burden of responsibility on the searcher, but part of the blame must also fall on the index language which, in this case, fails to direct the searcher from the general term ORAL MANIFESTATIONS to the specific oral manifestation terms in the vocabulary.

The more help the vocabulary gives in displaying possible useful relationships among terms, the more the intellectual load on the searcher is reduced, and the less likely he is to overlook alternative approaches to retrieval. Most controlled vocabularies are reasonably good at presenting formal hierarchical relations between terms, but some fail in the presentation of valid relationships that cut across the hierarchical structure of the vocabulary. There are several possible terms, from various categories (anatomy, pathology, diagnostic techniques), that might indicate

"oral involvement" or "joint involvement" as examples; but does the vocabulary relate them sufficiently well that the searcher has no doubt as to which terms he needs to use to express one of these viewpoints comprehensively?

A number of evaluation studies have produced valuable data on the effect controlled vocabularies have on the overall retrieval function. Most notable among these are probably the MEDLARS investigation previously cited, the evaluation of the Western Reserve system by Aitchison and Cleverdon,[1] and the studies of the *Universal Decimal Classification* in computer-based systems conducted by the American Institute of Physics.[2, 3, 4, 5] Strangely enough, very little experimentation has been conducted on the actual value of the controlled vocabulary in aiding the construction of search strategies; i.e., how much better is a strategy after the searcher has used the vocabulary to expand his original set of search terms? An exception is an early and frequently overlooked paper by Wall,[14] which presents a quantitative comparison of search results obtained with and without the assistance of a thesaurus. This study presented an interesting methodology, but was of limited scope. The experimental collection consisted of 9,802 chemical patents, and the thesaurus tested was the *Chemical Engineering Thesaurus*. The study was conducted on the basis of a single request for patents on "accelerators for foaming of plastics." The unaided search was carried out simply on the words of the request, as used in the thesaurus (i.e., using the thesaurus prescriptively only), with word form variations of these words, as:

ACCELERATION *and* FOAM *and* PLASTICS
ACCELERATING   FOAMING

This search retrieved only three patents, all judged to be highly relevant. The search strategy was then expanded by using the thesaurus. To each of the original search terms were added the terms the thesaurus showed to be related (e.g., ACCELERATORS brought in such terms as CATALYSIS and CATALYSTS; FOAMING brought in AERATION, BUBBLING, FOAMS, and BUBBLES, among others; and PLASTICS brought in POLYMERS). The expanded, thesaurus-aided search retrieved a total of 62 patents, of which 26 were judged highly relevant, 9 peripherally relevant, and 27 irrelevant.

The results were exactly as expected. A search conducted only on the exact words of the request, translated into approved terms (i.e., using the thesaurus as a prescriptive agent only), achieves a high precision (100 percent in this case) but a very low recall. When the original request terms are expanded with the aid of the thesaurus, and additional related terms are incorporated into the strategy (here the

thesaurus is used as a suggestive agent), recall increases considerably, although precision inevitably deteriorates. For a high-recall requirement the thesaurus has played a very valuable role, although for the low-recall (a few good documents) requirement the unaided search would probably suffice. Of course, we could argue that the searcher, even without the thesaurus, might have thought of this set of related terms. This is beside the point. The thesaurus exists to lighten the intellectual burden on the searcher, to reduce the possibilities of human error, and to improve both the effectiveness and the cost-effectiveness of the searching operation. A well-constructed thesaurus, or other form of vocabulary control, will certainly do this.

A more recent study by Hargrave and Wall [6] measured the impact made by the introduction of a thesaurus into a system for the Selective Dissemination of Information (SDI) operated by NASA. The results tend to indicate that the thesaurus significantly improved performance, especially in the area of recall.

THE VOCABULARY IN USER-SYSTEM INTERACTION

Before we close this chapter we should consider a closely related matter: the role of the controlled vocabulary at the user-system interface. A very important problem plaguing most information systems is that of user-system interaction. Users interact with the system in order to make their needs known. A search can only be conducted for a user after his needs have been verbalized; i.e., put in the form of a stated request. This stage of the complete retrieval process (illustrated in Figure 3) is critical. If a user submits a request that inadequately represents his real information need, the subsequent search is largely doomed to failure, however adequate the indexing, vocabulary, and search strategies may be. Unfortunately, it is frequently difficult for a user to be explicit in his request, and the system must give him as much help as possible in this. I have dealt with the problem of user-system interaction and some possible solutions in more detail elsewhere.[8, 9, 10]

The MEDLARS evaluation indicated fairly conclusively that the requests that best represent information needs are usually those the requester phrases in his own natural-language terms. These requests are not constrained by the logic and language of the system. They should be recorded in writing by the requester, preferably on a well-designed search request form. It was discovered, rather unexpectedly, that requests resulting from an interview between the user and a librarian or information specialist tend

to be further removed from the actual information need. The reason, apparently, is that an unconscious distortion may take place in a face-to-face interview of this type. This is particularly true if the information specialist tries to get the requester to use the language of the system in formulating his request. This places a linguistic constraint on the user that is highly undesirable. As a result, he may settle for less than what he really wants. Under such conditions he is more likely to ask for what he thinks the system can give him rather than precisely what he is seeking. In the situation where the user records his request in writing in his own terms he is unconstrained by the logic and language of the system; hence, he is much more likely to ask for what he really wants.

It is highly undesirable to require a user to make his request, at least initially, in the controlled vocabulary of the system. There are two principal reasons for this:

1. It imposes an artificial constraint upon the system user and may cause him to ask for what he feels the system can supply rather than what he really needs.

2. If requests are always made in terms selected from the present controlled vocabulary, there is very little opportunity to improve the vocabulary by making it more responsive to user requirements. In other words, we are given no evidence that the vocabulary needs to be more specific. Suppose we have the term WELDING in our vocabulary but no terms for specific types of welding, and that the user must always phrase his request in controlled vocabulary terms. We learn that many users request searches on welding of various metals or products, and we evaluate our searches on this basis.

However, we fail to discover that many of these requesters are really interested only in specific welding processes—shielded arc welding, argon arc welding, resistance welding, spot welding—and that many of the searches conducted are unsatisfactory to the user because they produce very low precision. It is important that the request statement record the precise topic that the user is interested in *even when the vocabulary of the system will not allow searching at this precise level.* If a requester is seeking information on nephrogenic diabetes insipidus, this is how his request should be recorded even if the vocabulary will only allow us to be as specific as DIABETES. How else can we discover inadequacies in our vocabulary, and how else can the vocabulary be developed to the level of specificity required to satisfy the majority of demands placed upon the system?

Searching, as indexing, involves both conceptual analysis and translation steps. The requester should be concerned with the conceptual analysis stage. Only when we have an adequate conceptual analysis of an information need should we consider how best to translate this into the controlled terms of the system. Natural-language search systems have certain advantages in this respect because they do not impose linguistic constraints on the user. On-line systems with controlled vocabularies present special problems which we will consider in a later chapter.

REFERENCES

1. Aitchison, J. and Cleverdon, C. *A Report on a Test of the Index of Metallurgical Literature of Western Reserve University.* Cranfield, England: College of Aeronautics, ASLIB Cranfield Research Project, 1963.

2. Atherton, P. et al. *Evaluation of the Retrieval of Nuclear Science Document References Using the Universal Decimal Classification as the Indexing Language for a Computer-Based System.* New York: American Institute of Physics, May 1, 1968. Report AIP/UDC—8.

3. Freeman, R. R. *Evaluation of the Retrieval of Metallurgical Document References Using the Universal Decimal Classification in a Computer-Based System.* New York: American Institute of Physics, April 1, 1968. Report AIP/UDC—6.

4. Freeman, R. R. and Atherton, P. *AUDACIOUS—An Experiment with an On-Line, Interactive Reference Retrieval System Using the Universal Decimal Classification as the Index Language in the Field of Nuclear Science.* New York: American Institute of Physics, April 25, 1968. Report AIP/UDC—7.

5. Freeman, R. R. and Atherton, P. *Final Report of the Research Project for the Evaluation of the UDC as the Indexing Language for a Mechanized Reference Retrieval System.* New York: American Institute of Physics, May 1, 1968. Report AIP/UDC—9.

6. Hargrave, C. W. and Wall, E. "Retrieval Improvement Effected by the Use of a Thesaurus." *Proceedings of the American Society for Information Science* 7 (1970): 291-294.

7. Korotkin, A. L. et al. *Indexing Aids, Procedures and Devices.* Bethesda, Md.: General Electric Co., 1965. AD 616 342.

8. Lancaster, F. W. *Evaluation of the MEDLARS Demand Search Service.* Bethesda, Md.: National Library of Medicine, 1968.

9. Lancaster, F. W. *Information Retrieval Systems: Characteristics, Testing, and Evaluation.* New York: Wiley, 1968.

10. Lancaster, F. W. "Interaction Between Requesters and a Large Mechanized Retrieval System." *Information Storage and Retrieval* 4 (1968): 239-252.

11. Slamecka, V. "Classificatory, Alphabetical and Associative Schedules as Aids in Coordinate Indexing." *American Documentation* 14 (1963): 223-228.

12. Slamecka, V. *Indexing Aids. Final Report.* Bethesda, Md.: Documentation, Inc., 1963. AD 294 859.

13. Slamecka, V. and Jacoby, J. *Effect of Indexing Aids on the Reliability of Indexers. Final Technical Note.* Bethesda, Md.: Documentation, Inc., 1963. RADC-TDR-63-116.

14. Wall, E. *Information Retrieval Thesauri.* New York: Engineers Joint Council, 1962.

21 Supplementary Vocabulary Tools

It is sometimes desirable for an information system to introduce supplementary vocabulary-related tools to aid the indexing and searching processes. Indexing using a controlled vocabulary involves constant look-up (unless the vocabulary is sufficiently small that it can be committed to memory) and recording of selected terms. Anything that can be done to reduce or simplify the look-up and recording activities will improve the efficiency of the indexing process.

VOCABULARY DISPLAY FOR INDEXING

A Mooers descriptor schedule is usually sufficiently small that it can be reproduced *in toto* on a few large sheets of paper (Table 51). Such conciseness has certain advantages. Look-up is fast and simple. The entire vocabulary can be taken in at a glance (or two), and this allows the indexer to consider the relevance of virtually every term against every document. A very small controlled vocabulary in a highly specialized area is best presented in this way. The U.S. Patent Office uses some small retrieval systems, implemented mainly by optical coincidence (peek-a-boo) techniques, and restricted to a single class, or limited number of classes, in the patent art. Specialized vocabularies have been devised for these areas, and they are small enough to be printed on one or two sheets. Figure 66 illustrates such a vocabulary for the subject of chemical testing. As with the Mooers descriptor schedules, the entire vocabulary can be easily scanned, preventing the indexer from overlooking an important term, and eliminating the need for the indexer to write or type terms on an indexing sheet. In this case multiple copies of the term list are available, and a patent is indexed merely by circling the appropriate terms or their codes on a copy of the list. All subsequent processing is clerical. The "microthesaurus" of the Air Pollution Technical Information Center, as described by Tancredi and Nichols,[5] is also designed for use by circling of terms. A portion of this microthesaurus is illustrated in Figure 67.

Of course, a large vocabulary cannot be presented in this way in its entirety, but perhaps portions can be. If certain classes of terms are potentially relevant to most documents in a system, it is efficient and economical to preprint these on an indexing form and allow the indexer merely to check them when they should be applied. This practice, followed by the National Library of Medicine, reminds the indexer that these terms must be assigned when they are appropriate, and it reduces the amount of writing or typing he must do. A MEDLARS indexing form (Figure 68) contains "check-tags" for such items as age, sex, and type of study. Terms from this group *must* be assigned to all documents for which they are relevant. The indexer assigns check tags simply by checking the appropriate box. These terms are treated in this way because they are potentially applicable to virtually all articles in the biomedical field.

191

U. S. DEPARTMENT OF COMMERCE
Patent Office

CHEMICAL TESTING CODING SHEET

csg

D.P.	H		Document Number										Accession Number				
REISSUE	E								230.000 253.000	256.000							
PATENT	A	US						023	231.000 254.000	258.000					C 4		
									232.000 255.000								
Col.	1	23	4	5	6	7	8	9	10	11-3	14-9	21	22	23	24	25-6	

MATL BY USE/FUNCTION/SOURCE

27 8 Adulterant
27 9 Amino-acid
28 Y Biological
YX .Blood
YX0 ..Albumin
YX1 ..Hemoglobin
YX2 ..Rh or blood type
YX3 ..Sugar
YX4 ..Oth sp blood test
Y5 .Breath
Y6 .Gastric juice
Y7 .Glandular
28 Y78 ..Thyroid
29 X .Urine + 28/Y
X0 ..Sugar + 28/Y
1 .Oth biol + 28/Y
2 Veg (non-food)
23 .Cellulose, cork
4 Bldg or road
45 .Brick or rock
46 .Cement or concrete
47 .Glass or oth ceramic
48 .Soil
29 49 .Other bldg
30 5 Catalyst
6 Coating
7 Enzyme
8 Explosive
30 9 Fertilizer
31 0 Food
01 .Beverage
31 02 .Dairy or eggs
03 .Fish or meat
04 .Vegetable
05 .Other food
6 Fuel
7 Gas
8 Ink, paint or dye
31 9 Leather
32 0 Lubricant
1 Oil
2 Process stream
3 Resin
4 Rubber
5 Textile
56 .Animal fiber
7 Water
32 8 Other

CONDITION OR PROPERTY

32 9 Acidity
33 Y Age dating
X Aroma or odor
0 Corrosion
1 Decay
2 Defect, flaw, leak
3 Fertility
4 Geochem explor
5 Interferent
6 Lubricity
7 Pregnancy
8 Viscosity
33 9 Other

MATERIAL ANALYZED

34 Y Inorganic
YX .Radioactive cpd
Y0 .Inert gas
Y1 .Rare earth cpd
Y2 .B and cpds
Y3 .P and cpds
Y4 .Si and cpds
Y5 .N and cpds
Y6 .C and cpds
Y7 .Hal and cpds
Y8 .Se, Te and cpds
34 Y9 .S and cpds
35 7 .O and cpds + 34/Y
8 .H and cpds + 34/Y
35 9 .Met + 34/Y
36 X Organic
X0 .Metal
X1 .Boron
X2 .Sulfur
X3 .Silicon
X4 .Nitrogen
X45 ..Aromatic
X46 ..Aliphatic
X7 .Halogen
X8 .Oxygen
36 X89 ..C,H, O
37 2 .C, H +36/X
23 ..Unsat + 36/X
37 4 .Other nonmet + 36/X

ANALYZER BY USE

37 5 Color
6 Catalyst
7 Enzyme
8 Indicator dye
37 9 Liquid crystal
38 2 Special form
23 .Laminated
4 Surfactant
5 Tracer mat add
56 .Radioactive
57 .Phys detecable
58 .Reactable
38 9 Other

ANALYZER (CHEM)

39 Y Inorganic
YX .Radioactive
Y0 .Inert gas
Y1 .Rare earth
Y2 .B and cpds
Y3 .P and cpds
Y4 .Si and cpds
Y5 .N and cpds
Y6 .C and cpds
Y7 .Hal and cpds
Y8 .Se,Te and cpds
39 Y9 .S and cpds
40 7 .O and cpds +39/Y
8 .H and cpds +39/Y
40 9 .Met +39/Y
41 X Organic
X0 .Metal
X1 .Boron
X2 .Sulfur
X3 .Silicon
X4 .Nitrogen
X45 ..Aromatic
X46 ..Aliphatic
X7 .Halogen
X8 .Oxygen
41 X89 ..C,H, O
42 1 .C,H + 41/X
12 ..Unsat + 41/X
42 3 .Other nonmet +41/X

BASIS FOR ANALYSIS

42 4 Sorption
45 .Ion exchange
46 .Paper or thin
7 Calorimetry
8 Chemilumin
42 9 Color reaction
43 0 Combustion
01 .Plasma
2 Comparison
3 Condens nucl
4 Displacement
5 Evol gas
6 Extraction
7 Flame analysis
8 Pptn coagn
43 9 Titration
44 Y Phys meas
YX .Time var
Y0 .Lgth or ar
Y1 .Vol, wt or d
Y12 ..Appendage
Y3 .Pressure
Y4 .Temperature
Y45 ..Gradient
Y6 .Thermal cond
Y7 .Viscosity
44 Y8 .Flame ioniz
45 Y .Optical
YX ..Color/absorb
Y0 ..Spectroscopy
Y1 ..Sensor
Y12 ...Photocell
3 .Non-visible wave
34 ..Infra-red
35 ..Ultra-violet
36 α/β/γ
37 ..Sensor
8 .Elec cond
45 9 .Other phys

index also 44/Y index also 44/Y

MANIPULATION OR DEVICE THEREFORE

46 Y Preparation
YX .Sepn or purif
YX0 ..Centrif or seb
YX1 ..Demist fog
YX2 ..Distill
YX3 ..Dry
YX4 ..Impurities
YX5 ..Other sepn
Y6 .Phase change
Y7 .Heat or cool
Y8 .Digest or cook
46 Y9 .Irradiate
47 X .Pressure
0 .Chem react
01 ..Catalytic
02 ..Neutralize
3 .Control flow
4 .In train
5 .Titration
6 .Aliquot
7 .Permeable
8 .Pump
47 9 .Carrier gas
48 0 .Holding vessel
01 ..Trans vessel
02 ..Trans contents
03 ..Mix or stir
04 ..Empty
05 ..Rack
056 ...Trans racks
7 Environmental
8 Capillary
48 9 Det station

index also 46/Y
indx also 46/X

49 Y Automated anal
YX .Train
Y0 .Central
Y01 ..Multiple
Y02 ..Program
Y03 .Decoder
Y04 .Computer-assist
Y5 .Process control
Y56 ..Chem process
Y57 ..Non-chem proc
..Signal generated by:
Y58 ...T, P or concn
49 Y59 ...Liquid level
50 1 ...Flow rate
2 ...pH,cond
3 ...Summary
..Signal fed:
4 ...Back
5 ...Forward
6 ...To detn pt takeoff
..Signal affects:
7 ...Input feed
8 ...Other conditions
50 9 ..Computer-assist
51 5 .Monitoring + 49/Y
6 .Other use + 49/Y
7 Treatment after detn
78 .Dump sample
51 79 .Cleanup

index also 49/Y5

INDEXER ________

DATE ________

Form PO-1100 (1-70)

USCOMM/DC

FIGURE 66 U.S. Patent Office vocabulary on chemical testing.

BK-65	BIOMEDICAL TECHNIQUES & MEASUREMENT
BK-66	ABSENTEEISM
BK-67	ATTACK RATES
BK-68	BIOCLIMATOLOGY
BK-69	EPIDEMIOLOGY
BK-70	GENETICS
BK-71	HEALTH STATISTICS
BK-72	HEMATOLOGY
BK-73	BLOOD CHEMISTRY
BK-74	BLOOD GAS ANALYSIS
BK-75	CARBOXYHEMOGLOBIN
BK-76	HEMOGLOBIN INTERACTIONS
BK-77	IMMUNOLOGY
BK-78	ANTIBODIES
BK-79	ANTIGENS
BK-80	LIFE SPAN
BK-81	MORBIDITY
BK-82	MORTALITY
BK-83	OCCUPATIONAL HEALTH
BK-84	OUTPATIENT VISITS
BK-85	PATHOLOGICAL TECHNIQUES
BK-86	RADIOLOGICAL HEALTH
BL-48	TISSUE CULTURES
BK-87	TREATMENT & AIDS
BK-88	ARTIFICIAL RESPIRATION
BK-89	BREATHING EXERCISES
BK-90	DIAGNOSIS
BK-91	AUTOPSY
BK-92	BIO-ASSAY
BK-93	BIOPSY
BK-94	SKIN TESTS
BK-95	DRUGS
BK-96	ANTIDOTES
BK-97	BRONCHODILATORS
BK-99	INHALATION THERAPY
BL-00	MEDICAL FACILITIES
BL-02	PHYSICAL THERAPY
BL-03	RADIOGRAPHY
BL-04	SURGERY
BL-05	VETERINARY MEDICINE
BK-22	URINALYSIS

BL-06	BODY CONSTITUENTS & PARTS
BL-07	BODY FLUIDS
BL-08	BONES
BL-13	CELLS
BL-14	BLOOD CELLS
GR-41	LEUKOCYTES
BL-17	LYMPHOCYTES
BL-15	CHROMOSOMES
BL-16	CILIA
BL-18	SPERMATOZOA
BL-09	CIRCULATORY SYSTEM
BL-10	BLOOD VESSELS
BL-11	HEART
BL-19	DIGESTIVE SYSTEM
BL-20	ESOPHAGUS
BL-21	INTESTINES
BL-22	LIVER
BL-23	MOUTH
BL-24	STOMACH
BL-25	ENZYMES
BL-46	EPITHELIUM
BL-26	EXCRETIONS
BL-27	EYES
BL-28	GLANDS
BL-29	HISTAMINES
BL-30	HORMONES
BL-31	KIDNEYS
BL-32	LIPIDS
BL-33	MEMBRANES
BL-34	NERVOUS SYSTEM
GY-29	NUCLEIC ACIDS
BL-35	PROTEINS
BL-36	AMINO ACIDS
BL-37	RESPIRATORY SYSTEM
BL-38	BRONCHI
BL-39	LARYNX
BL-40	LUNGS
BL-41	ALVEOLI
BL-42	NOSTRILS
BL-43	SINUSES
BL-44	TRACHEA
BL-45	SKIN
BL-46	EPITHELIUM
BL-47	TISSUES

BL-49	BODY PROCESSES & FUNCTIONS
BL-50	ADAPTATION
BL-52	BLOOD PRESSURE
BL-53	CELL GROWTH
BL-54	CELL METABOLISM
BL-55	DIGESTION
BL-56	INGESTION
BL-57	INHIBITION
BL-58	METABOLISM
BL-59	PULSE RATE
BL-60	REPRODUCTION
BL-61	RESPIRATORY FUNCTIONS
BL-62	BREATHING
BL-63	COMPLIANCE
GY-51	DEPOSITION
GY-98	LUNG CLEARANCE
BL-64	OXYGEN CONSUMPTION
BL-65	PULMONARY FUNCTION
BL-66	OXYGEN DIFFUSION
BL-67	PULMONARY RESISTANCE
BL-68	VENTILATION (PULMONARY)
BL-69	RETENTION
BL-71	SYNERGISM
BL-72	THRESHOLDS
BL-73	TOXIC TOLERANCES

BL-74	DISEASES & DISORDERS
BL-75	ALLERGIES
BL-76	ANEMIA
BL-77	ANOXIA
BL-79	ASPHYXIATION
Y-71	BERYLLIOSIS
BL-80	BLINDNESS
BL-81	CANCER
BL-82	BRONCHIAL
BL-83	LEUKEMIA
BL-84	LUNG
BL-85	SKIN
BL-86	TRACHEAL
Y-78	CARCINOGENS
BL-87	CARDIOVASCULAR DISEASES
BL-88	ERYTHEMA
BL-89	EYE IRRITATION
BL-90	FLUOROSIS
BL-91	HEADACHE
BL-92	HEALTH IMPAIRMENT
BL-93	HYPERSENSITIVITY
BL-94	HYPERVENTILATION
BL-95	HYPOXIA
BL-96	INFECTIOUS DISEASES
BL-97	LACHRYMATION
BL-98	METAL POISONING
BL-99	MUTATIONS
GR-00	NAUSEA
GR-01	ORGANIC DISEASES
GR-02	RESPIRATORY DISEASES
GR-03	ADENOVIRUS INFECTIONS
GR-04	ASTHMA
GR-05	BRONCHITIS
GR-06	BRONCHOCONSTRICTION
GR-07	BRONCHOPNEUMONIA
GR-08	COMMON COLD
GR-09	COUGH
GR-10	EMPHYSEMA
GR-11	HAYFEVER
GR-12	INFLUENZA
GR-13	LARYNGITIS
GR-14	PLEURISY
GR-15	PNEUMOCONIOSIS
P-84	ANTHRACOSIS
BL-78	ASBESTOSIS
S-72	BYSSINOSIS
S-84	FARMER'S LUNG
GR-18	SILICOSIS
GR-16	PNEUMONIA
GR-17	PULMONARY EDEMA
GR-19	TUBERCULOSIS
GR-20	STERILIZATION
GR-21	TUMORS

FIGURE 67 Section of microthesaurus of the Air Pollution Technical Information Center.

JTA

ARTICLES   INDEXER   ⑧ PAG

⑩ and ⑪ AUTHOR DATA

⑫ AUTHOR AFFILIATE

⑬ TITLE (English or Translation)

⑭ TITLE (Vernacular or Transliteration)

⑳ SUBJECT TERMS

1
2
3
4
5
6
7
8
9
10
11
12
13
14
15
16
17
18
19
20
21
22
23
24
25
26
27
28
29
30
31
32
33
34
35

㉒ COMMENTS:

☐ ENG ABST

NIH-1416

INDEXED CITATION FORM

⑨ AUTHOR TYPE
A ☐ Anonymous
E ☐ Editor
C ☐ Compiler

⑮ LANGUAGE
ENG___

⑯ Abstract _____
⑰ Refs

⑱ SPECIAL LIST
D ☐ Dental
N ☐ Nursing

⑲ CITATION TYPE
A ☐ HISTORICAL ARTICLE
B ☐ HISTORICAL BIOGRAPHY
C ☐ CURRENT BIOG-OBIT
D ☐ REVIEW
E ☐ SYMPOSIUM
F ☐ PROCEEDINGS
G ☐ TECHNICAL REPORT
H ☐ MONOGRAPH

㉑ CHECK TAGS
A ☐ PREGNANCY
B ☐ INFANT, NEWBORN (to 1 mo)
C ☐ INFANT (1-23 mo)
D ☐ CHILD, PRESCHOOL (2-5 yr)
E ☐ CHILD (6-12 yr)
F ☐ ADOLESCENCE (13-18 yr)
G ☐ ADULT (19-44 yr)
H ☐ MIDDLE AGE (45-64 yr)
I ☐ AGED (65-___ yr)

J ☐ CATS
K ☐ CATTLE
L ☐ CHICK EMBRYO
M ☐ DOGS
N ☐ FROGS
O ☐ GUINEA PIGS
P ☐ HAMSTERS
Q ☐ MICE
R ☐ MONKEYS
S ☐ RABBITS
T ☐ RATS

U ☐ ANIMAL EXPERIMENTS
V ☐ HUMAN
W ☐ MALE
X ☐ FEMALE
Y ☐ IN VITRO
Z ☐ CASE REPORT
a ☐ CLINICAL RESEARCH
b ☐ COMPARATIVE STUDY
c ☐ ANCIENT
d ☐ MEDIEVAL
e ☐ MODERN
f ☐ 15th CENTURY
g ☐ 16th CENTURY
h ☐ 17th CENTURY
i ☐ 18th CENTURY
j ☐ 19th CENTURY
k ☐ 20th CENTURY
l ☐ ENGLISH ABSTRACT

FIGURE 68 MEDLARS indexing form.

In some systems a form is designed to help the indexer structure his indexing in terms of the syntax of the system. Figure 69 shows such a form used with links and role indicators in the SHARP system (Ships Analysis and Retrieval Project) of the Bureau of Ships.[2] Note several features:

1. Each row of the coding sheet can be used to represent a single link.
2. Descriptors can be entered in columns to indicate the role indicators that apply to them.
3. The form is designed for ease of interpretation by a keypunch operator for input to the system.

Such a form should greatly facilitate the application of links and roles to the indexing process.

Caless [1] has described a somewhat similar form used in indexing documents on seismology by means of the *Universal Decimal Classification*; it is illustrated in Figure 70. The rows again represent conceptual links. The columns list the major facets, although not in the exact order in which they are to be cited. The indexer should ask himself if each facet is present in the document at hand. If it is, he should account for it by entering the appropriate term in the matrix. The form is intended to aid the intellectual analysis of a document and to help in the structuring of a correct UDC number. In the illustration given, the document in question describes shallow-depth earthquakes related to California aftershock sequences of short duration. In entering his conceptual analysis the indexer has linked the concept "shallow" with "earthquakes," and the "short term" with "aftershocks" and "California." From this form the full UDC number is constructed, using the facet sequence: thing, kind, part, material, processes, properties, operations, agents. The full number resulting from this analysis is 550.348.436.098.23: 550.348.433 (#AFTER)(794)"403." Obviously such a form can be used equally well to aid in the intellectual analysis of a request made to the system.

ENTRY VOCABULARIES

We have already stressed the importance of a good entry vocabulary. A published thesaurus will usually incorporate a limited entry vocabulary in the form of *see, use,* or *see under* references. A large information

BUSHIPS TECH. LIBRARY-PROJECT SHARP Doc. Subj. Processing Sheet (Rev. 8-63)	NOTE: (1) Record the link identification before each phrase. (2) Record the role number after each term.	DOCUMENT ACCESSION NUMBER: DOCUMENT SECURITY CLASSIFICATION:

- - - - - - - - - - Detach here - - - - - - - - - - Detach here - - - - - - - - - - Detach here - - - - - - - - - -

BUSHIPS TECH. LIBRARY-PROJECT SHARP. Document Coding Sheet (Rev. 8-63)

	ROLE 8	ROLE 1	ROLE 2	ROLE 3	ROLE 4	ROLE 5	ROLE 6	ROLE 7	ROLE 9	ROLE 10	Sec. Class	ROLE 0	Linkage	Card No.	Subcard No.	
	Primary Topics Principal Subjects	Inputs	Outputs	Undesirables Unnecessaries	Present, Possible, and Later Uses	Media; Adverbs; Adjectives Geog. Loc's	Independent Variables Causes	Dependent Variables Effects	Passive Recipients Location	Means of Accomplishment		Accession Number (Bib Data)				
	1-7	8-14	15-21	22-28	29-35	36-42	43-49	50-56	57-63	64-70	71	72-77	78	79	80	
1														1		1
2														1		2
3														1		3
4														1		4
5														1		5
6														1		6
7														1		7
8														1		8
9														1		9
10														1		10
11														1		11

FIGURE 69 Indexing form used in SHARP system of the Bureau of Ships.

	THING	MATERIALS	PROCESSES	OPERATIONS	AGENTS	KINDS	PARTS	PROPERTIES
1	Earthquakes					Shallow		
2	Aftershocks							
3								
4								
5								
6								
7								

	PLACE	TIME	VIEWPOINT	FORM	LANGUAGE			
1								
2	California	Short-Term						
3								
4								
5								
6								
7								

FIGURE 70 Form used in indexing documents on seismology by means of the *Universal Decimal Classification.*

center may also issue a separate entry vocabulary for in-house use by indexers, searchers, and lexicographers. Such a vocabulary may be available in several forms: card file, loose-leaf, machine-readable for printout or on-line display, or microfilm. The MEDLARS entry vocabulary exists in the form of a card file and also in loose-leaf format. It is known as the Integrated Authority File; a specimen page is illustrated in Figure 71. The file includes definitions or scope notes for descriptors (in upper case). For nondescriptors it presents indexing directions, and it may also give definitions. Foreign terminology is included along with English terms. Note that much of the mapping is one-to-many mapping. Bertielliasis, for instance, must be indexed by the term CESTODE INFECTIONS *and* BERTIELLA. The joint use of these terms defines this infection uniquely, and we can therefore regard "bertielliasis" as a specifier in the vocabulary. BF1 virus, on the other hand, is only an entry term since it is mapped to the more general VERTEBRATE VIRUSES and is thus not uniquely defined in the vocabulary.

The entry vocabulary concept has been carried further at the National Library of Medicine by the issuance of booklets of MEDLARS indexing instructions related to specific subject areas. Figures 72 and 73 illustrate sample pages from such a compilation dealing with the indexing of steroids. The publication discusses steroid chemistry in simple terms, with appropriate illustrations, and discusses the problems involved in indexing in this subject field. Use of the steroid terms from *Medical Subject Headings* is illustrated in the text (Figure 72). A complete list of MeSH steroid terms with entry terms and definitions, where appropriate, is included (Figure 73). Such a booklet is prepared by an indexer who is a subject specialist in the topic involved. Similar publications have been issued in the fields of pharmacy and pharmacology, respiration physiology, genetics, and parasitology. They are of obvious value to indexers and are particularly useful in training activities. Figure 74 shows another specimen page, this time from the issue on respiration physiology.

Where a well-established published authority exists on the terminology of a particular branch of medicine, this is accepted by NLM and used as a kind of extension of the system entry vocabulary. Such publications include the *Manual of Tumor Nomenclature and Coding* published by the American Cancer Society, and the *Enzyme Nomenclature* issued by the International Union of Biochemistry. In addition, as described in Chapter 18, various medical microthesauri exist (e.g., in rheumatology and in Parkinsonism).

BERTIELLA

bigarrure

BERTIELLA (B1)   1967
   genus under Cestoda; tapeworms found
   in primates and occasionally in
   domestic animals and man (MeSH
   definition)

bertielliasis
   Index CESTODE INFECTIONS (IM) (68)
         BERTIELLA (IM) (68)

 Bertolotti's syndrome
   (Ruhl & Sokoloff: A Thesaurus of
   Rheumatology)
   Index SCIATICA (IM) (68)
         SPINAL DISEASES (IM) (68)

BESNOITIASIS (C1,C15) 1968
   syn. globidiosis
   infection with protozoa of the genus
   Besnoitia (Globidium) (MeSH definition)

Bessau's nutrient
   an infant nutrient facilitating the
   growth of intestinal Lactobacillus
   bifidus flora (Gyermekgyogyaszat
   9:299 Oct-Nov 58)
   Index LACTOBACILLUS *growth &
           developement (IM) (68)
         INTESTINES *microbiology (IM) (68)

 beta-inhibitor
   a virus inhibitor which migrates
   electrophoretically with the fast
   gamma globulin or the slow-moving
   beta-globulins (Proc Soc Exp Biol Med
   126:176, Oct 67)
   Index VIRUSES (IM) (68)
         VIRUS INHIBITORS (Prov) (NIM)
                                    (68)

 beta-radiography
   utilizes the effect of the emission of
   electrons in the absorption of x-rays
   to produce a charge pattern on an
   insulating plate placed in contact with
   a lead surface (Radiography, Lond 23:
   281, Oct 57)
   Index RADIOGRAPHY (68)

 Betz cells
   cerebral cortical neurons with efferent
   axons in the medullary pyramids
   (J Physiol 166:313, Apr 63)
   Index CEREBRAL CORTEX *cytology (IM)(68)
         NEURONS (IM) (68)

beutacultura (It)
   ℮ submerged cultures ⊃
   Index CULTURE MEDIA (68)

Bewegungsbestrahlung
   ℮ moving-beam irradiation ⊃

Bezold-Jarisch reflex
   respiratory arrest, bradycardia and
   lowering of blood pressure
   Index RESPIRATORY INSUFFICIENCY (IM)(68)
         BRADYCARDIA (IM) (68)
         BLOOD PRESSURE (IM) (68)

BF1 virus
   virus isolated from bovine feces which
   is cytopathogenic for tissue culture
   cells (C R Soc Biol (Par) 153:1653
   1959)
   Index VERTEBRATE VIRUSES (68)

BGA virus
   blue-green algae virus (J Bact 88:771,
   Sep 64)
   Index PLANT VIRUSES (IM) (68)
         ALGAE (NIM) (68)

bharal
   Index ARTIODACTYLA (68)

BHK cells
   cell cultures of hamster cells
   Index TISSUE CULTURE (68)

BICUSPID (A3) 1965
   (premolar) one of the eight teeth in
   man, four in each jaw, between the
   cuspids and the first molars; usually
   has two cusps; replaces the molars of
   the deciduous dentition (MeSH definition)

Biesalski-Mayer technic
   tendon transplant in peroneus
   muscle (Afrigue Fr Chir, Jun-Aug
   54)
   Index TENDONS *transplantation (68)

bigarrure (Fr)
   ℮ mottled enamel ⊃
   Index MOTTLED ENAMEL (68)

FIGURE 71 Excerpt from MEDLARS Integrated Authority File.

Other Steroid Compounds

In addition to hormones, a number of other natural products possess the cyclopentano-perhydrophenanthrene ring nucleus. They include vitamin D, the bile acids and their salts, various cardiac glycosides and some alkaloids.

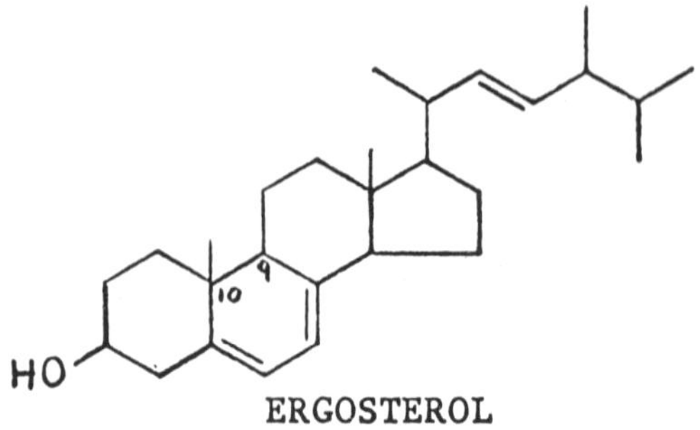

The D vitamins are formed by irradiation of ergosterol (Figure 21) usually producing a break in ring B between carbon atoms 9 and 10. As was mentioned earlier, such a fission of the ring structure produces a secosteroid. Ergosterol itself is indexed as VITAMIN D, and three specific D vitamins are also currently available as MeSH terms. They are ERGOCALCIFEROL, or vitamin D₂, CHOLECALCIFEROL, which is vitamin D₃ and DIHYDROTACHYSTEROL. In Figure 22 it can be seen that they differ only by the presence or absence of a double bond between C-10 and C-19, and at C-22.

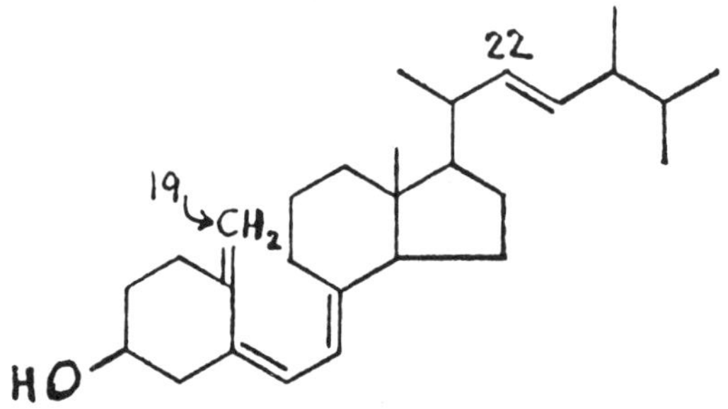

ERGOSTEROL

Figure 21

ERGOCALCIFEROL

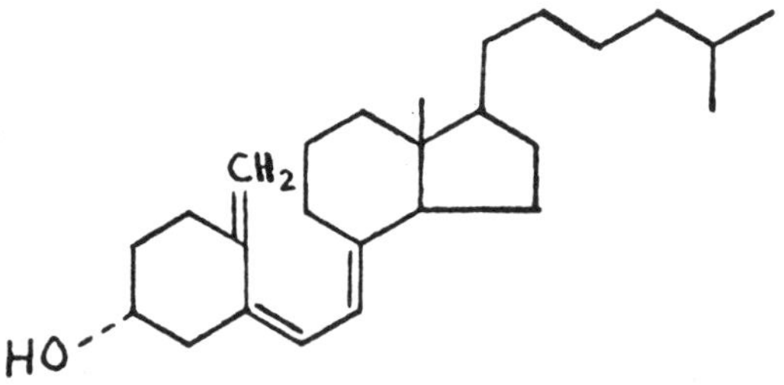

CHOLECALCIFEROL

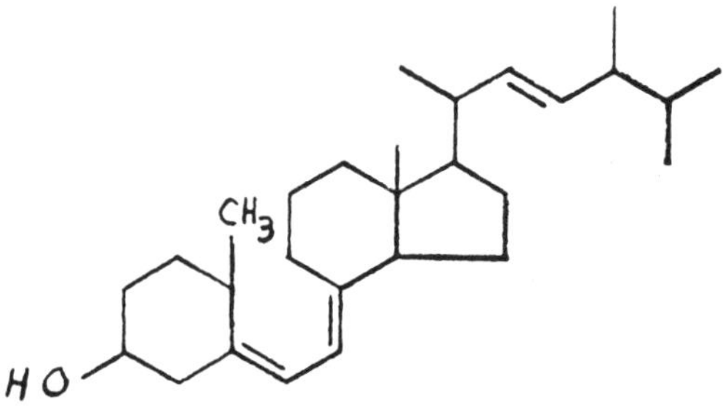

DIHYDROTACHYSTEROL

FIGURE 72 Page from MEDLARS indexing instructions relating to steroid terms.

CHOLESTANES (D2) (68)
    Steroids with methyl groups at C-10
and C-13 and a branched eight-carbon
chain at C-17. May include: Any degree of hydrogenation; hetero substitution in any of the rings; any
non-carbon derivatives and carbon
derivatives except as specified.

5α-cholestan-3α-ol
    see epicholestanol

cholest-5-en-3α-ol
    see epicholesterol

5α-cholest-7-en-3β-ol
    see lathosterol

CONVALLARIA (B6, D5)
    Syn. lily of the valley.
Produces a cardiac glycoside,
convallatoxin.

CORPUS LUTEUM HORMONES (D8)
    Steroid hormones (progesterone and
estrogens) secreted by the corpus
luteum during the normal human men-
strual cycle. If fertilization occurs, these hormones from the corpus
luteum maintain gestation during the
first trimester of pregnancy.

corticosteroids
    Index ADRENAL CORTEX HORMONES (IM)
                (68)

CYCLOSTEROIDS (D2) (68)
    Steroids containing a three-mem-
bered ring within the parent
steroid.

22-dehydrocholesterol
    Syn. cholesta-5,22-dien-3β-ol
    Found in red algae.
    Index STEROLS (IM) (68)
          CHOLESTANES (IM), (68)

11-dehydrocorticosterone
    Reg. 72231
    Syn. 21-hydroxypregn-4-ene-3,11,20-
trione
    Index PREGNANES (68)

21-dehydrocortisol
    Syn. 4-pregnene-11β,17α-diol-3,20-
dione-21-al
    Index PREGNANES (IM) (68)
        17-HYDROXYCORTICOSTEROIDS (IM)
                (68)
      STEROLS (NIM) (68)

DEHYDROEPIANDROSTERONE (D2, D8)
    Reg. 53430
    Syn. dehydroisoandrosterone;
    3β-hydroxy-5-androsten-17-one

dehydroisoandrosterone
    see DEHYDROEPIANDROSTERONE

desmosterol
    Reg. 313042
    Syn. 5,24-cholestadien-3β-ol
    A major sterol of red algae.
    Immediate precursor of cholesterol
in the biosynthetic pathway.
    Index STEROLS (IM) (68)
          CHOLESTANES (IM) (68)

DIGITALIS GLYCOSIDES (D5)
    Derivatives of plants of the fox-
glove family, sterols (cardanolides)
with from one to four sugars in
glycoside linkage with a hydroxyl
group at C-3 of the steroid nucleus.
They act to stimulate the heart
muscle directly.

DIGITOXIN (D2, D5)
    A cardiotonic glycoside obtained
from Digitalis purpurea and D.
lanata. Its aglycone is digitox-
igenin.

DIGOXIN (D2, D5)
    A cardiotonic glycoside obtained
from the leaves of Digitalis
lanata. Lanatoside A is digitoxin,
lanatoside B is gitoxin, lanatoside
C is digoxin.

dihydrotestosterone
    see STANOLONE

3α,11β-dihydroxy-5β-androstan-17-one
    see 11β-hydroxyetiocholanolone

epiandrosterone
    Reg. 438233 (5β); 481298 (3β)
    Syn. 3β-androsterone; isoandrosterone;
3β-hydroxy-5α-androstan-17-one;
androstane-3β-ol-17-one
    Naturally occurring androgen in man.
    Index ANDROSTERONE (68)

epicholestanol
    Reg. 516950
    Syn. 5α-cholestan-3α-ol
    Index STEROLS (IM) (68)
          CHOLESTANES (IM) (68)

FIGURE 73 Page of terms from MEDLARS steroid vocabulary.

The terms marked with an asterisk are expanded further; for example, the individual paranasal sinuses are named. The main problem here is that it is not possible to specify respiratory airways, a concept commonly used, for instance, in papers on airways resistance or airways obstruction. Papers on airways obstruction should be indexed under RESPIRATORY TRACT DISEASES.

The walls of the trachea, bronchi and bronchioles contain smooth muscle which can contract, narrowing the diameter of the airways. The terms bronchoconstriction and bronchodilatation are frequently seen in the literature. They are indexed as BRONCHI *physiology and the provisional heading CONSTRICTION, and BRONCHI *physiology and the provisional heading DILATATION, respectively. Note, however, that bronchial constriction at a clinical level is sometimes the disease term BRONCHOSPASM. The isolated trachea or bronchus is sometimes used as a test preparation for studying tracheal or bronchial smooth muscle. Papers on this topic should be indexed with TRACHEA or BRONCHI and MUSCLE, SMOOTH. The slant of the article will determine which is IM and which NIM.

The lungs are not connected with the chest wall. They lie in the pleural cavity. (Figure 9)

Figure 9 PHARYNX

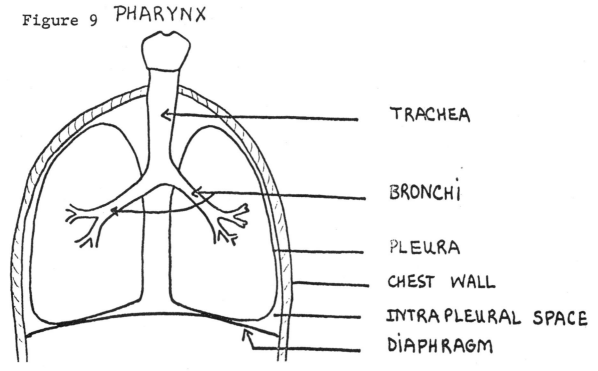

FIGURE 74 Page from MEDLARS indexing instructions relating to respiration physiology.

In these, the terminology of a specialized subject field is mapped to the approved terms in *Medical Subject Headings*.

These vocabulary-related tools are intended primarily to aid the indexer, but they should also be of value in the conduct of searches. Now we should consider some further tools designed specifically to assist the searching function.

SEARCH FRAGMENTS

In discussing causes of search failure (Chapters 13 and 20), we mentioned that recall in a search may be adversely affected by the fact that the searcher fails to cover all possible approaches to retrieval. The index language should give the maximum possible help to the searcher in the construction of comprehensive strategies. A useful concept that has emerged in MEDLARS is that of the *hedge* or *search fragment*. A search fragment is really a pre-established search strategy designed to retrieve documents on a particular topic or aspect. It is an agglomeration of terms, possibly including some built-in search logic, that cuts across the conventional genus-species hierarchies of the vocabulary. A search fragment is constructed by a search analyst and recorded with the understanding that it may be useful again (i.e., it covers a topic that is likely to recur in the future). For example, suppose a searcher has constructed a strategy for the topic "oral manifestations of neutropenia." The search has two aspects: the pathological condition, and the viewpoint from which it is being examined (oral manifestations). To cover the "oral manifestations" aspect comprehensively, the searcher creates a strategy which draws terms from several hierarchies: anatomical terms, diagnostic terms, pathology terms. The group has the characteristic that each member, in some way, indicates involvement of the oral cavity. Having constructed the strategy, and conducted the search with apparent success, the searcher recognizes that "oral manifestations" is likely to occur again in future searches. For example, a request may be made for literature on oral manifestations of leukemia. Once an "oral manifestations" strategy is constructed, it is wasteful to abandon it and reconstruct again where needed. This is particularly true in a very large system, with many search analysts involved, where certain elements or aspects of a search are likely to recur fairly frequently.

The searcher therefore records the strategy in the form of an "oral manifestations" search fragment (Table 55) so that it can be used again in the future with the minimum of additional intellectual effort. Preferably, such a fragment will be approved by a

TABLE 55 Search Fragment on Oral Manifestations (partial)

ORAL MANIFESTATIONS	MONILIASIS
or	*or*
DIAGNOSIS, ORAL	RANULA
or	*or*
MOUTH DISEASES	PAROTITIS
or	*or*
GINGIVAL DISEASES	MOUTH MUCOSA
or	*or*
HEMORRHAGE, ORAL	MOUTH
or	*or*
TONGUE DISEASES	LIP
or	*or*
TOOTH DISEASES	PALATE
or	*or*
STOMATITIS	TONGUE
or	*or*
SALIVARY GLAND DISEASES	TOOTH
or	*or*
PERIODONTAL DISEASES	SALIVARY GLANDS
or	*or*
CHEILITIS	PERIODONTIUM
or	
LUDWIG'S ANGINA	
or	

review group before it is accepted as "standard." The fragment may be recorded in any of several forms. It would probably be reduced to machine-readable form to allow printout and ease of updating, and also to allow on-line display. The fragment will be given a name and a unique identifying number. It will appear on the machine-readable master vocabulary file. This will allow a searcher to incorporate it into a strategy by number. For example, LEUKEMIA *and* SF204 would indicate the search is to be conducted on the term LEUKEMIA *and* all terms in the 204 search fragment, where 204 is the fragment for "oral manifestations."

Search fragments of this type are probably most useful in covering "aspects" or "points of view" in relation to a main search topic (e.g., "nutritional aspects," "genetic aspects," "epidemiology," "oral manifestations," "joint manifestations"). Although such pre-established strategies may not be 100 percent transferable from search to search, they should nevertheless have fairly general applicability. The major advantages of search fragments are:

1. They lighten the intellectual burden on the individual searcher and reduce the possibility of missing relevant documents because of a searcher's inability to think of all necessary approaches to retrieval.

2. They improve the cost-effectiveness of the searching process by avoiding duplication of effort; that is,

they avoid the repetitive construction, by many searchers, of strategies or partial strategies that tend to recur fairly frequently in a subject field.

TREE STRUCTURES

Another searching tool of obvious value is a complete hierarchical display of the vocabulary, in printed or on-line form. A page from the MEDLARS *Tree Structures* is illustrated in Figure 41. In any system in which the primary vocabulary display is alphabetical, it is important that a full hierarchical presentation also be available as an aid in the search process. The hierarchical display will be particularly useful in the conduct of generic searches. The hierarchical structure of the vocabulary should be recorded on the machine-readable master vocabulary tape. This allows the searcher to conduct a generic search without the need to list all the specific terms. For example (see Figure 41) it is possible to conduct a generic search on "tuberculosis" simply by stating "C1.90 (explosion)." The notation "C1.90" represents the tuberculosis tree, and "explosion" indicates that all terms in the tree are to be used. The machine search programs automatically expand the strategy to include all the tuberculosis terms, and the searcher is spared the need to list them all individually. To facilitate generic searching in MEDLARS, certain "dummy nodes" have been introduced into the tree structures. These dummy nodes bring together groups of related specific terms under an artificial generic term. The artificial terms are never, in themselves, used for indexing, but they provide useful "containing heads" for the conduct of generic searches (explosions). One example is found in the MEDLARS trees at C16.49, where "eye abnormalities" appears as a dummy node (non-MeSH term), and another, "environmental hazards," at G3.24.

TERM FREQUENCY DATA

A further supplementary tool we should consider, and a very important one, is a machine printout (or on-line display) of descriptors with an indication of how many times each has been used in indexing. Statistics on frequency of descriptor usage in indexing are generally referred to as "postings" or "tallies." They are obviously useful (as are statistics on frequency of use in searching) in vocabulary updating activities (see Chapter 12). Indexing tallies are also valuable in searching. They allow the searcher to estimate how many citations are likely to be retrieved if a particular strategy is used. To take a very obvious and trivial case, suppose we have a search strategy as follows:

A *and* B *and* C

The tallies indicate that term A has been used 1,016 times in indexing, B has been used 94 times, and C 103 times. Clearly, the search cannot retrieve more than 94 references, and the total retrieval will probably be very much less than this because it is unlikely that all items indexed under term B will also have been indexed under term A and under term C. In a machine-based retrieval system, usage tallies should be recorded on the master vocabulary file. This allows the automatic optimization of search procedures. In the foregoing example, the search optimization procedure would reorganize the strategy to place the terms in ascending order of frequency: B, C, A. Term B, being least heavily posted, is searched first, and the 94 document numbers recorded under this term are matched against the 103 under term C. Only the document numbers common to B and C are compared with the 1,016 postings under A. This is clearly much faster and more efficient than dealing first with the heavily posted term A.

Rolling[4] has described the use of term-frequency data in searching at the Centre for Information and Documentation, EURATOM. The use of frequency-of-assignment statistics as applied to a query is shown in Table 56. The descriptors chosen to represent the query are arranged into groups corresponding to their facets or functions in the query. The cumulated assignment frequencies of the descriptors in the groups are taken into account for the selectivity ranking of the term groups (the least heavily posted group is the most selective). The order of magnitude of the number of references to be retrieved in the search can be determined in advance, according to Rolling, by the formula:

$$R_n = \frac{f_1 f_2 \cdots f_n}{V_{n-1}} K_n$$

where

n is the number of descriptor groups in the query,
f_1 is the sum of the frequency of use of the descriptors in group 1,
V is the number of items in the collection, and
K_n is the association factor.

The association factor owes its existence to the fact that only a minor fraction of all possible associations of *n* descriptors is meaningful; its value is determined statistically. If the number of references R_n is not of the same order of magnitude as the number derived, or expected to be pertinent, the search strategy can be modified ("tightened" or "loosened") before the search is carried out.

A printout of descriptor frequencies is usually main-

TABLE 56 Assignment Frequencies

Wording of the Query	Deterioration of Zirconium and Its Alloys, Films, and Monocrystals in Diphenyl Environment		
Facets	Descriptors	Assignment frequency	Selectivity ranking
Materials (A)	ZIRCONIUM	2077	
	Zirconium alloys	1106	
	Zirconium oxides	524 } 4669	2
	Zircaloy	962	
Processes (B)	CORROSION	3457	
	Oxidation	2620	
	Reduction	1754 } 10095	4
	Electrical conductivity	2081	
	Corrosion protection	183	
Environment (C)	POLYPHENYLS	265	
	Organic coolant	203 } 618	1
	Organic moderator	150	
Shapes (D)	FILMS	2004	
	Crystals	4409 } 6955	3
	MONOCRYSTALS	542	

SOURCE: L. N. Rolling.[4]

TERM HISTORY

tained as an internal tool by an information center. Occasionally, however, they are made widely available. Statistics on the use of DDC descriptors were published in 1966.[3]

TERM HISTORY

The final vocabulary tool we should mention is the term history file. The vocabulary of a large operating information system will not be static. It should be constantly updated to make it optimally responsive to demands placed upon the system. As a vocabulary changes it becomes necessary to maintain records to show the historical development of the vocabulary. This is important for the vocabulary control group; it is also important for searchers. Suppose we are conducting a search relating to circadian rhythms. We need to know that this term was only introduced on 5/9/65, and that for earlier material, we must search on PERIODICITY. Unless we know this, we miss any material indexed before CIRCADIAN RHYTHM became a descriptor. Machine printouts can be generated to show the date on which each descriptor was added to the vocabulary and, more importantly, the descriptor that was used for the topic in the past (if any). This printout will be an in-house tool for use by searchers; the same printout may also contain the term tallies. The searcher may use the printout to ensure that all terms necessary to retrieve items on a particular topic

have been used, compensating for vocabulary changes over time. It is preferable, however, that automatic term substitution procedures be adopted; that is, the term history information will be recorded in machine-readable form (on the master vocabulary file), and this information will be used to add to a search strategy automatically. The searcher, in this case, will use only the latest term. In the previous example the searcher will use CIRCADIAN RHYTHM, and the term PERIODICITY will be substituted automatically to retrieve material (albeit with somewhat low precision) indexed prior to 5/9/65.

REFERENCES

1. Caless, T. W. "Subject Analysis Matrices for Classification with UDC." In *Proceedings of the First Seminar on UDC in a Mechanized Retrieval System.* Copenhagen: Danish Centre for Documentation, 1969. FID/CR Report No. 9.
2. Johanningsmeier, W. F. and Lancaster, F. W. *Project SHARP (Ships Analysis and Retrieval Project) Information Storage and Retrieval System: Evaluation of Indexing Procedures and Retrieval Effectiveness.* Washington, D.C.: Bureau of Ships, 1964. NAVSHIPS 250-210-3.
3. Klingbiel, P. H. et al. *DDC Descriptor Frequencies.* Alexandria, Va.: Defense Documentation Center, 1966. AD 632 600.
4. Rolling, L. N. "A Computer-Aided Information Service for Nuclear Science and Technology." *Journal of Documentation* 22 (1966): 93-115.
5. Tancredi, S. A. and Nichols, O. D. "Air Pollution Technical Information Processing—the Microthesaurus Approach." *American Documentation* 19 (1968): 66-70.

22 Vocabulary Use and Dynamics in a Very Large Information System

This chapter discusses the construction, structure, and change of a controlled vocabulary for a very large information network, with a central facility and remote network nodes, and offering multiple products and services. The system is designed to accommodate both on-line and off-line implementation. The word "lexicodynamics" has been coined to describe the total concept of vocabulary control and change in such a system. The discussion in this chapter is based upon a report prepared to provide an overall conceptual framework for the vocabulary aspects of "MEDLARS II"; i.e., the second-generation MEDLARS system.[1] However, the concepts discussed are equally applicable, with appropriate modifications, to other large multipurpose information systems.

The system exists to produce printed indexes (a general monthly index, with an annual cumulation, and a regular series of recurring bibliographies in specialized subject areas) as well as to offer retrospective search capabilities. Documents are processed at the rate of about 250,000 per year. The vocabulary has the following major characteristics:

1. Certain specific terms assigned by the indexer are used only in computer searching and never appear as access points in a printed index.

2. The indexer indicates under which terms (of all those he assigns) a citation is to appear in the monthly printed index. This may be viewed as a crude form of weighting since it reflects the indexer's decision as to which terms he considers best represent the major aspects of the document.

3. Mapping from one class of terms to another, particularly mapping from terms not used in printed indexes to terms that are used, is effected automatically by computer through the use of machine-readable conversion tables.

Seven classes of terms are recognized in the system:

1. *Major descriptors*. Terms used to describe documents, searchable, and may be displayed in a publication to head a list of citations.

2. *Minor descriptors*. Terms used to describe documents, searchable, but generally not displayed in publications. They permit useful distinctions to be made for retrieval purposes, but are not considered necessary access points for the printed index.

3. *Subheadings*. Words with a general modifying power over broad subject areas which may be used to qualify terms of types 1 or 2 in a syntactic relationship.

4. *Major entry terms ("Public" entry terms)*. Terms not used to describe documents, but which serve to direct the user, in publications or otherwise, towards terms in classes 1, 2, or 3.

5. *Minor entry terms ("Nonpublic" entry terms)*. Terms not used to describe documents and not used in publications, but which serve to guide indexers and searchers to terms in classes 1, 2, or 3.

6. *Pending terms.* Terms proposed for inclusion in one of the foregoing classes but awaiting a decision.

7. *Rejected terms.* Terms considered for inclusion in one of the foregoing classes but rejected.

The system includes a conventional alphabetical display of terms (thesaurus), a full hierarchical display (tree structures), and "search fragments" (Chapter 21).

The distinctions among the various classes of terms are best illustrated by examples. An indexer may use major descriptors, minor descriptors, and entry terms, with subheadings where indicated, in describing a document. To those terms that best represent the major aspect of the document he gives a *weight*. When the indexing record is put into machine-readable form various possible actions occur, depending upon the types of terms assigned and the weighting of these terms:

1. *Major descriptor, unweighted.* The descriptor is stored on the unit record for the document and is searchable.

2. *Major descriptor, weighted.* The descriptor is stored on the unit record for the document and is searchable. When the printed index is produced the document citation is printed under this descriptor.

3. *Minor descriptor, unweighted.* The minor descriptor is stored on the unit record and is searchable.

4. *Minor descriptor, weighted.* The minor descriptor is stored on the unit record and is searchable. When the printed index is produced, the citation prints under the equivalent major descriptor or descriptors. The machine-readable Master Vocabulary File (MVF) contains mapping instructions and effects the required term substitution automatically.

For example, an indexer may assign the minor descriptor SHIVERING, which is a searchable term and is stored on the document unit record. The term is weighted to indicate an important aspect of the document. When the citation is processed for inclusion in the monthly printed index, the term SHIVERING is checked against the Master Vocabulary File where it is shown to be a minor descriptor. For printing purposes only, the appropriate major descriptor, in this case BODY TEMPERATURE REGULATION, is substituted. The specific descriptor SHIVERING is retained permanently on the unit record.

On the Master Vocabulary File (MVF) certain minor descriptors are coded to indicate that they should be used as cross-references in the printed index. In this example the reference SHIVERING *see* BODY TEMPERATURE REGULATION is generated automatically and appears in the printed index.

5. *Entry terms.* A major entry term is always used as a cross-reference in the printed index. It will usually be an exact synonym of a descriptor (e.g., ACETYLSALICYLIC ACID *see* ASPIRIN). A minor entry term is never used in a printed index, but may be used internally by indexers and searchers. Minor entry terms include abbreviations. Indexers and searchers may use minor entry terms, but these are merely replaced by the appropriate descriptors from the MVF when the indexing record or search strategy is input to the system. For example, as a convenience an indexer may use PATHOG as a subheading and this will be replaced by PATHOGENICITY.

These various mapping processes are carried out:

(a) To allow a specific vocabulary to be used for machine retrieval and a relatively more general one for printed indexes.

(b) To allow cross-references to be generated automatically for printed indexes.

(c) To allow both the machine retrieval and printed index functions to be achieved through one indexing operation.

Mapping may include one-to-one mapping and one-to-many mapping. Entry term mappings are *use* mappings, whereas minor descriptor mappings are *add* mappings, as in the following examples:

MOUSE *use* MICE (the former is merely replaced by the latter).

PANADOL *add* ACETAMINOPHEN (the former is retained on the unit record, the latter is used in the printed index).

ARTIPHAKIA *add* LENSES *and* CATARACT EXTRACTION (the former is retained on the unit record, the latter two terms are used in the printed index).

In some cases mapping cannot be fully automatic because a human choice has to be made. For example, in the case ARTERIAL STENOSIS *add* VASCULAR DISEASES *and* ARTERIES *or* specific artery term, the indexer must choose the term ARTERIES if the document discusses arteries in general, but a specific artery term if the discussion is restricted to a single artery. In this case the indexer must assign the minor descriptor ARTERIAL STENOSIS and an artery term, the artery term being recorded on the unit record for the document along with the minor descriptor. In the printed index the artery term will be selected as an entry point, as well as VASCULAR DISEASES, which will be generated automatically.

Some mapping may involve the use of subheadings. A subheading is only carried over to a mapped-to term if it is valid with this term. For example, for printing purposes PANADOL/METABOLISM becomes ACETAMINOPHEN/METABOLISM. However, SHIVERING/PREVENTION AND CONTROL cannot be converted to BODY TEMPERATURE REGULATION/PREVENTION AND CONTROL because the

subheading is unacceptable with this descriptor. In this case the subheading is merely dropped for printing purposes.

MASTER VOCABULARY FILE

The Master Vocabulary File plays a very important role in the system. This machine-readable file will include descriptors, entry terms, and subheadings. The following data are recorded:

1. *Accepted form* of the term itself.
2. *Identification code* (an alphanumeric code for purposes of machine manipulation).
3. *Tree numbers.* These numbers indicate the exact position of the term in the hierarchical structure of the vocabulary and permit the generation of printed displays of the hierarchy.
4. *Search fragment codes.* These codes indicate in which fragments, if any, a particular term occurs. They permit the generation of search fragment printouts.
5. *Microthesaurus codes.* These codes indicate in which microthesauri a term appears. They can be used to generate printed microthesauri (specialized thesauri within the framework of the general thesaurus).
6. *Permitted subheadings.* For each subheading, codes are used to show with which categories of descriptor it may be used. Each descriptor carries a category designator. The subheading ADVERSE EFFECTS is accepted, for example, if it is used in conjunction with a drug or chemical term, but rejected if it is used with an anatomical term (e.g., we cannot say HEAD/ADVERSE EFFECTS).
7. *Publication indicators.* These indicators show in which of the printed indexes a term may be used. A descriptor used as an access point in the monthly index is a *major descriptor*. But certain minor descriptors (i.e., not used in the main printed index) may be acceptable as access points in one of the specialized printed indexes and are so coded on the MVF. Publication indicators also show which entry terms and minor descriptors are to be used as cross-references in the various printed indexes.
8. *See-to-from codes.* These codes give the identification code or address of entries that cross-refer to this entry.
9. *See-also-related codes.* Similarly, these codes point to entries for generating *see also* cross-references.
10. *Mapping directions.*
11. *Definition* (where available).
12. *Tallies.* Two tallies are recorded: frequency of use in indexing, and frequency of use in searching.

Entry terms as well as descriptors carry tallies. When an entry term is used by an indexer or searcher the tally for both entry term and the descriptor to which it is mapped are updated. Comparison of these numbers gives an indication of how the vocabulary is actually being used.

13. *Term history.* The date on which the term was added to the vocabulary is recorded, with an indication of which descriptor or descriptors (if any) were previously used for the concept. This permits comprehensive searches of the data base over several years and allows automatic term substitution for this purpose.

VOCABULARY DYNAMICS

The system vocabulary will be dynamic and constantly growing. However, the growth is likely to occur largely among the minor descriptors and entry terms rather than in the major descriptors. Moreover, very few major descriptors will begin in the system with this status. It is more likely that a major descriptor will first enter as a minor descriptor or conceivably as an entry term.

The principal input of new terms into the vocabulary will be an internal input from the system itself. This input will come from the following major sources:

1. *Indexers.* An indexer may propose a new minor descriptor or entry term for any concept encountered in the indexing operation and not adequately covered by existing terminology.
2. *Searchers.* A searcher may propose a new minor descriptor or entry term for a concept occurring in a request that cannot be adequately covered by existing terminology.
3. *Vocabulary Control Group (VCG).* The VCG may, itself, generate new descriptors or entry terms. This type of generation will largely emanate from two sources:
   (a) Mapping of microthesauri and other specialized vocabularies to the main thesaurus.
   (b) Splitting descriptors, or status change of descriptors, on the basis of use-statistics provided by the system.

All proposals made by analysts will be reviewed by the VCG before being accepted as bona fide minor descriptors or entry terms. While awaiting review, these proposals will be carried, on-line or off-line, in a *pending file.* The pending file will carry the proposed minor descriptor or entry term (with mapping instructions), possibly a provisional definition, the identity of the proposer, and the identifying number of the citation or search that generated the proposal. Once

reviewed by the VCG, a term, if accepted, will be removed from the pending file and transferred to the MVF. If rejected, it will be transferred to the *rejection file*. The *rejection file* will contain entries for all terms proposed and rejected. It will be coded to indicate reasons for rejection, the two principal categories being for:

1. Violating a general system rule (e.g., on spelling or singular versus plural form).
2. Some other (intellectual) reason.

It is conceivable that, over a period of months, the same proposal may be made by a number of different analysts. In the on-line mode, such a proposal would be automatically checked against the rejection file and again rejected. For Type 2 rejections, however, a tally would be maintained to record the number of times a proposal had been made. Once this tally exceeds some pre-established threshold, the proposal would be automatically replaced on the pending file for reconsideration by the VCG.

An indexer or searcher will make a proposal in one of the following forms:

X *use* Y   (for entry terms)
X *add* Y   (for minor descriptors)

These proposals may be recorded at the console in the on-line mode. Off-line, they would be recorded on the indexer's data form or a special proposal form (in the case of proposals from searchers). On-line, the proposal will be automatically checked against the rejection file and, if found, rejected a second time as previously described.

If the work of the analyst making the proposal is normally checked by a senior indexer or searcher, the proposal will be reviewed by this person before it is placed on the pending file. In other cases, the proposal will be immediately recorded on the pending file. In the case of a proposed minor descriptor, this descriptor will be stored provisionally as part of the unit record for the citation.

The contents of the pending file will be periodically printed out or displayed on-line for review by the VCG. Frequency of review will depend on the volume of proposals. However, new terms should be reviewed and incorporated into the system as early as possible to allow their use in indexing and searching. Because the most time-consuming aspects of a review process are usually those involved in defining a term and positioning it in the hierarchical structure, a two-stage review process may be adopted. The first review, a group action by the VCG, would merely accept or reject the term. If accepted, the term would be transferred from the pending file to the MVF, thus allowing its immediate use by analysts. At a later time, the term would be given the additional elements that require further research (e.g., tree and hedge designations and definition). Ideally, the VCG would be an "executive" group representing searchers, indexers, and vocabulary specialists.

In reviewing a proposal in the pending file, the VCG will take one of three possible actions:

1. *Accept the term and mapping instructions as proposed.* In this case, the term is transferred to the MVF, and a directory * is set up in the case of a minor descriptor.

2. *Reject the proposal.* In this case, the term is transferred to the rejection file and coded to indicate the reason(s) for rejection. In the case of a minor descriptor, the term will be deleted from the unit record for the citation to which it has already been attached.

3. *Amend the proposal.* In this case, the amended version will be transferred to the MVF, and a directory will be set up in the case of a minor descriptor. The citation unit record may or may not require change, depending on the type of amendment made. A change in the mapped-from term will require a change in the unit record, while a change in the mapping instructions will require a change in postings in the directories.†

Few major descriptors will be introduced initially into the vocabulary. Rather, they will become major descriptors by first being minor descriptors or, less often, entry terms. The principal criteria for justifying change in status to that of a major descriptor will be:

1. The term must represent current usage.
2. It must be a heading under which people will be likely to look in the printed index.
3. The volume of usage per annum must be within suitable limits. A term used infrequently probably will not be justified for use as a major descriptor in a printed index. However, a term so general that it applies to many documents will tend to collect too many citations to be useful and should be split into more specific terms.

Major descriptors are most likely to result from one of the following:

1. Splitting an existing major descriptor,

---

* Inverted term file, random access, for machine-searching purposes.
† An alternative procedure would put a proposed minor descriptor on the pending file only, with the citation number attached. Directory-posting and addition to the unit record would occur only after the minor descriptor has been accepted by the VCG.

2. Upgrading the status of a minor descriptor, or

3. Interchange of a major descriptor with an entry term.

In each case, the principal justification for change will be the tallies for usage of the terms. A major descriptor used more than x times per year in indexing automatically becomes a candidate for splitting into something more specific. A minor descriptor used more than y times per year automatically becomes a candidate for change of status to that of a major descriptor. An entry term used more frequently than the major descriptor to which it maps automatically becomes a candidate for interchange with the major descriptor. For example, some years ago the literature of ophthalmology tended to use the expression Vogt-Koyanagi Syndrome for the syndrome of bilateral retinal detachment accompanied by encephalitis, vertigo, and alopecia. Later, some writers began to refer to this as the uveomeningoencephalitic syndrome. At that time, the latter term would be a useful entry term mapping to Vogt-Koyanagi Syndrome. Now, however, "uveomeningoencephalitis" appears to be commonly accepted, and usage tallies would indicate that this term should become the major descriptor, relegating Vogt-Koyanagi Syndrome to the status of entry term. Changing the status of an entry term or minor descriptor to a major descriptor, or splitting major descriptors into more specific descriptors, is a responsibility of the VCG.

Tree structures are likely to grow, particularly by the addition of descriptors at the lowest tree levels, but completely new trees are less likely to be needed. The principal structural elements that will continue to be added to the vocabulary will be microthesauri and hedges (search fragments). Microthesauri will be incorporated by mapping existing specialized vocabularies (e.g., from other information centers). Mapping of microthesauri to system descriptors is a time-consuming intellectual task which will be conducted by analysts as a specially assigned function, usually with the assistance and guidance of subject specialists. If indexing and searching on minor descriptors is possible, mapping is likely to be relatively simple because much of it will be a one-to-one mapping rather than a one-to-many mapping. Most terms introduced via microthesauri are likely to be minor descriptors, although some will be entry terms, and some could conceivably be introduced as major descriptors. Once mapped to system descriptors, a microthesaurus becomes a subset of the system vocabulary, fitting into the same overall hierarchical structure. Descriptors will be tagged on the MVF as belonging to various microthesauri. This will allow the printing of various specialized vocabularies as indexing and searching aids.

Suggestions for new hedges or search fragments will be made by search analysts. This can be done at the time of creating a search formulation. For example, a searcher assembles a collection of terms, in a logical sum relationship, which collectively expresses the search element "oral manifestations." He recognizes that this search fragment is likely to be needed and useful in future searches and therefore identifies it in some way on the search formulation, on-line or off-line, as being a proposal for a new hedge. He also names it, in this case, the ORAL MANIFESTATIONS fragment.

The proposed hedge will be printed out at some stage for review by a Search Fragment Review Group (SFRG), a small review group of senior searchers. It is essential that hedges incorporated for future use by search analysts should be reviewed and accepted as standardized hedges. Search analysts should not be allowed to introduce unreviewed fragments into the system for their own personal use. "Hedgehogs" will thus be excluded.

The SFRG will take one of three possible actions in reviewing a proposed hedge:

1. *Accept it intact.* In this case it will be given an identifying number and stored in a hedge file (possibly part of the MVF). This will allow it to be displayed on-line, incorporated into a search strategy by name or number, and printed out in desk-top tools.

2. *Modify it.* In this case the modified version will be given an identifying number and stored in the hedge file.

3. *Abandon it.* This action would be taken when the SFRG feels that the proposed fragment has little general applicability.

Having accepted a hedge, the SFRG will inform the VCG of its existence. The VCG will have the responsibility for incorporating the hedge into the tree structures as a dummy node (Chapter 21). Newly accepted hedges will be printed out in multiple copies for dispatch to search analysts at distant centers. They will be incorporated, in loose-leaf form, into a desk-top tool.

Tallies will be maintained on the use of hedges. These tallies will represent both the number of times a hedge has been incorporated into a strategy and also the number of times it has been called up for display purposes. A hedge that proves to be used infrequently may subsequently be eliminated from the system.

Hedges (search fragments) and microthesauri are groups of terms of interest to the searcher in constructing searches. Changes in these, therefore, should have

no impact on the unit record files. However, a much more difficult problem arises when new descriptors are added to the system. The difficulty is in deciding whether these new descriptors should be added to any existing hedges or microthesauri. While this decision must ultimately be a human one, it is desirable that the system should give assistance in identifying cases for review. In particular, when a new specific term is added at the foot of a hierarchical tree, the system should check to determine whether the immediate generic term is a member of any hedges or microthesauri. If it is, the system should generate a query as to whether the new term should also be included. However, since, by definition, hedges are structures cutting across the tree structures, this can only be a partial solution.

Descriptors newly added to the vocabulary should be printed out and routinely reviewed by analysts responsible for maintaining hedges and strategies for the production of recurring bibliographies. The SFRG will have the responsibility for modifying hedges as a result of vocabulary changes. In addition, hedges may be modified or even discarded on the basis of usage statistics or usage experience. For example, if it is found that a certain hedge is rarely called-up for display or incorporated into a strategy, it could well be eliminated from the system. Alternatively, experience may indicate that certain portions of a hedge are used and others are not. In this case, there would be good justification for the SFRG to undertake some hedge pruning.

Changes in mapping instructions may also occur. The effect of these changes is illustrated by the following cases:

1. It is decided that an entry term and a major descriptor should change places; e.g., ASPIRIN *use* ACETYLSALICYLIC ACID changes to ACETYLSALICYLIC ACID *use* ASPIRIN. Here the simplest answer is to keep the identification number the same and alter the status of the terms with no file maintenance.

2. The mapping of an entry term is changed because of descriptor changes; e.g., suppose that we change RENAL AMYLOIDOSIS *use* KIDNEY *and* AMYLOIDOSIS to RENAL AMYLOIDOSIS *use* KIDNEY DISEASES *and* AMYLOIDOSIS. If entrance is made into the system at RENAL AMYLOIDOSIS for search purposes, the use of date history and historical link data from the Master Vocabulary File will enable one to search on either combination without needing to resort to file maintenance.

3. Changes of mapping from minor to major terms; e.g., a change from APHONIA *add* VOICE to APHONIA *add* VOCAL CHORDS. No file maintenance is needed in this case because one can search under APHONIA.

DESK-TOP TOOLS

Although the system is designed for on-line implementation, desk-top tools will also be necessary, at least for use by outlying centers. These desk-top tools will need careful design to make them of maximum utility and effectiveness. Alternative methods of display and presentation should be investigated. The following desk-top tools are needed as a minimum:

1. *Public Thesaurus.* This will include all the major descriptors plus all "public" entry terms; i.e., all entry terms deemed of sufficient importance to be of general utility to users of the public thesaurus and the printed indexes.

2. *In-house Thesaurus.* Although searchers will require certain data not needed by indexers (e.g., tallies and term history), it will be preferable to produce a single in-house tool for use by both types of analyst. The in-house thesaurus will include all major descriptors, minor descriptors, and entry terms. In addition, it will include: (a) tallies, (b) term histories, (c) names of hedges or search fragments with identifying numbers, and (d) mapping instructions. To conserve space and to make the tool less cumbersome, definitions will not appear in the thesaurus itself. The in-house tool will be printed as frequently as necessary for purposes of currency. Because minor descriptor and entry term vocabularies are likely to grow rapidly, the in-house thesaurus probably will require printing on a quarterly basis, whereas the public thesaurus may be issued annually or even less frequently.

3. *Alphabetical list of descriptors with definitions.* The definition file will be maintained in machine-readable form to allow generation of printouts and on-line display, where needed.

4. *Book of search fragments, loose-leaf, to allow continuous updating.* This volume will be organized alphabetically by name of fragment, possibly with cross-references.

5. *Permuted descriptor index.* This index is of minor importance, but could be of some utility. It would allow immediate recognition of term combinations in which a particular word (e.g., NODE or DUCT) occurs. The principle could be extended to allow a permutation on word roots (e.g., to show every descriptor in which the sequence HYDRO occurs).

6. *Microthesauri.* Specialized microthesauri, within the vocabulary framework, should be printed out as separate desk-top tools for the convenience of indexers specializing in particular subject areas. In this context, specialized indexing guides (e.g., in steroids and in respiration physiology) could be regarded as special forms of microthesauri.

These procedures may sound highly complex. They would certainly be unnecessarily complex in a small organization. They illustrate, however, some of the problems that may arise in the utilization and maintenance of a large controlled vocabulary in a large enterprise in which many indexers and searchers, possibly geographically dispersed, are employed, and in which multiple products, including printed indexes and on-demand services, are provided.

REFERENCE

1. Harley, A. J. and Lancaster, F. W. *Structure and Uses of Vocabulary in MEDLARS II*. Silver Spring, Md.: Computer Sciences Corporation, 1969.

23 *Vocabulary in the On-Line Retrieval Situation*

The first computer-based information retrieval systems were all off-line, batch-processing systems. In a batch-processing system, a request for literature on a particular topic is translated into a search strategy, usually in the form of a Boolean algebraic expression. The search strategy is put into machine-readable form and is then matched against the machine-readable file of indexed citations. Searching is carried out when computer time is available (only in extremely large information-processing agencies is a computer dedicated solely to information retrieval activities), and a number of searches are "batched" and run simultaneously.

Machine retrieval by batch processing has the following limitations:

1. The end user (i.e., the person with the information need, or requester) usually cannot conduct his own searches. Instead he delegates the searching task to an information specialist who acts as an intermediary between the requester and the system. The search strategy is prepared by this intermediary who, in this capacity, is usually referred to as a searcher or search analyst. While search delegation may have certain advantages, it has one fundamental disadvantage: there is a danger that an analyst will misinterpret a requester's information need or that the requester himself will not be able to express his need verbally with sufficient accuracy to effect a successful search.[14]

2. It is difficult, if not impossible, to browse in this type of system.

3. The searcher has essentially only one chance to conduct a successful search. He cannot readily experiment with various possible search approaches. The search strategy must be all-embracing. The analyst must think in advance of alternative approaches and must incorporate them into his strategy; there is little opportunity for the development of a truly heuristic strategy. If the results of the search are disappointing he can obviously try again, but this will usually mean a further delay while waiting for the availability of machine time once more.

4. A batch-processing system almost inevitably involves time delays. Under the very best of conditions this will usually mean a response time of 24 hours. In many systems the response time (from submission of a request to obtaining an appropriate response) will be several days or even weeks. There is no possibility that a user can visit an information center and obtain an immediate ("real time") response to his request.

Most computer systems now being designed or implemented are intended for the on-line mode of operation (or at least partial on-line and partial off-line), and most early machine-based systems are moving toward conversion to the on-line mode. An on-line system differs from an off-line system in that the searcher, via some type of terminal, has immediate access to the data base (in theory at least!) and can interrogate it directly, structuring his strategy at the terminal, receiving responses from the system, and modifying the strategy on the basis of responses (e.g., tallies

or specimen citations) received. The entire search can be conducted in a matter of minutes, and the output (of citations, abstracts, or possibly full text) displayed on a video console or typed out at a machine-controlled typewriter which is part of the user's terminal. For a search retrieving very many citations, the searcher, once he is satisfied with his strategy and has received some specimen printouts or displays on-line, can request that the full search results be printed out off-line and sent to him at a later time.

On-line retrieval systems avoid many of the disadvantages of off-line, batch-processing systems. Browsing is possible. The search strategy can be developed at the terminal heuristically, and the searcher can experiment with various approaches. Results can be obtained virtually immediately (at times in which the system is available for this particular function), and the requester himself may, if he wishes, be given the opportunity to conduct his own search at the terminal without the need to delegate to a system intermediary.

This chapter will not discuss or describe on-line retrieval systems per se (an entire book could be written on this subject alone) but will restrict itself to considering some of the implications of on-line systems for vocabulary control concepts. The on-line mode of operation may be applied to indexing, to searching, and also to the vocabulary control function itself. The actual searches can be conducted by information specialists or by requesters themselves. We will consider each of these possibilities in turn.

ON-LINE INDEXING

On-line indexing implies that the indexer prepares an indexing record for a document at the on-line terminal. The descriptors are keyboarded at the terminal by the indexer. Preferably, the terminal should provide the capability of video display (cathode ray tube) of this record to the indexer. Once the record is completed to the indexer's satisfaction, already being in machine-readable form, it may be input to the system data base immediately. The process has certain obvious advantages:

1. Writing or typing of forms is avoided.
2. The clerical task of converting an indexer's work to machine-readable form (e.g., by punched cards or paper tape) is eliminated.
3. Record formatting can be done by the computer while indexing is taking place.
4. Indexing delays are reduced because the record is immediately available for input to the data base.

In addition to these obvious advantages, on-line in-dexing may offer certain other advantages, including economy of indexing time, the provision of additional indexing aids, and possibly the presentation of certain indexing cues. It is these aspects that we should consider in greater detail.

To aid the indexing process, the vocabulary can certainly be displayed on-line. An indexer may key-in a word or phrase and request one of several possible displays, including:

1. *Alphabetical*. The term, if recognized, is displayed along with other terms alphabetically adjacent in the system vocabulary. Even when not recognized, the appropriate alphabetical display can be generated. For example, the indexer may erroneously ask for MONGOLOIDISM. This is not a valid descriptor, but the alphabetical display closest to this spurious descriptor is generated, as follows:

MOLONEY VIRUS

MOLTING HORMONE

MOLYBDENUM

MONASE

MONGOLISM

MONGOLOID RACE

MONIEZIASIS

MONILIA

MONILIALES

The indexer recognizes that MONGOLISM is the term he is seeking and accepts it accordingly.

2. *Hierarchical (tree structure) display.*
3. *Term with cross-references.* For the term first entered, if recognized, a display of terms referred to and referred from is generated.
4. *Permuted.* The indexer may keyboard a word, say ISOTOPE, and ask for all descriptors containing it.

The indexer may select terms from any of these displays by depressing an appropriate key or by pointing to the terms with a light pen. These terms are recorded and are subsequently displayed when the indexer recalls his index record.

The on-line retrieval system should incorporate an extremely large entry vocabulary. Any term recognized in this vocabulary should be accepted and automatically converted to the appropriate descriptor. Thus, if an indexer keys-in DOWN'S SYNDROME, which appears in the entry vocabulary, the approved descriptor MONGOLISM is substituted (and displayed) automatically. Likewise, if CERVICOTOME is entered, the approved descriptors, CERVIX/PATHOLOGY and BIOPSY, are automatically substituted from the Master Vocabulary File.

The indexer should also be spared the need for keyboarding a descriptor in its full form. The system

should recognize unique "minimum character" strings and automatically complete the display of a descriptor once this minimum string has been keyed. For example, an indexer can begin to key-in the string SUBG, this being the beginning of a descriptor he is seeking. When he reaches the G, before he adds any additional characters, the program takes over and displays SUBGINGIVAL CURETTAGE, which is the only descriptor in the vocabulary beginning with the string SUBG. The indexer may also type in a root with a truncation symbol and ask for a display of all descriptors beginning with the string, say TRICH. This is particularly useful if the indexer remembers a term imperfectly or is not quite sure of the spelling.

The indexer may also browse rapidly in the data base. He may, for example, wish to find out how a particular descriptor has been used in the past. He can do this very easily by requesting a sample display of titles (or abstracts) indexed under this term. The potential value of such indexing precedents has been discussed by Herr.[10] An author search can be used to find how a particular citation has been indexed. A certain author may write a series of related papers, and the indexer would like to recall the descriptors assigned to earlier papers in the series. Obviously, tallies of indexing usage can be displayed. The indexer may thereby avoid a term already used very heavily in favor of another more discriminating term. This aspect has been discussed by Bennett.[2]

The on-line mode makes the introduction of new or proposed descriptors very easy. The indexer may suggest a new descriptor that appears to be needed and incorporate it into the index record for the document that generated it. The descriptor is marked with a special code to indicate its provisional nature. On a regular basis, the Vocabulary Control Group can call up for display or printout all new suggestions (from the Pending File—see Chapter 22), and can review the proposal in the context of the complete index record and the appropriate citation or abstract. Indexers are more likely to contribute substantially to the indexing process in this way than they would if they were required to complete a suggestion form. Moreover, the proposed descriptor is immediately available and can be used by another indexer before it has been officially approved. In the on-line system the indexers should make substantial contributions to the growth of a dynamic vocabulary. And this is where most of the healthy growth should come from (bibliographic warrant again!).

The console can be used to display any kind of indexing "form." The "check-tags" mentioned in Chapter 21 can be shown, allowing the indexer to incorporate selected tags by depressing the necessary keys or by use of a light pen. Structured formats with links and roles can be used to aid indexing or to assist the correct facet analysis of the subject matter.

Appropriate checking programs may be designed to avoid certain types of indexing errors. Common misspellings should be recognized and corrected automatically. Completely unrecognized terms will be rejected and thus brought immediately to the indexer's attention. Certain unacceptable combinations should be recognized and rejected by the system. For example, the indexer may use an unacceptable main heading/subheading combination. Providing the descriptors are placed into broad categories (e.g., the COSATI fields), and that certain subheadings are applicable only to designated categories, the recognition of unacceptable combinations in this way is relatively straightforward.

Carried to its logical conclusion, the on-line indexing program should be capable of making suggestions to the indexer or providing him with appropriate cues. Suppose, for example, he assigns the descriptor TUBERCULOSIS/DRUG THERAPY, but forgets to assign a term to represent the drugs involved. When the indexer has indicated completion of the indexing of the item, a cue is presented to him in the form "No drug term used." The indexer may accept the cue, and act on it or reject it. The point is that a possible error of omission has been brought to his attention. Whenever the subheading DRUG THERAPY occurs, normally a drug term should also be present in the indexing bearing the subheading THERAPEUTIC USE. Providing that the drug terms are identified by category number, this cue is relatively easy to generate. Cues of this type are potentially quite valuable and can be generated automatically whenever possible reciprocal relations exist between descriptors and descriptors, descriptors and subheadings, subheadings and subheadings, or role indicators and role indicators (e.g., "property given" and "property given for," "agent" and "patient"). Statistical association links can also be generated. Thus, the indexer can see which descriptors have been used most frequently in the past with a particular descriptor already assigned, and this may draw his attention to terms that he would otherwise have overlooked. Some preliminary experiments with this concept have been reported by Rosenberg.[20] In video console indexing procedures described by Margolies,[15] an "adaptive interface" will accept the indexer's set of terms and will generate a second set of terms related to the starting terms on the basis of statistical association. The indexer may then modify his original selection.

Finally, most large information systems use senior indexers to check or revise the work of junior analysts. Such checking is greatly facilitated by on-line opera-

tion. A reviser can call-up the work of an indexer on a daily basis, and examine it at his own terminal. Corrections or recommendations can be made immediately. It is possible that even notes can be recorded. The indexer, in turn, can call back and review any indexing records in which changes have been made or recommended by the senior indexer. The whole revision process is thus streamlined and expedited, and delays that might otherwise result (e.g., in passing forms backwards and forwards) are successfully avoided. In an information network a reviser at a central location could review the work of indexers geographically dispersed at a number of specialized information centers, possibly on a sampling basis. Some experiments in on-line video console indexing for MEDLARS have been described by Armenti et al.[1] Descriptive cataloging, subject indexing, and revision were all conducted in an on-line mode. Dual screen and split screen modes of operation were investigated, the former being preferred in indexing and the latter in revising. Average total times for descriptive cataloging, indexing, and revising were 5, 14, and 21 minutes per article, respectively.

A novel approach to computer-aided on-line indexing, also using a portion of the MEDLARS data base, was investigated by Gray and Harley.[9] The hypothesis upon which this work is founded is that the index terms relevant to a new paper to be indexed should be "similar" to the index terms previously assigned to the papers referred to (in the list of references) in the new paper. The experiments were conducted as follows.

When a new paper is to be indexed, the articles cited by it as references are retrieved from the machine data base, assuming that they are present. Then, according to Gray and Harley,

The descriptors assigned to these references are noted. Each descriptor assigned to one or more of the references is given a score equal to the number of references in which it appeared. A threshold value is set and the descriptors whose score is greater than this threshold constitute a list of possible descriptors for the new article. This threshold value can vary according to the maximum number of descriptors wanted, the number of papers contributing to the scores, or a combination of both of these criteria.

These procedures were used to produce a list of "suggested terms" for each of 66 articles, and these term lists were then compared with the terms originally assigned to the articles by MEDLARS indexers. The automatic procedures suggested 50-55 percent of all terms used by the human indexers, and 68.6 percent of the major terms. The automatic method also suggested additional terms not used by the human in-

dexers. For a sample of 41 articles, an experienced MEDLARS indexer decided that 56.7 percent of these additional terms were in fact relevant to the subject content of the papers in question. Treating the complete set of relevant terms for these 41 articles as consisting of the 344 terms humanly assigned plus the additional 143 terms assigned automatically, Table 57 presents a comparison of the two approaches. The performance of the automatic method is only slightly inferior to the performance of the human indexers on the basis of these data. Note that the machine suggested a considerable number of pertinent terms that the human indexer overlooked. The percentage agreement between man and machine increased with the number of references used to generate the suggestion lists.

Gray and Harley believe that, while the human indexer should have final say on which terms are to be assigned, an on-line system working on references to cited papers could make a significant contribution to the improvement of the overall indexing quality by suggesting additional terms that the indexer would otherwise overlook. Clearly, a process involving the keyboarding of citations and the viewing of suggestion lists is unlikely to reduce indexing costs, but it may improve indexing quality and/or reduce the amount of training needed by human indexers. With documents that can be captured inexpensively in machine-readable form, as a by-product of some other operation and for which the suggestion lists can be generated automatically and spontaneously (i.e., without the need for the indexer to keyboard references), the process obviously becomes much more attractive economically.

ON-LINE SEARCHING

The major advantages of on-line searching are obvious and were mentioned briefly earlier. Searching in an on-line system is an interactive process. The searcher can try various terms, term groups, or term combinations and immediately find how many citations match

TABLE 57 Comparison of Automatic and Human Indexing Performances

Total relevant terms for 41 articles (machine and indexers)	487
Number of these assigned by indexers	344 (70.6%)
Number of these assigned by machine	322 (66.1%)
Number assigned by both	179 (36.8%)

SOURCE: W. A. Gray and A. J. Harley.[9]

the exploratory strategy. He can then broaden or narrow the scope of the search by adding descriptors, or he can try a completely different search approach. He can browse in the data base to determine the type of document retrieved by a particular strategy. When he finds a relevant item, he can view all the descriptors assigned to it. Possibly he will find further terms that can be incorporated into his search formulation.

The searcher may browse in the system vocabulary, calling up alternative displays (alphabetical, hierarchical, permuted, cross-referenced). From these displays he should be able to incorporate any term (or hierarchy) into his search strategy simply by hitting a key or using a light pen. Search fragments will also be available for on-line display (Chapter 22), and these too can be incorporated by a unique identifying number. Alternatively, the searcher may select certain portions of a tree or certain portions of a search fragment.

The on-line system is susceptible to alternative forms of vocabulary display not frequently used in the more conventional printed tools. Graphic displays of the EURATOM type seem particularly suitable for implementation on-line. Statistical association data may be used to display groups of terms related in the sense that they have been used together in indexing.

Like the indexer, the search analyst may contribute directly to the growth of the vocabulary. When a search has proved unsatisfactory through lack of an appropriate specific term, the searcher can document this, recording on-line the descriptor that appears to be necessary. This descriptor will then become a candidate descriptor for subsequent review by the Vocabulary Control Group. New hedges or search fragments can be created by identifying on the terminal a particular set of terms used in a strategy and giving this group a descriptive name (the unique fragment number will be assigned automatically). Newly introduced fragments will also be reviewed on a regular basis by an appropriate review group.

Clearly, the searcher should be allowed to use entry terms in the same way that the indexer can use them, and should also be allowed the "minimum character lookup" facility. In browsing in the data base, and most particularly when reviewing the results of a search, the searcher may discover instances of apparent indexing error. He should be allowed to identify incorrect term assignments or obvious errors of omission at the terminal with a mechanism provided to bring these cases to the attention of the indexing group.

The literature on on-line retrieval systems is now becoming extensive, and most of it discusses the search function. The BOLD system of the System Development Corporation is described by Burnaugh[4] and by Borko;[3] the TIP program at M.I.T. is described by

Kessler;[13] use of the UDC in on-line retrieval experiments is discussed by Freeman and Atherton;[8] the Lockheed DIALOG system is described by Summit;[23] the RECON system (NASA) is described and evaluated by Meister and Sullivan.[17] Tutorial programs for operation of on-line systems are presented by Caruso,[6] and useful summaries of system characteristics have been prepared by Seiden[21] and by Katter and Blankenship.[12] These various reports include valuable background material, but they do not deal specifically with the vocabulary question.

VOCABULARY CONTROL ON-LINE

The Vocabulary Control Group can itself obtain valuable benefits from the on-line mode of operations. Proposed new descriptors generated by indexers and searchers can be called up and displayed on a regular basis. These proposed descriptors can be reviewed within the context of the citations or search strategies from which they were generated. Vocabulary review should be a more efficient activity in the on-line system, and newly approved terms should get into the vocabulary and be available for use faster than is usual in the off-line mode of operation. The lexicographer can browse among the various vocabulary displays, including displays of term definitions, in the way the indexer and searcher can browse. Tallies on the use of descriptors in indexing and searching can be reviewed on-line. The term history file, showing obsolete and discarded terms and the dates on which existing descriptors were introduced, will also be available for viewing at the console.

On-line text editing programs may be available to help the lexicographer in editorial work (for example, in introducing or amending term definitions). Words in newly introduced definitions can be checked against existing definitions in order to locate similarities and to reveal possible redundancy or overlap.

The main advantage of the on-line system for the lexicographer may, however, be its possible amelioration of the thorny problems of file maintenance. The on-line facility should make it considerably easier to introduce terms into the appropriate places in the hierarchies, to delete terms, or to amend them. It will also facilitate the correction of document unit records to reflect vocabulary changes (e.g., the splitting of descriptors), if such file updating is considered practicable and desirable.

Before we leave the subject of vocabulary control on-line it is worth considering the idea of the "growing thesaurus" as advocated by Reisner.[18, 19] Reisner proposes a freely growing thesaurus built up from re-

lationships used by searchers in querying a system in on-line mode. The initial system vocabulary is formed freely from a natural-language data base, and a human "thesaurus" of the most obvious inter-term relations is superimposed upon this. The searcher uses words contained in the system vocabulary and is led by the thesaurus to other related terms. These he can accept and incorporate into a strategy at will. In developing his search strategy heuristically, any additional useful relationships that he himself thinks of are automatically recorded. His own trail of word associations is then added to the "informal thesaurus" and can thus be used by later searchers.

Reisner justifies this approach on the grounds that "people differ significantly in their personal semantic roadmaps." A general-purpose thesaurus is a compromise that attempts to serve everyone. The general thesaurus may represent a "common potential stock of semantic associations." Individuals, however, will select differently from this common pool in constructing thesauri and in using them. The proposal has obvious merit: a thesaurus developed in this way has "warrant" (search warrant rather than bibliographic warrant), represents multiple viewpoints, and is constantly updated.

A similar approach has been described by Higgins and Smith.[11] They propose a thesaurus that will display a set of related words for each word in the vocabulary. "In a search the computer will display to the user the set of related words and ask if any of these can be used in place of the one he has suggested. The user will also be encouraged to supply any other related words he knows. Registers will keep stored evidence of the usage of these related words, and only those employed frequently will be displayed if the number of related words becomes too large. Related words given by the user will be stored. . . . In this way the thesaurus will change and grow with user interaction."

USE OF THE ON-LINE SYSTEM
BY REQUESTERS

While an on-line system has great potential benefits for members of an information staff, ultimately it should also be usable by the people who have information needs (i.e., the practitioners in a discipline). An on-line system should give the requester the opportunity to conduct his own browsing interactive searches in a large data base without the need to delegate to a system intermediary. But, in a large information system with a controlled vocabulary and long-established indexing protocols, the requester cannot be

expected to acquire overnight the search sophistication of a trained analyst. We must help this requester as much as we can and make it as easy as possible for him to query the data base. For the unsophisticated searcher, vocabulary displays may need to be presented spontaneously. For example, the searcher uses term X and is immediately shown its scope note, hierarchy, and set of related terms, thus allowing the user to confirm his choice or to abandon it in favor of something more appropriate (possibly more specific) gleaned from the new display. A split-screen technique can be used: the spontaneous displays occupy one portion and the searcher's term list another. Fail-safe mechanisms need to be built in to compensate for common user errors—misspellings, invalid combinations, illogical constructions. The on-line system must do more than reject an incorrect term or construction; it must lead the user to the correct form. Techniques of computer-aided instruction appear suitable for guiding a user in the construction of strategies. Preliminary work in this area has been conducted by Caruso.[6]

The user will, of course, be able to examine the surrogates of documents responding to his search requirements. He may thus be able to find new search terms in the profiles of items he has already retrieved. Ideally, once the user has found one or more relevant items in his on-line search he should be able to ask the system to find others that have been indexed similarly (algorithms can be devised to compare the descriptor profiles of documents and to rank them on the basis of similarity). If he already knows of some relevant documents when he first approaches the system, the citations to these can be used as his initial entrée into the data base.

The practitioner's search is likely to be more successful if he is spared the necessity of using controlled-language terms and putting these together into Boolean search statements. The closer we can get to complete natural-language querying (as permitted, for example by SMART) the better the results may be. Obviously, a very complete entry vocabulary is a necessity.

A full-entry vocabulary will be particularly important in an on-line system for users who are not information specialists. Cain[5] has described the construction of such an entry vocabulary for an on-line MEDLARS data base operated as part of the Biomedical Communication Network of the State University of New York. For on-line searching Cain uses a modified version of *Medical Subject Headings*. In particular, alternative word orders are used. The straight natural-language approach is preferred (e.g., INBORN ERRORS OF METABOLISM replaces METABOLISM, INBORN ERRORS, which is the MeSH term for this concept). The entry vocabu-

lary provides approaches from alternative word sequences, from spelling variants (e.g., English versus American usage), from abbreviations, and from common misspellings (e.g., OPTHALMOLOGY). The object is to provide an entry point from whatever term the user might think of when sitting at the on-line terminal. Cain's procedures added approximately 23,400 entry terms to the 8,000 MeSH terms.

Natural-language searching systems appear particularly attractive for on-line implementation. But even if the data base is not a natural-language data base, the user should be able to query it in natural-language terms and have the free text of his query mapped automatically, or as automatically as possible, to controlled terms. On-line systems for use by noninformation specialists should be designed, if possible, to avoid the use of Boolean algebra in the formulation of search strategies. Term or group weighting procedures have greater flexibility and are easily comprehended.[16, 22] This type of system has been implemented by Arthur D. Little, Inc. and described by Curtice and Jones.[7] The search program will accept English-language queries entered at the terminal and will subject them to an automatic indexing routine, reporting back to the user those words or word pairs found in the system vocabulary. The requester then builds up lists of terms describing his interests. This initial list of terms may be expanded by the use of statistical association, the new terms thus derived being added to the list and displayed for confirmation. All necessity for specifying logical combinations of terms is removed from the requester. The search strategy is constructed automatically: the query terms are automatically weighted, and the records in which they occur are identified and sorted prior to presentation on the display. The retrieved records are shown to the user in decreasing order of a calculated weight based on the sum of the weights of the terms in the query that the record contains.

REFERENCES

1. Armenti, A. et al. *An Experiment in On-Line Indexing Using LISTAR.* Lexington, Mass.: MIT, Lincoln Laboratory, November 1970.
2. Bennett, J. L. "On-Line Access to Information: NSF as an Aid to the Indexer/Cataloger." *American Documentation* 20 (1969): 213-220.
3. Borko, H. "Interactive Document Storage and Retrieval System—Design Concepts." In *Mechanized Information Storage, Retrieval and Dissemination.* Edited by K. Samuelson. Amsterdam: North-Holland Publishing Co., 1968, 591-599.
4. Burnaugh, H. P. *The BOLD User's Manual for Retrieval.* SDC Tech Memo TM-2306/004/00. Santa Monica, Calif.: System Development Corporation, 1966.
5. Cain, A. M. "Thesaural Problems in an On-Line System." *Bulletin of the Medical Library Association* 57 (1969): 250-259.
6. Caruso, D. E. "Tutorial Programs for Operation of On-Line Retrieval Systems." *Journal of Chemical Documentation* 10 (1970): 98-105.
7. Curtice, R. M. and Jones, P. E. *An Operational Interactive Retrieval System.* Cambridge, Mass.: A. D. Little, Inc., 1969.
8. Freeman, R. R. and Atherton, P. *AUDACIOUS—An Experiment with an On-Line, Interactive Reference Retrieval System Using the Universal Decimal Classification as the Index Language in the Field of Nuclear Science.* New York: American Institute of Physics, April 25, 1968. Report AIP/UDC—7.
9. Gray, W. A. and Harley, A. J. "Computer Assisted Indexing." Paper presented at the Second International Conference on Mechanized Information Storage and Retrieval Systems. Cranfield, England, 1969.
10. Herr, J. J. "Use of Data-Base Access for Interindexer Communication and for Indexer Training." *Proceedings of the American Society for Information Science* 7 (1970): 163-166.
11. Higgins, L. D. and Smith, F. J. "On-Line Subject Indexing and Retrieval." *Program* 3 (1969): 147-156.
12. Katter, R. V. and Blankenship, D. A. *On-Line Interfaces for Document Information Systems: Considerations for the Biomedical Communications Network.* Santa Monica, Calif.: System Development Corporation, 1969. TM-(L)-4320.
13. Kessler, M. M. "The M.I.T. Technical Information Project." *Physics Today* 18 (1965): 28-36.
14. Lancaster, F. W. "Interaction Between Requesters and a Large Mechanized Retrieval System." *Information Storage and Retrieval* 4 (1968): 239-252.
15. Margolies, R. F. *Video Console Indexing.* Paper presented at the Seventh Annual Information Retrieval Colloquium, Philadelphia, May 1970.
16. Matthews, F. W. and Thomson, L. "Weighted Term Search: A Computer Program for an Inverted Coordinate Index on Magnetic Tape." *Journal of Chemical Documentation* 7 (1967): 49-56.
17. Meister, D. and Sullivan, D. J. *Evaluation of User Reactions to a Prototype On-Line Information Retrieval System.* Canoga Park, Calif.: Bunker-Ramo Corporation, 1967. NASA CR-918.
18. Reisner, P. "Construction of a Growing Thesaurus by Conversational Interaction in a Man-Machine System." *Proceedings of the American Documentation Institute,* Short Papers, Part I, 1963, 99-100.
19. Reisner, P. *Evaluation of a "Growing" Thesaurus.* Yorktown Heights, New York: IBM, Thomas Watson Research Center, 1966. Research Paper RC-1662.
20. Rosenberg, V. "A Study of Statistical Measures for Predicting Terms Used to Index Documents." *Journal of the American Society for Information Science* 22 (1971): 41-50.
21. Seiden, H. R. *A Comparative Analysis of Interactive Storage and Retrieval Systems with Implications for BCN Design.* Santa Monica, Calif.: System Development Corporation, 1970. TM-4421.
22. Sommar, H. G. and Dennis, D. E. "A New Method of Weighted Term Searching with a Highly Structured Thesaurus." *Proceedings of the American Society for Information Science* 6 (1969): 193-198.
23. Summit, R. K. *Remote Information Retrieval Facility.* Palo Alto, Calif.: Lockheed Missiles and Space Co., 1968.

24 Some Cost-effectiveness Aspects of Vocabulary Control

It is certainly costly to construct a large controlled vocabulary. Hammond [2] quotes a figure in excess of half a million dollars as the total funds appropriated for construction of the *Thesaurus of Engineering and Scientific Terms*. In addition, some 328 volunteer panelists contributed their own time to the project and paid their own travel expenses. On the other hand, Rolling [5] has described the construction of a thesaurus in metallurgy that required only four months of effort. While exact figures are not generally available, a large national information service, such as MEDLARS or ERIC, spends a considerable amount of money on initial vocabulary construction and on continued maintenance and updating activities. Cummings [1] quotes personnel costs of $55,658 for Fiscal Year 1966 in maintenance of *Medical Subject Headings*, the controlled vocabulary used in MEDLARS. The annual personnel costs for 1971 must be considerably above this figure. Surace [7] has stated that a complete thesaurus maintenance program may cost between $50,000 and $75,000 to design and code, although some packaged programs can be purchased for about $15,000.

These significant costs make it necessary to give some consideration to the cost-effectiveness of vocabulary control in information retrieval and dissemination systems.

Cost-effectiveness analysis is applicable to the design and application of index languages, but it is rather difficult to apply in this area, and the results are more difficult to express in tangible terms than they are in many other applications.

We can improve the cost-effectiveness of an index language either by (a) altering the language in such a way that system costs are reduced while the present level of search effectiveness is maintained; or (b) making changes that improve search effectiveness with no measurable increase in overall system costs.

It is expensive to develop and maintain a highly sophisticated index language for vocabulary control in large information retrieval systems. In fact, the more sophisticated the vocabulary, the more expensive it is likely to be to apply and maintain. An important economic consideration is vocabulary size. Generally speaking, the more terms in the vocabulary, the greater the number of document classes that can be uniquely defined, the greater the specificity of the vocabulary, and the greater the precision capabilities of the system. However, a large, highly specific controlled vocabulary will tend to be costly to develop, costly to apply, and costly to update. A highly specific vocabulary will change much more frequently than one with relatively broad terms. Most changes will occur at relatively low levels in term hierarchies, particularly to accommodate new concepts. The specificity of the vocabulary must be related directly to the specificity of the requests made to the system. It is certainly uneconomical and inefficient to develop and use a vocabulary considerably more specific than the level of

specificity required by the demands placed upon the system. Thus, there is a strong economic necessity for conducting a careful analysis of representative requests at the stage of system design. In considering vocabulary specificity we must, of course, make allowances for growth of the data base and the effect of this on the average number of citations retrieved per search. A precision of 20 percent may be tolerable when the average search output is 12 citations, but it may be completely intolerable when the average output is 125 citations.

A closely related consideration is the need for additional precision devices such as links, role indicators, subheadings, and term weighting. These devices are intended to improve system precision by reducing the number of unwanted items retrieved in a search as a result of false coordinations, incorrect term relationships, or highly exhaustive indexing. They are usually costly to apply. Role indicators, in particular, are likely to add substantially to indexing costs and search formulating costs, and they may add to actual search processing costs. The productivity of indexers (i.e., the average number of items indexed a day) is likely to be reduced considerably in a system employing links and roles. Sinnett [6] found that roles added substantially to indexing cost, to the number of postings, to search formulating and processing times, and to actual searching times. Montague [3] reported that the assignment of links and roles consumed 15.6 percent of the total 36 minutes spent, on the average, in indexing a patent. Moreover, the use of role indicators was found to increase file size by about 50 percent. Mullison et al. [4] found that inexperienced indexers took 30 percent longer when indexing with roles than they did when indexing without them.

Because they increase specificity of the vocabulary, role indicators almost invariably cause reduced consistency of indexing. They frequently have a devastating effect on recall. Subheadings, which may function simultaneously as links and as roles, also add to indexing costs and reduce indexer consistency. However, they tend to have a less drastic effect than the use of role indicators. In mechanized and semi-mechanized retrospective search systems, such devices serve to reduce the number of irrelevant citations one must examine to find each relevant citation. They can only be justified economically if they prove cheaper than alternative methods of achieving the same results for the end user. Role indicators, for example, will reduce or possibly eliminate one particular type of unwanted retrieval, namely, the incorrect term relationship (the situation, in post-coordinate systems, in which the terms causing retrieval are related but not in the way the requester wants them related). A cost-effectiveness analysis may well reveal that it is more economical not to use role indicators (thereby saving indexing and searching time), to allow some incorrect term relations to occur, and to eliminate the irrelevant citations thus retrieved through a postsearch screening operation conducted by a member of the information staff.

A very important but usually sadly neglected component of an index language is the entry vocabulary; i.e., a vocabulary of natural-language expressions, occurring in documents or requests, that map onto the controlled vocabulary of the system. Usually, the entry vocabulary will consist of terms which, for indexing and retrieval purposes, are either considered synonymous with controlled vocabulary terms or are more specific than controlled vocabulary terms (e.g., HELIARC WELDING *use* SHIELDED ARC WELDING). Although an extensive entry vocabulary may be relatively expensive to construct and update, it can have a significant effect on improving performance (by reducing recall failures), particularly of large retrieval systems. It can also have significant long-term benefits to the cost-effectiveness of the system by reducing the intellectual burden on both indexers and searchers. An entry vocabulary is really a collection of records of intellectual decisions made previously by indexers. Unless an intellectual decision made by an indexer (topic X index under term Y) is recorded, the decision will have to be made again (not necessarily with the same mapping results, hence inconsistency) by other indexers or by the same indexer at a later date. Moreover, the system searchers will also have to make intellectual decisions (not necessarily agreeing with the indexers) when they come to search for literature on topic X. The larger the entry vocabulary, the fewer current intellectual decisions need to be made by indexers and searchers (thus reducing indexing and search time), the greater the consistency in indexing, the better the recall of the system, and (possibly) the lower the professional level of the staff needed in the indexing operation.

Index language factors are as relevant to the cost-effectiveness of published indexes as they are to the cost-effectiveness of machine retrospective searching. Again, specificity of the vocabulary must be related to the type of demands placed upon the system (i.e., to the specificity of searches conducted in the index). Index terms should not be so broad that they accumulate a large heterogeneous collection of citations in each issue of the index, thus making the manual search a tedious, time-consuming process. Because most published indexes do not employ post-coordinate principles, it is important that sufficient pre-coordination be present to allow the conduct of reasonably specific, high-precision searches. This may be achieved by pre-coordinate subject headings with subheadings

(as in *Index Medicus*), by an index term (entry point) supplemented by a modifying phrase (an articulated index of the *Chemical Abstracts* type), or by specific, tailor-made headings constructed by adherence to a strict citation order (as in the *British Technology Index*). In a printed index the specificity required in headings is partly determined by the type of document surrogate provided because, with certain types of indexes, the heading itself acts as a specific content indicator for the document. An index using highly specific headings (such as the *British Technology Index*) may have less need to include abstracts than an index using relatively broader headings. If the heading is broad, the document surrogate must provide the indication of specific content. Without abstracts the user is entirely dependent upon the quality of a document title for determining its probable relevance, although some indexes include tracings (i.e., a record of all the index terms assigned to a document) in place of the document abstract.

INPUT COSTS VERSUS OUTPUT COSTS

As with other aspects of information retrieval systems, in considering the cost-effectiveness of a controlled vocabulary we need to balance input costs against output costs as well as against retrieval effectiveness. Economies in input procedures will almost invariably result in an increased burden on output processes and thus increased output costs. Conversely, greater care in input processing (which usually will imply increased input costs) can be expected to improve output efficiency and reduce output costs. Two possible trade offs relating to vocabulary control are:

1. *A carefully controlled and structured index language versus free use of uncontrolled keywords.* The controlled vocabulary requires effort in construction and maintenance and is more expensive to apply in indexing. It takes longer, on the whole, to select terms from a controlled vocabulary, which may involve a look-up operation, than it does to assign keywords freely; moreover, keyword indexing may be done by less qualified personnel than indexing involving the use of a more sophisticated controlled vocabulary. The controlled vocabulary, however, saves time and effort at the time of output. Natural-language or keyword searching, without the benefit of a controlled vocabulary with classificatory structure, puts increased burden on the searcher, who is virtually obliged to construct a segment of a controlled vocabulary each time he prepares a search strategy (e.g., he must think of all possible ways in which "petrochemicals" or

"textile industry" could be expressed by keywords or in natural-language text). Likewise, the uncontrolled use of keywords may lead to reduced average search precision and thus may require additional effort and cost in output screening.

2. *A highly specific, controlled vocabulary versus a relatively more broad, controlled vocabulary.* The former is generally more expensive to create, maintain, and apply. The more specific the vocabulary, the more difficult it becomes to achieve indexing consistency, and the higher the level of personnel needed to apply it. On the other hand, a highly specific vocabulary may allow high search precision and thus save on output screening time. A particular form of specificity is achieved by role or relational indicators, and these comments apply equally to the use of such devices.

These are merely obvious examples of possible trade offs between input effort and output effort. Other possibilities exist. Table 58 presents a trade-off comparison of two hypothetical information systems. In System A, great care and expense is put into the input operation with a resulting economy in output effort and costs. In System B, on the other hand, deliberate policies designed to economize on input costs are in effect with the inevitable result that output effort and costs are increased. System A is not necessarily more efficient than System B, or vice versa. The approach taken in System B may be more cost-effective than that taken in System A, if we can show that it achieves an acceptable level of performance for the end user with overall costs less than the costs associated with System A.

Many different factors enter into the decision whether to emphasize the input processes or the output processes of an information system. The most important considerations are probably the following:

1. *Volume.* The volumes of concern are the volumes of documents indexed and the volumes of requests processed annually. In the extreme situation of many documents indexed but comparatively few requests handled, it would be rational (all other things being equal) to economize on input costs and put an additional load on the output function. In the reverse situation—comparatively few documents input but many requests handled—the opposite would be true, and savings would be best effected at the output stage.

2. *Required input speed.* In certain situations it is imperative that documents get into the system as rapidly as possible. This is certainly true, for example, when the information system serves a dissemination (current awareness) function, as in certain intelligence situations. Under these circumstances it

TABLE 58 Trade-off Comparison of Two Hypothetical Information Systems

System A	System B
Input characteristics	*Input characteristics*
A large, carefully controlled vocabulary.	A small controlled vocabulary supplemented by the free use of keywords.
Indexing of medium exhaustivity (an average of 10 terms per document).	Low exhaustivity of indexing (5 terms per document).
Highly trained indexers at a high salary level.	Less highly trained indexers without college degrees.
An indexing revision process.	No indexing revision.
Average indexer productivity of 40 items per day.	Average indexer productivity of 100–125 items per day.
High input costs.	Low input costs.
Relatively long delay between publication and actual input to system.	Fast throughout.
Output characteristics	*Output characteristics*
Reduced burden on the searcher in preparation of strategies.	Greater burden on the searcher in the preparation of strategies.
High precision of raw output.	Low precision of raw output.
Tolerable recall.	Tolerable recall.
No screening needed.	Screening of raw output needed to raise precision to tolerable level for end user.
Fast response time.	Delayed response.
Relatively low search costs.	Relatively high search costs.

SOURCE: F. W. Lancaster. "The Cost-Effectiveness Analysis of Information Retrieval and Dissemination Systems," *Journal of the American Society for Information Science* 22 (1971): 12-27.

is likely that required speed of input would outweigh other considerations, and that indexing economies would be adopted.

3. *Required output speed.* In other situations, rapid and accurate response may be vital (e.g., the case of the Poison Information Center), and no economies at input will be justified if these are likely to result in delayed response or reduced accuracy of output.

4. *By-products.* Under certain conditions it may be possible to obtain a searchable data base very inexpensively. For example, we may be able to acquire a machine-readable data base, perhaps in natural-language form, which is a by-product of some other operation (e.g., publishing or report preparation) or has been made available by some other information center. Even though the input format and quality may not be ideal for our requirements, if the data base is available at nominal cost it might be desirable, in terms of cost-effectiveness, to make use of it (possibly with some slight modifications) and to expend greater effort on the searching operation.

Cost-effectiveness analysis may be applied to any of the various subsystems of a complete information system: indexing, index language, searching, and user-system interaction. In actual fact, in the analysis of cost-effectiveness, just as in the evaluation of effectiveness, it is unrealistic and dangerous to consider any one of the subsystems in isolation. All of these

components are very closely interrelated, and a significant change in one will almost certainly cause repercussions throughout the system as a whole. We must be aware of this; and in any cost-effectiveness analysis, we must consider the long-term, indirect effects of any system changes as well as the immediate, direct effects. For example, suppose we make the decision to move away from a carefully controlled, sophisticated index language to something much simpler. We can expect the immediate effects to be:

1. A reduction in vocabulary control and maintenance costs.
2. A reduction in indexing time.
3. Improved throughput time.

There will also be some long-term, less direct effects:

1. The time required to prepare search strategies may increase, resulting in a rise in searching costs.
2. Search precision may be reduced, and we may find we need an output screening operation.
3. If we now need output screening we may also need to improve the quality of the document surrogates in the system. Perhaps we will need to include abstracts although these were previously unnecessary.

Similar phenomena may occur if we increase the average exhaustivity of indexing. As immediate effects we would expect an increase in indexing time and costs, an increase in the average number of documents

retrieved per search, an improvement in recall, and a drop in average precision. Again, the long-term effects may be that we need an output screening operation to keep precision (to the end user) at a tolerable level, and that we may need improved document surrogates to effect the screening operation. An information system is a complex organism, and we must not expect any change to have only local effects.

There are many possible ways to implement a successful retrieval system. Aesthetically we may prefer to use a very carefully controlled vocabulary to allow greater search precision and to economize on output screening time and costs. This approach, however, is not necessarily the most cost-effective approach. We may be able to operate an effective system much more economically through less stringent vocabulary control, with less time spent on indexing and more effort allocated to the output stages of searching and screening. The Central Intelligence Agency, in a very large intelligence retrieval system, has deliberately abandoned careful, complete vocabulary control in favor of uncontrolled keyword indexing (expanded titles), with a very broad subject code and a geographic code superimposed. This approach has proved much more satisfactory in terms of cost-effectiveness. Although different situations dictate different procedures, there is clearly a general trend toward simplification in information systems at the present time.

REFERENCES

1. Cummings, M. M. "Needs of the Health Sciences." In *Electronic Handling of Information: Testing and Evaluation*. Edited by A. Kent et al. Washington, D.C.: Thompson Book Company, 1967, 13-23.
2. Hammond, W. "Satellite Thesaurus Construction." In *The Thesaurus in Action: Background Information for a Thesaurus Workshop at the 32nd Annual Convention of the American Society for Information Science*. San Francisco, Calif., October 1969: 14-20. AD 694 590.
3. Montague, B. A. "Testing, Comparison and Evaluation of Recall, Relevance and Cost of Coordinate Indexing with Links and Roles." *Proceedings of the American Documentation Institute* 1 (1964): 357-367.
4. Mullison, W. R. et al. "Comparing Indexing Efficiency, Effectiveness and Consistency With or Without the Use of Roles." *Proceedings of the American Society for Information Science* 6 (1969): 301-311.
5. Rolling, L. "Compilation of Thesauri for Use in Computer Systems." *Information Storage and Retrieval* 6 (1970): 341-350.
6. Sinnett, J. D. *An Evaluation of Links and Roles Used in Information Retrieval*. Dayton, Ohio: Air Force Materials Laboratory, Wright-Patterson Air Force Base, 1964. AD 432 198.
7. Surace, C. J. *The Displays of a Thesaurus*. Santa Monica, Calif.: Rand Corporation, 1970. P-4331.

25 *Synopsis*

In this final chapter, I will highlight some of the most salient points on vocabulary control that this book has attempted to illustrate.

1. The effectiveness of a retrieval system is largely dependent upon the size and composition of the document classes existing in the system. Class size and composition are controlled by the labels we assign to classes; that is, by the vocabulary used to describe (index) documents. (*Chapter 1*)

2. The name (label) that we give to a document class may be a word, a group of words, a notation from a classification scheme, or some other symbol (e.g., a randomly assigned trigraph). The name itself has no effect on the performance of the system. The important thing is what we put into a class (i.e., how we define its scope), not what we call it. (*Chapter 3, Chapter 19*, and elsewhere)

3. A controlled vocabulary exists primarily to control synonyms, near-synonyms, and homographs; to link semantically related terms; and to provide sufficient hierarchical structure to allow the conduct of generic searches. (*Chapter 1, Chapter 20*)

4. A controlled vocabulary used for indexing must be synthetic; i.e., it must provide facilities for combining terms in order to be able to represent any subject discussed in documents. Post-coordinate vocabularies are, by definition, synthetic. (*Chapter 2*)

5. Classification schemes, subject headings, and thesauri are all capable of satisfying the requirements of a controlled vocabulary. (*Chapters 3, 4, 5*)

6. While pre-coordinate systems, through synthetic features, can express any degree of subject complexity, they are unable to provide a multiple-access approach to documents efficiently and economically because of the essential linearity of their file structure. Pre-coordinate systems can provide multiple-access points only by providing multiple entries or multiple references. This leads to bulky search files and increases the costs of producing and maintaining the index. (*Chapters 3, 4*)

7. A controlled vocabulary is likely to be most effective if it has *literary warrant* and *user warrant;* that is, if it is built up from the language of the documents of a subject field and from the terms employed by users and potential users to describe their subject interests. Vocabularies produced solely by the committee approach are likely to be less effective. (*Chapter 6*)

8. The methods used to organize and display a vocabulary are not critical to the performance of a retrieval system. The size and composition of the document classes are much more important than how these classes are organized. (*Chapter 13*) Nevertheless, certain forms of display are likely to be more helpful than others to indexers and searchers. (*Chapter 7*)

9. The process of facet analysis is extremely useful in the generation and organization of a controlled vocabulary of any type, including a thesaurus. (*Chapters 6, 7*)

10. Graphic display is attractive in many situations. It may be particularly suitable for use in on-line systems using video consoles. This type of display has

been somewhat neglected in the United States. (*Chapter 7*)

11. Perhaps an ideal controlled vocabulary, from the viewpoint of providing maximum assistance to indexers and searchers, is a combination of a thesaurus and a faceted classification. The *Thesaurofacet* is a controlled vocabulary of this type. (*Chapter 8*)

12. For purposes of consistency, and to facilitate cooperation between various centers and services, a thesaurus needs to be constructed and presented according to certain guidelines. The rules and conventions adopted by COSATI are those most generally followed in thesaurus construction in the United States. (*Chapter 9*)

13. Certain thesaurus conventions (e.g., the degree of pre-coordination in the terms) will have a significant impact on the performance of a retrieval system, while others (e.g., direct versus inverted entry) should have very little effect on system performance. (*Chapter 9*)

14. A computer can be used to:

a. Manipulate and edit thesaurus input data, generate reciprocals, sort and print the thesaurus.

b. Facilitate thesaurus updating and maintenance.

c. Store a machine-readable thesaurus to facilitate the conduct of generic searches, to allow certain mappings and term substitutions to be made automatically, and to provide statistics useful in indexing, searching, and vocabulary control functions. (*Chapter 11*)

15. A controlled vocabulary must be updated continually to reflect new terminology occurring in documents and in requests made to a system. (*Chapter 12*)

16. The specificity of the vocabulary is the single major factor determining the *precision* capabilities of a retrieval system. (*Chapter 13*)

17. Searching failures in a retrieval system attributable to the vocabulary are likely to be of two major types:

(a) Failures due to lack of specificity, or

(b) Failures due to ambiguous and spurious relationships between terms. (*Chapter 13*)

18. A complete index language, like any other language, will have a vocabulary, a syntax, and rules for use. (*Chapter 14*)

19. A vocabulary for indexing and retrieval may contain three types of terms: descriptors, specifiers, and entry terms. These terms serve different functions and have varying effects on system performance. (*Chapter 14*)

20. A complete entry vocabulary, consisting of natural-language words occurring in documents and requests, is very important to the effectiveness and efficiency of a retrieval system (*Chapter 14*)

21. "Syntax" in a retrieval system may be provided by a series of devices designed to facilitate achievement of high recall or high precision, or both. (*Chapter 15*)

22. In most subject areas and with most document collections, regardless of size, it is usually possible to implement a successful retrieval system with a minimum of syntax. Role indicators have usually been shown to have a deleterious effect, overall, on the performance of a system. In most situations term coordination (class intersection) is sufficient to reduce potential ambiguities. (*Chapter 15*)

23. While a controlled vocabulary, used in both indexing and searching, is virtually essential for non-mechanized systems, there is considerable evidence to suggest that computer-based retrieval systems can operate effectively on the natural language of documents or abstracts. (*Chapter 16*)

24. It is possible to use a thesaurus as a searching aid without applying it in indexing. (*Chapter 16*)

25. Adoption of a controlled vocabulary for indexing precludes the possibility of complete specificity in searching. Natural-language searching, on the other hand, allows complete specificity. (*Chapter 16*)

26. The combination of free-text input plus a thesaurus as a searching aid may provide the most functional base for operation. With this combination the user has complete flexibility to achieve great specificity (on the text words) or to conduct a broad search (on thesaurus groups), as the requirements of the individual request dictate. (*Chapter 16*)

27. Highly successful retrieval systems can be operated by a "two-level" searching approach; that is, on a combination of uncontrolled keywords with a small, broad controlled vocabulary imposed upon them as a kind of superstructure. (*Chapter 16*)

28. A computer may be used to index a document automatically, using statistical criteria and other characteristics of the words contained in the document itself. (*Chapter 17*)

29. Automatic indexing may be achieved by word and phrase *extraction* or by *assignment* of terms from a controlled vocabulary. The latter process has usually been less successful than the first and is, in any case, less worth undertaking. (*Chapter 17*)

30. A computer can also be used to group terms together, on the basis of term co-occurrence statistics, in order to form term classes automatically. These classes have potential value in retrieval applications and, in certain circumstances, can substitute for the classes formed by a conventional, humanly prepared thesaurus. (*Chapter 17*)

31. For maximum effectiveness, a controlled vocabulary must be carefully tailored to the requirements of a particular organization or user community. (*Chapter 18*)

32. Increasing inter-agency cooperation and processing necessitate that procedures be developed to effect compatibility or convertibility between controlled vocabularies. This convertibility may be achieved by use of a common subsumption scheme or intermediate lexicon, by procedures for automatically mapping one vocabulary to another, or by the deliberate construction of a microthesaurus to fit within the hierarchical framework of some larger thesaurus. (*Chapter 18*)

33. An index language should (a) allow indexers to represent the subject matter of documents in a consistent way, (b) bring the vocabulary of the searcher into coincidence with the vocabulary of the indexer, and (c) provide means whereby a searcher can vary a search strategy to provide high recall or high precision as differing circumstances demand. (*Chapter 20*)

34. A controlled vocabulary may directly cause system failures by lacking term specificity and by allowing ambiguous or spurious term relationships to occur. (*Chapter 13*)

35. A controlled vocabulary may be *prescriptive* or *suggestive,* or both. The more *prescriptive* the vocabulary the greater the indexing consistency that is likely to result. (*Chapter 20*)

36. It is possible to provide various supplementary tools, including preprinted term lists, entry vocabularies of various types, term history files, statistics on term usage, and files of search fragments. (*Chapter 21*)

37. In a very large, multipurpose information system it may be necessary to develop procedures for automatically mapping from one set of terms to another (e.g., for publication purposes). Fairly complex procedures for continuous updating of the vocabulary will probably be needed. (*Chapter 22*)

38. The on-line system may offer new approaches to vocabulary display, to vocabulary maintenance, and to the use of vocabulary in indexing and searching. (*Chapter 23*)

39. A very complete entry vocabulary is likely to be particularly important in an on-line system used in a nondelegated search mode. (*Chapter 23*)

40. The on-line mode appears particularly suitable for the implementation of natural-language searching systems. (*Chapter 23*)

41. Controlled vocabularies are expensive to construct and to maintain. Some of the less sophisticated approaches to vocabulary control may be justifiable on the basis of a cost-effectiveness analysis. (*Chapter 24*)

Appendix:
Some Controlled
Vocabularies for Study
or Examination*

AERONAUTICS

Facet Classification Schedules and Index (of aeronautics). Cranfield, England: College of Aeronautics, 1960.

NASA Thesaurus. Washington, D.C.: National Aeronautics and Space Administration, 1967.

FAA Thesaurus of Technical Descriptors. 3rd ed. Washington, D.C.: Federal Aviation Administration, 1969. AD 686 837.

AGRICULTURE

Agricultural/Biological Vocabulary. Washington, D.C.: National Agricultural Library, 1967.

ATOMIC ENERGY

EURATOM Thesaurus. 2nd ed. Brussels: European Atomic Energy Community, 1966-67.

INIS Thesaurus. Vienna: International Atomic Energy Agency, 1970. IAEA-INIS-13.

Isotopes Information Center Keyword Thesaurus. Oak Ridge, Tenn.: Oak Ridge National Laboratory, August 1970. ORNL-IIc-24. (Rev. 1).

NSIC Keyword Thesaurus. Oak Ridge, Tenn.: Oak Ridge National Laboratory, Nuclear Safety Information Center, 1967. ORNL-NSIC-35.

* This list is not intended to be complete. Many other specialized vocabularies exist, including thesauri prepared by industrial organizations for their own internal use (e.g., the *Thesaurus of Manmade Fiber and Textile Terms* of the Celanese Fibers Co.). Most of these are not generally available. This list represents vocabularies that are generally available or vocabularies that contain special features making them particularly worth examining.

Nuclear Science and Technology: A Documentation Thesaurus. Experimental edition. Stockholm: AB Atomenergi, April 1966. Report FTI-13.

Subject Headings Used by the USAEC Division of Technical Information. 10th rev. ed. Oak Ridge, Tenn.: U.S. Atomic Energy Commission, 1971. TID-5001 (10th Rev).

BIOMEDICINE

Medical Subject Headings. Bethesda, Md.: National Library of Medicine, 1971. (Revised and re-issued annually.)

Medical and Health Related Sciences Thesaurus. Bethesda, Md.: National Institutes of Health, Division of Research Grants, 1970. Public Health Service Pub. No. 1031 (1970 ed).

A Thesaurus of Rheumatology. Compiled by M. J. Ruhl and L. Sokoloff. In *Arthritis and Rheumatism*, vol. 8, no. 1, Part II, February 1965.

Thesaurus for the Visual Sciences. Compiled by M. M. Eichhorn et al. Boston: Harvard Medical School, Vision Information Center, 1969.

DATA PROCESSING

Technical Information Center Thesaurus. 2nd ed. Poughkeepsie, N.Y.: IBM Systems Data Division, 1964.

EDUCATION

Thesaurus of ERIC Descriptors. 2nd ed. Washington, D.C.: Office of Education, Educational Resources Information Center, 1969.

Information Retrieval Thesaurus of Education Terms. Compiled by G. C. Barhydt and C. T. Schmidt. Cleveland, Ohio: Case Western Reserve University, 1968.

The London Education Classification. Compiled by D. J. Fos-

kett. London: University of London, Institute of Education, 1963.

ENGINEERING

Subject Headings for Engineering. New York: Engineering Index, Inc., 1970.

Thesaurus of Engineering Terms. New York: Engineers Joint Council, 1964.

Chemical Engineering Thesaurus. New York: American Institute of Chemical Engineers, 1961.

A Faceted Subject Classification for Engineering. Compiled by J. Binns and D. Bagley. 3rd ed. Whetstone, England: English Electric Co., 1961.

Thesaurofacet: A Thesaurus and Faceted Classification for Engineering and Related Subjects. Compiled by J. Aitchison et al. Whetstone, England: English Electric Co., 1969.

Engineering Index Thesaurus. New York: Engineering Index, Inc., 1971.

FINE ARTS

Classification of the Performing Arts. Compiled by A. Croghan. London: the Author, 1968.

Thesaurus of Coordinate Index Terms for Literature Related to Experimental Research in the Arts. Columbus, Ohio: Ohio State University, Center for Experimental Research in the Arts, 1968.

MANAGEMENT

Management Information Retrieval: A New Indexing Language. Compiled by J. F. Blagden. London: British Institute of Management, 1969.

The London Classification of Business Studies. Compiled by K. C. C. Vernon and V. Lang. London: Graduate School of Business Studies, 1970.

METALS

ASM Thesaurus of Metallurgical Terms. Metals Park, Ohio: American Society for Metals, 1968.

Thesaurus della Siderurgia. Compiled by V. Canepa and M. Trigari. Rome: Centro Sperimentale Metallurgico, 1966. (Versions existing in Italian, English and German.)

Thésaurus Chimie-Métallurgie. Paris: Centre National de la Recherche Scientifique, 1968.

Thesaurus of Terms Related to the Iron and Steel Industry. Compiled by M. R. Van Smaalen. 2nd ed. Pretoria, South Africa: South African Iron and Steel Industrial Corporation, 1968. (A 3rd ed., known as the *ISCOR Thesaurus* was issued in June 1970.)

A Thesaurus for Welding and Allied Processes. Cambridge, England : The Welding Institute, 1969.

Thesaurus of Terms on Copper Technology. 3rd ed. New York: Copper Development Association, 1966.

NATURAL RESOURCES

Thesaurus of Descriptors: A List of Keywords and Cross-References for Indexing and Retrieving the Literature of Water Resources Development. Denver, Colo.: Bureau of Reclamation, 1963.

Water Resources Thesaurus. Washington, D.C.: Department of the Interior, Office of Water Resources Research, 1966.

PACKAGING

Classification Schedule and Alphabetical Index for Packaging Documentation. London: European Packaging Federation, 1966.

PAINT

Thesaurus of Paint and Allied Technology. Philadelphia: Federation of the Societies for Paint Technology, 1968.

PAPER

Thesaurus of Pulp and Paper Terms. Compiled by J. E. Tasman and P. M. Nobbs. Pointe Claire, Quebec: Pulp and Paper Research Institute, 1965.

PETROLEUM SCIENCE

Exploration and Production Thesaurus. 4th ed. Tulsa: University of Tulsa, 1970.

Subject Authority List. 7th ed. New York: American Petroleum Institute, 1970.

PHOTOGRAPHY

Thesaurus of Photographic Science and Engineering Terms. New York: Society of Photographic Scientists and Engineers, 1967.

PUBLIC AFFAIRS

The New York Times Thesaurus of Descriptors. New York: New York Times Co., 1968.

SCIENCE AND TECHNOLOGY. GENERAL

Thesaurus of Engineering and Scientific Terms. Washington, D.C.: Office of Naval Research, Project LEX, 1967.

NASA Thesaurus. Washington, D.C.: National Aeronautics and Space Administration, 1967.

Thesaurus of DDC Descriptors. Alexandria, Va.: Defense Documentation Center, 1966.

Bureau of Ships Thesaurus of Descriptive Terms and Code Book. 2nd ed. Washington, D.C.: Bureau of Ships, 1965. NAV-SHIPS 0900-002-0000.

TDCK Circular Thesaurus System. 3rd ed. The Hague: Netherlands Armed Forces Technical Documentation and Information Center, 1964.

TEXTILES

Textile Technology Terms. Compiled by R. S. Merkel and W. C. Harris. Charlottesville, Va.: Institute of Textile Technology, 1966.

Thesaurus of Textile Terms Covering Fibrous Materials and Processes. Compiled by S. Backer and E. I. Valko. 2nd ed. Cambridge, Mass.: Massachusetts Institute of Technology, 1969.

URBAN AFFAIRS

Thesaurus Landesplannung. Zurich: Eidgenossische Technische Hochschule Bibliothek, 1970.

Urban Thesaurus. Compiled by J. E. Rickert. Kent, Ohio: Kent State University, Center for Urban Regionalism, 1968.

Urbandoc Thesaurus. New York: The City University of New York, Project URBANDOC, 1967.

Index

229